O

SERIES EDITORS

David E. Johnson, *Comparative Literature, University at Buffalo*
Scott Michaelsen, *English, Michigan State University*

SERIES ADVISORY BOARD

Nahum Dimitri Chandler, *African American Studies, University of California, Irvine*
Rebecca Comay, *Philosophy and Comparative Literature, University of Toronto*
Marc Crépon, *Philosophy, École Normale Supérieure, Paris*
Jonathan Culler, *Comparative Literature, Cornell University*
Johanna Drucker, *Design Media Arts and Information Studies,*
University of California, Los Angeles
Christopher Fynsk, *Modern Thought, Aberdeen University*
Rodolphe Gasché, *Comparative Literature, University at Buffalo*
Martin Hägglund, *Comparative Literature, Yale University*
Carol Jacobs, *German and Comparative Literature, Yale University*
Peggy Kamuf, *French and Comparative Literature, University of Southern California*
David Marriott, *History of Consciousness, University of California, Santa Cruz*
Steven Miller, *English, University at Buffalo*
Alberto Moreiras, *Hispanic Studies, Texas A&M University*
Patrick O'Donnell, *English, Michigan State University*
Pablo Oyarzun, *Teoría del Arte, Universidad de Chile*
Scott Cutler Shershow, *English, University of California, Davis*
Henry Sussman, *German and Comparative Literature, Yale University*
Samuel Weber, *Comparative Literature, Northwestern University*
Ewa Ziarek, *Comparative Literature, University at Buffalo*

O

Apostrophic Ghosts and the Disappearing Acts of Lyric Poetry

DAVID BEN-MERRE

Published by State University of New York Press, Albany

EU GPSR Authorised Representative:
Logos Europe, 9 rue Nicolas Poussin, 17000, La Rochelle, France
contact@logoseurope.eu

For information, contact State University of New York Press, Albany, NY
www.sunypress.edu

Library of Congress Cataloging-in-Publication Data

Name: Ben-Merre, David, author.
Title: O: Apostrophic ghosts and the disappearing acts of lyric poetry /
    David Ben-Merre, author.
Description: Albany : State University of New York Press, [2025] | Series:
    SUNY series, literature . . . in theory | Includes bibliographical references and
    index.
Identifiers: ISBN 9798855804089 (hardcover : alk. paper) | ISBN 9798855804102
    (ebook) | ISBN 9798855804096 (pbk. : alk. paper)
Further information is available at the Library of Congress.

for my parents

It [is] not the present but the thought that counts.

—James Merrill, "The Will"

A globe in the window tilts like a coloured *O*.

—Seamus Heaney, "Alphabets"

Contents

List of Illustrations

Acknowledgments

The debts I have—personal and professional—since my first attempt at writing acknowledgments with SUNY Press have grown beyond measure. Who could have figured? Many thanks go out to my epilogic coconspirator Manu Samriti Chander, whose friendship continues to be a cure for many of this world's ills, and to the folks at SUNY Press, especially the inestimable Rebecca Colesworthy. Thanks to the manuscript readers for their feedback and support. I am indebted to Cristanne Miller—when I could not see to see—for her resoluteness in helping me see the Emily Dickinson chapter through. Many thanks to Dawne McCance, who, years ago, took the W. B. Yeats chapter out of its silences. The Wallace Stevens chapter would still be more Xs than Os if not for the eyes and ears of Bart Eeckout and Henry Weinfield. I thank Marie Olivier, the star in every circle, and Université Paris-Est Créteil for indulging some early ideas about Elizabeth Bishop. Beyond my gratitude for permission to reprint his work, I am very grateful to Terrance Hayes for helping a modernist join the twenty-first century. Finally, the reimagined chapter on Carly Simon would not have been possible without the initial assistance of Karin Kukkonen and Sonja Klimek, the frame-breaking editors of *Metalepsis in Popular Culture*. The early life of that chapter, and so much else, would not have been possible without the support of Keri Holt.

I cannot imagine a greater group of colleagues than what I have at Buffalo State. I am grateful for the advocacy of Lisa Berglund and Kelly Frothingham, and for the friendships of Ann Colley, Lorna Perez, Natalie Szymanski, and Roy Bakos, among many, many others. Raul Neira, Mary McBride, and Maribel Garrett have now become family. I am particularly thankful to Jason Grinnell for our long conversations about the value and possibilities of a liberal arts education, even in these, our darkest days.

And, to come full circle, to the family: along with my parents, Diana and Aaron, I want to thank Howard and Ann, Emily and Josh, Shira, Danna, and Ron. Most of all, I am grateful for the patience of my wife, Rebecca, and the impatience of our son, Adam. With apologies to Platonic precision, there is perfection in every Crayola™ circle he draws.

And finally to Mutlu Blasing and Robert Scholes, who hide all throughout these pages—I think you would've enjoyed this book.

An earlier version of Chapter 1 was published as "Falling into Silence: Giorgio Agamben at the End of the Poem" in the special issue *Between Poetry and Philosophy* of *MOSAIC*, volume 45, number 1 (March 2012), pages 89–104. An earlier version of Chapter 2 was published as "Xs and Os": Chiasmus, Apostrophe, and the Lyric in Wallace Stevens" in *Wallace Stevens Journal*, volume 45, number 2, Fall 2021, pages 199–217. Parts of Chapters 3 and 4 were published as " 'Circles Surrounding Stars': The Optics of O in Elizabeth Bishop and James Merrill" in *TIES Revue de littérature: Textes, Images et Sons*, number 4, 2019. Parts of Chapter 6 were published as "I'm so vain, I bet I think this song is about myself: The Problematic 'I' of Lyric Poetry" in *Metalepsis in Popular Culture*, edited by Karin Kukkonen and Sonja Klimek (De Gruyter, 2011), 65–82.

Introduction

Once up against the sky it's hard
to tell them from the stars—
planets, that is. . . .[1]

—Elizabeth Bishop, "The Armadillo"

You'll recall "The Armadillo," Elizabeth Bishop's poem, dedicated to her friend Robert Lowell, in which she describes a Saint's Day festivity in Brazil where celebrants send fire balloons into the night sky.[2] The majesty of the scene—that transcendent beauty toward which artists strive—captivates until we are forced to realize, slowly, through a somewhat detached speaking voice, that the wind sometimes tosses these beauties back toward the earth.[3] The self-immolating balloon "splattered like an egg of fire" (l. 22), Bishop's speaker almost too casually relates, before telling us how it scorched an owl's nest, rabbit, and armadillo. The ritual gives way to horror. What appeared to be a visual harmony of stars ascending toward a heavenly constellation

---

1. Bishop, *Complete Poems 1927–1979*, 103.

2. James Longenbach (*Virtues of Poetry*, 108) and Lloyd Schwartz correct the widespread misunderstanding that the poem was written as a response to Robert Lowell, especially his "Skunk Hour." (The influence went the other way, and Bishop's dedication was added years after the poem was written.) Schwartz sees "a Cold War metaphor: a dazzling display of airborne fire that mimics missiles of mass destruction dropping on innocent civilians" (121).

3. Compare this to P. B. Shelley's Sonnet [To a balloon, laden with Knowledge] and its metaphorical "fire": "Bright ball of flame that through the gloom of even / Silently takest thine etherial way / . . . Unlike the Fire thou bearest, soon shalt thou / Fade like a meteor in surrounding gloom . . ." (98).

is destroyed, and poetic words themselves, along with the speaking voice and the listening ears—*our* listening ears—are suddenly and dangerously caught in the crossfires.[4] Only then, are we given this final italicized stanza:

> *Too pretty, dreamlike mimicry!*
> *O falling fire and piercing cry*
> *and panic, and a weak mailed fist*
> *clenched ignorant against the sky!* (104)

The dreamlike mimicry of the poetic act—itself "too pretty"—is gusted away and the full, dangerous scope of humanity's ritualistic actions are exposed to the gasping air of the immediate scene. Amid the noncomprehension of the armadillo, the powerless poet, now with her own ignited eyes, turns away from detached, representational attempts to capture the scene and begins to address the blazing projectiles themselves: "O falling fire." Is this the voice of invocation, of resignation, of an exasperated shout against something that doesn't have ears to listen? What, exactly, happens to the lyric speaker at this moment, and what are we to make of that graphic balloon of an O, which falls a bit too conspicuously into the opening of the antepenultimate line?[5] It is within this absence, within this failure of speech to save the animals or even simply to capture the immediate visceral horror of the event, that something like a poetic voice begins to materialize.

---

4. In a 1955 letter to Anny Bauman, Bishop explains, "It is pouring rain which is too bad because it's a day for fireworks and bonfires, etc.—but very good, really, because there may not be so many forest fires and accidents. Fireballoons are supposed to be illegal but everyone sends them up anyway . . . They are so pretty—one's of two minds about them" (qtd. in Costello 76).

5. Various readers have tried to make sense of this inward turn at the end of the poem. "The question for the critic," Penelope Laurens writes, ". . . is how Bishop shapes the reader's response to this beautiful and cruel event. One could say that the poem, by its factual presentation alone, asks us to recognize the chaos these illegal balloons generate. Yet, until the final stanza, there is little to indicate that Bishop's involvement in the scene is anything more than an aesthetic one" (77). We are left with more questions than answers, as the poet "hold[s] the poem back from any easily paraphrasable meaning [in order] to give it moral resonance" (77). Bonnie Costello hears "a strong moral voice break[ing] in to oppose the stance of transcendence and aesthetic mastery"; in its place, Bishop "dramatizes this aesthetic distance and the inevitable return to the rage of the suffering body" (75). C. K. Doreski notes how "[i]nvocation and resignation collapse together in an impotent outcry as rage displaces epiphany," leaving only an angry gesture and grieving voice (39).

This book is about such attempts of lyric speakers to constitute their own subjectivity within the apostrophic address or, rather, what I want to consider here as the language of the poetic O. Understandably, the vocative aspect of apostrophe is central to how the trope and the trope's intimate relation to lyric poetry is understood. Jonathan Culler calls it "the very figure of voice" ("Reading" 99). In Barbara Johnson's phrasing, "Apostrophe situates its fictive entities in the field of direct address, so that the spoken voice is what knits utterance together" (*Persons* 7). But I want to suggest that there is often more to the poetic O than its silently voiced performance of vocalization. Bishop's final stanza, not originally included in early drafts of the poem, first added an "Oh" before she finally settled on the "O" hovering beneath the two circles of "Too"—her intentional choice appearing in a draft manuscript (beside a reminder to italicize the lines):

> Too pretty, dreamlike mimicry!
> Oh falling fire and piercing cry
> and panic, and the a weak mailed fist
> clenched ignorant against the sky.[6]

If this O, as I suggested, visually captures the poem's balloons, its egg of fire, and generally whatever circular shape sent up into the sky (the stars— / planets, that is . . .), it is no apostrophic accident. It is a call to put in graphic form a painful cry that could not pop the ritualistic balloon. Pushing back against the overwhelmingness of the vocative, my book's central argument is that scholarly discussions connecting apostrophe to lyric subjectivity have ignored the trope's grounding in written language. I hope to rethink, as poets have done and continue to do, how the various symbolic, iconic, archetypical, and material guises of O intersect its tropological presence. This, despite my own habit (too late to break) of calling words in a poem brought together into the presence of a subject a "speaker." Without trying to be too provocative here, I argue that poets playing with this circular figure (as circle, shout, ring, even a mouth in ecstasy), frequently locate its appearances in the tension between the doodles of its round shape and what Anglo-European poetic practice has taught us to understand as a

---

6. "The Owl's Nest Armadillo," Elizabeth Bishop Papers, Vassar College Library Special Collections, box 57, folder 13. Bishop originally considered the more delicate "dainty" before settling on "pretty," and the poem was originally titled "The Owls' Nest."

traditional apostrophic address.[7] Accordingly, their lyric voices often find themselves delicately balanced between the possibility of the spoken word and the materiality of the written page.

It is here that two deconstructive impulses come to a head, as the "presence" supposed by the vocative apostrophic address calls into question the iterability of an always-already written system. In other words, I do not understand how the de Manian ode to lyric apostrophe and the Derridean elegy for phonocentrism never quite had it out.[8] "The principle of intelligibility, in lyric poetry," de Man writes, "depends on the phenomenalization of the poetic voice. Our claim to understand a lyric text coincides with the actualization of a speaking voice" (*Rhetoric* 55).[9] But for Derrida, such will always be an oral fixation: "the voice is always already invested, undone, required, and marked in its essence by a certain spatiality" (*Of Grammatology* 290). And this is not even to ~~speak~~ write of the way poetic occasions are generally valued in the world: a poetry reading is an *event* and the poet gets paid—presence is how the words on the page are marketed. But this, of course, varies according to different social marketplaces composed of very different groups of critics, audiences, and poets themselves.[10] I will discuss

---

7. The term "doodle" memorably takes shape in Northrop Frye's *Anatomy of Criticism*, which also gives voice to the counterpart, "babble." When these terms are invited to a fancier dinner party, they are called *melos* (the music of poetry) and *opsis* (the visual element). Culler sees "[t]he empty 'O' of apostrophe, which has no semantic force . . . implicitly to allude to all other apostrophes of the tradition" (*Theory* 217).

8. While their work is often conflated, the two have a very different metaphysics (or antimetaphysics) underlying their interpretive modes. Although the ins-and-outs (if there were such a thing) of their philosophical relationship has been explored thoroughly since Rodolphe Gasché's *Wild Card*, his early words still focus a critical, *ahem*, difference: "While the Derridean reading . . . shows understanding to depend for its possibility on the medium of undecidability of writing . . . de Man's theory of reading . . . [is concerned with] the possibility of understanding altogether" (9).

9. "Now it is certainly beyond question," de Man continues, with his own rhetorical flair, "that the figure of address is recurrent in lyric poetry, to the point of constituting the generic definition of, at the very least, the ode (which can, in its turn, be seen as paradigmatic for poetry in general)" ("Lyric Voice" 61). Joining de Man, Culler writes, "To interpret a sequence as a lyric is to find ways of hearing in it a speaking voice" ("Reading Lyric" 99). Voice is figural for both de Man and Culler. For a long line of critics, actual voicing is what matters. Over sixty years ago, Francis Berry could call poetry "essentially a spoken form" (112), centering around the poet's voice.

10. What the literal and figurative senses of "voice" mean to various philosophers, critics, poets, and individuals naturally complicates the simplistic writing/speech binary, which is already encoded for Derrida and de Man in certain ways. Without any quantitative

deconstructive impasses further in the following chapter but, rather than readjudicate an older generation's debates, my main thrust in this study goes to how various poets, in vastly different ways, have connected the possibilities of the poetic gesture of "O" to its graphic and iconic existences.

---

data to back this up, I imagine it would be safe to say that most twentieth-century U.S. poets and those teaching the craft in both academic and community institutions had no problem advocating for the inverse of (at least the second half of) Polonius's admonition: "give every man thy ear, but few thy voice." (See Rasula.) LANGUAGE poets, as the story tells ourselves, would stake a poetics on decentralizing the voice. In Marjorie Perloff's words, they refused "the outward sign of a spoken self-presence" and saw "the dismissal of 'voice' as the foundational principle of lyric poetry" (412, 405). Looking at the poetry reading as its own medium, Charles Bernstein stresses aurality, "the sounding of the *writing*," over orality with its "emphasis on breath, voice, and speech—an emphasis that tends to valorize speech over writing, voice over sound, listening over hearing" (13). Disputes—quite vocal ones—linger. "Short of 'lyric' itself," Christopher Spaide writes, " 'voice' has become the most contentious term in lyric studies today, with lyric readers celebrating voice for cohering an original and individual identity, and anti-lyric readers shaming voice for its egocentric pretensions to authority" (255). Even with the easy borders of contention, though, it is unclear exactly what voice implies, as the debates bring a microphone not so much to what "voice" entails or ought to entail but to a fluctuating cultural marketplace. Beyond recitals, readings, and performances of poetry, "voice," as Lesley Wheeler writes, "is also a metaphor for originality, personality, and the illusion of authorial presence within printed poetry"; it is political, as in "as the right or ability to speak or write" (3). And this is not even to touch on how voice, as I imagine, now includes AI dictional pastiches of remarks never uttered. Such is the danger of language speaking without a person behind it, or, as we will soon learn all too quickly, with an avatar of voice ("ChatGPT—write a chapter on apostrophe as would XXX").

Still, for Wheeler, "[t]o address sound in poetry is to invoke a body—whether the body belongs to the poet, the audience, or both" (23). Accordingly, a poem and its invocations remain a mere site of potentiality until their voicing becomes more than figural: "The figurative nature of voice remains a limit for printed poetry. . . . Poems on the page cannot complete the circuit between poet and audience unless or until the poem is physically voiced" (126). This became a particular problem for various Victorian poets, as Eric Griffiths makes the point (*Printed Voice*), trying to navigate the ambiguities inherent in presenting their voice in written texts, and, one imagines—given the vastly different ways of trying to map intention afterward—the problem has remained. For Jean-Jacques Rousseau, who will join the conversation in the following chapter, one answer meant creating a different punctuation system—forsaking the question mark for a new mark of vocative address: "one [able] to distinguish, in writing, between a man one mentions and a man one addresses" (22). Alas, given speed, tone, intonation, pitch, and inflection—a vocative mark might fall a breve short. Not every professional reader, it should be noted, reduces sound to voice. In different ways, both Garrett Stewart's paradoxical "silent textual sounding" (*Reading Voices* 1) and Culler's "enunciative apparatus" (*Theory* 16) focus on nuances of meaningful poetic sound, as it exists away from voicing and revoicing.

In addition to whatever calling the trope dramatizes or melodramatizes, it will always also be a circular O on a page. My focus on poetic playfulness surrounding this address does not belie the seriousness of what is at stake in this tropological gesture: death of another, death of the self, pain, longing, the misguided hope of resurrection, and—what is possibly of most significance, as Barbara Johnson and others have convincingly argued—individual subjectivity and legal personhood itself.[11]

A scholarly generation ago—always so distant and yet so present—apostrophe became a bit of a poetic celebrity, and debates about it brought up some old feuds about the status of poetry and its relationship to the world. Tied to both sentiment and voice, apostrophe, as you know, is the turning away to address another, which is usually an absent person (Whitman's "O Captain! My Captain!"), inanimate object (Juliet's "O happy dagger"), or abstraction (Céline Dion's [*et al*'s] "O holy night"). That those three very different types of address—a crying out for the departed, a message to a chunk of metal that cannot hear, and a yuletide hymn that helps Target™ shoppers ease their grip on wallets—can be tied so easily together gestures toward the trope's romantic hopefulness. It can seem a bit trivial to find apostrophe with each turn of the O—"the most sonorous vowel," as per Edgar Allan Poe (157)—as if every time one were to eat a bowl of Cheerios, one would encounter Oatic nature itself speaking. O, of course, does not necessitate apostrophe, and apostrophe does not necessitate an O. Critics such as J. Douglas Kneale and William Waters have rejected the passionate O as apostrophe (preferring the Greek term *ecphonesis*) and rejected the conflation of apostrophe with prosopopoeia or anthropomorphism, which, for them, are more about animation than "turning away" in order to address anew. Others have critiqued the confusion of apostrophe with *exclamatio* (heightened emotion) or with the temporal immediacy created by speech acts.[12] Rhetoric handbooks—mostly to torment undergraduates before exams—give simple definitions of poetic

---

11. "The notion of 'person,'" she writes, following Émile Benveniste, "has something to do with the presence at the scene of speech and seems to inhere in the notion of *address*. 'I' and 'you' are persons because they can either address or be addressed, while 'he' can only be talked *about*. A person who neither addresses nor is addressed is functioning as a *thing* in the same way that being an *object* of discussion rather than a *subject* of discussion transforms everything into a thing" (*Persons* 6).

12. William Waters (*Poetry's Touch*) cautions against conflating the nuances among modes of address. Apostrophes, for him, are addressed to "unhearing entities" (3 n.5). For Kneale, "The current problem with apostrophe stems from associating it with voice rather than with a movement of voice" (142). Other critics have taken these concerns

apostrophe, give or take a word, like the one I provided earlier. But there is no definite critical consensus. Some stress the address, others the absent hearer or the supposed animation, still others the turn itself. The critical nonconsensus about apostrophe—as if it were something floating out in the world, unheeding—echoes the ambiguous desires with which poets treat it: longing for presence or self-presence, outcry and celebration, ecstasy and absence. Questions abound. Does the simple grammar of the I/you relationship necessitate an address? Not all second-person addresses—and we might think of the epistle—are usually considered apostrophic. One wonders if the addressee, unlike Juliet's dagger, must be absent. For that matter, Juliet's dagger isn't "unhearing" until it is anthropomorphized to have ears that no longer work. Is the addressee itself what matters (as it was for Quintilian, Culler reminds us, who stressed the address away from the judge)[13] or is it the turn to address—a shift in posture, a break in discourse that occurs outside signification, in that sudden space between words? As it often happens, it is within the absence of consensus that we might better learn what is at stake in each of the interventions.

Paul de Man who understood lyric itself as "the instance of represented voice," was perhaps most responsible for crossing apostrophe with prosopopoeia, "which posits the possibility of the latter's reply and confers upon it the power of speech. Voice assumes mouth, eye, and finally face" (*Rhetoric*, 75–76).[14] In this pre-face of sorts, de Man distinguishes prosopopoeia from personification and anthropomorphism, two tropes that figure or animate a nonliving thing but don't necessarily give it a voice. Jonathan Culler,

---

in new directions: Eva Zettelman links apostrophe to possible worlds theory and challenges Culler's presumption that apostrophe categorically denies to lyric the potential to reposition the reader in a language-induced mimetic scenario; Gavin Hopps contests the notion that apostrophe is non-representational by offering a "theologically-grounded reading of apostrophe" (224); and David Shaw sees apostrophe as central not only to the lyric but also the vocatives of the dramatic monologue, which depends just as much—if not more—on the discursive speech act and the poet's rhetorical "words of power" (325).

13. *Institutio Oratoria*, IV, I; qtd. in Culler, *Pursuit* 135.

14. Importantly, for de Man, prosopopoeia gives the face (or a figure) but not the essence of the thing, because it is "the *fiction* of an apostrophe to an absent, deceased, or voiceless entity, which posits the possibility of the latter's reply and confers upon it the power of speech" (*Rhetoric* 75–76; emphasis my own). Ann Keniston writes, "Apostrophe thus persists in address that its speaker knows to be unheard, while demanding that both speaker and reader pretend that this absent other is in fact present and capable of hearing" (298).

following de Man, has perhaps been the greatest steward of apostrophe over the last generation, linking it to the essence of the lyric itself—ironically so, given what we have come to think of, in the last couple hundred years, as a private utterance that is not heard but rather "overheard."[15] Apostrophe, for Culler, has to do with the vocative, with vocal performance, and with a distinctive *lyric* temporality. It "makes its point by troping not on the meaning of a word but on the circuit or situation of communication itself" (135), focusing us on the moment of *discourse*, rather than the time of *narrative*, belying the story one wants to tell (or tell oneself) with the sudden conscious realization that one is speaking, perhaps to no end. It is not simply the demonstration of a moment of realization, however, that has grabbed one's attention. Suddenly, poetry becomes magical. "To apostrophize," Culler writes, "is to will a state of affairs, to attempt to call into being by asking inanimate objects to bend themselves to your desire" (139).[16] Such is what the lyric aspires to—to will an actual world with words. Culler distills this apostrophic energy to the poetic signpost O, as in the celebrated final lines of W. B. Yeats's "Among School Children":

> O chestnut tree, great rooted blossomer,
> Are you the leaf, the blossom or the bole?
> O body swayed to music, O brightening glance,
> How can we know the dancer from the dance?
>
> (*Collected* 217)

The romantic couplings of art and artist, object and voice, which the lines in most readings rhetorically understand to connote a metaphysical

---

15. The well-known characterization comes from John Stuart Mill, who contrasts it with eloquence: "eloquence is *heard*, poetry is overheard" ("Thoughts" 95). The intersubjective grounding of the lyric derives, in part, through the influence of a Hegelian structure of individuation dependent (as most things in Hegel) on a mediating force of otherness—otherness, as one would understand it now, in a very abstract way.

16. "Apostrophes invoke elements of the universe as potentially responsive forces, which can be asked to act, or refrain from acting, or even to continue behaving as they usually behave" (Culler, *Theory* 215–16). Mark Smith writes, "where there is lyric, there is apostrophe . . . [which] names not a codified rhetorical device or trope, but a demand that lyric poems lay upon their readers" (411). Daniel Albright sees lyric as "magical, and the proper history of lyric is the history of incantation" (viii). David Shaw reminds us that "[t]he paradigmatic narrative of all ghostly conjuring is Jesus' call to Lazarus—'Lazarus, come forth'" (320). Geoffrey Hartman can ask whether it is optative (expressing a wish) or imperative, voice speaking out or attempting an invocation (Hartman 193; qtd. in Culler *Pursuit*, 139).

coherence,[17] echo the illusory logic of that simple circular grapheme—the closed harmonious circuit of O—which, cast from the speaker's mouth, can supposedly do more than offer mere narrative descriptions of the absent tree and dancer. In one sense, Yeats's apostrophic O seems to gesture toward an actual attempt at conjuring, for why else would there be an address? This is the abracadabric hope and necessary failure of the lyric—that a word or even a letter uttered aloud in the right intonation or projected deep into the heavens can somehow change the world. Nowhere, perhaps, was such apostrophic yearning more visually apparent than in the graphic for a (non-poetic) opinion piece lamenting the tumultuous political present (fig. I.1).

There is hope, in Mikey Burton's visual calling out, that someone will heed this manner of bat-signal cast into the sky, as if the receiver could simply be conjured by the address. The absent addressee is hailed but unconjured; still, the overheard, or rather, *overseen* graphic sign can generate a community around its message, so long as the light remains in the night sky.

Despite its pretensions, poetic apostrophe cannot but fail in this regard. Yeats's chestnut tree and mid-swayed dancer can be hailed from afar, but they cannot hear the call. To believe otherwise in this animistic power, as Sigmund Freud reminds us, would be delusional.[18] The apostrophic address can only voice its own real hopefulness—"a performance of fantasmatic intersubjectivity" (25) in the words of Lauren Berlant—suddenly overwhelmed by an unexpected awareness.[19] This, for Culler, who hopes to

---

17. For an alternative reading, one which relishes the paradoxical tension between the literal and rhetorical as they relate to the mythical unity of language, see the "Semiology and Rhetoric" chapter of de Man's *Allegories of Reading*.

18. While Freud mostly writes about thought processes (rather than vocalizations), the parallel is clear. He calls such narcissistic wish-fulfillment a "magic," which hopes to "subject the processes of nature to the will of man . . ." (137). He writes of "compulsion neurotics" (150) for whom the mention of another causes something to happen to the other, and of "the savage who believes he can change the outer world by a mere thought of his" (153). Rather than effecting a change in the world, such gestures illustrate a "longing of the absent" (172). Interestingly, the one exception is art where "it still happens that man, consumed by his wishes, produces something similar to the gratification of these wishes, and this playing, thanks to artistic illusion, calls forth effects as if it were something real" (158).

19. Apostrophe "is actually a turning back, an animating of a receiver on behalf of the desire to make something happen *now* that realizes something *in the speaker*, makes the speaker more or differently possible" (Berlant 25–26). Part of this "cruel optimism" allows the speaker to act as if she were "affectively and mentally in sovereign control over the ways that [those absent] are 'in' her" (252).

Figure I.1. *New York Times* 08/24/2017. *Source:* Mikey Barton, *New York Times.*

President Obama, Where Are You?

By CAROLINE RANDALL WILLIAMS   AUG. 24, 2017

recapture the enunciative structure of the lyric address, becomes, beyond delusion, the partial enchantment of the trope.[20] Percy Shelley's "Ode to the West Wind," for example, does not describe but rather invokes the wind, or, more precisely, invokes a voice hoping to invoke the wind:

> O wild West Wind, thou breath of Autumn's being!
> Thou, from whose unseen presence the leaves dead
> Are driven, like ghosts from an enchanter fleeing. . . .
>
> (401)

Linguistically speaking, there ought to be little distinction between the poet/speaker uttering those words and their iteration today.[21] There is both a violence and a charm to the reader being asked to step into another's voice,

---

20. See Culler "L'Hyperbole," 94. Because lyric poems presume an address (even if it is to oneself), even the first words (as in Shelley's "O wild West Wind") can be seen as a turning away of sorts from a previous situation.

21. Johnson writes, "Shelley spends the first three sections demonstrating that the west wind is a figure for the power to animate: it is described as the breath of being, moving

performing—even in quotation marks—the same invocation. The wind hasn't actually been conjured, but a voice reaching out to it (and accordingly failing to reach it) has. "What is really in question," Culler writes, noting W. H. Auden's famous elegy for Yeats, "is the power of poetry to make something happen" (*Pursuit* 140):

> Now Ireland has her madness and her weather still,
> For poetry makes nothing happen: it survives
> In the valley of its making where executives
> Would never want to tamper, flows on south
> From ranches of isolation and the busy griefs,
> Raw towns that we believe and die in; it survives,
> A way of happening, a mouth.
>
> ("In Memory of W. B. Yeats," *Collected* 248)

Looking closer at one of the most mis-contextualized poetic lines of the twentieth century ("poetry makes nothing happen"), one finds that the "surviving" poetry seems to make quite a lot here: valleys, rivers, and then ranches and towns. In his own way, Auden is saying that we built this city on rock and roll. Moreover, the event of the poem itself becomes its own happening, a type of performative magic that draws Culler to the apostrophic trope: "Nothing need happen because the poem itself is to be the happening" (149)—a happening that, in an extended conceit running throughout the poem, is effected by the possibilities of the open "mouth."[22]

One would be remiss if one did not mention the original refrain of the poem and its own lamenting "O"—now mostly lost to history but still lingering—which captured the speaker's initial pang about the febrile earth. Before settling on the more familiar refrain seen today ("What instruments we have agree / The day of his death was a dark cold day"), Auden had composed the lines as: "O all the instruments agree / The day of his death was a dark cold day" (247). In both versions, the lines suggest a thermometer placed in the open mouth of the day, a mouth reshaped into its own O to

---

everywhere, blowing movement, and energy through the world, waking from its summer dream, parting the waters of the Atlantic, uncontrollable. Yet the wind animates by bringing death, winter destruction" (*World* 187).

22. Does poetry, Sara Guyer asks, "survive as a mouth? Does it survive in our mouths? Does it survive because of our mouths or because it gives us mouths? And if it is a mouth, a mouth that survives, what survives is us, us insofar as in voicing it we are made to speak and to live, to live on in a figure, a figure of address" (105).

receive the instrument. The speaker seems to engage in the pathetic fallacy, believing that the earth, too, so stricken by this loss, brings about a coldness across its face. But the earth, no more than the plaints, as Skeeter Davis will always remind us, cannot change the weather.[23] Paradoxically, Auden's act of revising seems to belie the artifice of the whole enterprise, the constructed nature not of anguish but of the *voice* of anguish. The poet is calmly choosing one refrain instead of another, not in any way burdened by the moment. It is as if the Hollywood director, following Wordsworth's admonitions in the *Preface*, were shouting into her bullhorn: "*O* isn't real! Use fewer poetic devices to get authenticity!" Still, we might ask, *is it all artifice?* Although the apostrophic address cannot create the unhearing object being hailed, it can (and does) fashion and refashion a voice hailing it, which, in Auden's poem, seems to be a voice in anguish at its own inabilities to change the season or summon the departed. It is the address to the Other, which here constitutes the speaker, in this "act of radical interiorization and solipsism" (Culler *Pursuit* 146), this usurious lending of presence.

"The speech situation—presence—is about the poet, and his or her feelings about the object," Barbara Johnson writes, adding that "addressing something reveals the nature of the subject, not of the object" (*Persons* 9). Working with Walt Whitman's overloaded circuit of a poem "Apostroph," Johnson calls attention to the performative aspect of the trope: "The complete thought [Whitman] utters is not 'X is Y,' but 'I invoke X.' The problem of poetic authority does not depend on what the poet says but on his capacity to *call*" (9). As Whitman, himself, seems to put it in the poem, "O present! I return while yet I may to you!"[24] Oftentimes, it feels

---

23. The stark division between the inside emotion and the outside world is perhaps nowhere more felt (at least in 1962 America) than in Skeeter Davis's (Mary Frances Penick's) popularization of the Arthur Kent and Sylvia Dee song "The End of the World": "Why does the sun go on shining? / Why does the sea rush to shore? / Don't they know it's the end of the world? / 'Cause you don't love me anymore. . . ." One might also be reminded of Lee Hazlewood's remembrance of his brother, "Cold Hard Times": "I heard the preachers said God must have a sense of humor / 'cause when they put him in the grave it didn't even rain." Emily Dickinson's version ("It makes no difference abroad / The Seasons—fit—the same— / The Mornings blossom into Noons— / And split their Pods of Flame") similarly fails to reconcile inside and outside in a harmonious way, because the outside just doesn't care the way we wished it did (F686; J620; M332). Over the years, the weather at Mozart's funeral—raging storms in most biographies—seems to have taken on more and more allegorical significance, however much it may have been fabricated (see Nicolas Slonimsky, "The Weather . . .").

24. "Apostroph" (accessed through the Walt Whitman Archive: https://whitmanarchive. org/about/index.html). It is a line that is repeated in "O Sun of Real Peace."

as if the only actual magical conjuring of apostrophe would be in its failure or what Johnson calls "a form of ventriloquism through which the speaker throws voice, life, and human form into the addressee, turning its silence into mute responsiveness" (*World* 185). Walt Whitman's "Out of the Cradle Endlessly Rocking," where the mockingbird's apostrophe for his lost love goes unanswered, provides an instance: *"O throat! O throbbing heart! / And I singing uselessly, uselessly all the night. . . . / But my mate no more, no more with me! / We two together no more"* (176). The conjuring, the attempt to voice a thing into being fails, but in doing so brings about the immortal presence in the boy of "a thousand warbling echoes . . . never to die" and a sense of identity that hadn't existed before. In this, the performativity of the apostrophic gesture ("not the representation of an event . . . [but] a fictive, discursive event" itself [Culler 153]) is very close to onomatopoetic language or the divine Word, where (as it is written) voicing means doing.

George Herbert was not a stranger to apostrophe's theological possibilities—prayer, perhaps, being the greatest of all apostrophic acts.[25] When he writes of the effectiveness of sermonizing in *A Country Parson*, and lists the five characteristics of "Holiness," he includes, among others, "making many apostrophes to God."[26] His heavenly poetic phone call, "Deniall," is a testament to the yearning of divine apostrophe:

When my devotions could not pierce
Thy silent ears,
Then was my heart broken, as was my verse . . . .

"Come, come, my God, O come!
But no hearing."

O that thou shouldst give dust a tongue
To cry to thee,
And then not hear it crying! All day long

---

25. Apostrophe is, per Val Cunningham, "the fundamental trope of prayer" (392). More recently, Jahan Ramazani explores poetry and prayer's "many interconnections" (128). See Ramazani, 126–83.

26. Herbert: "When he preacheth, he procures attention by all possible art. . . . [B]y turning often, and making many Apostrophes to God, as, Oh Lord blesse my people, and teach them this point; or, Oh my Master, on whose errand I come, let me hold my peace, and do thou speak thy selfe; for thou art Love, and when thou teachest, all are Scholers. Some such irradiations scatteringly in the Sermon, carry great holiness in them" (*English Works*, 224–25).

> My heart was in my knee,
> But no hearing. . . .

(English Poems, 288)

As the unrhymed final line of each of the stanzas but the last makes clear, there is no responsive echo from the one the speaker is reaching out toward. God, in a sense, has swiped left. The poem hinges on this failure of apostrophe. That is until the hopeful final lines ("They and my minde may chime / And mend my ryme") (289), when the sound of the Word begins harmonically to resonate, as if by prosopopoeia, in the concluding rhyme.[27] But is this turn to address really an instance of poetic conjuring—here, of a deity that presumably does not need a direct address for its own omniscience—or a mere example of wish fulfillment? If a lyric speaker prays in the woods, are her prayers overheard? *O ye, of little face.* Far from the *Quinque Viæ*, the echo of one's own words falls short of offering proof that someone is listening, but it does perform a manner of faith in the speaker. Such ritualistic iterations, ideological interpellation aside, achieve the very faith presupposed by the authenticity of divine address. Making any presumption about the efficacy of this speech act would already mean having resolved a theological debate, and that is not a space I will tread on tonight.[28]

It is difficult, perhaps, in our contemporary age to take the poetic posturing of, say, "O chestnut tree" seriously. The lines themselves seem to force their iterator into a physically different face, one that needs to eyebrow-raise a feigned seriousness or otherwise half-smirk at the fabricated utterance. Culler,

---

27. Not only in "Deniall" can Herbert be seen negotiating the hopes and disappointments of this divine figure. The opening of his "Affliction" (III) seems to turn Culler's sense of apostrophe inside-out: "My heart did heave, and there came forth, *O God!* / By that I knew that thou wast in the grief" (265). Here, the "O God" isn't the discursive moment of apostrophe but a narrative story about an apostrophe (or perhaps, as he writes, about a "sigh"), which is then followed by Herbert "interpreting" his own exclamation.

28. Gavin Hopps writes, "faith has its being and is a wagering *in advance of* such [truthful, confirmable] conditions, which may or may never arrive, or may paradoxically arrive in never arriving" (235). Freud, for his part, writes, "the conjuration of spirits avails nothing unless accompanied by belief, and that the magic effect of prayer fails if there is no piety behind it" (148).

29. Embarrassment can become a particularly poignant sentiment when apostrophe intersects a theological belief. Hopps writes, "Indeed, it is not the *occurrence* of embarrassment that is in dispute or even its meaning . . . but rather the tyrannical authority accorded to it as arbiter of the real. Whereas embarrassment might be seen as policing the boundaries of secular reason, theology might be said to think and act—and perhaps even centrally to have its being—in the space beyond, or *in spite of,* such embarrassment. We might therefore say that embarrassment is the response of reason to that which exceeds it or

notably, has been acutely conscious of apostrophe's tendency to provoke a feeling of embarrassment.[29] This is, after all, an outdated poetic trope that forces its listeners not toward laughter or tears, not toward ecstasy or terror, but toward eye-rolling amid titters for an age of belief that certainly never quite existed as we conjure it now. Apostrophe is "the pure embodiment of poetic pretension," he writes (*Pursuit* 143), noting how "the craft of poetry would be demeaned if it were allowed that any versifier who wrote 'O table' were approaching the condition of sublime poet" (152). Tables, alas, didn't even dance in Marx's day.[30] Culler's remark seems specifically reserved for the poetic O; other, less dramatic apostrophic addresses can still be found across the spectrum of contemporary poetry. But the embarrassment surrounding that O is such that, in a line of Wallace Stevens cited by Culler, the modern poet wants nothing to do with it: ". . . apostrophes are forbidden on the funicular."[31] Despite this embarrassment, despite what Culler—tongue-in-cheek—finds as the tendency of literary critics to "*turn aside* from the apostrophes they encounter in poetry" (136, emphasis my own), Culler can still isolate apostrophe as the central trope of the lyric, precisely because it will not allow for the easy reduction of poetry to paraphrase: "Apostrophe resists narrative because its *now* is not a moment in a temporal sequence but a *now* of discourse, of writing" (152). The poet, as in the opening plea I quoted from Bishop, turns away from her descriptions on the page to cry out a loss, and thereby constitutes, in the process, her own lyric subjectivity.

Too pretty, dreamlike mimicry. My statement concluding the previous paragraph gestures toward the romantically humanizing drive of both the trope and critical reading practices, while underscoring the ideologically problematic transhistorical posture of both—conjuring acts, in their own right. A label like "lyric subjectivity" presumes a historical stability and the willful forgetting of gender, racial, and class difference, where people, *real people*—their pain and pleasure and the violence around them—are turned

---

goes over its head—its retaliation, we might say, not at being refused admission, but at being asked to forego its accustomed dominion" (239).

30. Here is Marx memorably describing the mystical character of the commodity: "A commodity appears at first sight an extremely obvious, trivial thing. But its analysis brings out that it is a very strange thing, abounding in metaphysical subtleties and theological niceties. . . . [A]s soon as [the table] emerges as a commodity, it changes into a thing which transcends sensuousness. It not only stands with its feet on the ground, but, in relation to all other commodities, it stands on its head, and evolves out of its wooden brain grotesque ideas, far more wonderful than if it were to begin dancing of its own free will" (163–64). My own fetish, for the moment, is tropological.

31. Culler is quoting Wallace Stevens's "Botanist on Alp (No. 1)" (*Collected Poetry and Prose* 109; hereafter cited as CPP).

into figures, misrecognized through iterations upon iterations of faceless poetic tropes.[32] Critical theory, from various directions but pressured most notably from historicist, materialist, and identity studies has pushed back on such romantic ideals, already complicated as they were in their own time. More on this in a moment. Whether or not "lyric" is a genre and/or ontological condition and/or practice of reading still remains one of the central disputes in lyric studies, as has been the case over the last generation. Though nuanced, the genre status of lyric, for Culler, still thrives; for de Man, lyric is closer to an ontological condition. Upending lyric studies, Virginia Jackson and Yopie Prins reject the supposed genre status (let alone any privileged ontological status) for the lyric, seeing it instead as a reading practice, as they recontextualize various genres in their historical modes.[33] De Man and Culler's figuration, as Virginia Jackson argues in *Dickinson's Misery*, "is bound up with an idea of the lyric as an ideal, ahistorical genre" (157). Instead, she sees the lyric speaker as a "trope" (230), enacted by a process of tautological reading she and Yopie Prins term "lyricization": "to be lyric is to be read as lyric—and to be read as a lyric is to be printed and framed as a lyric" (8, 6).[34] Interestingly, one might detect in the textual unconscious of Jackson's book, that the (lyric) desires behind lyric forces are neither limited to the act of reading nor to the occasion of verse forms.[35]

---

32. "[O]ne cannot assume address without gender and race," Johnson crucially reminds us (*Persons* 15).

33. See Jackson and Prins; and the special issue on "The New Lyric Studies" (Yaeger 2008).

34. She writes, all the poetic forms and occasions "considered lyrical in the Western tradition before the early nineteenth century were lyric in a very different sense than was or will be the poetry that the mediating hands of editors, reviewers, critics, teachers, and poets have rendered as lyric in the last century and a half" (7).

35. Three moments, "here," in Jackson's book—neither terribly significant nor conspicuously singular—might offer a clue as to how a specifically lyric presence exists somewhere between reading/writing practices and textual forms. Such lyric desires are an integral process of composition—even that of prose—and, depending on how they are taken, they might confirm or complicate some of the various senses of "lyric." The first moment has to do with Jackson's occasional turns to address an absent person. One such apostrophic turn fittingly occurs when she is discussing a leaf pinned to a letter Dickinson wrote to her brother Austin: "[B]y the time that you (whoever you are) encounter the image of the leaf in this [Jackson's] book about Dickinson you will understand it instead as a reminder of what you cannot share with Dickinson's first readers, an overlooked object lyrically suspended in time" (12). Jackson's book is not a lyric poem, and I—David, the figure actually(?) addressed by her prose—have not been trained to read scholarly works as lyric spaces, and yet the reading response (to Jackson, not Dickinson) is still brought about by the centripetal desire of the apostrophizing subject.

In a way, the critical dispute has, in the last generation, become one of the disciplinary proxy wars between "history" and "theory," with the figure of apostrophe central to the debate. Jackson writes, "The idea that the figure of apostrophe generates the lyric imaginary is not just a post-structuralist pose that needs to be historicized; it has been taken to be common sense" ("Apostrophe" 657). Conversely, Culler and others have pushed back on the conflation of a romantic ideology with so-called New Critical tendencies

---

The second moment is an acknowledgement that the presumed solitary critical voice is actually (and unconsciously so, at times) doubled . . . or more. She writes, "Since 'lyric reading' is an historically theorized process that Prins and I have thought out together (lyrically), her ideas on the subject will frequently subtend my own—more frequently, I fear, that [sic] I will be able to note often or explicitly enough in this book. For an explicitly co-written statement of some of these ideas, see Virginia Jackson and Yopie Prins, 'Lyrical Studies' " (244 n.22). The multiplicity of voice is not limited to conscious acknowledgement. This is as true of prose as it is of what one treats as a lyric work. Following Bakhtin, one normally associates such multiplicity with prose, but the dialogic "[s]tratification," as William Watkin compellingly contends, "belongs with poetry in the first instance; prose is merely borrowing it" ("The / Turn" 55). The desires behind both of Jackson's quasi-asides—playful and apologetic, though they be—might be historically or institutionally motivated, but they also come from a *lyric* subject uncertain about how her (critical) address will be understood. These lyric gestures would seem to reside in the text whether or not one wants to read them as such.

The third moment appears in the "Acknowledgements" section of *Dickinson's Misery*, where the author acknowledges that "[a]n early version of chapter 3 appeared as 'Dickinson's Figure of Address' in *Dickinson and Audience*, edited by Martin Orzeck and Robert Weisbuch (Ann Arbor: University of Michigan Press, 1996): 77–103; it is reprinted in expanded form by permission of the University of Michigan Press" (xiii). It is a typical book gesture, usually borne out of courtesy and/or obligation. Against the conventional monograph, which still retains its own lyric illusions of voice and coherence, the edited collection is the space of conversation and contrast. As is typical of the scholarly form, the editors of *Dickinson and Audience* took it upon themselves to introduce each addition to the collection. Jackson's chapter was summarized as follows: "For Jackson 'Dickinson's privileged self-address entitles her to the definition of lyric poet in its purest form,' whose 'structure of address . . . is one in which saying "I" can stand for saying "you"' " (Weisbuch and Orzeck 5). They quote from a passage in the chapter but leave off an important prefatory clause. Here is that passage from Jackson's "Dickinson's Figure of Address" as it appears in the edited collection and then (revised) in *Dickinson's Misery*:

If the notion of a published privacy—a privacy that circulates—has proven immensely attractive ever since, perhaps this is because we still share with that first public the assumption that Dickinson's privileged self-address entitles her to the definition of lyric poet in its purest form. (*Dickinson and Audience* 77)

(themselves codified years after their time and never really as ahistorical as is re-presented today). This is not even to note the more nuanced sense of various scholars of romanticism—those who have refused to take Wordsworth at his word, instead dismissing the notion of a solitary lyric speaker detached from political and social history.[36] This, as my book title takes it, would be the other "disappearing act" of lyric poetry. Some, like Mutlu Blasing, see the lyric "as old as recorded literature" (*Lyric* 20 n12) and essential to how subjects are constructed through language.[37] Others, like Paul Allen Miller

---

> If the notion of a published privacy—a privacy that circulates—has proven immensely attractive ever since, perhaps this is not because of the way we read Emily Dickinson, but because of the way we read lyrics. (*Dickinson's Misery* 127)

The revision (I imagine) came about because the editors, in lifting only part of the passage, did not address the rhetorical thrust of the argument and thereby presented it as the opposite of what it actually is. In their quoting, they left off the crucial first part of the sentence: ". . . because we still share with that first public the assumption that. . . ." The "entitlement," here, is a comment on the historical development of how the poems have come to be read, not a comment on their supposed ideal genre status—the whole point of Jackson's intervention. What was lost was the presence of voice behind the words, which are rhetorically saying "because we [*mistakenly*] still share. . . ." The letter in souffrance did get lost, but its issuer was able to recapture and readdress it in the monograph. This is all a long way of saying that individual desires—called, over the years, *lyric*—reside in texts whether or not one chooses to read them lyrically.

36. Andrea Brady hopes to rethink lyric possibility away from romantic and New Critical ideologies. She writes, "the perception of lyric as fundamentally individuated obscures the collective nature of poetic practice" (xi). According to Gillian White, "Much of the modern and postmodern shame of lyric identification assumes the caricatured figure of the Romantic lyric . . . supposing 'lyric' to be defined by unmitigated individualistic subjectivism, self-absorption, leisured privilege, and ahistoricism" (5). White's project locates "shame" at the heart of the debate, acknowledging "how widely the issue of the 'lyric I'—as problem, preoccupation, and source of shame—shapes thinking about poetry in the field" (25). In a less than charitable review of both Jackson and Prins's lyric anthology and White's book, Lytle Shaw notes how "many poems deemed lyric aren't airtight instantiations of the closure and expressivity attributed to them but scenes of projection of that closure and expressivity" (407), adding that writing shamed as lyric "isn't *actually* so, but has just been rendered so by reductive acts of projection" (409).

37. Blasing's theory of the lyric is based on the material nature of language acquisition. "To dismiss the materiality of language is to dismiss the emotionally charged history that made us who we are—subjects in language, which is the subject of the lyric" (*Lyric* 6). For her, "the disciplinary censoring of lyric poetry . . . is a determined evasion of

locate the beginnings of the lyric to the movement from oral to written texts in ancient Greece. Still others, like Stephanie Burt, are not so troubled by an anachronistic sense of the lyric.[38] That the debate keeps going in circles is not to say that there isn't something crucial at stake. Whether the lyric exists, doesn't exist, or only exists by way of certain hermeneutic apparatuses, the cultural structures of social exclusion and dominance are still at play, and this is something that always ought to make us listen when it calls out. Jackson critiques the privileging of lyric as a romantic ideal, coming at the expense of other poetic forms and the voices behind them. Post-structuralism's "full-throated apostrophic ease," in Jackson's phrasing, "assume[s] a long arc in which the figure of Romantic lyric address becomes increasingly poetic and transhistorical," and this idealized lyric speaker "tends to be White" ("Apostrophe" 659, 660).[39] But variations on how this trope

---

the special status of poetic language as such" (4), and she (rather counterintuitively) locates ideological weights behind recent historicist work, which, self-professedly, ought to be aware of its own ideological structures. "Historicizing the lyric as essentially a late eighteenth and nineteen-century European invention," she writes, "in effect universalizes a historically and geographically specific model of a subject" (4). Rather than see the lyric embrace as reactionary, Blasing understands it as possibly politically advantageous, because understanding a specifically *lyric* logic counteracts the mimetic theory of poetry, through which discursive structures reign. Lyric poetry, thus, "is not mimesis . . . [I]t is a formal practice that keeps in view the linguistic code and the otherness of the material medium of language to all that humans do with it. . . . It offers an experience of another kind of order, a system that operates independently of the production of the meaningful discourse that it enables" (2).

38. Whether or not the lyric is a "real thing," it does, according to Stephanie Burt, have "non-self-contradictory implications and effects" ("What is . . ." 437). As to the charge of anachronism, just because the sense of the word didn't exist as it does now does not mean that poets weren't composing in a similar mode across history.

39. Jackson meticulously shows how Frederick Douglass's newspaper, the *North Star,* "resignified apostrophic lyric address as an inherently racialized fiction" (664), where even Whitman's celebrated democratizing apostrophes hinge on "anxieties repeatedly expressed in the work of his Black contemporaries" (655). Poets such as James Monroe Whitfield, in a lesson not just to his contemporaries, but moreover to ours, "demonstrates that the speaker created by the figure of apostrophe is . . . always already personified and thus always already raced" (670). A revised version of this article was printed as chapter two of Jackson's *Before Modernism,* where the author's twenty-first-century ethically optimistic account of the cultural history of the American lyric traces its roots not to the subgenres of European romanticism but to (what would later be called) lyric subjectivity—always already mediated by racialized narratives.

constitutes a political subject abound.[40] It can be tough for those studying (or writing) in the lyric mode to abandon what feels like the lyric speech act, even when acknowledging the pervasive ideological contexts. It is a Pyrrhic if not a lyric victory. While Culler, for his part, acknowledges a romantic sensibility, he is still able to push back on the New Critical reduction of the lyric to dramatic monologue and thus on the depersonalization of the lyric mode—crucial for ignored voices. I cannot offer any resolution to this critical marathon but rather join a chorus advocating that we listen to what is at stake in these different voices addressing us. I do hope to show, though, that because of the demands of tradition and form and history, what is or could be "lyric" remains a dynamic question for poets and any poetics working through the ideological space of language. This, of course, is not to deny what Johnson calls "the political dimensions of the scholarly study of rhetoric" (*World* 184).

"Contemporary US black poetics," Jess Cotton writes, "exposes the ways in which 'lyric' is a fictional production that has been historically mobilized to bolster ideals of transcendent white humanity, particularly as they constellate around the fantasy of the universal lyric speaker who operates as the stand-in for the sanctity of white interiority against which blackness is cast as otherness" (529). Anthony Reed and Kevin Quashie, in different ways, see the lyric as a more nuanced, contested site. If scholars have collectively fallen into a trap of "lyricization," Reed makes the convincing case that they have also fallen into the trap of "racialized reading." He cautions against such reactive, prescriptive reading, instead embracing what he sees as a postlyric, "aesthetic break" (22), which features a "more radical literary politics . . . not rooted in the biography or politics of the author or in the determinant political situation to which the work 'responds' " (5–6).[41] Quashie takes issue with "[t]he politics of representation, where

---

40. Lloyd Pratt sees the apostrophic acts of the mid-nineteenth-century *Les Cenelles* poets of New Orleans as a form of "apostolic invitation," replacing the romantic "stranger witness" with the "poetry of stranger-with-ness" (75, 67). The communal figuration—what he calls "apostolic apostrophe" (80)—ventur[es] a version of lyric that does not reproduce the privatized self-enclosure that will come to be associated with lyric utterance. . . . [T]he *Les Cenelles* poets engage practices of citation, revision, and address that disaggregate the sense of self without destroying it" (69).

41. Reed references what Erica Hunt ("Notes for an Oppositional Poetics") calls an aesthetic of "unrecognizable speech," where, in Reed's words, "the hiatus of unrecognizability can spur new thought and new imaginings, especially the (re)imagining of collectivities and intellectual practices" (1).

black subjectivity exists for its social and political meaningfulness rather than as a marker of the human individuality of the person who is black"(4).[42] In this critical model he critiques, the dominant framework for understanding black culture, becomes "resistance" (11). The result is the hollowing out of any sense of interiority, of a complicated (*lyric*, I would say) subjectivity, that is, of course, responsive to but not entirely dependent on social and political discourse. There is something worth holding on to here.

The rejection in toto of the lyric, as Sonya Posmentier convincingly makes the point, comes with its own challenges.[43] For centuries, poets of color were denied such lyric presence and transcendence in the same manner people of color were denied legal citizenship and humanistic subjectivity. Now that this lyric space (albeit a problematic one) has been opened, critics (poets, poststructuralists, and poetry scholars—for very different reasons, operating in very different social and cultural marketplaces) come along and claim what might be a very productive door for many has now been closed. This has a Kafkaesque resonance. Recent work aligned with the critique of "lyric" still shows how (good) readings of specific poets excuse those poets from the naïve sense of the lyric subject. It is a (worthwhile but exhausting) exercise in faith. One feeling more pessimistic about resistance would claim that "the system" allows countercultural critical narratives to expand or contract the balloon that would otherwise pop. One feeling even more pessimistic would call this a ruse of power, a limited vision of choice decorating the two bookshelves in the university library that haven't yet been turned into a Starbucks. As one may gather, I am more reluctant to embrace not the politics but rather the *promise* of an anti-lyric mode, which (importantly) decries the ideological baggage of the transcendental lyric but then optimistically—and cruelly so—conjures a manner of resistance in an aesthetic (or antiaesthetic—I am unsure of the difference) alteration of the very same form. Too often, this ends up fetishizing difference or romanticizing a supposed subversive aesthetic.

---

42. He continues, describing a narrative all too familiar: "[a]s an identity, blackness is always supposed to tell us something about race or racism, or about America, or violence and struggle and triumph or poverty and hopefulness" (4).

43. Rather than "invok[ing] the qualities of lyric poetry as 'givens' inherited from a much older European classical tradition," she explores how they act "as vital modern concerns about the capacities of literary genre . . . generated on the margins of American and European modernity" (4). For her, Black writers in what has come to be called a lyric tradition, have importantly "countered the alienation brought about by social and environmental catastrophe by voicing a poetics of survival, repair, and generation" (3).

More crucially, beyond being a reactionary, embarrassing, or passé trope, apostrophe can seem to exult in its privileged deafness to actual voices crying out for help. Listening to, but countering, such charges of critical deafness, Johnson asks whether there is "any *inherent* connection between figurative language and questions of life and death, of who will wield and who will receive violence in a given human society" (*World* 184). She turns to Gwendolyn Brooks's difficult poem "The Mother," whose opening line is the grammatically end-stopped but unrelenting "Abortions will not let you forget." Refiguring the problematic of apostrophe away from the privileged romantic "I," Johnson explains how Brooks's speaker is ambiguously conflated with the addressee. The opening address "you" is really a "one" but really the "I," and the speaker is "simultaneously eclipsed, alienated, and confused with the addressee" leaving in doubt a "clear cut distinction . . . between subject and object, agent and victim" (189).[44] Rather than using the apostrophic address to constitute the self, "Brooks is representing the self as eternally addressed and possessed by the lost, anthropomorphized other" (189). The ground of Johnson's intervention has been heavily trodden under strong poetic feet, but I do want to turn to one of the less-addressed moments in her essay, which subtly invokes the elephant in the stanza and one of the dedicatees of Johnson's book—the recently departed Paul de Man, branded by Marc Redfield as "the allegory and allergen of theory-in-America, who haunts the archive as the figure for theory's half-obliterated, never quite eradicable or forgettable or entirely present-to-itself *event*" (14).[45] Here is an extended excerpt from Johnson's final two pages:

---

44. Johnson goes further to ask "[w]hat happens when the lyric speaker . . ." isn't "sure of the precise degree of human animation that existed in the entity killed? What is the debate over abortion about, indeed, if not the question of when, precisely, a being assumes a human form?" (189). It is not that Johnson is simply politicizing figuration or the lyric. We only have the political because of the undecidability. Elucidating Johnson further, Judith Butler notes how "the poem articulates that state of suspended animation ('living person' or not?), indeed, of undecidability that governs debates on the life or personhood of the fetus" (xxii–xxiii).

45. Much more politely than one ought, Redfield rends Evelyn Barish's and David Lehman's accounts of de Man, which predictably "run counterclockwise to the desire to understand what [de Man's] theoretical texts are saying" (15). He writes, "Both biographers approach their subject with an odd blend of anger, fascination, and ignorance—seemingly inexhaustible anger; near-obsessive fascination; an ignorance that can at times seem almost willed" (15). While Barish is "driven by a desire to disqualify through ad hominem argument *the theory she admits she does not understand*" (15), Lehman's book "feeds its fires almost entirely with caricatural versions of the threat of unreadability" (17).

The verbal development of the infant, according to Lacan, begins as a **demand** addressed to the mother, out of which the entire verbal universe is spun. Yet the mother addressed is somehow a personification, not a person—a personification of presence or absence, of Otherness itself.

> **Demand** in itself bears on something other than the satisfactions it calls for. It is **demand** of a presence or of an absence—which is what is manifested in the primordial relation to the mother, pregnant with that Other to be situated *within* the needs that it can satisfy. . . . Insofar as [man's] needs are subjected to **demand**, they return to him alienated. This is not the effect of his real dependance . . . , but rather the turning into signifying form as such, from the fact that it is from the locus of the Other that its message is emitted.[46]

If **demand** is the originary vocative, which assures life even as it inaugurates alienation, then it is not surprising that questions of animation inhere in the rhetorical figure of apostrophe . . . there is precisely a link between **demand** and animation, between apostrophe and life-and-death dependency. If apostrophe is structured like **demand**, and if **demand** articulates the primal relation to the mother as a relation to the Other, then lyric poetry itself—summed up in the figure of apostrophe—comes to look like the fantastically intricate history of endless elaborations and displacements of the single cry "Mama!" (198–99; emphasis my own)

It would not be odd, in view of Johnson's ethical turn in this essay, to repeat the word "demand," even less so while working in this specific Lacanian mode. Yet, given the context and the density of the word here, it is difficult to ignore the demand/de Man parallel. This is a paronomasia that runs deeper than a simple twinkle in the letters. The word appears as a refrain, as in prayer or conjuring, a subtle, *graphic* invocation, yet one picked up by the ear. The call isn't poetry, but perhaps it takes part in what we have come to understand—rightly or wrongly—as lyric address.

---

46. Quoting Lacan, 286.

It is not the only time in the book she plays with the word "demand," which is sprinkled here and there throughout. She puns explicitly on the name in the "Rigorous Unreliability" chapter, which is ostensibly on the values and evaluation of deconstruction, but veers to poke at the knot between grammar and subjectivity. Her section heading "Demanding Anacoluthons" (manners of syntactical veering off) shows how de Man's texts themselves "inscribe signs of subjectivity in the absence of any grammatical subject," perhaps as part of his "will to erase" (24). That chapter begins with a quotation of his: "Literature as well as criticism—the difference between them being delusive—is condemned (or privileged) to be forever the most rigorous and, consequently, the most unreliable language in terms of which man names and transforms himself" (*Allegories* 19; qtd. in Johnson 17). Most critical glosses (*pace* the delusive non-difference) of this have focused on the aporia between literature and criticism, text and interpretation—or what de Man would call reading. Johnson (I think) is ultimately interested in another part of this phrasing, which is often overlooked: "of which man names." There is something about the particular performativity of naming that tickles Johnson's and de Man's attention—the subjectivity attached to having a name and the agency attached to self-naming, the hailing of another by calling out a name or a metaphorical third-person invocation, itself a sign of absence but one that still chills.[47] Rather than her own anacoluthon, the apostrophic effect of naming takes a performative turn, as in the invocation of "Rumpelstiltskin," which saves the queen's firstborn or the mentioning of "Calaf" from Turandot's mouth ("O giovinetto!") that would spell his death. "The act of 'calling,'" Johnson writes, ". . . correlates a lack of name with a loss of membership" (195). As she was writing—and perhaps even more so now—the invocation of the very name "de Man" would have been enough to trigger deaf ears in many academic circles. It was enough to make her preface her book with an apologia of sorts, addressing what had by then been named the "de Man affair." Flipping the mother/child model in the passage she quotes from Lacan, a model which might as well also name the teacher/student relationship, Johnson is able to issue her demand: that

---

47. Elsewhere, Johnson makes the connection between the proper name and the epitaph, noting (uncoincidentally) that it was Dr. Johnson who "emphasizes the identificatory importance of the deceased's proper name" (*Persons* 11). "The impulse to epitaph," she writes, "is thus the same as the impulse to write: to mark something that can communicate with any passer-by," and, "like all lyric poetry, [the epitaph] depend[s] on the creation of a poetic voice" (13, 14).

an old teacher appear now, at the conclusion of her book, to listen. "De Man's subversive teaching," she writes elsewhere, "certainly unsettled many of the assumptions that have accompanied the humanist understanding of the canon, but he did nothing to unseat the traditional white male author from his hiding place behind the impersonality of the universal subject, the subject supposed to be without gender, race, or history. . . . It is up to us to open the subversiveness of teaching further—*without* losing the materialist conception of language that remains de Man's truly radical contribution" ("Poison or Remedy" 369). This feels more a just response than a simple celebratory thumbs-up or dismissive thumbs-down—each too frequent in our day.

It feels off, decades into the twenty-first century, to spend one's time writing and thinking about a no-longer-au-courant trope, let alone to do so through the alleged hocus-pocus of a poetical-theoretical lens, when there is so much more that needs to be done. This is not even to address the tiredness one feels in defending whatever lurks in what is now the quotation-marked "deconstruction" let alone in explaining away what has never lurked within it.[48] "What would it mean," Anahid Nersessian asks, "to continue to think about arcane topics like apostrophe or lyric address in the face of charges that this is a worthless and even a damaging pursuit?" (135).[49] This is a challenge for all such academic projects today and feels even more so for this book: how a tropological, poetic balloon of "O" and a discussion about it can have a meaningful place in our world. Better than I am able, Barbara Johnson articulates how it is a mistake to conceive of the figure outside figuration, and how focusing on a poetic trope today must not be at the expense of history, of what Fredric Jameson called "what hurts" (102). The two—figure and history—have never been exclusive, despite the allure of the humanist gesture or the metaphysical glance. But it is not just what is supposedly outside or behind or beneath the cultural apparatus that hurts. "Not long ago," Claudia Rankine remembers, "you are in a room where

---

48. I would have to disagree, here, with earlier words of Kwame Anthony Appiah, a thinker I greatly admire. But his phrasing, given my own figurative contexts, is worth repeating: "If I were Derrida, I might, perhaps, add that the 'O' which mediates between the names [Sunday O. Anozie's] is a zero, an absence . . ." (127).

49. If scholars have identified apostrophe with lyric itself, she proposes, "that may be because apostrophe so explicitly concerns the activity of things that seem hardly to exist at all" (132–33). Chapter 4 of her *The Calamity Form* connects poetic apostrophe to visual art.

someone asks the philosopher Judith Butler what makes language hurtful. You can feel everyone lean in. Our very being exposes us to the address of another, she answers. We suffer from the condition of being addressable. . . . Language that feels hurtful . . ."—and this, as life has shown over and over, does not fall equally—"is intended to exploit all the ways that you are present" (*Citizen* 49).

I hope, here, to continue the important study of the poetic desire of address without being blind to the politics behind the figure, while explaining why it all matters beyond our academic circles, even to family and friends who still think this is a book about "apostrophe s" or that its sequel will be on the letter "p." Despite my framing, my ostensible argument, and the theorists cited in this introduction and what will briefly follow, this book is not really about deconstruction. It is about poems and poetics, about how the dramatized turn to call out to an absent friend or idea, which generates a lyric voice, is made possible by the graphic sign it pretends not to acknowledge. We turn at moments that are deeply human, this immediacy of the moment calling forth an alternative to the present. There is a social function in turning outside oneself, even if it is to an imaginary projection of that very same self. Wary as I am of reinventing the wheel, I hope to grasp the circularity of the turning address of O as it exists between trope and sign, between the illusion of voice and the graphic on the page, between metaphysical longing and the texture of language.

Many poets, acutely aware of both the possibilities and embarrassment of apostrophe, have wandered in this poetic space. My own chapters, which have now taken on the sitcom familiarity of a domestic partnership ("oh, you"), are mostly chronological, and they range from W. B. Yeats, Wallace Stevens, Elizabeth Bishop, James Merrill, Emily Dickinson, Carly Simon, Terrance Hayes, to the Cure. In some of the chapters, my attention will be on one poem or verse, while in others it will be more of a gathering of multiple poems. My mostly twentieth-century historical grounding is not meant as a universalizing claim about either twentieth-century poetics or modern incarnations of apostrophe. Rather, these following chapters are simply what has been fitted to my circle. If one "historical" argument need be ripped from these pages, it would be the self-evident claim that with the explosion of print culture in the nineteenth and twentieth centuries the reach of talking to "no one" becomes vaster than previously imagined. This, notwithstanding, the individual chapters in this book will not posit a new ontological claim or reaffirm a truism about apostrophe or literature or history. Instead, it is my hope that they will enlarge the discussion of their intersections. So very many other poets and poems, of course, deserve to be part of the discussion and might, perhaps, be in the future. I think of Marianne Moore's tentacled O of a mountain "Completing a circle, / you have been deceived into thinking that you have progressed" or the performativity of argument in Edna St. Vincent Millay's "Oh, oh, you will be sorry for that word!" which invokes by iterating a husband's speech only to have the speaker be the one to will her own absence. And this is to say nothing of Olga Broumas's erotically O-charged "Artemis" or Langston Hughes's "O Blues!" predictably (or unpredictably?) interrupting the drowsy syncopation of the line or T. S. Eliot's jazz-inspired "O O O O Shakespeherean Rag."[50] One might even go back a few years to the consoling address of John Donne's compass-drawn love circle and its trepidated spheares.[51] The one chapter that, alas, for me, never came full circle intended itself to be on the geographical climate of Seamus Heaney, a /poet very much invested in the material shapes and sounds of letters.[52]

---

50. Moore, "An Octopus," 71; Millay, ["Oh, oh, you will be sorry for that word!"], 54; Olga Broumas: "I work / in silver the tongue-like forms / that curve round a throat // an arm-pit, the upper / thigh, whose significance stirs in me / like a curviform alphabet / that defies // decoding, appears / to consist of vowels, beginning with O, the O- / mega, horseshoe, the cave of sound" (*Beginning with O* 23); Hughes, "O Blues!" 33; Eliot, "The Waste Land," 34.

51. The well-known conceit of "A Valediction: Forbidding Mourning" parallels the separation of morning lovers to the geometric compass: "But trepidation of the spheares, / Though greater farre, is innocent. . . . / And though it in the center sit, / Yet when the other far doth rome, / It leanes and hearkens after it, / And growes erect, as that comes home. . . . / Thy firmnes drawes my circle just, And makes me end where I begunne" (38–39).

52. "The shower / gathering in your heelmark" he tells us or, rather, tells the acquaintance he was walking with, "was the black *O* / in *Broagh* . . ." (*Poems* 105). He is punning, perhaps on the sound of brogue, lingering in the traces of his poetic feet. The spinning globe of a O in "Alphabets" offers another example of letters fitting themselves to the shapes of the world:

A globe in the window tilts like a coloured *O*. . . .

As from his small window
The astronaut sees all that he has sprung from,
The risen, aqueous, singular, lucent O
Like a magnified and buoyant ovum—

Or like my own wide pre-reflective stare. . . . (*The Haw Lantern* 1–3).

Some of the readings within the following chapters are less about apostrophic address than related conversations about lyric poetry (or, if you would have it another way, about lyric reading), especially regarding the materiality of printed verse. In searching this relationship as a way into language itself, I have found it useful to turn to the Italian philosopher Giorgio Agamben's sense of verse, which understands linear enjambment as "the necessary and sufficient condition of versification" ("Idea of Prose" 40). Many significant pictures—whole eschatological systems, the relationship of philosophy to poetry, the possibility of the lyric—stem from this starting point, and I will consider them further in the Interlude and first chapter, which follow this introduction. For my own turn or return to poetic apostrophe, focusing on enjambment shows how lyric addresses might compel and be compelled by the turns of a writing system. Although it cannot provide the "answer" to unanswerable, dynamic questions about the cultural production we have come to call poetry, enjambment, for me at least, has become a way to think about how the intersections of culture and history and social life are mediated, in part, by this *otherness* within language. And that has often been a compellingly enough way to talk about what poetry is and does. I do not believe that this is *the* way one ought to read poetry, but it is another path one might take. Although there are notable, important exceptions to Agamben's framing of poetry, his thoughts align very well with my own continued interest in how an often-arbitrary language sets the parameters for thought. Despite his recent pronouncements, which are similarly difficult to comprehend, Agamben's poetical-philosophical model helps us, as William Watkin persuasively argues, "to return art back to life [in order to ask] what it means for a living being to speak" ("The / Turn" 51).

As much fun as it would be to write about the circular figure of the moon for two hundred pages, I try to shift the apostrophic focus of each chapter. The first chapter—a revisioning of an article bringing W. B. Yeats alongside Giorgio Agamben—offers an extended reading of Yeats's early

---

Very often, "O" for Heaney becomes, as he phrases it in "Wheels within Wheels": "an orbit coterminous with longing." We might see this in the final section of "Clearances," written after his mother's passing: "I thought of walking round and round a space / Utterly empty . . ." (*The Haw Lantern* 31). For the intersection of apostrophe and politics in Heaney's work, see Kevin McGuirk, "Questions": Heaney's apostrophes seek "to redress a sense of loss and breakdown, to stop time, to induct us into a fictional but whole presence in poetry; each works to resolve the fear and uncertainty expressed in the urgent questions posed by the poet" (75).

poem, "The Stolen Child." Now recontextualized in terms of the apostrophic address, I consider what it means for the (dramatic) speakers—kidnapping fairies from Celtic folklore—to shift their focus from describing an enchanting landscape to address directly their desired children. Presumably, only the children can hear the fairies, who shroud a very different, very threatening lyric disappearing act: the loss of identity in the call of another. The poem moves between circular shapes and the force of circular rituals, returning often to the performatively mesmerizing refrain "Come away, O human child." The poem's rhetorical drive finds itself amid competing desires, and this too pulls at the heart of the reader, ever eager to escape from a world that, in Yeats's time and in ours, doesn't make much sense.

"Oh! Blessed rage for order. . . ." I hear Wallace Stevens's words from "The Idea of Order at Key West" at every turn, voicing "The maker's rage to order words of the sea . . . / And of ourselves and of our origins, / In ghostlier demarcations, keener sounds" (*CPP* 106). One hears in the "words of the sea" the Stevensian comedian "C"—ever arch, always arching—never wanting to complete the circle. Moving between Os and Xs, the chapter on Stevens considers how the apostrophic and the chiastic (the rhetorical figure of repetition and reversal) intersect, and in doing so reveal how we are constituted from without by the materiality of language, its keener sounds.[53] It is the address or interaction with radical otherness—the rebounding of an echo that has been there all along—that ends up constituting the lyric subject, a figure framed, as in Da Vinci's Vitruvian Man, by X and O. Stevens's echo is not merely of voice, but moreover derived from the ghostlier demarcations of letters.

Punning not so much on apostrophe and chiasmus, but on the homonyms of letters, Elle King, in a chart-topping hit, connects the passionate "oh" to the lingering presences of former lovers: "Ex's and the oh, oh, oh's they haunt me."[54] Elizabeth Bishop, in her time, would never be so explicit,

---

53. Eve Sedgwick connects chiasmus to the diacritical differences and temporal displacements of Derridean *différance*: "These senses of chiasmus also have an affinity with *différance*, a word coined by Derrida (in *Writing and Difference*) to link together the features of *deferral* and *difference* in the structure of language (i.e., the ways that meanings are not self-present in words, but depend on both a system of diacritical differences across the language as a whole, and also on the temporal displacements involved in iterative utterance and grammatical contextualization)." The quotation comes from course material Sedgwick assembled for her students. It was accessed through the website: https://eveksedgwickfoundation.org/teaching/rhetorical-devices.html.

54. Elle King, "Ex's and Oh's," *Love Stuff*, RCA, 2015.

but more than lyric longing frequents the shape of her O and the agony of her voicing. O, as Catharine Stimpson makes the point more generally about female sexuality, is the space and impossibility of Bishop's desire.[55] But for the asthmatic poet, like her fish "breathing in / the terrible oxygen," it is also the difficult space of inspiration, as if the world around her were always on ritualistic fire. As I touched on briefly in this introduction, the final lines of "The Armadillo" show the dangerous scope of humanity's ritualistic actions and call into question the ethical import of the lyric act (or of lyric reading) itself. I suggested that it was within this failure of speech that something like a poetic voice, always teetering, materializes. The chapter on Bishop tracks these circular hesitations, always seemingly through a visual image, and always seemingly deferring any sense of a cohesive "I," through what Victoria Harrison calls the poet's relational poetics (9).

Like Bishop, James Merrill was often viewed in his time as too lyrically detached.[56] His utterances weren't just overheard; they were sanded down and gilded with four coats of paint. Behind his immaculate façade of form, though, always lurked his "chronicles of love and loss." As many of his later poems suggest, there is a terrifying roundness to the interlocking spirals of DNA. "Look closely at the letters," he insists in his enigmatic poem "b o d y": ". . . how like a little kohl-rimmed moon / o plots her course from b to d." Y or "why," standing outside the lines of life, gives us a final pun, but the joke is on us—we who are conjured by the verse—as we try to listen for an answer that will never come. Merrill's figuration—always more trope than body—has us asking what one loses when one looks too closely at letters? And yet for decades, that is what Merrill did. "With his Ouija board and [his partner David] Jackson's willing hand to help," Langdon Hammer writes, "Merrill renewed poetry's ancient task of soliciting speech from the gods. He activated a source of inspiration existing in language itself, inviting us into that basic mystery by which voice and presence . . . emerge from the letters on a page" (xv). Contrary to romantic notions of lyric solitude, Merrill's séance-inflected poetic voice, as Lesley Wheeler shows, is "intrinsically choral, multiple, and allusive," and it thereby "presents its lyric

---

55. O, for Stimpson, "can stand for both the zero of impossibility and for the possibilities of female sexuality" (100). See her *Where the Meanings Are*, especially chapter 9 "Zero Degree Deviancy."

56. Working from Multu Blasing's developmental-materialist model of lyric poetry, Claudia Ingram argues against this simplistic reduction. Instead, Merrill's "work shimmers with the plural senses, and nonsense, produced by the play of language's materials. . . . His habit of mind and extravagance of style play out in the work's seemingly casual subversion of reductive cultural myths and easy polemics. In this, Merrill tends to outdistance his critics" (45).

speaker as a fragile piece of artifice" (14).[57] Underlying all this harmless fun with word games lies a glimpse into the dark recesses of our staged being and the impossibly worthwhile lettered attempts to recover the world.

At the heart of the book and outside its general chronological order is my chapter on Emily Dickinson. The hope is that, following Bishop and Merrill, Dickinson's playfulness with the circular trope might project just a little more. Here, I consider the morphing shapes and shades of Dickinson's O amid and outside any apostrophic turns. Loosely speaking, the first half is about the appearances in her work of the circular form, whether as a zero, a circumference, or a contour of the natural world—pivotal for how Dickinson understood her world and how we are asked to understand it too—and the second half is about her varied forms of address, which circulated often through her epistolary poetics. The two naturally intersect, although never, at least for my own sense of balance, come full circle. (Thankfully) Dickinson's verse does not ever seem to accommodate what one wishes to find in it. Still, there is enough to be said. As many of her readers have noted and as she herself winks at us, reading Emily Dickinson's verse often feels like circling and circling around an object and voice that is never decipherable. The only hope, as Dickinson phrases it, in a complicated moment, is finding "an Ampler Zero." This chapter and the chapter on Elizabeth Bishop draw on archive material, which, especially in recent years, has complicated critical notions of the lyric as much as of the output of individual poets. The fact one generally does not look at the multiple false stops and starts of drafts means that to a great extent—even in those self-professed anti-New Critical approaches—one is still romanticizing the published/finished text as some manner of atemporal organic whole. At the end of the chapter on Dickinson, I offer an extended reading of an unrealized pause of address in one of the manuscript pages and consider how Dickinson's written script mediates the desire lurking somewhere between circular gestures and her unusual apostrophic poetics.

"Lyric," we sometimes remind ourselves when it fits the critical tune we hope to hum, derives from the Greek *lyrikos* (λυρικός) for a song that was sung to a lyre. But even this sense, as Virginia Jackson makes the point, was prompted by absence: "lyric was from its inception a term used to describe a music that could no longer be heard" ("Lyric" 826).[58] Historically, Jahan

---

57. She reminds us of Merrill's (and others') position that "No voice is as individual as the poet would like to think" (*Collected Prose* 122).

58. Detailing this historical transition, Matthew Bevis writes that "scholars of the Alexandrine library sought to preserve poems on the page whose musical settings had been lost" (n.p.).

Ramazani explains, the term loses its musical connotation with the shift from an oral poetic tradition to a written one. He writes, "The primal unity between song and lyric poetry . . . is often said to have been fractured long ago by written texts and then exploded by print culture" (184). Whereas song developed to encompass words, music, and what Roland Barthes called "the body in the voice as it sings" (188; qtd in Ramazani 192), the written poem could only proffer another ghostly specter of voice; quite unsurprisingly, the modern sense of aesthetic authenticity would come to be tied more toward song and its bodily presence.

In Chapter 6 and the epilogue, I explore how songs and song lyrics can intersect, in different ways, pseudo-apostrophic addresses, and consider what such intersections might tell us about the cultural networks around them. "Deracinated from their musical, vocal, and social contexts," Ramazani warns, "song lyrics often seem skeletal, diminished, caricatured by expectations of semantic, graphic, syntactic, imagistic, allusive, psychological complexity and imaginative reach" (193).[59] What happens, though, when the performance becomes reified in the recording, and the supposedly "original" extemporaneous moment—in reality, quite calculated—returns as scheduled in its dissemination? The chapter on Carly Simon circles back to a mediated performance of a song I critically habituated years ago.[60] The performance of songs—either actual or hypothetical—complicates many of the questions about lyric subjectivity and poetic apostrophe that I will have turned to in this book. Are songs meant to be heard or overheard? Is the "you" to whom they are often addressed an actual "you" or a generic one? Or what about the audience member who (grammatically, at least) feels summoned by the second-person address? What, in a sense, happens when the singer wants to hold on to the path of the "you" after the voice has left the mouth? Carly Simon's 1972 hit "You're So Vain" is a perfect enactment of a spurned woman not wanting to give her "vain" former lover the time of day even in the testimonial that decries him. The second person address ("You're so vain / You probably think this song is about you") puts listeners in the awkward position of being asked to believe that the person to whom

59. Conversely, "Musical accents are often at odds with poetic rhythms and enjambments, and the music forces the poetry to follow a different tempo, typically slowing it down and even obscuring the text's intricate semantic networks . . ." (Ramazani 189).

60. At the time, the ostensible institutional "vanity" of those upholding the flame of "literature" still necessitated, in some circles, a good deal of defensive posturing for those who wanted to examine texts of popular culture. If, as Horace pointed out, even Homer sometimes nods—the first epic fail—thankfully, we might now say that Homer Simpson (or another stand-in for popular culture) at times rouses.

the song is addressed is not the person to whom the song is addressed. This shifting "you" of the song mirrors the shifting "I" of the lyric speaker, and both represent a sort of vanity: the lover, because he seems always to be looking at himself, and the speaker, because she thinks she can control each instance of the apostrophic "you," as though the actual "you" has become part of her song. In considering the relationship of deixis to apostrophe, I now ask whether the song is an authentic "voicing" or in the end just another rhetoric guise, fit and fitted for its marketplace.

Beyond the big-stakes political (legal subjectivity) and the small-stakes political (MA program tussling about aesthetics), the ethical dangers of the "lyric wars" come more into focus in the chapter on Terrance Hayes, a poet who is less poetically embarrassed by the realities of social politics than most of the other writers in this study, and not necessarily in the ways that are read onto him. In an interview with Charles Rowell, Hayes pushes back a bit against the critical embrace of the subversive antiaesthetic, arguing in favor of a more nuanced version, not somehow outside the lyric. "Maybe the generation after [the Civil Rights generation]," he ventures, "moved even closer to the internal, to the idea that black power could be achieved through the personal, the lyric *I . . .*" (1079). In interviews, he calls his ambivalence about this stance his "schizophrenia." Without revisiting the politics of the lyric wars, my chapter on Hayes takes it for granted that his lyric voice is far more complicated than the critical discussions about lyric potential have been. His lines turn with the hesitancy of a driver entering a roundabout, watching for other words that might want to drive through. And suddenly, he is in another car, going the other way. Unlike Donne's compass-drawn shape, Hayes's "perfect circle" is a dream and a nightmare, and his voyage through O becomes its own *Divine Comedy*.

My monograph, in returning to song, concludes with a very different sort of critical epilogue. If literary criticism has developed in remarkable ways (and I count "Theory" among the productive paths), it has also too often idled under the tyranny of its own semi*lyric* modes, rather than dancing to the songs it hears. "The trope of the organic whole," as Mary Poovey, makes the case, "continues to organize most of the strains of criticism that now dominate U.S. practice" (432).[61] That was 2001, but the pressure, in

____

61. Modern literary criticism (in the manner of Henry James) "embodies *lyric* features" (426). Poovey lists five features of criticism echoing lyric identity: embedded quotations and close reading are the most convincing; the diachronic developmental narratives (one critic building on another's work) and a critical sphere that extends the whole to discussions with other critics (a mode of critical "self-reflexivity" but one that extends "outside") are not as persuasive.

some ways, still feels tangible. Of course, critical engagements usually have a beginning, middle, and end—a wholeness not unlike that found in other pre-romantic conceptions. Still, there's a deeper sense that, like the new critical idea of a lyric poem, monographs ought to cohere top to bottom. Ephemeral, they are not, but, for the most part, they do remain unspeakably individualized experiences, structured by a single voice (however much in conversation with other critics). Their pretense of organic coherence is met by a pretense of mastery (not how I understand the lyric, but how others often treat it), and a rejection of affective subjectivity, which, in Poovey's phrasing, "threatened to undermine the possibility that criticism could ever be considered systematic, rigorous, or sophisticated enough to require expertise" (430). The epilogue will turn away from these institutional pressures and instead embrace the more dynamic modes of lyric possibility and address—uncertainty, multivocality, and an "organic" weight that comes from living beings and not from the pretense of a coherent whole. As the history of both (lyric) poetry and criticism can attest, sometimes when one calls out, another is able to respond, never more so than when the call can be memorialized in graphic form. The second half of this epilogue was cowritten with the Romanticist scholar Manu Samriti Chander, composed across distance, during the pandemic when the gravity of calling out to another who wasn't there could not always be embellished poetically. We offer intersecting readings of a ventriloquizing act in The Cure's "Just Like Heaven," and a reframing of the lyric in terms of mutual presence. Betrayed by a capricious titling, as providence would have it, we continue the dialogue alongside another contemporaneous song. What would it mean, we ask, not to keep pretending that the lyric was and will always be an utterance that is overheard when we might otherwise think of it as something necessarily written down because a poet knows that her solitary voice will, in time, be heard? Text gives the possibility for future voices in conversation, for new communal spaces that are more than the absence of presence. So sing to us, O Muse. This, at the very least, is what poetic possibility is owed.

An Interlude

Some Horsing Around

An introduction should not intrude.

—Jacques Derrida, The Archeology of the Frivolous, 108

Buried deep under the entry "Horse" in Volume XIII, Slice VI of the eleventh edition of the *Encyclopædia Britannica* ("Home, Daniel Dunglas" to "Hortensius, Quintus (dictator of Rome)"), one finds the following lineage:

> Shakespeare was the son of Hobgoblin by Aleppo, and consequently the male line of the Darley Arabian would come through these horses instead of through Bartlett's Childers, Squirt, and Marske; the *Stud-Book*, however, says that Marske was the sire of Eclipse. . . . In Eclipse's pedigree there are upwards of a dozen mares whose pedigrees are not known, but who are supposed to be of native blood. Eclipse was a chestnut horse with a white blaze down his face; his off hind leg was white from the hock downwards, and he had black spots upon his rump—this peculiarity coming down to the present day in direct male descent. His racing career commenced at five years of age, viz. on the 3rd May 1769, at Epsom, and terminated on the 4th October 1770, at Newmarket. He ran or walked over for eighteen races, and was never beaten. It was in his first race that Mr O'Kelly took the odds to a large amount before the start for the second heat, that he would place the horses. When called upon to declare, he uttered the exclamation, which the event justified, "Eclipse first, and the rest nowhere."

> Eclipse commenced his stud career in 1771, and had an enormous number of foals, of which four only in the direct male line have come down to us, viz. Potooooooooo, or, as he is commonly called, Pot-8-os (1773), his most celebrated son, King Fergus (1775), Joe Andrews (1778), and Mercury (1778), though several others are represented in the female line. Pot-8-os was the sire of Waxy (1790) out of Maria (1777) by Herod out of Lisette (1772) by Snap. Waxy, who has been not inaptly termed the ace of trumps in the *Stud-Book*, begat Whalebone (1807), Web (1808), Woful (1809), Wire (1811), Whisker (1812), and Waxy Pope (1806), all but the last being out of Penelope (1798). . . .

It goes on. Biblical in its genealogy, Borgesian in its orotundity, with an oblivious touch of Dickensian wit, the passage chronicles a late eighteenth-century equine pedigree, or what we might call a very different sense of bred and circuits. Putting aside the revelation that Shakespeare was the son of Hobgoblin by Aleppo (a trying aside to put), we might see the importance of lineage itself, not unlike a certain promulgated poetic tradition, itself "in the direct male line come down to us." Potooooooooo (or Pot-8-os or "Potatoes")—a homophone literalized, a writing turned into speech turned into writing—himself a partial Eclipse, sired Waxy and a whole lot of W-grandchildren.[1] Two centuries later, the spectral protuberance of an alphabetic witticism remains. Willard Espy quips:

> Who of vodka distilled from potooooooooo partake,
> Heed this warning;
> You'll be jolly at night, but oooooooooooo when you wake
> In the morning. (26–27)

Eleven Os, we learn, is *more* than the eight of pot-8-o. Hence: morose when you wake [pause] In the morning.

*　　*　　*

---

1. It is neither here nor there, but, since we are already running a foal of the circuit, one might as well note that Potooooooooo was apparently owned by Percy Shelley's first wife's aunt's husband. Thomas Medwin, *The Life of Percy Bysshe Shelley*, Humphrey Milford (Oxford), 13.

Pour exprimer l'idée d'un homme ou d'un cheval, on représenta la forme de l'un ou de l'autre, et le premier essai de l'ecriture ne fut qu'une simple peinture. . . . Toward the end of *Of Grammatology*, after most have already given up, Jacques Derrida returns, without having left, to Jean-Jacques Rousseau's linguistic phylogenesis. Calling Rousseau's dismissal of Homer's possible knowledge of writing sus, as it were, Derrida resolves that "[s]uch is the situation of writing within the history of metaphysics: a debased, lateralized, repressed, displaced theme, yet exercising a permanent and obsessive pressure from the place where it remains in check" (270). Before showing just how permanent and obsessive this pressure of writing is, Derrida tracks Rousseau's thought as it derived from Étienne Bonnot de Condillac and William Warburton.[2] Derrida (ahem) writes,

> Under the name of writing, Condillac thinks readily of the possibility of such a subject, and of the law mastering its absence. When the field of society extends to the point of absence, of the invisible, the inaudible, and the immemorable, when the local community is dislocated to the point where individuals no longer appear to one another, become capable of being imperceptible, the age of writing begins. . . . Since the operation of writing reproduces that of speech here, the first *graphie* will reflect the first speech: figure and image. It will be pictographic. Again a paraphrase of Warburton:
>
> > Their imaginations then represented nothing more to them than those same images, which they had already expressed by gestures and words, and which from the very beginning had rendered language figurative and metaphorical. The most natural way therefore was to delineate the images of things. To express the idea of a man or of a horse, they represented the form of each of these animals; so that the first essay towards writing was a mere picture. (282)

2. Derrida's engagement with Condillac and Warburton spans his oeuvre, but see especially Derrida, *Archaeology of the Frivolous: Reading Condillac*, translated by John P. Leavey, Jr., U of Nebraska P, 1987 [originally published as *L'archéologie du frivole* (1973)]; and Derrida, "Signature Event Context" [1972], translated by Samuel Weber and Jeffrey Mehlman, in *Limited Inc*, Northwestern UP, 1988, 1–23.

The first forms of writing for Condillac and Warburton, and subsequently iterated by Rousseau, were pictorial—what Charles Sanders Peirce would later (much later) term an icon. The representation in the imagination, here, is thus the first translation, the first sign, writing that exists before writing. The simple cave drawing of the horse, chalked or carved in a wall of stone—still of this first form—would be the second translation, a sign of the sign in the imagination.[3] Following Condillac, as Derrida summarizes, "writing does not have a different origin from that of speech: need and distance. Thus it continues the language of action. But it is at the moment that the social *distance*, which had led gesture to speech, increases to the point of becoming *absence*, that writing becomes necessary" (281). The absence of the actual horse, as Condillac makes the point, allows for this first writing and for the subject utilizing it (and being utilized by it). Writing hence "has the function of reaching *subjects* who are not only distant but outside the entire field of vision and beyond earshot" (281). No longer is speech possible. The distance of horses and men has guaranteed as much. Writing is "law mastering its absence."

The second stage of writing, like the Chinese ideogram, is a type of demotic shorthand, which "paints sounds" and is "ideo-phonographic" (291). A rebus provides another example for Derrida: "The picture puzzle [*rebus à transfert*]; a sign representing a thing named in its concept ceases to refer to the concept and keeps only the value of a phonic signifier" (299). It is not quite potatooooooooo, but close. "According to Warburton, it was already for economic reasons that cursive or demotic hieroglyphics were substituted for hieroglyphics properly speaking or for sacred writing"—an "effacement of the signifier [that] led by degrees to the alphabet" (284, 285). This third stage—the alphabetic—follows initially the boustrophedonic furrows of the ploughman. It is economical.[4] The system of the hand (that of the scribe)

---

3. Derrida: "If supplementarity is a necessary indefinite process, writing is the supplement par excellence since it marks the point where the supplement proposes itself as supplement of supplement, sign of sign, *taking the place* of a speech already significant: it displaces the *proper place* of the sentence, the unique time of the sentence pronounced *hic et nunc* by an irreplaceable subject, and in return enervates the voice. It marks the place of the initial doubling" (281).

4. "The furrow," Derrida writes, "is the line, as the ploughman traces it: the road—*via rupta*—broken by the ploughshare. The furrow of agriculture . . . opens nature to culture (cultivation). And one also knows that writing is born with agriculture which happens only with sedentarization" (287).

soon replaces the system of the eye (that of the reader).[5] "In a word," Derrida promises, but gives us more: "it is more convenient to read than to write by furrows" (288). Essentially, writing has become a "linear phonography" (289).

In a materialist bent, the possibility of a language is conditioned by societal order. An Exergue to Derrida's book quotes Rousseau: "These three ways of writing correspond almost exactly to three different stages according to which one can consider men gathered into a nation. The depicting of objects is appropriate to a savage people; signs of words and of propositions, to a barbaric people; and the alphabet to civilized people" (3). The development of writing is further tied to that of money, which also "[r]eplaces things by their signs" (300), and to political representation, wherein, for Rousseau, a people's sovereignty disappears alongside the presence that effectuated it.[6] Writing "naturalizes" or tames culture by "articulat[ing]" it, "working to efface a difference it has opened" (301). It is more efficient because "its rationality distances it from passion and song, that is to say from the living origin of language" (301). Because of its basis in the phonetic, alphabetic writing is paradoxically a little closer to speech, to presence: "In losing a little more presence, it restores it a little bit better"; writing "is more apt to fade before the voice, more apt to let the voice be" (295). But the historical movement tends away from this. The emerging science of alphabetic writing ("the mutest possible")—what we would call today linguistics—doesn't speak a specific language (and is hence "alien to the voice"); rather, its fidelity to uttered sound ends up "represent[ing] it better" (300). The horse that became a picture of a horse and then "horse" will soon become, in the march of a logico-scientific system, "hôrs." "Science"—or "philosophy in Condillac's and Warburton's terms—"the *epistémè* and eventually self-knowledge, consciousness would therefore be the movement of idealization: an algebrizing, de-poeticizing formalization whose operation is to repress—in order to master it better—the charged signifier or linked hieroglyph" (285). This, Derrida

---

5. Even the split between the eye and the hand is unstable. In an almost throwaway line, Derrida writes, "one reads a little blindly, guided by the order of the hand" (289). The abyss at the end of a scribe's line seems to necessitate a manner of tactile faith, in order, as it were, to make ends meet.

6. Rousseau: "the moment a people allows itself to be represented, it is no longer free: it no longer exists" (qtd. in Derrida 297). Derrida calls this "the perfect alienation of the instrument of civil order" (312).

links to consonantal language, in essence a form of algebra, a sign devoid of any voice that once was—"speech degree zero" (303).

Derrida's project, as we have come to know it (if one may borrow, a moment, from the logic it deconstructs and also posit such subjects), is to rethink the de-scription central to all metaphysical thought, here epitomized by Rousseau's phonocentrism.[7] Languages, for the earlier philosopher "are made to be spoken, writing is nothing but a *supplement* of speech. . . . The analysis of thought is made through speech, and the analysis of speech through writing; speech *represents* thought through conventional signs, and writing represents speech in the same way; thus the art of writing is nothing but a mediated *representation* of thought, at least in the case of vocalic languages, the only ones that we use" (qtd. in Derrida 295). Classically understood, writing is "derivative," "*reduc[ing]* the dimensions of presence in its sign" (281), while speech presumably offers presence, despite being a "fictive immediacy" (280).[8] "Rousseau attempts to recapture a sort of happy pause," Derrida writes about this "language without discourse, a speech without sentence, without syntax, without parts, without grammar. . . . It is the moment when there are words . . . which do not yet function as they do 'in languages already formed'" (279–80; quoting *Discourse* 177). Rather than having an existence exterior to or as an appendage of speech, the "originary supplement" (313) that is writing, as per Derrida, is always already its condition—"infecting" it, enabling the economy of the sign.[9] "One wishes," he writes, "to go back *from the supplement to the source*: one must recognize that there is *a supplement at the source*" (304). Speech and writing are both empowered by the same force of iterability, and one cannot have speech without the possibility of *language*—the spacing of words, the syntax of arche-writing—already built in. "But is not a mark," (even an oral one), Derrida asks, "wherever it is produced, the possibility of writing?" (302).

Alongside this inside-out binary of speech and writing, amid the historical march toward writing systems which more and more lose their traces

---

7. Rousseau's critique of representation as well as "the entire history of metaphysics" come under fire: "But at the same time—and here the entire history of metaphysics is reflected—this critique depends upon the naivete of representation. It supposes at once that representation follows a first presence and restores a final presence" (296).

8. Derrida quoting Rousseau's *Emile*: "the letter killeth" (304).

9. "For the voice is always already invested, undone, required, and marked in its essence by a certain spatiality," even though "Rousseau could not think this writing, that takes place *before* and *within* speech" (290, 315).

of speech (however closer they move toward it at the same time),[10] comes an analogous movement in the vocality of words and a concomitant break at the heart of language itself between poetry and prose—something to which Giorgio Agamben will also attune his ears. "Expression is the expression of affect, of the passion at the origin of language," Derrida writes, "of a speech that was first substituted for song, marked by *tone* and *force*. Tone and force signify the *present voice*: they are anterior to the concept, they are singular, they are, moreover, attached to vowels, the vocalic and not the consonantic element of language" (314). Earlier forms of language carried verse aspects (rhyme and sound echoes), which served as mnemonic patterns, creating furrows in the field of the mind. Condillac called the character of this foundational speech "originally poetical" and Rousseau saw in it "the tongues of poets" (qtd. in Derrida 273). "When writing appears, one no longer needs rhythm and *rhyme* whose function is, according to Condillac, to engrave meaning within memory" (287), Derrida summarizes, before clarifying: "But if Rousseau could say that "words [*voix*], not sounds [*sons*], are written," it is because words are distinguished from sounds exactly by what permits writing—consonants and articulation. The latter replace only themselves. Articulation, which replaces accent, is the origin of languages" (315). As they develop, the signifiers become more abstract, and the traces of an origin are obscured. Hence, "[t]he history of philosophy is the history of prose; or rather of the becoming-prose of the world. Philosophy is the invention of prose" (287). The binaries compound. On one hand: speech / poetry / accent / vowels / southern Europe / language-as-song; and, on the other: writing / prose (philosophy & science) / articulation / consonants / northern Europe / language-as-precision.[11] At the heart of (in the gap of?) the columns is the sense (or non-sense) that poetry (albeit on a historical model) has been specifically romanticized as an oral form.

Now that Derrida is not here to scold us with a letter, we might posit a question of difference. In most senses, the metaphysics underlying the metaphysics of presence is very different than a lyric act. But what would

---

10. Once again, Derrida: "Phonetic writing, however abstract and arbitrary retained some relationship with the presence of the represented voice, to its possible presence in general and therefore to that of a certain passion" (312).

11. Rousseau links "articulation" to the Northern European countries, "accent" to the southern ones. Once again, material circumstance—here, climate—conditions possibility. Noting these temperature-controlled utterances, Derrida temporalizes the spatial difference as a seasonal consequence.

it mean to say that the turn in speech (Culler's moment of discourse or "presence") is always already conditioned by the written or that the syntactical space of emotion is always already a part of its own condition? Both apostrophe—as Culler, Johnson, and others make the point—and speech—as Rousseau's ghost in Derrida makes the point—are not so much about the unhearing and unheeding object of address but rather about the reassuring/effecting performance of the speaking subject. Phonetic writing, Derrida, ventriloquizing Rousseau, suggests, "keeps an essential relationship to the presence of a speaking subject *in general*, to a transcendental locutor, to the voice as the self-presence of a life which hears itself speak" (303). Rousseau—and we might say the same about the apostrophizing speaker—is "less interested in the present, in the being-present, than in the presence of the present, in its essence as it appears to itself and is retained in itself" (309–10). It is not so much about a return to what never was, but instead about presence as self-proximity.[12] For a lyric speaker, this would mean a return to oneself, and perhaps to a previously unrealized moment of grief. Rousseau, along this line, turns to a moment of reexperiencing a nonexperience—something about being knocked down by a dog by the water cooler (Rousseau, following a divine finger, was trying to be sociable). The split in experience—one might be reminded of Walter Benjamin's (or, earlier, Wilhelm Dilthey's) distinction between *Erfahrung* and *Erlebnis*—always seems to come at a moment of a downturn, of a *catastrophe* for Rousseau: "That the return to the presence of the origin is produced after each catastrophe, at least in so far as it *reverses* the order of life without destroying it" (310).[13]

What is that pseudo-originary moment underlying apostrophe, forcing a lyric sound out of the rhythmic furrows of language? Fear? Realization? Despair of loss somehow constituted as sign in the imagination? Phonetic outburst? *Exclamatio* without writing, without rhetoric? Whatever it is, it gives us the presence of *presence*. Like Santa.

∗　∗　∗

---

12. Derrida: "It is this that the metaphysics of presence as self-proximity wishes to efface by giving a privileged position to a sort of absolute now, the *life* of the present, the living present" (309).

13. [*"Ce retour à la presence de l'origine se produit après chaque catastrophe, dans la mesure du moins où elle renverse l'ordre de la vie sans le détruire"* (437)]. The "catastrophic" event for Agamben, as I will explore before long, comes precisely at the end of the poem.

If the historical march of the gesture-turned-sound-turned-hieroglyph-turned-alphabet-turned-variable proceeded as per Rousseau, we wouldn't have poetry, which still operates in the furrows of language, between sound and sentiment. Searching this gap between prose language and poetic language as a way into language itself, Agamben puts forth the idea that linear enjambment is "the necessary and sufficient condition of versification" ("Idea of Prose" 40). Poetry is distinguished from prose by this possibility of enjambment—not by quantity, rhythm or syllabic count ["Né la quantità, né il ritmo, né il numero delle sillabe" (23)], and certainly—[pause] thankfully—not by any romanticized idea we have of it today.[14] "[W]e shall call poetry the discourse in which it is possible to set a metrical limit against a syntactical one," he writes, noting that prose, on the other hand, "is the discourse in which this is impossible" (39). The non-voice of enjambment, a "hanging back . . . [a] sublime hesitation between meaning and sound" shows itself to be "the poetic inheritance with which thought must come to terms" (41). For Agamben, enjambment

> reveals a mismatch, a disconnection between the metrical and syntactical elements, between sounding rhythm and meaning, such that (contrary to the received opinion that sees in poetry the locus of an accomplished and a perfect fit between sound and meaning) poetry lives, instead, only in their disagreement. In the very moment verse affirms its own identity by breaking a syntactic link, it is irresistibly drawn into bending over into the next line to lay hold of what it has thrown out of itself. It hints at a passage of prose with the very gesture that attests its own versatility. By this headlong dive into the abyss of meaning, the purely sonic unit of verse transgresses its own identity as it does its own measure. (40)[15]

---

14. Original Italian quotations from *Idea della prosa*. Agamben designates verse in which enjambment isn't present (but which isn't prose): as having "zero enjambement" (39).

15. "In this way," he continues, "*enjambement* brings to light the original gait, neither poetic nor prosaic, but boustrophedonic, as it were, of poetry, the essential prose-metrics of every human discourse. . . . The *versura*, the turning-point which displays itself as *enjambement*, though unspoken-of in treatises on metrics, constitutes the core of verse. It is an ambiguous gesture, that turns in two opposed directions at once: backwards (*versus*) and forwards (*pro-versa*)" (40–41).

This hesitation, this disjunction between sound and sense can be seen in two "poetic" (but they are surely more than that!) terms Agamben juxtaposes: enjambment and caesura, which, each in its own way, shows how thought and words can unsettle each other. He turns to the halting verse of Sandro Penna to show "the breaking action of the caesura" (43):

> Io vado verso il fiume su un cavallo
> che quando io penso un poco un poco egli si ferma.

> I go towards the river on a horse
> which when I think a little a little he stops. (43)[16]

The horse stops a little when its rider thinks a little. But the towardsness of verse has a different mechanic than the towardness of prose, of thought. The pause—the little pause—between the two *un poco* ought not do anything, ought not be meaningful, and yet it, bridled as it is in the space between words, stops the voice, a little, in its tracks. The repetition—what one thinks ought to keep the horse moving at the same pace—instead halts the movement. Did the thought (or the thought about the thought) trigger the hand, which triggered the rein? And yet, somehow, just as the thought stops the horse, the cadence of words, rather the hesitating cadence between words, stops the poet's thought. "For the poet," Agamben writes, "the element that arrests the metrical impetus of the voice, the caesura of voice, is thought. . . . The parallelism between sense and metre is again reconfirmed by the repetition of the same word on either side of the caesura, almost as if to give to the pause the epic density of an atemporal interstice between two moments, which suspends the gesture halfway in an extravagant goose-step" (43–44).

Following the exegetical tradition of the Apocalypse of St. John, Agamben ties the horse to "the sound and vocal element of language . . . in which logos is described as a 'faithful and honest' knight astride a white horse" (43).[17] He—Agamben (not the knight or the horse)—then connects the early theology of Origen of Alexandria with the poetically chivalric process of the early troubadour Guillaume d'Aquitaine. Referencing Origen, he writes that "the horse is the voice, the word as utterance, which 'runs with more verve and swiftness than any steed' and which only logos makes clear and intelligible. It is while asleep on such a horse—*durmen sus un chivau*—that

---

16. Michael Sullivan and Sam Whitsitt's translation, slightly modified.

17. Apoc. 19.11: "Now I saw heaven opened, and behold, a white horse. And He who sat on him was called Faithful and True. . . ."

Guillaume d'Aquitaine, at the very beginning of Romance poetry, claims to have composed his *vers*" (43). Putting aside these embryonic self-driving cars, such poetic journeys are importantly without necessary destinations. They become ways to access the *it* of language. "But what is it that is being thought in this caesura that brings the horse of verse to a halt? What does this interruption of the rhythmic transport of the poem reveal?" Agamben asks. Invoking Friedrich Hölderlin (and not naming, but surely riding atop Walter Benjamin's workhorse), he retrieves an answer: "The tragic transport, in fact, is quite empty and that which is the truly free. This is why in the rhythmic succession of representations where the tragic transport is displayed, the pure word, the anti-rhythmic interruption, in meter called caesura, becomes necessary so as to block the enchanting succession of representations at its height in such a way as to make manifest no longer the alternation of representation, but representation itself" (44).[18] The tragic transport, a non-moment of representation or what Agamben calls representation itself, bridges two different realities separated by a hesitation. But is it representation itself, as he would have it, or the representation of *representation itself*, as seems more likely? Or is there indeed a difference anymore between the two? Hölderlin can bring the moment of peripeteia to the lyric, where we find not quite hamartia but a sudden shift in the tragically lyric hero. The break in narrative is similar to the discursive turn of apostrophe but without the address, unless one wants to claim that discourse itself is being addressed. I won't travel so far to make that claim, but within the caesura's nonvocal temporality, it is difficult to say that an event of language isn't taking place.[19] It is not the O of apostrophe, of course, but rather an aorgic circling around a void of representation. "The

---

18. See Walter Benjamin, "Two Poems by Friedrich Hölderlin" (*Selected Writings Volume 1: 1913–1926*, 18–36). See also Kevin McLaughlin, "Walter Benjamin's Philology of Life: Methodological Reflections on 'Two Poems by Friedrich Hölderlin'" *Modern Language Notes*, volume 135, number 3 (April 2020), 746–69, for the relationship to what McLaughlin terms Benjamin's "philology of life"; and Beatrice Hanssen, " 'Dichtermut' and 'Blödigkeit': Two Poems by Hölderlin Interpreted by Walter Benjamin" *Modern Language Notes*, volume 112, number 5 (December 1997), 786–816, for the relationship to German idealism, as reimagined through Theodor Adorno's intervention.

19. Apostrophe, Culler reminds us, "makes its point by troping not on the meaning of a word but on the circuit or situation of communication itself" (*Pursuit* 135). For Agamben, following Émile Benveniste, "language can *show* itself, or can *indicate* the present instance of discourse as its own taking place, through shifters" (*Language and Death*, 31). Deixis becomes the instrument for "the conversion of language into discourse" (Benveniste, *Problems*, 220). David Johnson explains how "[s]hifters indicate the locutionary possibility of language; without any material reference, deictics site language, instantiate it, and thus

rhythmic transport that gives the verse its impetus is empty, is only the transport of itself," Agamben writes, continuing: "And it is this emptiness which, as *pure word*, the caesura—for a little—thinks, holds in suspense, while for an instant the horse of poetry is stopped. As Raymond Lully writes, 'Astride his palfrey, the squire went to court to be dubbed, but lulled by the sway of his mount, he fell asleep as he went. Arrived at a fountain, however, the beast stopped to drink, and the squire woke up, because in his sleep he perceived the horse no longer moved' " (44). The mesmerizing cadence of poetry has the world fading away, akin to a lullaby inducing sleep. A pause in the rhythmic narcotic reactivates thought and the rhythm is broken. "The poet, here asleep on his horse," Agamben writes, "awakens and contemplates for an instant the inspiration that carries him—he thinks nothing else but his voice."[20] It is a voice without content or with content but a little.

*　*　*

Finding himself on a horse headed to his lover's house following what one can only now imagine as some late-night sexting, the speaker of Wordsworth's "Strange fits of passion have I known" begins to fall half asleep. Thankfully, the horse, like that of Lully's squire, knows how to get there. One gathers that the horse (as well as much of the dear paths of the more-traveled verse) has made this trip more than a few times. Eyes drooping, mind wandering, the rider begins to watch the moon, which moves relative to the traveler—or seems to from the traveler's perspective (Eppur si muove!)—until it plunges behind the lover's cottage as the horse nears. The rider is suddenly overwhelmed with the direst of thoughts—the death of his beloved:

> What fond and wayward thoughts will slide
> Into a Lover's head!
> "O mercy!" to myself I cried,
> "If Lucy should be dead!" (72)

She's not, of course, because the indifferent world doesn't care about the wanderings of our individual minds the way we sometimes wish . . . or

---

mark the conversion from a general language that never takes place to the instance of discourse" ("As If the Time Were Now" 271). Because of this, shifters like *I* and *you* "are intimately related to the voice, to the presence of the voice" (271).

20. In *Potentialities*, Agamben elaborates on this "pure taking place of language without any determinate event of meaning," which is effected by "a voice that, without signifying anything, signifies signification itself" (42).

fear.[21] But how did he get there? And how have we been asked, night after night, to get there too?

We've been told for too long to make sense of the economy of a poem, pulling the same feed from the same saddle we've been telling ourselves the poet was asked to draw from. We've been told for too long that there must be connections among the rider and Lucy and the horse and the moon in these twenty-eight simple lines, lines with a rhythmic repetitiveness even a child could discern. The rider wants to get to Lucy; the horse takes him there. But what of the lunar enlightenment? Here—risking the lunacy of a mixed metaphor—the hermeneutic feedbag is the ominously backdropped moon, which, rather than set the romantic scene, seems to overpower the poem until it is (not that unexpectedly) out of sight. The rider, unaware of his own semiconscious connections, can't help but personify this moon, which is all along reflecting the light of another body. Hence, the threat of disappearance, hence the imaginative jump to Lucy's death. The rider, no doubt, gets it wrong; he will have a typical night with his love. The reader, stepping on the same trodden ground, might also get it wrong (who are we to know?); her or his punishment is a "D" on a paper or a lambasting from a romanticist scholar. (It is not altogether clear which hermeneutic misstep is worse.)

Barbara Johnson's brilliant reading of Wordsworth's poem contrasts the commonly (mis)understood version of his naturalistic poetics with Edgar Allan Poe's ostensibly more mechanical version of his own: "spontaneous overflow versus calculation emotion versus rigid consequence, feelings versus letters of the alphabet . . . primacy to the *signified* . . . [versus] primacy to the *signifier*" (91). Wordsworth, as the story goes, thinks poetry is about lived experiences, while Poe thinks it's about putting the letter O next to the letter R. These two seemingly polar opposite senses of creativity, as Johnson compellingly demonstrates, cannot exist without the other, as Wordsworth's "attempts to prevent the poetic figure from losing its passion . . . involves just such a blind mechanical repetition of the lost language" while Poe's ostensibly pure-signified "engenders its own compulsion to sense . . . [and] cannot remain empty" (99). For Johnson, it is neither about an equivocal poetics nor about getting it—the poetic imagination—right. The very nature

---

21. The published versions of this poem omit a final verse, which was included in the version Wordsworth sent to S. T. Coleridge: "I told her this: her laughter light / Is ringing in my ears: / And when I think upon that night / My eyes are dim with tears." The poet's ultimate decision to omit the stanza does indeed leave the matter a bit more ambiguous, but to assume the worst recreates the great imaginative leap of the speaker. (See *The Letters of William and Dorothy Wordsworth*, rev. ed., edited Chester L. Shaver, Mary Moorman, and Alan G. Hill, Oxford UP, 1967–93, 1:238.)

of poetry's fond and wayward thoughts lies buoyantly in this uncertain space: "If it were possible to differentiate clearly between the mechanical and the passionate, between the empty and the full, between the fit and the fit, between 'real' language and 'adulterated phraseology,' there would probably be no need for extensive treaties on the nature of poetic language. But there would also be no need for poetry" (99). Johnson's reading of Wordsworth focuses on two strangely contrasting senses of "fit" in "Strange fits. . . ."—one oxymoronically connoting an odd framing, the other an unexpected paroxysm. The poem, as does Wordsworth's spontaneous-overflow/recollected-tranquility poetics, navigates both senses, each of which must "fit" the wayward thoughts of the imagination into a poetic form. It is here that Johnson's journey through the poem marches, foot after foot, right up to the precipice of catastrophic wonder. Even though she showed us what was below, in that breathtaking chasm of poetic inspiration, I wish, sometimes, that she had taken that final step.

By the end of William Wordsworth's "Strange fits of passion have I known," the hypnotizing clipclop of balladic iambs leads the drowsy travelers—rider and reader—into an unexpected but almost inevitable end. Against most of the readings (or trotting beside them), which propose a psychological or metonymic link between Lucy and the moon, I would propose a semiotic cause.[22] "What fond and wayward thoughts will slide / Into a Lover's head! 'O mercy!' to myself I cried . . ." *if Lucy should be fed? if Lucy were in bed? if Lucy were beet red? if Lucy had street cred?* Here, the poem sets up the imagination not solely derivative of image or referent but moreover mediated by expectations within the patterned sounds of language and cultural expectation. One might even question whether the moon is there because it's night and IRL the moon comes out at night—hence an authenticity of experience—or whether the moon is there because the poetic cliché of June/moon always already forces the imagination of English speakers into it—a chance paroxysm of the semiotic.

One might be reminded of what, in another context, Cleanth Brooks called Wordsworth's "paradox of the imagination," but Brooks's focus on how poems dramatize questions rather than answer them might be more

---

22. Geoffrey Hartman notes how the rider "has been psychically able to establish a link between Lucy and the moon" and hence "between the moon's drop and Lucy's death" (*Wordsworth's Poetry* 23). Ian Balfour ties Lucy etymologically to "lux" or the light of the moon.

apt here.[23] Along similar lines, the poem, as Adela Pinch argues, "stages a debate over the origins of emotions and their appropriateness to their causes" (106).[24] For Johnson, Wordsworth's imagination—and pretty much poetic imagination itself—is not simply mechanical and not simply (or ideologically, one might add) free. The poem, instead, dramatizes how the nonsemantic aspects of language have etiological stakes in the movement of the imagination—a movement, which, from time to time, no doubt, follows that of the horse, hoof after hoof. Going in circles gets the poet nowhere, just as going in circles stays the horse from its destination. And yet, the verse is all sound moving in circles: Ba-bum ba-bum ba-bum ba-bum / Ba-bum ba-bum ba-bed / "O mercy!" to myself I cried, / "If Lucy should be dead!" The rider closes his eyes and still knows how many steps his horse is to take, but he loses himself in the process. In the end, his exclamation "O mercy!" (rather than an apostrophic address to a personified being) is some manner of performative outburst in which the speaker seems to be hailing himself back into the reality of the scene.[25] And then it ends, as if the destination were never significant. In its place lingers the David Byrne-esque *how did I get here*: "here" being the state of an imaginative mind rather than a lover's cottage, "here" being wherever the non-semantic horse of language—those "fond and wayward thoughts"—wanted to take him.[26]

This wilder suggestion that the circular face of the moon might have just as easily provoked the O than any unconscious psychological cause hopefully doesn't eclipse a curious interest in how various things seem to converge at

---

23. See Brooks, 124–50. Albeit a different context, I. A. Richards's romantic turn to language (mainly regarding his reassessment of S. T. Coleridge) feels apt. As Richard Foster summarizes, "It is note-worthy, finally, that in [Richards's] account of how the mind works with words there is a total absence of the mechanist's jargon of 'interests' and 'impulses' and that, as the syntax of the passage makes clear, words seem to be endowed with a kind of life of their own, apart from that of him who uses them" (97).

24. She reminds readers how Wordsworth's early readers had similar difficulties connecting his poetic emotions to their causes. The poem "features a speaker who seems as perplexed by his own wayward emotions as some of Wordsworth's readers were with his" (106).

25. Pinch suggests that we "connect the speaker uttering 'O Mercy' to Wordsworth's warning in the Preface that poetry can leave us 'utterly at the mercy' of 'those arbitrary connections of feelings and ideas with particular words, from which no man can altogether protect himself'" (109).

26. Mary Jacobus calls apostrophe, "a stalking-horse for Wordsworth's conception of lyric voice in *The Prelude*" (*Romanticism* vii). It is the "signal instance of the rupture of the temporal scheme of memory by the time of writing" ("Apostrophe" 171–72).

this moment: the movement of O, the performative act of turning, and a lyric presence, which at this moment seems very different than the shifting tense and fictionally limited audience puzzling the opening of the poem. But there are also other questions we might want to ask now about the poem's enabling contexts. One thinks of this placeholder "Lucy," who, as line three makes clear, still hasn't heard about his embarrassing exclamation. She, professedly, will be the only one granted access to his story, months, maybe years, after the fact. Was he too mortified to tell her his story that night? Was he too overcome by her figure at the door? Did he forget his waking call, as he tied up his horse beside her cottage? Or was he worried that two hundred years hence she wouldn't be particularly pleased to be his muse of a moon, the absent occasion for this rider's poetic journey. When we stare too long at the sky, it's easy to forget what's on earth.[27]

*   *   *

One more ride around the track. Amid some of Emily Dickinson's other end-of-days reflections, the following fragment, in Marta Werner's phrasing, gives us "a present so dilated" (111) as if we were already removed from mortal time:

> We must travel
> abreast with
> Nature if we
> want to know
> her, but where
> shall be obtained
> the Horse—
> A something
> over takes the
> mind—we do
> not hear it
> coming.[28]

---

27. "I have never known the police of any country to show an interest in lyric poetry as such," Langston Hughes writes, "But when poems stop talking about the moon and begin to mention poverty, trade unions, color lines, and colonies, somebody tells the police" ("My Adventures" 9).

28. Dickinson, Fragment A879, *The Letters of Emily Dickinson*, Thomas H. Johnson, ed.; qtd. with facsimile reproduction in Werner 111–12.

How can one keep up with this velocity of the world? On a horse, moving at the same pace, perhaps, as those of the Apocalypse. Unlike Wordsworth's horse who wouldn't deign take a step out of turn, Dickinson's mare isn't headed anywhere specific. It just needs to keep going. Was this horse never found or could it just not keep pace? Because, in that space of a dash, the mental ground had shifted from under. The "barely lyrical" fragment, Werner writes—"so far misclassified by Dickinson's editors as a 'prose aphorism'—is in fact verse contracted to its most essential elements: caesura and enjambment" (111, 114). Poetic silence, astride its own horse, overtakes the semantic. We do not hear it [pause] coming. Abreast of the semantic unhearing is the silence following the final line; Werner calls it "enjambment degree zero" (114).

"Listen always to the silence before a poem begins" Allen Grossman implores, before embarking on Dickinson's "I cannot live with You."[29] *This silence, though, can only be heard once the poem has been completed, once Dickinson has found ampleness in the "White Sustenance / Despair—" following the deictic separation of "You there—I—here—". . . even if the "I"—dashed away from both "there" and "here"—feels as if it isn't even quite present in the latter. Something must impel this turning toward (an imagined) speech. Without naming such a cause save for the vital absence of past lives, W. B. Yeats, in "After Long Silence," finds a counter-inertial energy with which to begin: "Speech after long silence; it is right, / All other lovers being estranged or dead. . . ." The two, one presumes, are left alone, finally in their imagined private space to "descant"—conversing but also musically voicing above others. The poem concludes with a very Yeatsian chestnut: "Bodily decrepitude is wisdom; young / We loved each other and were ignorant." But what happens, now, with this poetically gleaned knowledge after the ultimate retreat into silence? What, exactly, happens in that still space after the poem ends?*

---

29. Dickinson, F706; J640; M343. "Allen Grossman—Poetry Lectures #6 [Part 1]—Emily Dickinson's 'I Cannot Live With You'" (accessed via https://www.youtube.com/watch?v=9CZt-tICoTk). A similar phrasing of his, from my own undergraduate days, has stayed with me, even if it has not or not yet been immortalized in print: "Every poem comes out of the silence before it." Sharon Cameron, at her most Grossmanian, tells us that "all lyrics oppose speech to the action from which it exempts itself, oppose voice as it rise momentarily from the enthusiasm of temporal advance to the flow of time that ultimately rushes over and drowns it" (*Lyric* 23). Following Cameron's query that the renounced "you" of F706 seems to occupy a great bit of space in the poem, Virginia Jackson re-elaborates her position that "what is renounced is the performative affect of apostrophe, the trope that brings 'You' into the moment of speech" (*Dickinson's Misery* 154; see *Lyric* 78).

Chapter 1

W. B. Yeats

"Come away, O human child!"

All over Ireland are little fields circled by ditches, and supposed to be
ancient fortifications and sheep folds. These are the raths or forts. Here,
marrying and giving in marriage, live the land fairies.

—W. B. Yeats, "The Sociable Fairies" (1889), *Uncollected Prose I*, 133

In the italicized intermezzo propelling this chapter, W. B. Yeats's "After
Long Silence" presents life as an uncomplicated movement from bodily bliss
(albeit with ignorance) to knowledge (albeit with bodily decay). A *movement*,
perhaps, in the musical sense would be more appropriate than the implied
slower passage of a lifetime, because the speaker seems to have reawakened
one evening in this opposite ontological space, with no apparent memory
of how he got there. That Being is comprised of dichotomous forces and
conditions and awarenesses—especially between young and old—is not, as
one would presume, an isolated thought in the work of that comfortable
kind of old scarecrow, Yeats. The younger poet could be just as bleak in
casting an imagined older self as a desolate landscape. Yeats's speaker and his
eavesdropping reader are often confronted with such dichotomous choices
about worlds of knowledge and pain, even when they are not isolated to
a difference in age.

His "The Stolen Child," for instance, asks both its textual addressee (a
child) and its extratextual listener to choose between two worlds: a mortal
world that is real but full of pain and a fairy world that is painless, yet

deceitful. It is not a difficult poem, as far as things go, but it is caught among dissimilar narrative, dramatic, and lyric voices, each seemingly desiring a different rhetorical end—whether that be a warning, a beckoning, or an aesthetico-political stage setting. Such rhetorical deceits are based on contexts of invitation (*beware before you click on that link!*) and expectations of closure. They can also be poetic. Take, if you will, the opening mise en scène:

> WHERE dips the rocky highland
>   Of Sleuth Wood in the lake,
> There lies a leafy island
>   Where flapping herons wake. . . .[1]

We encounter a seemingly typical portrait of Yeats's mistily breathtaking western Irish landscape—the wooded hills surrounding Lough Gill (the County Sligo lake in which the famous Innisfree isles). Behind the words, we might also hear the patterned rhythm of the ballad meter, which—as it does for Wordsworth and un-does for Dickinson—depends as much upon anticipations and resolutions of stanzaic closure as upon iambic regularity. The "wake" at the end of the fourth line resolves the expected echo of the "lake," and, because of this phonetic resolution, we expect a semantic one.[2]

---

1. "The Stolen Child" in *The Irish Monthly* (December 1886), 646–47. The complete poem in listed in my book's Appendix A. I quote from this version unless otherwise noted.

2. The semantic pressure exerted by these chance sound similarities has been taken up across major twentieth-century critical engagements, and, as Agamben illustrates, it goes back many hundreds of years. "Although rhyme by definition is based on a regular recurrence of equivalent phonemes or phonemic groups, it would be an unsound oversimplification to treat rhyme merely from the standpoint of sound," Roman Jakobson writes, "Rhyme necessarily involves a semantic relationship between rhyming units" (81). By inviting a metaphoric association between the cola, rhyme disrupts the syntactic structure of the stanza, "link[ing] syllables, and thereby words, and thereby lines, and thereby larger versified structure," John Hollander writes, adding that "at each level of linkage, it performs another sort of 'musical' or 'rhetorical' work" (*Vision* 199). Rene Wellek and Austin Warren call rhyme "an extremely complex phenomenon," noting that "aesthetically far more important [than its euphonious function] is its metrical function signaling the conclusion of a line of verse, or as the organizer, sometimes the sole organizer, of stanzaic patterns. But, most importantly, rhyme has meaning and is thus deeply involved in the whole character of a work of poetry. Words are brought together by rhyme, linked up and contrasted" (161). By wresting words from their true calling, rhyme, according to W. K. Wimsatt, "impose[s] upon the logical pattern of expressed argument a kind of fixative counterpattern of alogical implication" (153).

There lies a leafy island whereon herons wake *themselves*. This, however, would be a misreading, because behind this rather benign geography and behind the expectation of stanzaic closure hides something much more sinister. Just how we read this opening is contingent on the forced poetic silence between lines four and five, in that semantic-semiotic disruption called enjambment. The sentiment is not "Where flapping herons wake" [stop] but rather "Where flapping herons wake / The drowsy water-rats," as the semantic continuation onto line five reveals. The flapping herons, it turns out, are not waking themselves; they have already been up and moving in the silence before the poem has started. Instead, they are waking the drowsy water-rats, for an end that one imagines won't be good.

Stealing a line from William Watkin's Agambenian wink to the strophic realm of language and recasting it to Yeats's seabirds, we might say that the enjambment of line four shows us "the tern" of verse. The (false) pause at the end of this line, exacerbated by the invitation and closure of the rhyme, hides, in grammatical terms, the ambiguity between the transitive and intransitive senses of "wake." Just who happens to be waking up whom might not be such an issue but for the fact that the poem spotlights the kidnapping tendencies of some Irish fairies. Here, the waking of another, as opposed to the waking of oneself, comes across as the ominous threat of losing one's body. This disappearing act, as the poem will unveil, is one of the dangers lurking beneath apostrophic address. The drowsy water-rats, still in recovery from whatever previous night's affair, will soon find themselves perilously exposed.

Yeats's choice of "wake" arouses other connotations of the word. The sense of coming alive again at the dawn of the day is shadowed by the forewarning of the funerary ritual, just as each of these senses might give way to a planar disturbance in sound water, the trace of a past event. More poetically significant, perhaps, than the various definitions of "wake" that one can drum up, is its ritualistic thump, as if it were a punchline reverberating at the end of its expected place. Recast the lines for their informational content (*In the lake beside the rocky highland of Sleuth Wood, there lies a leafy island where flapping herons wake the drowsy water-rats*) and there is no punchline, no expectation of closure. The semiotic disjunction is typographical, but it derives, very importantly, from the unsoundness of a sound event. Yeats's rather remarkable enjambment—that stutter, or slight hesitation between lines four and five—allegorizes the disruption between sound (enchanting fairy rhetoric) and sense (disheartening human understanding) that will envelop this poem, threatening a terrifying silence at its end.

As I previewed in the opening of this book, Giorgio Agamben's sense of poetry—that other, less understood aspect of Language writ-large—depends upon the disjunction between the semiotic and semantic. Poetry is "the discourse in which it is possible to set a metrical limit against a syntactic one" while prose is "the discourse in which this [limit] is impossible" (*Idea of Prose* 39). That the above distinction is not actually the philosopher's own phrasing (it comes by way of translation) demonstrates the semantic force of prose at the expense of any metrical limit. Although it is not so much on Agamben's radar, we ought to note that one is conditioned to read these limits; it is not inherent. One might pause alongside the appositive phrases of a prose sentiment or catch a breath at its logical turns; but, except in the rarest instances, one will not be sidetracked by the blank spaces on the page. Agamben returns to his characterization of poetry in his all-too-short but frighteningly dense essay "The End of the Poem," where he reiterates that poetry exists "only in the tension and difference [. . .] between sound and sense, between the semiotic and the semantic sphere" (109).[3] In order to situate his thinking, he turns to some well-worn patches of a seven-hundred-year tradition of poetics. He notes the caesural definition of poetry by Paul Valéry, who writes, "Le poème, hésitation prolongée entre le son et le sens" ("The poem, a prolonged hesitation between the sound and the sense"), and goes back to the fourteenth-century scholar Nicolò Tibino: " 'It often happens that the rhyme ends, without the meaning of the sentence having been completed' (*Multiocens enim accidit quod, finita consonantia, adhuc sensus orationis non est finites*)" (110). Reading Valéry alongside Tibino, Agamben concludes that—across geographies, cultures, and time—the odd typographical nuance known as enjambment becomes *the* defining quality of poetry. "All poetic institutions participate in this noncoincidence," he writes, "this schism of sound and sense—rhyme no less than caesura" (110). The turncoat of logos, enjambment shows the schism in language for what it is.

In focusing on this non-sense, Agamben moves away from the more prevalent and generally more ambiguous definitions of poetry, which are typically based on some variation of a logos/mythos binary. The binary—whether objective/subjective, literal/metaphorical, or informational/emotional—is traceable, in the end, to what Plato called an "ancient quarrel

---

3. See Düttmann (28–42) and Heron (97–113) in Murray et al.'s *The Work of Giorgio Agamben.*

between [poetry] and philosophy" (*Republic* X: 607b).[4] Despite the fact that subsequent philosophers and poets from Aristotle to Jacques Derrida have reminded us that this was really *Plato's* quarrel all along, definitions of poetry with ethical (and disciplinary) claims on both sides of the equation have mostly adhered to Plato's dichotomy. Sir Philip Sidney's neo-Aristotelian reconsideration of Plato's mimesis—"art of imitation . . . a representing, counter-feiting, or figuring forth to speak metaphorically, a speaking picture with this end, to teach and delight" (25)—is only one such notable example. Sidney and others in this tradition set poetry (understood in the larger sense of what one would today call "Literature"—however sticky that term) against philosophy, history, or the later incarnation "science." Other attempts at defining poetry, specifically of the lyric kind, have set it off not so much against the nonliterary as against fictive prose. William Wordsworth's "spontaneous overflow of powerful feelings . . . recollected in tranquility" and John Stuart Mill's "utterance that is overheard" seem to navigate the waters between these differential systems. Agamben's posited definition, on the other hand, is formal—in the sense that it is based on a formal property of verse—and it is unequivocal: we know a poem when we see one or when we hear one, provided the graphic or phonic hesitation is retained. This unstable totality of sound-sense experience, however, is unlike the romantic proportional harmony of, say, Samuel Taylor Coleridge (318), or the elaborate forms of organicism that cropped up years later for the New Critics. Poetry, for Agamben, is a negative system or potentiality where harmony is possible but never achieved. What matters is disproportion, difference, tension. As he writes, "The poem is an organism grounded in the perception of the limits and endings that define—without ever fully coinciding with, and almost in intermittent dispute with—sonorous (or graphic) units and semantic units" (*End* 110).

There are various ways to speak of the semiotic-semantic tension in poetry, all of which seem to circle around the same schism. Roman Jakobson, referenced by Agamben, discusses tension in terms of "equivalence," whereby

---

4. To Plato, poetry is *mimetic* in a pejorative sense; it is a copy of a copy, or an imitation of "appearances," furthest from the ideal truth it is copying (X: 598b). It is not just that it is based on an epistemological deficiency but moreover that it leads to an ethical decrepitude as well. Poetry, he charges, "nurtures and waters" all of the baser emotions and desires "and establishes them as rulers in us when they ought to wither and be ruled" (X: 606d).

the poetic function projects *"the principle of equivalence from the axis of selection into the axis of combination"* (71). Poetry, for him, adds a temporal dimension to the principle of equivalence, which is ordinarily reserved for the metaphoric axis (selection). Rhyme counterbalances expectation with resolution, defying the pressures of the semantic sphere. "Wake" falsely closes "lake" before one sees the period. Still, where we expect meaning, we find a mere semblance of sound. "For what is rhyme," Agamben concludes, "if not a disjunction between a semiotic event (the repetition of a sound) and a semantic event, a disjunction that brings the mind to expect a meaningful analogy where it can find only homophony?" (*End* 110). For Agamben, the prospects of rhyme and other modes of equivalence all boil down to the figure or, rather, the possibility of enjambment, which becomes the prototypical instance of poetic hesitation: " 'Poetry' will then be the name given to the discourse in which this [semantic-semiotic] opposition is, at least virtually, possible; 'prose' will be the name for the discourse in which this opposition cannot take place" (109). The translated opening "The End of the Poem," for example ("My plan, as you can see summarized before you in the title of this lecture, is to define a poetic institution that has until now remained unidentified: the end of the poem" [109]), is prose, because there is apparently no meaningful relationship between the semantic end of the sentence and the semiotic ends of the lines. The apparent relationship between the two in prose is determined by how much marginal room the publisher decides to leave.

I bring together this essay by Agamben and Yeats's "The Stolen Child" in the hope that their juxtaposition or co-incidence sheds some light on how the desires inherent in apostrophic address are situated between philosophy and poetry, between the longings of an intentional language and the reverberations of speech captured on the page. Agamben's demarcation of poetry undermines the great philosophic myth of the logos, the dream in which saying equals meaning. Ironically, though, it performs as an act of philosophy, made possible by a unity of Idea, a *logos* of "enjambment." Enjambment, or the running on of semantic meaning from one line to the next, calls attention to the poetic sound/sense disjunction by fiddling with the gap between rhetorical anticipation and literal understanding.[5]

---

5. While Agamben (thankfully) moves away from emotionally ambiguous definitions of poetry, he does not account for things like prose-poems or "enjambed" magazine advertisements or for how the potentiality of such discourse might be metonymically tied to culturally determined locations. Nonetheless, he does point to what is commonly a central cross-cultural distinction between prose and poetry.

To read Yeats's poem, however, as an allegory of Agamben's thought is to misread both Yeats's poem and Agamben's thought by subsuming poiesis to logos, poetry to philosophy, and sound to sense. And yet, refusing to take Yeats's poem as an instance of Agamben's thought would be to deny that the philosopher is making a claim about poetry in general, a claim that is paradoxically bound up in a semiotic network of poetic specificity (sound events), which, by practice, must deny any claim to universality. Unable to navigate this paradox and yet embracing the encounter between philosophy and poetry, Watkin finds the space for this Agambenian juxtaposition-without-hierarchy between the universal (*logos*) and particular (*phone*) in his neologism "logopoiesis," or "thinking as such through poetry" (*Literary* 196). Although it clings onto a different etiological narrative, Agamben's project of recovering Language as such is reminiscent of Walter Benjamin's.[6] Both depend upon the reconcilable potential of the irreconcilable schism between poetry and philosophy. For Agamben specifically, as we will see the further we descend, those two monstrous cliff faces come together in the silence at the end of a poem.[7]

In "The End of the Poem," an essay in a book of the same name, Giorgio Agamben sets out to "define a poetic institution that has," in his words, "until now remained unidentified: the end of the poem" (109).[8] Agamben's essay is short but its breadth is staggering; what is at stake is not merely another comment on a concluding couplet, but the very possibilities of . . . well, everything. The essay is about indefinable spaces: the spaces between lines of verse, the spaces between verse and prose, and the spaces between poetry and philosophy. As a philosopher whose reflexive style, realizing the unrealizable realm of language as such, plays against what he is trying to convey, Agamben naturally leaves many of his own loose

---

6. In "Language and History" (*Potentialities* 48–61), Agamben explicitly compares his project to Walter Benjamin's in "On Language as Such. . . ." (*Selected Writings Volume I: 1913–1926*, 62–74). However, while Benjamin's language is tied to a prelapsarian, pre-Babel mythology, Agamben finds his "fall" with the schism of philosophy and poetry. See "Introduction" and "The Perverse Image" in Agamben's *Stanzas: Word and Phantasm in Western Culture.* For the relationship among Agamben, Benjamin, and Martin Heidegger regarding Agamben's critique of modern "indifferent" aesthetics, see Durantaye (26–54) and Mills (35–58).

7. Agamben's "Frenhofer and His Double" explores the relationship among silence, Rhetoricians, and Terrorists (*The Man Without Content*, 8–12).

8. For other major critical intersections of formal and eschatological "ends," see Kermode's *The Sense of an Ending: Studies in the Theory of Fiction* and Herrnstein Smith's *Poetic Closure: A Study of How Poems End.*

"ends." He takes up what he sees as the negative ontological state of the final line of a poem, but also the eschatological end of lyric poetry in the twentieth century (as in Theodor Adorno's oft-cited pronouncement),[9] and the mythological end of poetry, which comes by way of that millennia-old exile from Plato's Republic. There, with the threat of poetic rhetoric at an end, comes that mythological harmony of the logos, the possibility of accord between sound and sense, between the semiotic and the semantic—or what, for millennia, has been called philosophy. Agamben's fascination with teleology might seem odd at first, given that his body of work deals with navigating around one. Still, even here, the end is not a type of Hegelian Absolute but is, instead, turned around once again as a potentiality that defines in its nonidentity the jagged spaces of existence.

Yeats's "The Stolen Child" was first published in *The Irish Monthly* in December of 1886 and later included in his 1888 collection *Fairy and Folk Tales of the Irish Peasantry*.[10] Its title—definite article ("The"), verbal past participle acting as adjective ("Stolen"), noun ("Child")—is unmistakably ominous. The definite article signifies that what is about to be read was a singular occurrence; "stolen" implies that the occurrence in question has already happened and continues to underscore the present; finally, "child" makes the occurrence locally contextual—there exists a child who has been taken, either through force or coercion. The occurrence could now be labeled a "kidnapping," an unlawful bringing of a person from one locale to another.[11] Fifty-three lines long, "The Stolen Child" is composed of four

---

9. There are different versions of Adorno's frequently misconstrued assertion. In "Cultural Criticism and Society," he writes: "Cultural criticism finds itself faced with the final stage of the dialectic of culture and barbarism. To write poetry after Auschwitz is barbaric" ("Cultural" 34). In later interviews, Adorno specified that he meant lyric poetry. Agamben discusses Adorno's pronouncement extensively in *Remnants of Auschwitz*.

10. "The Stolen Child" borrows from two William Allingham's poems Yeats chose to include in *Fairy and Folk Tales of the Irish Peasantry*. From "The Fairies," he adopts Allingham's vivid landscaping ("Up the airy mountain, / Down the rushy glen, / We daren't go a-hunting / For fear of little men. . . ."), and from "Twilight Voices" he takes and repurposes the enchanted appeal. A verse from this latter poem echoes the fairy address in Yeats's poem: "I hear strange voices, flitting, calling, / Wavering by on the dusky blast,— / 'Come, let us go, for the night is falling; / Come, let us go, for the day is past!'" "I . . . took from Allingham and Walsh their passion for country spiritism," Yeats acknowledges (*Essays* 248). Allingham, "The Fairies" in *Sixteen Poems by William Allingham*, 12; Allingham, "Twilight Voices," 164–66.

11. In an 1889 article for the *Scots Observer*, Yeats regards the trooping fairies as "kidnappers." Reprinted as "Kidnappers" in *Writings*, 39–43.

stanzas: twelve, fifteen, fourteen, and twelve lines, respectively. No stanza has the same rhyme scheme, though, in an unusual strophic arrangement, each begins with interlocking couplets and ends with a refrain. The first three stanzas all situate fairy rhetoric within the naturally stunning space of western Ireland, which becomes a magical land of enchantment, somewhere between domesticated country life and the mythical realms of Celtic lore. The opening, concerned as it is with geographical positioning, taunts with its mystical movement of locales:

> WHERE dips the rocky highland
>   Of Slewth Wood in the lake,
> There lies a leafy island
>   Where flapping herons wake
> The drowsy water rats;
> There we've hid our fairy vats
> Full of berries
> And of reddest stolen cherries.
> Come away, O human child!
> To the woods and waters wild
> With a fairy, hand in hand,
> For the world's more full of weeping than you can understand.

Those familiar with the poem are more likely to know the crisper second line of the refrain as "*To the waters and the wild.*" This line, along with various lines from most of the poem, would be constantly revised over the next half century, as was Yeats's custom.[12] Most of the changes, though, were slight alterations of punctuation. Along with the one I just noted, the most significant changes found in the final version, as it appeared posthumously in the 1950 *Collected Poems*, included an italicized refrain, a couple word substitutions and deletions, and what Yeats thought were more Gaelic spellings of places ("Sleuth" instead of "Slewth")[13] and beings ("faery" instead of

---

12. Between 1886 and 1950, the poem underwent countless changes, which are detailed in "The Stolen Child" in *The Early Poetry Volume II: "The Wanderings of Oisin" and Other Early Poems to 1895 Manuscript Materials*, George Bornstein, ed., Cornell UP, 1994), 183–86.

13. A. Norman Jeffares writes, "Yeats commented that when he wrote most of the poems in Poems . . . he had hardly considered seriously the question of the pronunciation of the Irish words. He had copied at times somebody's fanciful spelling, and at times the ancient spelling as he found it in some literal translation, pronouncing the words as they were spelt" (520). The history of Yeats's manuscripts is marked by the often-perplexing

"fairy"), which, although likely inadvertent, might have an impact on how this poem is sounded.[14]

The rhetorical-geographical positioning of the first word of the stanza "Where"—as both the place of no-place and the apparent answer to the uncertainty introduced by the title—will be repeated at the beginning of the next two stanzas. The word seems doubly significant given the spatial context of kidnapping and what became, for Yeats at the end of the nineteenth century, the mythological space of western Ireland. Commonly referred to as Slish or Slesh Wood, Yeats's "Slewth" Wood derives from the Irish word *slios* which means "sloped." Located along the underside of the Killery Mountains, the forest approaches the south shore of Lough Gill, in the vicinity of Sligo and the town Dromahair, which means the "ridge of

spelling choices the author had made. "Deciphering the words in a Yeats manuscript is only the first step," William O' Donnell writes, "for then the editor must decide how to treat the many misspelled words. Some of those spelling errors can be presciently entertaining, as in a letter written the day after Yeats first met Maud Gonne, in which he misspelled her name as 'Miss Gone'" (89; the letter to Miss 'Gone' appears in *The Collected Letters of W. B. Yeats*, 134).

14. Yeats's pronunciation of faery/fairy is uncertain (see "The Pronunciation of the Irish Words" in *Poems* [1899]). If "faery" were three syllables, the line would be iambic tetrameter and, in keeping with this rhythm, the two previous lines would tend to have an initial anapestic foot ("Come awáy"; "To the woóds"). If faery were pronounced as the two-syllable "fairy," the three lines of the refrain might alternatively be read as catalectic trochaic tetrameter ("Cóme awáy o húman chíld"). This is the mesmerizing song-meter of Byron's Tyger, London Bridge, and the English alphabet, and it easily becomes lodged in a child's unconscious memory. Allowing that semantic meanings are not inherent in stress patterns, one might still hear the catalectic trochaic tetrameter lines almost as ritualistic feet stomping around a circle. Yeats himself would locate stress patterns in the performance rather than written text. This meant that stress patterns would necessarily vary given the fluctuations of different reading voices. He writes, "If I repeat the first line of *Paradise Lost* so as to emphasize its five feet I am among the folk singers—'Of mán's fírst dísobédience ánd the frúit,' but speak it as I should cross it with another emphasis, that of passionate prose—'Of mán's fírst disobédience and the frúit,' or 'Of mán's fírst dísobedience and the frúit'; the folk song is still there, but a ghostly voice, an unvariable possibility, an unconscious norm. What moves me and my hearer is a vivid speech that has no laws except that it must not exorcise the ghostly voice. I am awake and asleep, at my moment of revelation, self-possessed in self-surrender; there is no rhyme, no echo of the beaten drum, the dancing foot, that would overset my balance" (*Essays* 524).

the air-demons" or "ridge of the two demons."[15] In answering this initial call of "where," the poem twice offers "there" in unanticipated rhymes at the beginning of lines three and six. But where "there" in line three functioned initially as an unnecessary rhetorical posture of exposition, here in line six "there" acts as deixis, an instance of discourse, as if someone or something were present and pointing.[16] We soon find out just who is pointing, but not before another semantic disturbance. The ambiguity of "fairy vats" leaves us wondering for a moment whether we are encountering vats belonging to fairies or vats filled with fairies. Although we find out quickly that it is the former, the ambiguity has the lasting effect of foregrounding the coerced relationship between belonging and containment. Being "a part of" means being a part of a space one might not altogether control. This, as the misty

---

15. In "The Heart of the Spring," Yeats describes Sleuth Wood as though it looked "cut out of green beryl, and the waters that mirrored it shone like pale opal" (*Mythologies*, 175). He recalls an old countryman who speaks of mystical events and the romance of warriors fighting "dragons among the blue hills" (64), and responds that he is "not certain that [the old countryman] distinguishes between the natural and supernatural very clearly" (61). *Gleann an Chairthe* or "Glen of the Standing Stone" is a lake and a vale near Drumcliff. In "Towards Break of Day," Yeats describes one of its waterfalls: "I thought: 'There is a waterfall / Upon Ben Bulben side / That all my childhood counted dear. . . .' / I would have touched it like a child / But knew my finger could but have touched / Cold stone and water" (*Collected* 185).

16. This, of course, relates directly to Agamben's thoughts on deixis ("shifters" or "indication"), which, although they come up again here and there every now and then, are most fully explored in *Language and Death*. There, Agamben glosses Hegel's critique of sense-certainty and the "apparent contradiction [. . .] that the most concrete and immediate thing ["this" "now" "here"] is also the most generic and universal" (17), "signifiable and determinable through an act of indication" (22). Émile Benveniste's sense of deixis as an instance of discourse brings Agamben once again to the relationship between philosophy and poetry and the idea of language as such. See Watkin (*Literary* 20–23) and Clemens in Murray et al. (43–65). David Johnson (pointing to Agamben pointing to Émile Benveniste), notes the contextual difference between the spoken and written instances of shifters: Benveniste's "consideration of personal pronouns, which constitute a specific set of shifters, leads him to argue for a distinction between the spoken instantiation of discourse and the written one: 'A linguistic text of great length . . . can be imagined in which I and you would not appear a single time; conversely, it would be difficult to conceive of a short spoken text in which they were not employed'" (271; quoting Benveniste, 217–18).

second and third stanzas of the poem make clear, is the space of "unearthly resort."[17] Here are the stanzas (sans refrain but including the lines Yeats subsequently revised in brackets):

> Where the wave of moonlight glosses
>   The dim gray sands with light,
> Far off by furthest Rosses
>   We foot it all the night,
> Weaving olden dances,
> Mingling hands and mingling glances
>   Till the moon has taken flight;
> To and fro we leap
>   And chase the frothy bubbles
>   While the world is full of troubles.
>   And is anxious in its sleep. . . .
>
> Where the wandering water gushes
>   From the hills above Glen-Car,
> In pools among the rushes
>   That scarce could bathe a star,
> We seek for slumbering trout
>   And whispering in their ears
>   We give them evil dreams,   [Give them unquiet dreams]
>   Leaning softly out
> From ferns that drop their tears
>   Of dew on the young streams. . . .   [Over the young streams]

---

17. In *Mythologies*, Yeats describes this distant land beside Slewth Wood: "Drumcliff and Rosses were, are, and ever shall be, please Heaven! places of unearthly resort. I have lived near by them and in them, time after time, and thereby gathered much faery lore. . . . At the northern corner of Rosses is a little promontory of sand and rocks and grass: a mournful, haunted place. Few countrymen would fall asleep under its low cliff, for he who sleeps here may wake 'silly,' the Sidhe having carried off his soul" (88). The poet then offers his own near-death experience: "Once, before the sand covered it, a dog strayed in, and was heard yelping helplessly deep underground in a fort far inland. These forts or raths, made before modern history had begun, cover all the Rosses. . . . Once when I was poking about there, an unusually intelligent and 'reading' countryman who had come with me, and waited outside, knelt down by the opening, and whispered in a timid voice, 'Are you all right, sir?' I had been some little while underground, and he feared I had been carried off like the dog" (88–89).

The cascade, a magical façade of cold stone and water, becomes a delectable hunting ground for the fairies, the Sidhe of lore, who had been hiding behind the ecology of each stanza's opening. Trawling its waters "for slumbering trout," they cradle those abed, anxious in their sleep. That we take the trout figuratively, as a metonym for children, shows the fairyland speakers engaging the dislocating power of rhetoric. Rather than simple metonymy, though, we might also see the power of a performative language at work, invoking an actual metamorphosis brought about by the druidic power of the furtive rushes. The fairies seem almost exuberant in their confession: "whispering in their ears / We give them evil [unquiet] dreams." Not all the Glen-Car ecology, it should be noted, is comfortable with its complicity in the abduction. In a line that was stolen from later versions of this poem, "tears / Of dew" fall, in the manner of the cataract, from the ferns onto the young streams. The personified ferns, which keep the fairies concealed, seem disheartened by their own deception. And yet, even this enjambed antiptosis asks that we confuse "teary dew" with "dewy tears"—each a saline mixture, though with a different agent and, more importantly perhaps, agenda. Following the phrase "whispering in their *ears*," we might wonder whether the ferns, themselves charmed by the rhetoric and the semiotic expectation of (what shall we call it?) a will-to-rhyme, can do anything but "drop their *tears*" (emphases my own). Agamben, addressing the relationship between *topos* and *topoi* in *Language and Death*, calls this semiotic pressure on the semantic sense "the metrical-musical element" of verse (77).[18] Nowhere is this more prevalent in the poem than in the refrain, which, like the words of the fabled druid Niamh Chinn Óir who lured Oisín to Tir na nÓg,[19] promises eternal rewards on the other side of the world.

----

18. "Poetry," he writes, "contains in fact an element that always already warns whoever listens or repeats a poem that the event of language at stake has already existed and will return an infinite number of times. This element, which functions in a certain way as a super-shifter, is the metrical-musical element" (77). In *The Man Without Content*, Agamben's analysis of an artistic *Gestalt*, which depends upon the radically other, "something else" (96) of Form, leads him to see structure as rhythm, which is as much enjambed disruption as continuity. He writes that rhythm "appears to introduce into this eternal flow a split and a stop . . . almost . . . the presence of an atemporal dimension in time" (*The Man Without Content* 99). See also Watkin, *Literary* 135–44 and 189–93.

19. In Yeats's "The Hosting of the Sidhe," Niamh calls "Away, come away: Empty your heart of its mortal dream" (*Collected* 55).

Save for a slight (but significant) variation at the end of "The Stolen Child," the last four lines of each stanza turn to offer, as the poem's eerie refrain, an address which may or may not be apostrophic, depending on how one understands not only the rhetorical term but moreover what exactly is happening in the poem and by whom. (Yeats, after all, collected hundreds of different Irish fairies in his own literary vats, and their rhetorical schemes differ accordingly.[20]) The refrain that Yeats finally settled on, italicized for effect, has the communal fairy voice calling out:

> *Come away, O human child!*
> *To the waters and the wild*
> *With a fairy, hand in hand,*
> *For the world's more full of weeping than you can understand.*

The sound and rhetorical repetition partake of the "dissociative and incantatory" (126) effects of what Northrop Frye calls "charm poetry," and for good measure.[21] The speaking voice is presumably the same as the more narrative/lyrical one opening the stanza (one that could claim "There we've hid our fairy vats"), but the tone shifts dramatically in the devocation. It is clear that the child hears this address but not the earlier strophes (the fairies, we presume, would not divulge their nightmarish method to one they are trying to beguile). What is unclear, though, is if the child being addressed is "there" on the leafy island, deceived by the fairy vats full of berries or in some safer place of the weeping world, able to hear an apostrophic call from a ghostly presence afar. Either way, the child seems unable to respond, as is the case in an apostrophic address.

---

20. *Fairy and Folk Tales of the Irish Peasantry,* Yeats's collection of lore and poetic works, became, in his own words, the "chief influence of my youth" (*Uncollected* 328). He distinguishes between "solitary" and "social" fairies, calling the latter "trooping fairies." Like a good lyric poet, the solitary fairies prefer to be alone, while the trooping fairies prefer company, making their "chief occupations . . . feasting, fighting, and making love, and playing the most beautiful music" (*Fairy* 2). As a subset of trooping fairies, Yeats lists "Changelings"—those fairies who carry mortals "away into their own country, leaving instead some sickly fairy child, or a log of wood so bewitched that it seems to be a mortal pining away. . . ." (47). "Most commonly," Yeats adds, "they steal children" (47). The poet appended his own "The Stolen Child" to this section titled "Changelings."

21. "[T]he rhetoric of charm," Frye writes, "is dissociative and incantatory: it sets up a pattern of sound so complex and repetitive that the ordinary processes of response are short-circuited. . . . Such repetitive formulas break down and confuse the conscious will, hypnotize and compel to certain courses of action" (126).

As the various semiotic-semantic tensions—including that poetic pun on "foot," which importantly implicates poetic practice in the thievery of words as much as the fairies in their thievery of infants—make clear, the poem is not only about the dangers of kidnapping fairies, but also about the dangers of ritualized rhetoric, one of which unsurprisingly includes lyrical tongues. Most haunting, perhaps, is the communal speaker—the "we" rather than the "I"—who, as an instance of discourse, conflates all subjects into a collective voice, as if it were a classical chorus.[22] In turning to address the child, the poem's refrain illustrates the dangers of such poetic rhetoric or what we might call music without an awareness of its semantic content. Like enjambment, the refrain's caesurae are modes of hesitation that exhibit a scission between thought and sound. As William Watkin succinctly explains, though, there's a significantly different pressure on each poetic mode: "the caesura [is] where thought interrupts poetry" and enjambment is where poetry interrupts thought (172). Seemingly, there should be no reason for a pause in the middle of a line but for a *semantic* disturbance. Yeats's caesurae, here—too balanced as they are (we might assume one even in the refrain's second line)—seem to do the reverse. Thought is overwhelmed by rhythm. The mellifluously alliterative "w"s, the tranquil "hand in hand," and the somnifacient anapests mesmerize the child. Blanketed by the rhythmic echoes of words, the child can hear sounds but cannot comprehend the world of weeping or the formless woods and illimitable wild of language as such. The iteration hypnotizes the child; he cannot refrain from following.[23] On the other hand, the reader—that other extra-poetic addressee "you"—need not entirely be seduced by the musical and rhythmic qualities of language because she or he ought to be able to note both the final line's conspicuous praeteritio (mentioning the world through the pretense of its omission) and its odd protractedness, which threatens to break the lyric bubble on the right-hand margin of the page. It is as if the world is too busy to bend what it needs to say to the metrical pattern. The graphic form breaks this extra-textual hypnotic glance, and the reader is sent out from the land of enchantment, up the rocky highland, and back into the world, however full of weeping it may be.

---

22. And yet, as an instance also of deixis, it evokes the Voice that is no longer but was never voice. See Agamben's *Potentialities* (260) and *Language and Death* (23–37).

23. Such enchantment very well captures what Agamben means by the opposing semantic-semiotic propulsions of poetic structure.

The kidnapping fairies must, in essence, be poets for their "unquiet" powers of language to work. Depending upon how this poem is understood, it either reinforces or undermines Plato's treacherous positioning of poetic rhetoric, the basis for exiling the poet.[24] While Yeats (of course) does not maintain the same distinction between philosophical Truth and poetic rhetoric as Plato, he does turn the classical philosophy/poetry binary around as a matter of ethics: Is it more desirable to maintain a poetics of understanding or one of escape? Yeatsian critics and readers are divided about the choice of worlds. Although he is generally thought to have preferred mythologies of escape in his younger years, Yeats himself was troubled by this choice. "Those who are carried away," he writes, "are happy, according to some accounts, having plenty of good living and music and mirth. Others say, however, that they are continually longing for their earthy friends" (*Fairy* 47). The influence of the fairy world "upon Yeats's youthful life and work was precisely that of the moon upon the tide," Frank Kinahan maintains, adding that "[a]t times its strong pull draws him out towards mystic depths; then the influence wanes, and an earthly counterpull brings him, as it brought Oisin, back to the shores on which the frailer tents are pitched" (63). The depiction of the fairy world, however, in "The Stolen Child" leaves little ambiguity for Kinahan, for whom "there is little really glamorous about [the fairies'] glamouring of the human child" (63).[25] Declan Kiberd agrees, arguing that the "vagueness" of the fairies' world is "no match for the concrete

---

24. "So we were right not to admit him into a city that is to be well-governed, for he arouses, nourishes, and strengthens this part of the soul and so destroys the rational one, in just the way that someone destroys the better sort of citizens when he strengthens the vicious ones and surrenders the city to them" (*Republic* X: 605B).

25. "The Stolen Child" for Kinahan becomes a "variation on one of the dominant motifs of nineteenth-century Irish fairylore: the lamia motif, the grin of malice masked by a face smiling welcome." He calls the sidhe "lords of deception" and sees "their happy other world as genuinely enticing but ultimately fatal to man" (63). William T. Gorski can similarly maintain: "Yeats is loathe to enter this 'other' world. By representing the passage into the spiritual dimension as an act of kidnapping, Yeats highlights the inimical and hazardous aspects of the human relation to the superhuman. In effect, the higher world poses a threat to the lower world: it can overcome and override human life. Its power is fatal" (52). The choice is a non-choice for Yeats's contemporary Lady Wilde, who insists that the countrymen "look on the sidhe as a race quite inferior to man," while it is the fairies who "look on mortals as of much higher race than themselves" (39, 73; referenced through Kinahan 48).

homeliness of feeling with which the poet renders the details of a country kitchen" (141).[26] The final stanza of the poem seems to endorse this reading:

> Away with us he's going
>   The solemn-eyed—
> He'll hear no more the lowing
>   Of the calves on the warm hill side,
> Or the kettle on the hob
>   Sing peace into his breast,
> Or see the brown mice bob
>   Round and round the oatmeal chest.
> For he comes, the human child,
> To the woods and waters wild
> With a fairy, hand in hand,
> For the world's more full of weeping than he can understand.

The dramatic shift from the initial oneiric tone of the previous stanzas indicates that there is no further need for seductive rhetoric. Where the reader anticipates another geographical positioning—the "Where" that opens the other stanzas—the speaker can only offer "Away," as if to say *there is no "where" there*. This dictional flight into fairyland is complemented by an actual vanishing of the child. "The solemn-eyed"—one of only two dimetric lines in the poem—gestures toward an omission. I take the short line as an aposiopesis (Greek for "becoming silent"), a noun-less epithet. In keeping with the regular metrical pattern, the line should have read "The solemn-eyed child," but the child has already faded "away." Again, it is the

---

26. By calling "attention to the homely things that the child, in going with the faery, must now abandon," Robert W. Caswell writes, the speaker is "aware of the simple beauty and value in the things of the child's world," and thus seems quite respectful of such a world. Following Yeats's own ambivalence, Caswell notes, "[i]f there is a solution between the desire of the spirit for immortality and the mortal desires of the body, Yeats does not try to state it," but, rather, leave it as a "problem for his reader" (Item 64). Resistant to the pedagogical ambiguities one loves to have in the literary classroom, Yeats, however, could also be quite critical of his own ambivalence. In an 1888 letter, the young poet writes to Katharine Tynan, calling his poetry—specifically "The Stolen Child"—"almost all a flight into fairyland from the real world, and a summons to flight. . . . [I]t is not the poetry of insight and knowledge, but of longing and complaint—the cry of the heart against necessity" (*Letters* 63).

anticipation of the rhyme at the end of the line that signals the finality of disappearance: "solemn-eyed" rhymes almost with "hill side" . . . but something is off. The speaker then turns to the world we have heard so much and so little about, the world more full of weeping than one can understand. Here, the day is real again and—with its calves and kettles and mice and warm, warm hillside—more importantly, present. Time emanates from this sun-baked hillock, where the lowing, as an onomatopoetic resonance, imparts a momentary illusion of unity between word and world, between the rhetoric of representation and performative possibility.[27] The details of the kitchen themselves are trapped between metonymic figuration—where any specificity is but a posture for sentiment—and the non-figural concreteness of time—where the mice will indeed snatch the oatmeal in order to survive. This duality seems the very enchantment of the actual world (and, for that matter, the very enchantment of lyric poetry), one in which literal time can be defined by its magical metonymic potential. The ritualized dance of the fairy world—its interminable music—is shown to be somewhat inadequate without the perpetual regeneration in the face of mortality that defines the real world. "Trapped within the flux of time," Frank Lentricchia writes, Yeats "could, at moments, intuit release from necessity and the innumerable afflictions dealt him in the everyday world. But for all his transcendental desires, Yeats often found life in the finite world attractive enough to lure him down from the occult towers, attractive enough, in fact, to make him wish he had never engaged in otherworldly pursuits" (89). "The Stolen Child" finds itself in the tension between these two possible worlds, asking what happens when a person is pulled by each, one comprehensible in its "wild," the other unintelligible in its domesticity.

A question remains: if the child has already been "stolen," why does the fairy speaker continue with the rhetorical refrain at the end of the final stanza? To answer this, we might return to Agamben, who finds a problem for poetry and, once the dots are connected, for all of philosophy, at the end of the poem. "[W]hat happens at the point at which the poem ends?" (*End* 112), he asks. "Clearly, here there can be no opposition between a metrical limit and a semantic limit" (112).[28] If enjambment, in his view,

---

27. Agamben compares onomatopoeia to glossolalia and calls the former "the poetics of the dead voice" and the latter "the poetics of dead language" (*End* 70).

28. One could do worse than bearing in mind Walter Benjamin's words comparing the novelist to the storyteller. At the end: "With such an insight the novel [*Éducation sentimentale*] reaches an end which is more proper to it, in a stricter sense, than to any

defines poetry, Agamben simply and astonishingly concludes that the end of the poem—the final line which is not enjambed, which is not between anything—cannot really be poetry. Because there can be no enjambment, "it follows that the last verse of a poem is not a verse" (112). The lack of in-between-ness casts the final line into a different ontological position, a sort of poetic state of exception, "a genuine *crise de vers*" in which the poem's very identity is at stake" (113).[29] He turns to Marcel Proust's and Walter Benjamin's various readings of the final poems of Charles Baudelaire's *Les fleurs du mal* as shocking, fragmentary, and "suddenly ruined," noting especially the impressionistic disorder at the end of "Le cygne" (a poem to which I will return in the next chapter): "As if the poem as a formal structure would not and could not end, as if the possibility of the end were radically withdrawn from it, since the end would imply a poetic impossibility: the exact coincidence of sound and sense. At the point in which sound is about to be ruined in the abyss of sense, the poem looks for shelter in suspending its own end in a declaration, so to speak, of the state of poetic emergency" (113).

Punning upon the many etymological links of agriculture and verse (*versure*, the "plow turning around"), Agamben offers an apocalyptic description of the final poetic line: "*una catastrofe*" ("La fine" 116) he calls it, linking "catastrophe" etymologically with the poetic unit of the strophe. Here, however, we have not a "turning," but a literal "against-turning," or an overturning, or the much more terrifying end-of-the-world pronouncement of a no-turning, because ultimately at the end of the poem (*pace* Aristotle) there's nothing left to turn into but the void.[30] "Suddenly it is possible,"

---

story. Actually there is no story for which the question as to how it continued would not be legitimate. The novelist, on the other hand, cannot hope to take the smallest step beyond that limit at which he invites the reader to a divinatory realization of the meaning of life by writing 'Finis' " (*Illuminations* 100).

29. Watkin calls this poetic space "no longer a pause but an abyss" ("The / Turn" 60).

30. Not yet a fan of postmodern literature, Aristotle's sense of a literary work had very concrete beginnings and endings. Tragedy, he calls, "an imitation of an action that is complete, and whole. . . . A whole is that which has a beginning, a middle, and an end. A beginning is that which does not itself follow anything by causal necessity, but after which something naturally is or comes to be. An end, on the contrary, is that which itself naturally follows some other thing, either by necessity, or as a rule, but has nothing following it. A middle is that which follows something as some other thing follows it. A well constructed plot, therefore, must neither begin nor end at haphazard, but conform to these principles" (*Poetics*, 1450b 25–30).

Agamben writes, "to see the inner necessity of those poetic institutions, like the *tornada* or the envoi, that seem solely destined to announce and almost declare the end of the poem, as if the end needed these institutions, as if for poetry the end implied a catastrophe and loss of identity so irreparable as to demand the deployment of very special metrical and semantic means" (*End* 112).[31]

Agamben treads very carefully here, mitigating his own claim of identity loss with the contagious uncertainty of its pronouncement. His "as if" [*come se*]—"as if the end needed these institutions" (112), "as if for poetry the end" (112), "[a]s if the poem as a formal structure" (113), "as if the possibility of the end" (113)—remind one of Immanuel Kant's "as if," which is needed to mediate the subject-object antinomy of aesthetic judgment, especially as it finds its way into Hans Vaihinger's later philosophy. But Agamben's "as if" is not Vaihinger's; Agamben's potentiality is "as not."[32] Such para-Messianic ontology for the time that remains mediates the poetic object's actual ending with the subject's desire for or anxiety about such an ending, while also leaving such a dialectic unresolved. Ends, desires, forms, and knowledge are ultimately all potentialities, as much "as not" as "as if." In this way, theological and ontological time partake of the same primordial form as poetic time or *kairos*, "the *time that the poem takes to come to an end*" (*The Time That Remains* 82–83).[33] "And the poem is like the *katechon* in Paul's Second Epistle to the Thessalonians," Agamben concludes, "something that slows and delays the advent of the Messiah, that is, of him who, fulfilling the time of poetry and uniting its two eons, would destroy the poetic machine by hurling it into silence" (*End* 114).

---

31. Agamben turns briefly to Raimbaut d'Aurenga's "No sai que s'es," a medieval love lyric that does not seem to know whether it is prose or verse. See Manning's "Game and Earnest in the Middle English and Provençal Love Lyrics."

32. Agamben critiques Vaihinger's "as if" ("all the vices of Neo-Kantianism"), while he defends Adorno's "as if" against Jacob Taubes's claim that Adorno "aestheticiz[es] . . . the messianic" (*Time* 35–43). See also Watkin on Messianic time, *klēsis*, *kairos*, and *chronos* (*Literary* 144–55).

33. Taking the asymmetrical sestina form as typical of poetic time, Agamben writes that the "retrieval of rhyming end words . . . transforms chronological time into messianic time. Just as this time is not other to chronological time or eternity . . . so too is the time of the sestina the metamorphosis that time undergoes insofar as it is the time of the end, the *time that the poem takes to come to an end*" (*The Time That Remains* 82–83).

Waiting patiently in line for their turn to speak are some words from Book II of Dante's *De vulgari eloquentia*. Here, Dante speaks of the related and unrelated rhyme, the *clavis*, meaning either a nail or a key. In Daniel Heller-Roazen's translation of Agamben's translation, Dante maintains that " 'the endings of the last verses are most beautiful if they fall into silence together with the rhymes' (*Pulcherrime tamen se habent ultimorum carminum desinentiae, si cum rithmo in silentium cadunt*)" (113–14). Agamben renders his Italian translation as: "bellissime sono le terminazioni degli ultimo versi, se cadono, con le rime, nel silenzio" ("La fine" 117). Heller-Roazen's translation ends with "the rhymes"; Agamben's translation ends in "silence"; Dante, more precisely, ends with the silent fall: "silentium cadunt." Poems do not end; they fall into a silence both semantic and semiotic. Silence, like translation, is the place of no-place—Stéphane Mallarmé's "rien n'aura lieu que le lieu" to which Agamben alludes (*End* 114)—either the divine space where the semiotic and the semantic can finally come together or the vacuum signaling that their union is, at last, impossible. The silent rhyme, Agamben mentions, is missing from Dante's "Così nel mio parlar voglio esser aspro" (I want to be as bitter in my speech [as this beautiful stone is in her acts]). "It is as if," Agamben notes, "the verse at the end of the poem, which was now to be irreparably ruined in sense, linked itself closely to its rhyme-fellow and, laced in this way, chose to dwell with it in silence" (115). That woman, "quella donna," like the stone and like *logos*, cannot be pierced by the poet's words. As the only way for togetherness is annihilation, the poet asks that his bitter words penetrate her heart as she had penetrated his.[34] The silent "fall" suggests divine implications, specifically the nonplace of Eden and its myth of a prelapsarian language, the perfect union of sound and sense. This silence, though, a silence that shrouds ethics onto eschatology, is closer perhaps to Cain than his parents. Because Cain knows not what happened to his brother—because, in effect, he cannot end his story—he must endlessly wander the earth. Whether we call it a "wandering" or a "turning against" or a catastrophe or a loss of identity, this crisis of verse causes poetry to "collapse . . . into silence . . . in an endless falling" (*End* 115). Language cannot communicate anything other than its

---

34. In "*Corn*: From Anatomy to Poetics" (*End* 23–42) Agamben traces the etymological kernels of another name for the unrelated rhyme. The "corn," unrhymed in one stanza, returns to rhyme in a later stanza, thereby ensuring that the phonetic echo, while deferred, is not left behind. On Dante's poem, see Mariann Sanders Regan (134–48).

own event—or what Agamben terms "itself"—"without remaining unsaid in what is said" (115).[35]

The silence following the final line of Yeats's poem seems to shout out as if for attention. The refrain of which it was a part has been altered slightly, so that it is no longer directed at the child. Here are these final lines (as revised for the *Collected Poems*):

> *For he comes, the human child,*
> *To the waters and the wild*
> *With a faery, hand in hand,*
> *From a world more full of weeping than he can understand.*

What remains, exactly, in the wake of this refrain? To begin to answer that, we might turn to John Hollander, for whom refrains can be "applied, like a brake, to the song's momentum . . . exercising control over the course of the song" (*Melodious* 132). Yeats's foot pedal, like each instance of a refrain, is partitioned into what Hollander terms an original, ritualistic "medieval carol burden" and the more modern "poetic" element: "Each occurrence of the danced-to burden increases its redundancy and tends to collapse it into a univocal sign: 'That was all full of meaning; now meaning stops for a while and we all dance again.' Poetic refrain, on the other hand, starts out by troping the literalness of the repetition, by raising a central parabolic question for all textual refrain: 'Does repeating something at intervals make it more important, or less so?' " (133).

As Yeats's final refrain loses its apostrophic O and moves from the second person to the third, we must ask, as Hollander does for each instance of poetic refrain, "What is it to mean *this* time around?" (133). Modes of repetition and the pseudo-chronological/pseudo-eschatological time of the poem go hand-in-hand for Agamben: "The poem is therefore an organism or a temporal machine that, from the very start, strains toward its end. . . . But for the more or less brief time that the poem lasts, it has a specific and unmistakable temporality, it has its own *time*" (*Time* 79). Such time, called *kairos*, is marked through nonlinear homologies like rhyme, or, as in Yeats's poem, the refrain. That the fairy-speaker needed three stanzas and three refrains to convince the child to leave the world testifies not to the semantic power of poetic language but rather to the rhetorical power of the *semiotic*; the expectation of closure following the sounds of words is more forceful in

---

35. "Silence is not [philosophy's] secret word—but rather philosophy's word perfectly leaves unsaid its own silence" (Agamben, *Idea of Prose*, 111).

the discursive realm of desire than any sense lurking around it. The child, now absent, is no longer addressed. With a turn of the pen, "for" becomes "from," the deictic "you" becomes the referential "he," and the claim about a more desirable world moves from rhetorical posture to fact. The child has been summoned by fairy language; there is no more need to apostrophize. Here at the end, language itself, like this sacred child, disappears into a silence of no-place. The nonsilence following the first three stanzas is disquieting as it waits for an answer it has not yet received. The falling into silence following the final line is sinister, more sinister, perhaps, than we can understand.

Given how much his poetic style interferes with what he is trying to say, it is difficult not to make much of Agamben's own hesitations—the caesurae, digressions, and losses of identity—which all pave the way for him to get to the end of "The End of the Poem." Naturally, his final commentary must ask: "How to conclude an essay that speaks of the impossibility of concluding?" Agamben, finding himself at wit's end, offers an extended parenthetical—his own metaphorical falling into silence:

> (Wittgenstein once wrote that 'philosophy should really only be poeticized' [*Philosophie dürfte man eigentlich nur dichten*]. Insofar as it acts as if sound and sense coincided in discourse, philosophical prose may risk falling into banality; it may risk, in other words, lacking thought. As for poetry, one could say, on the contrary, that it is threatened by an excess of tension and thought. Or, rather, paraphrasing Wittgenstein, that poetry should really only be philosophized). (115)

It is a rare essay that ends with a parenthetical. It is an even rarer speech—which does not even have the grammar for a parenthetical, and which Agamben's essay originally was—that does so. (Such speculations do not even include the very real, very anxious posturing that always seems to surround the event of the end of the speech. Without the trumpet call of the tornada, how will the audience know when to clap?) The bracketing of language in the curves of the parenthetical registers itself as a caesura or a turn, a different tonality of voice—thought disrupting words. Behind both Wittgenstein's and Agamben's claims is an ethical pronouncement (*dürfte, dovrebbe*)—that poetry and philosophy "ought really only" be done as the other. This commitment speaks volumes about the place of poetry at its end, whether we mean the Platonic one or the Adornian one or the Agambenian one, still unresolved in its potential. Taking Wittgenstein's "One really ought do philosophy as poetry-ing" and turning it on its head, Agamben tenders his own potentiality of "perhaps" [*forse*; translated as "rather" by Heller-Roazen] in searching for a philosophy that might be accountable to the totality of language as such, be it poetic language entering the realm of thought or philosophical language entering the realm of voice.[36] Perhaps the poet ought to be let back into the Republic. Perhaps only at the mythical end, the return of the Messiah, can we have the marriage of sound and sense. And yet, there is a sense of hesitation here in the formal parenthetical, as if the quieted sounds of Agamben's own rhetoric could not but spite the literal pronouncement that subsumes the poetic under the philosophical. The authority of Agamben's final line inheres not in the familiar assertion that poetry be philosophized, but, rather, in the sounds of its rhetoric, its con-verse—the inverted repetition of the refrain.

The ability to "paraphrase" Wittgenstein already presupposes the ability to locate the sense of Wittgenstein's statement within its sounds. The philosophical bind, here, is not with a mythical "end," but with a beginning; this is Jacques Derrida's critique of Plato and the imagined epistemological ground or beginning that must always be paradoxically "outside" or "before" itself. This bind might also make us think about the *crise de vers* at the other book end: the beginning of the poem. Where is the first line enjambed from? Where is the tension, the echo of hesitation between sound and sense? In Yeats's poem, it seems to be in the silence preceding the initial "Where"—that attempt to locate, within an actual geography, the natatory place of no-place. The poem (with apologies) is all about the mysterious loch of in-between-nesses: spaces between cultures, between people, between art and life, between ethics and cultural forms. There is a sense that the final moment, what Agamben would see as the irruption of prose, can be captured neither by poetry nor by philosophy, but only by something in-between—"Language." Perhaps the schism between philosophy and poetry—what Watkin labels "the false caesura at the founding of our philosophy" (16)—might be overcome in the nebulous space of nonpoetry/nonprose that the end of the poem provides.[37] According to Watkin,

---

36. Compare this to Agamben's statement (and rhetorical parenthetical) in "The Idea of Language": "Philosophy can only lead thought to the limit of voice; it cannot say the voice (or, at least, so it seems)" (*Potentialities* 43).

37. Quite interestingly, Yeats contrasts his own poetics of escape with a more territorialized prose. From his metaphorical tower (years before he moved into the literal one), he noted that the "folk-tales are full of simplicity and musical occurrences, for they are the literature of a class for whom every incident in the old rut of birth, love, pain, and death has cropped up unchanged for centuries: who have steeped everything in the heart: to whom everything is a symbol. The people of the cities have the machine, which is prose and a *parvenu*" (*Fairy* xii).

"Ending books on a call for the healing of the fracture between poetry and philosophy [. . .] becomes something of a habitual gesture" (47) for Agamben. Not a myth, but a refrain of sorts. Agamben's simple, positivistic definition of poetry gives us a notion of law, but it also gives us a notion of interference—that poetry lives where philosophy starts to break down. This difficulty, this incompatibility of language, resides in what the fairies might call a very "human" disjunction, and what we happen to call the trespass of poetry: the difference between what is said and what is meant.

Tornada

As the fairies weave olden dances, they "mingl[e] hands and mingl[e] glances"—their ritualistic evocation dependent as much on touch as on their mesmerizing circular movement. With the moon taken flight, the lunacy of one turn replaces another, and they are left "chas[ing] the frothy bubbles," almost otherworldly spheres washing over the dim gray sands of the Rosses. I would not go so far to say that there's an intentional connection between the "O" beckoning the human child and symbolic circles cropping up throughout the poem, but the latter do arise mysteriously and meaningfully. Fairy circles, James MacKillop writes, are "thought to have been caused by dancing fairies." "If a human steps into the ring," he explains, "he or she is compelled to join the fairies in their wild dancing, which would seem to occur in a few minutes but in fact lasts for seven years or more" (180).

Losing track of time is fatal in the mortal world. The mice, who, in their way, foot it all the day, dancing "Round and round the oatmeal chest," would lose themselves if they ever stopped moving. Above them, the kettle on the hob sings its peace in evaporation, contrasting the earlier "frothy bubbles" of the fairies with its own. "Hob"—short for hobgoblin—also denotes the act of making trouble. Yeats, courtesy of Lady Wilde's "formula," recounts the horrifying witch-trial-like thermal process necessary to expose a hobgoblin or changeling: "Many things can be done to find out in a child a changeling, but there is one infallible thing—lay it on the fire with this formula, 'Burn, burn, burn—if of the devil, burn; but if of God and the saints, be safe from harm'" (*Fairy* 47). That is faith gone too far, whatever its origins.

It feels like the world—the real one, *our* world—is more full of weeping than one can understand. The causes today are numerous, the understanding still fails. Some days, remembering to take the kettle off the hob can be too much. What would it mean, amid one's own poetic daydreaming, to stop and listen to the actual kettle crying on the hob? What would it mean to forsake the fairies and stay within our own world, even with all of its attendant pain? More still, what would it mean to hold on to our own versions of poetic ritual, but do so, nonetheless, in this world? Given too many machinations, the world would live without a soul; given too few, though, and the kettle might smolder. At least, this is what we tell ourselves. For Yeats, amid the middle ground of Sligo, where "everything is steeped in the heart," the magic can still be felt even if it goes untouched. In a kinder if not altogether uncondescending moment, he writes,

> We will not too severely judge these creatures of the imagination. There are worse things after all than to believe some pretty piece of unreason, if by so doing you keep yourself from thinking that the earth under your feet is the only god, and that the soul is a little whiff of gas, or some such thing. The world is, I believe, more full of significance to the Irish peasant than to the English. The fairy populace of hill and lake and woodland have helped to keep it so. It gives a fanciful life to the dead hillsides, and surrounds the peasant, as he ploughs and digs, with tender shadows of poetry.[38]

---

38. Yeats, not always aware of why his immediate world was full of weeping, concludes this thought with an old Irish adage: "No wonder that [the Irish peasant] is gay, and can take man and his destiny without gloom and make up proverbs like this one from the old Gaelic—'The lake is not burdened by its swan, the steed by its bridle, or a man by the soul that is in him'" (*Uncollected Prose* I, 181–82).

The twisting and turning of seductive fairy rhetoric plays out in the strophic whirlpool of the third stanza of Yeats's "The Stolen Child": "wandering water" in the opening is complemented by "young streams" at the end; further in, "gushes / From the hills above" is matched by "From ferns that drop their tears / Of dew"; and still further in toward the center, the metaphorical reach of "slumbering trout" is balanced by the catalepsy of "evil dreams." The chiastic encasing gives the impression of a tapering gyre, drawing all to the center, where the fairies are "whispering in their ears." The child never recovers. Writing about "My Descendants," Part IV of Yeats's "Meditations in Time of Civil War," Helen Vendler connects the circle to the figure of chiasmus: "This closing third stanza 'proves' its assertion of the superior value of circular form by shaping itself into the figure of speech which represents a circle, the abba figure of chiasmus, which bites its own tail." Within three lines, Yeats repeats and inverts love → friendship and friendship → love. Together, as Vendler writes, they "enclose[e] (the unnamed) Augusta Gregory and George Yeats within a wreath of love and friendship."[39] Not to be outdone, in one of the thirty-three cantos of "The Man with the Blue Guitar," Wallace Stevens offers a "duet / With the undertaker" whose song in the snow ends up "apostrophizing wreaths."[40] As duets go, this is more of a wait-for-your-line rather than a take-turns-leading situation. What will turn out to be a chiastic shape of apostrophe hasn't yet revealed itself, but its circular foundation is there. His is not so much love and friendship as it is the imagination and reality, but perhaps the two pairs, in the end, aren't so unalike.

---

39. Vendler, *Our Secret* 268–69.

40. Stevens, *Collected Poetry and Prose*, 145; hereafter cited as CPP.

Chapter 2

Wallace Stevens

"Ecce, Oxidia is the seed"

It is fatal in the moon and empty there.
But, here, allons. The enigmatical
Beauty of each beautiful enigma

—Stevens, "An Ordinary Evening in New Haven"

$$X_1$$

The flowery beginning of "Anecdote of Canna" pits "thought" against and alongside "sleep" until it (thought), fighting the dots of its own ellipsis, wanders back into the reality of daybreak. The canna, coming alive not with the light of dawn but earlier in "the dreams of / X," colors the optical white of the neoclassical columns and dome of the capital's Capitol, where Wallace Stevens (waking) had been walking (*CPP* 44).[1] A little wind, and the canes of the columnar canna bend, creating their own visual crossings, as does that mighty figure X whose mental architecture dominates the

---

1. In a letter to Hi Simons, Stevens relates, "Anecdote of Canna is the sort of poem that forms itself in one's mind. One afternoon I was walking around the terraces of the Capitol in Washington. These are unreal enough at the right moment, but they became completely unreal so that the thing was more or less somnambulistic. Then one never really thinks or thinks clearly in dreams and that thought was the end of the somnam-bulism. 'Now daybreak comes' is simply the return of reality" (*Letters* 464).

opening. The middle stanza of the poem—with its own crossings and repetitions—makes a quincunx of "thought . . . sleep . . . thought . . . sleep . . . thought." But by the final stanza, the senatorial (or is it stentorian?) figure X has been moved outside, where he is left to cross the wet, settled stones and observe the canna:

> Now day-break comes . . .
>
>   X promenades the dewy stones,
>   Observes the canna with a clinging eye,
>   Observes and then continues to observe.
>
> (CPP 44; ellipses in the original)

A walking daydream of sorts, the poem presumably turns from thought to reality, even if the final line, turned toward itself in obverse fashion, seems more invested in the act of observing than in what is ultimately observed. Reduced to the variable X, the figure of Stevens's imagination seems caught between the materiality of the letter and the world's unreality. If X is the detached lyric speaker, he is reflectively disembodied. If X is an object of observation, then the unnamed, unnoticed lyric speaker has been spending his time thinking about X's thinking. Either way, the alphabetic X remains the scaffolding of thought, legislating how the mind, from without, turns in on itself, thereby constituting the self.

Hidden behind the unfurling leaves of the canna lies the grammatical ambiguity of the final lines. One typically reads the subject-object relationship as: *X promenades the dewy stones. [X] observes the canna with a clinging eye. [X] observes and then continues to observe.* But we might just as well understand the lines as: *the canna* [deferred subject] *observes with a clinging eye [that] X promenades the dewy stones. [The canna] observes and then continues to observe.* X is here because it is observing. X is here because it may be observed. Subjectivity—that other clinging I—is found in this crossing. But enough of that for now, before we get too lost in the dream. It is not the "I" so much that concerns me as yet in this poem but the alphabetic movements at the beginnings of the lines:

>   O r thing . . .
>   X promenades . . .
>   O bserves . . .
>   O bserves . . .
>
> (CPP 44; initial separation is my own)

Here, in the openings of these final lines, Stevens has us almost playing noughts and crosses, as if the movement between the mind and reality were calculated placings on a giant gameboard, one always blocking the possibilities of the other's movement.

I have been wandering around a bit lately in parts of what Philip Furia and Martin Roth years ago marvelously called Stevens's "fusky alphabet." I have been curious about his peculiar Xs and Os or, as we might begin to see them, his figures of chiasmus and apostrophe—two ways of returning home, yet by vastly different paths. I am interested in how these figures—the rhetorical figure of repetition and reversal and the turning away to address another, usually absent, person, inanimate object, or abstraction—intersect, and in doing so, show us how we, as subjects, are constituted from without. In Stevens, we often see this complexity in variable subject-predicate relationships. As in many of his poems, the titular "of" of "Anecdote of Canna" (the title already its own phonetic chiasmus of sorts: *an-ec . . . ca-na*) obscures the subject-predicate relationship between "anecdote" and "canna." Is this the canna's anecdote or is this an anecdote about the canna?

Both apostrophe (as it is usually understood in a vocative way) and chiasmus (as it is usually understood in a spatialized way) provide the conceptual space and temporal immediacy for lyric speakers to create an other outside themselves, and it is the address to or interaction with the other—the rebounding of an echo that has been there all along—that ends up constituting their lyric subjectivity.[2] As I detailed in the introduction, the apostrophic gesture, especially in the hands of Jonathan Culler, is often signaled by the long "O" of poetic tradition. Chiasmus comes to us from the Greek *chi* as the lettered form X, which Furia and Roth call "the most frequently isolated letter in Stevens' poetry" (69).[3] Contrasting this X with Stevens's senses of metaphor, Bart Eeckhout sees the poet's X, specifically in "The Motive for

---

2. The enchanting and foreboding existential possibilities of poetic apostrophe, as I recounted in my introduction, have been well documented. But the deeper senses of chiasmus have not been as well explored. A recent notable exception is the collection edited by Anthony Paul and Boris Wiseman, *Chiasmus and Culture*, which hopes to move beyond chiasmus as mere rhetorical plaything and offer a foundation for what they see as the trope's theoretical "place in social interactions, cultural creation and more generally human thought and experience" (1).

3. If you are one of the sixty-seven people who "live[s] for this stuff" see also Jeffrey Nunberg's overview of political rhetoric (as in the more interesting sense of "rhetoric"): http://people.ischool.berkeley.edu/~nunberg/inaugural.html; and Richard A. Lanham's *Analyzing Prose*, 2nd ed., Bloomsbury, 2003, 119–36, *passim*.

Metaphor," as the "condition of all metaphoricity" (251).[4] While nearly all critical glosses of chiasmus take interest in the shape of the reversed repetition, most (phonocentric) understandings of the apostrophic, as I have been arguing in this book, not unexpectedly minimize the written sign in favor of the otherworldly possibilities of the vocative address.[5] As I argue, we also need to understand the graphic existences of these circular and crossed letters, because they shape the poetic and ontological possibilities of apostrophe and chiasmus, which seem always at play in the noughts and crosses of Stevens. His shifting sense of Xs and Os moves beyond the purely visual and the purely vocative in imagining how the shapes of such poetic gestures are already entangled in the turnings of their various symbolic, iconic, and material guises.

Naturally, the alphabetic appearances of Stevens's Xs and Os are not only subject to the turns of canna. Consider, for instance, the circular line openings beginning another of Stevens's poems:

> O ne's grand flights, one's Sunday baths,
> O ne's tootings at the weddings of the soul
> O ccur as they occur. So bluish clouds
> O ccurred above the empty house and the leaves
> O f the rhododendrons rattled their gold. . . .
> (*CPP* 205; initial separation is my own)

Poems such as this one, "The Sense of the Sleight-of-Hand Man," seem to glorify the fortuitousness of random events, which "Occur as they occur." This healthy form of unknowing, a mental state beyond logic, allows the imagination to map onto a natural world that is continually pleasing in its surprises. That inconspicuous word repeated twice in the first stanza—"so"—which can mean a logical "therefore," an "in this manner," a doubling down of "very," or the narrative turn to another topic ("anyway"), feints as if it could draw a logical connection between all the things the eye

---

4. See especially Chapter 11, "Between Metaphor and X," of his *Wallace Stevens and the Limits of Reading and Writing* for the relationship to metaphor.

5. Some rhetoricians distinguish between chiasmus and its cousin antimetabole, which is the repetition and inversion of the exact same words, whereas chiasmus might include repeated and inverted notions rather than exact words. An example of a chiasmus that is not an antimetabole would include this line from Stevens's "The Plain Sense of Things": "For this blank cold, this sadness without cause" (*CPP* 428). The external words/phrases ("blank" and "without cause") and the internal words/phrases ("cold" and "sadness") are close parallels.

sees. "Could you have said the bluejay suddenly / Would swoop to earth?" the speaker continues, leaving it uncertain whether he is invoking the absent reader or asking this question to himself (*CPP* 205). Either way, he takes the linearity we expect of narrative and desire in life to the inexplicable realities of slight movements. "Could you have said" is an interesting phrasing for this reflection, which when understood on a self-referential level, gestures toward the unexpected choices poets make: *I could have said. . . .* Some meaning seems to come together in this poem, however, around patterns of shapes—things that remind the eye of the eye's reminders:

> It is a wheel, the rays
> Around the sun. The wheel survives the myths.
> The fire eye in the clouds survives the gods.
>
> (*CPP* 205)

The rotational swooping of the bird conjures in the speaker images of the wheel, of the sun, of the disembodied eye. Or, as the sleight-of-hand man might paraphrase it, *now the coin is in my hand, now it is behind your ear.* Still, we are left wondering what is meaningful in these possibly connected events or whether all this is nature's metacarpal coin trick. Just as the shapes of the natural world outlive our mythologies, so the material shapes of our letters seem to outlive our intentions, and it is here that the imaginative misdirections of the sleight-of-hand man have us following the wave of the semantic hand rather than that to which it is pointing—that initial O, that accidental origin for the wandering of each turning line. Stevens's poetic prestidigitations seem to insist that the semiotic—the materiality of language—and not the semantic is, like the bluejay suddenly swooping, the real gift of poetic magic. But what, exactly, is that magic conjuring?

If the conman/magician's words are meant to distract from the actions of the hands, then there is something particularly threatening here about the poetic diversion that moves the focus in reverse: from the metonymical mouth of speech to the metonymical hand of writing. There is not, perhaps, a more terrifying fragment in the history of English poetry than John Keats's posthumous fragment "[This Living Hand]":

> This living hand, now warm and capable
> Of earnest grasping, would, if it were cold
> And in the icy silence of the tomb,
> So haunt thy days and chill thy dreaming nights

> That thou would wish thine own heart dry of blood
> So in my veins red life might stream again,
> And thou be conscience-calm'd—see here it is—
> I hold it towards you. (365)

One wonders: is the "it" at the end the warm capable hand or the icy one? Could it possibly even be the written fragment itself? Is the address to the thou turned by the poem into a type of apostrophe? Or is this a separate trope of prosopopoeia or anthropomorphism? We might even push these questions further and ask whether the very cutting up of this gesture into three separate tropes reenacts the threat of disembodiment the poem articulates.[6] Like Stevens's "Could you have said," which can conjure the disembodied "I" only by pointing to a "you," Keats's poem asks that we bring a voice to life by temporarily losing our own.

There is a terror that the listener-cum-reader-cum-newly-embodied-speaker feels in perceiving his or her own still-pulsing hand. The very unease of apostrophic frame-breaking brings second life to a voice that has traveled across two hundred years to find a new body, which will, in turn, ultimately find its own place in that icy silence of the tomb. Turning to Paul de Man, Culler notes the proleptic threat here of a very different "dead"-line than most are used to: the temporal chiasmus. "[N]amely," he puns, repurposing de Man's words, "by making the dead [sic] speak, the symmetrical structure of the trope implies, by the same token, that the living are struck dumb, frozen in their own death" (*Rhetoric* 78; qtd. in Culler, *Pursuit* 153).[7] And here the deictic language—this, now, thy, thou, thine, my, thou, here, it, I, you—typifies the grip that the once-living lyric voice still has on the reader, who is suddenly asked to voice the words of the dead, as if they were her or his own.[8] Barbara Johnson calls this a type of "ventriloquism,"

---

6. David Nowell Smith notes the likeness between the fragmentation thrust upon both the speaker and addressee, adding that "the uncanniness of voice is part of the poem's status as *fragment*" (45).

7. Interestingly, Culler misquotes and/or corrects de Man's original disembodying statement, which was "making the *death* speak" (emphasis my own).

8. "When we read a lyric," Culler writes, "aloud or silently, we utter the words, we temporarily occupy the position of the speaker. . . . We are not simply overhearing the speech of another, whom we strive to identify from this speech but are ourselves trying out, trying on this speech. And some of the embarrassment of apostrophe comes, I think, from the fact that we ourselves engage in this preposterous act of addressing clouds, birds, and the spirits of the dead" (*Pursuit* xv).

or "throwing one's voice," and she notes how "it manipulates the I/thou structure of direct address in an indirect, fictionalized way" (*World* 185). Or is it all just artifice, another guise of a ventriloquized address, mouthed by a puppet with a hand up its sleeve?

O₁

One can see how apostrophe is tied to both sentiment and voice in the concluding lines of Stevens's early send-off of trite romantic images, "Invective Against Swans":

> And the soul, O ganders, being lonely, flies
> Beyond your chilly chariots, to the skies.
>
> (CPP 4)

The speaker, presumably, having broken away from his lyric mode to address those clichéd ganders directly, returns along the way to the "O ganders" of the odd—though not poetically unusual—opening:

> The soul, O ganders, flies beyond the parks
> And far beyond the discords of the wind.
>
> (CPP 3)

But when these opening lines return at the end of the poem, they are now crisscrossed phonetically: "flies beyond" becomes "be-in . . . flies." One might also note the phonetic chiasmus in the phrases "beyond the par . . ." and "far beyond" in the first stanza. One golden quirk (among many here) is that the apostrophic invocation ironically harkens back to its own out-of-date ritual, as does the refrain—another burden of years past. Paradoxically, the emotional outburst is shown to be crafted, the artifice of a poet in tranquility calmly employing one rhetorical device over another. The unexpected couplet, with its rhyming of "flies" and "skies," offers some measure of harmonic closure, if not the always-hoped-for metaphysical answer. That, too, betrays a vestige of an older poetic desire to resolve things with the magic of sound, as if the swans could be stayed a moment longer with a plea, as if the speaker's world could be recreated with a mere "O."

An aquiline pedant hovering above the halls of rhetoric might note here that the "O ganders" is not actually an apostrophic act but rather is being confused with *exclamatio* (heightened emotion), or prosopopoeia (giving inanimate objects human qualities, notably that of the voice or the ability to hear), or with normal speech acts, which deceptively create a sense of temporal immediacy. The point is well taken, as voicing and turning and emotion only overlap so much, despite the borders among the three still wavering. And yet there is something that still feels a little magical about the lyric "O"—at least for Culler, who, following de Man, has directly linked apostrophe to the very magical possibility of the lyric address. As a time-shattering instance of voicing, apostrophe resists easy paraphrase and in turn shows the lyric to be something more than a fictional imitation of a real-life speech act. It is the performance of the act itself. "O ganders" does not describe but rather invokes the birds, or, more precisely, invokes a voice hoping to invoke the birds. That address to the other in turn constitutes the lyric subject, and, here, in Stevens's poem, this seems to be a voice coming to understand its own failures. Signifiers, of course, cannot conjure things (this holds true even for those of the poet), but, in a sense, the voice *is* conjured with its instantiation. Apostrophe becomes a moment outside narrative, outside representation; it provides a *now* that is constituted of discourse, its own discursive event.

Even if this were magical language and not an instance of representing voice, it still feels difficult in our own age to take seriously the poetic posturing of apostrophe—or what Culler calls the essence of "poetic pretension" (*Pursuit* 143). The embarrassment is such that, in a line Culler cites from the beginning of Stevens's "Botanist on Alp (No. 1)," the modern poet wants nothing to do with it:

> Panoramas are not what they used to be.
> Claude has been dead a long time
> And apostrophes are forbidden on the funicular.
>
> (*CPP* 109)

It is not just embarrassment but cliché that has Stevens prohibiting apostrophes on the funicular. (De Man, if I remember correctly, is forbidden on the funicular too.) Might we hear "forbidden in the vernacular" in this line as well? We are no longer in a world that can apostrophize unironically; we are no longer in a world that can believe that words have such power. But how in this new world, which is still unavoidably burdened by old language, Stevens's speaker earnestly asks, can the poet capture real sentiment? After all, we are not the operators of the funicular, forced to take the ascent yet again at each hour. Turning to exclaim "O beautiful mountains, O beautiful trees" seems so out of time, but there is the desire to say something more meaningful than "As Barbara Cartland would put it, 'O beautiful mountains!'" Once again for Stevens, sufficiency and propinquity seem the best (or only remaining) options:

> But in Claude how near one was
> (In a world that was resting on pillars,
> That was seen through arches)
> To the central composition,
> The essential theme.
>
> (*CPP* 109)

Like the poet, Stevens's botanist "live[s] by leaves." And as in many of Stevens's poems, the meditation cannot find its center: the poet stutters amid his own words, repeating the cloudiness of his own corridors. What does it all mean? The poet can conjure only failure: "I don't know what" (*CPP* 109). The poem concludes:

> What composition is there in all this:
> Stockholm slender in a slender light,
> An Adriatic *riva* rising,
> Statues and stars,
> Without a theme?
> The pillars are prostrate, the arches are haggard,
> The hotel is boarded and bare.
> Yet the panorama of despair
> Cannot be the specialty
> Of this ecstatic air.
>
> (*CPP* 109–10)

The world of Claude Lorrain was never real, resting as it did on its own pillars, however much it was framed through arches, however much beyond these arches was ignored. The poet again stumbles over the echoes of his own despondent sounds: **An A dria** tic **ri va ri** sing; pill **ars are pros trate**, the **ar** ches **are** hagg **ard**. The labor of the poet's work becomes apparent, as do the hidden forces—however mysterious—of language. Still, even without a center, even without a theme, even amid this modernist "panorama of despair," there remains an ecstasy of air, despite the inspiration the poet can no longer draw. With the turn to poetic self-reflection, the voice in doubt gives way to the real—whatever that is—behind it all. A final voicing of hope is suddenly conjured through the failure to summon the older scene and even through what immediately feels like the ruin of the anticipated new poem.

O₂

Positing another failure of apostrophe, Culler invokes Charles Baudelaire's "Le Cygne" (*Pursuit* 144–45), which begins with an apostrophe of its own, "Andromache, je pense à vous!" (Andromache, I think of you!) (Baudelaire 172–73). The thought of Hector's wife, whose tears swelled up the Simois river around Troy, sets Baudelaire's mind racing about how Paris (the *other* Paris) used to look. Now, he is almost like the idiomatic bird out of water he soon references:

> Près d'un ruisseau sans eau la bête ouvrant le bec
>
> Baignait nerveusement ses ailes dans la poudre,
> Et disait, le cœur plein de son beau lac natal:
> "Eau, quand donc pleuvras-tu? quand tonneras-tu, foudre?"
>
>
> (Close by a dried out ditch the bird opened his beak,
>
> Flapping excitedly, bathing his wings in dust,
> And said, with heart possessed by lakes he once had loved:
> "Water, when will you rain? Thunder, when will you roar?")
>
> (174–75)

"Water, when will you rain?" asks the swan that gandered alone into the heart of Paris. The direct address to the skies presumes that there is this thing, "rain," that could hear and, in doing so, answer the desperate plea. This plea, however, creates not rain but the voice of anguish itself, not just for the bird but for the analogical poet who also could be seen as flapping excitedly. Culler, with an eye to the ear, writes, "when [the swan] seeks something other than itself (*eau*), it finds only itself (*O*), which may also be nothing (*O*)" (*Pursuit* 144). Here, the swan's failure is the poet's failure, but the inability to summon enacts the nothing that is. As Culler spells it out, *cygne* becomes *signe*.

"Asides on the Oboe" has Stevens similarly playing upon the possibility of a hidden apostrophe. The poem proclaims in its own prologue that the past prologues—the unchanging cycles of life—are over and now, in an Emersonian vein, we must choose our own fictions. As in many of his other poems, Stevens tries to move beyond myth, beyond any form of mediation, and transparently find access to the world:

> The prologues are over. It is a question, now,
> Of final belief. So, say that final belief
> Must be in a fiction. It is time to choose.
>
> (*CPP* 226)

As if it were itself carried by the melancholic sounds of the oboe, this wartime poem is heavy, with mythical gods killed off, heroic monuments turned to gravel, and the jasmine islands bloodied. Yet, even faced with the sense of an end all around, Stevens can still find a heroic soul in the philosopher's man, the "man of glass":

> If you say on the hautboy man is not enough,
> Can never stand as god, . . .
>   . . . there is still
>   . . . the human globe, . . .
>   . . . the man of glass,
> Who in a million diamonds sums us up.
>
> (*CPP* 226–27)

The pun on "hautboy" ("oh, boy"), archaic French for oboe, brings us back to the high woods of Baudelaire's sonnet "Correspondances" and its own forest of symbols: "Il est des parfums frais comme des chairs d'enfants, / Doux comme les hautbois, verts comme les prairies" (There are perfumes as cool as the flesh of children, / Sweet as oboes, green as meadows) (18–19).[9] Stevens also moves to (haunted) forests, but, where Baudelaire embraces the columns of nature, Stevens instead turns to find a unity between two mysterious shapes: the

---

9. Paul de Man's reading of "Correspondences" and "Obsession" in "Anthropomorphism and Trope in the Lyric" (*Rhetoric* 239–62) concludes by understanding the couple not as lyric but as exemplifying the psychological projection of a hermeneutics: "The lyric is not a genre, but one name among several to designate the defensive motion of understanding" (261). See also Barbara Johnson's "Anthropomorphism in Lyric and Law" on de Man's reading (*Barbara Johnson Reader*, 236–43).

diamond and the globe. These shapes move throughout Stevens's poem—or rather, the poem seems to move alongside them until, at the end, Stevens can find a measure of solace in the notion that "we and the diamond globe at last were one" (*CPP* 227). These oddly combined shapes might remind the reader of the circularity and crossing in Leonardo da Vinci's Vitruvian Man. It is also possible that Stevens had the "diamond globe universal stand" of "Sanford's Assorted Inks" in mind—something that would more directly align the asides to the poetic vocation. While the specific design below from 1888 would not have been on Stevens's desk, other designs featuring the diamond and the globe were produced throughout the 1940s:

Figure 2.1. Sanford's Assorted Inks advertisement (1888). *Source:* The American Stationer, vol. 23, 1888, p. 696.

Whatever the inspiration for the shapes was, taken together, they bend Stevens's circle, as if the image he had in mind were that of a bow in the hands of an archer:

Figure 2.2. A "diamond globe." *Source:* Created by the author.

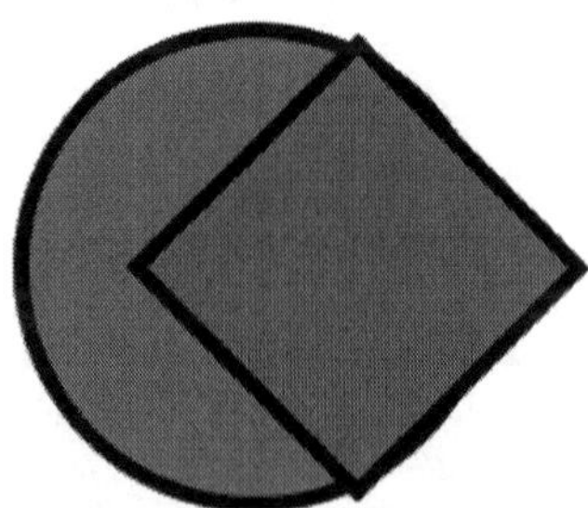

The odd reference to the "hautboy" (oboe) and all of its echoed sounds in the poem ("obsolete," "globe," "Boucher") come back within earshot (*CPP*

226–27), and the title might be heard again as an invocational aside on an "O Bow," a stringed counterpart to Baudelaire's high-wooded sound—here, whittled down from the forest of symbols and bent into the musical C of a counterpointed bow.[10]

If we flip Stevens's title around, we are left with "Oboes on the Aside," or "Oboes on the A-side," as if the entire poem were about the diamond stylus of language cutting through the spinning grooves of a record. Even "The central man, the human globe" is flattened into a circular "mirror with a voice" (*CPP* 227). If the lyric words are now music, they are "cold and numbered" in a very different way; they invoke and have us invoking "jazzman" through the mythic "jasmine." And Stevens, for his part, has us move from A to C, from the "a-side" to be "Still by the sea-side" until we are left "Climb[ing] through the night, because his cuckoos call" (*CPP* 226–27). Paronomastic letters, a measure of peace—the horrors of 1942 notwithstanding—still remain ("It was not as if the jasmine ever returned"), and while any invocation ("Him chanting for those buried in their blood") seems futile, it is the voice still able to cry out that lets us know that he is there (*CPP* 227). As a modern poet with romantic sensibilities who relishes the failures of the imagination, Stevens will never give us the harmonic circle or the cyclical return to how things once were. Besides, he is always operating within the humors of an almost-circle or, as he so often returns to it in his figuration, to the letter-comedian "C"—an incomplete ring, a movement that strives toward but can never find its mythological home.

In one of his very last poems, "Not Ideas About the Thing but the Thing Itself," Stevens, celebrating the circular sequence of the seasons ("At the earliest ending of winter, / In March" [*CPP* 451]), comes as close as he can to invoking the thing beyond words:

The sun was coming from outside.

That scrawny cry—it was
A chorister whose c preceded the choir.
It was part of the colossal sun,

Surrounded by its choral rings,
Still far away. It was like
A new knowledge of reality.

(CPP 452)

---

10. "The wind is never rounding O" (*CPP* 237), Stevens tells us in "Montrachet-le-Jardin." The pure sound remains inaccessible.

The movement of the circle, a different voicing of "choral rings," approaches the center, but can provide only an incomplete "as if" of O—the almost circular letter C.

$$X_2$$

We can find the letter X crawling all across Stevens's corpus. The poem following "Asides on the Oboe" in *Parts of a World*, "Extracts from Addresses to the Academy of Fine Ideas," shows us how

> The lean cats of the arches of the churches
> Bask in the sun in which they feel transparent,
> As if designed by X, the per-noble master.
>
> (*CPP* 230)

Not as haggard as they are in Claude's paintings, these arches—architecturally upright *Cs*—allow the church cats and other words that wander alliteratively into the scene to see the "eXquisite errors of time," augured by the titular "EXtracts from Addresses" (*CPP* 230; capitals added). We find the *X* in Stevens's letters as well—here, to his friend Henry Church: "I felt that I must have done something in Princeton that had offended you or Mrs. Church, and that you had x-ed me out" (*Letters* 400). It acts as a variable, as a presence, as a negation, as an indeterminacy.

Various other readers, considering the chiastic structure of Stevens's phonemes, lexicon, grammatical structures, and stanzaic themes, have tied his use of chiasmus to autistic perception, all manner of precognitive space, and to various modes of perception, especially to that nebulous space of metaphor.[11] The relationship between chiasmus and metaphor in Stevens is nowhere more apparent, perhaps, than in "The Motive for Metaphor":

> You like it under the trees in autumn,
> Because everything is half dead.
> The wind moves like a cripple among the leaves
> And repeats words without meaning.
>
> (*CPP* 257)

The poem memorably concludes with the terrifying desolation of "The vital, arrogant, fatal, dominant X" (*CPP* 257). Noting how "The Motive for Metaphor," in an abyss of reflection, moves from the opening "You" to the

---

11. For such readings of chiastic structure in relation to Stevens, see Bruhn; Lissner.

concluding "X," Robert Hariman finds a self-defeating quality to the "subject of the poem, the motive for metaphor." He writes, "Stevens was fascinated by the problem of how language mediated the relationship between mind and world. His poetry . . . could use the chiasmus . . . to suggest deep, paradoxical connections between meaning and reality that can be revealed but not quite grasped" (53).[12] An optimistic reader of Stevens might here see that everything under the trees must also be half alive.

A paratextual "X" marks the spot for the transition between section nine and section ten of "An Ordinary Evening in New Haven," the latter section containing one of Stevens's most beautiful and most enigmatic uses of chiasmus:

> . . . not merely the visible,
>
> The solid, but the movable, the moment,
> The coming on of feasts and the habits of saints,
> The pattern of the heavens and high, night air.
>
> X
>
> It is fatal in the moon and empty there.
> But, here, allons. The enigmatical
> Beauty of each beautiful enigma
>
> Becomes amassed in a total double-thing.
> We do not know what is real and what is not.
>
> (CPP 402)

There is a sense that a felt experience is occurring, however unable we are to understand its significance. Is that "X," that enigmatical crossing in the space between the sections *there*? Or does it sit outside or between the realities of the poem? Does the X gesture toward the beautifully enigmatical chiasmus that is to follow, as if to ground us for a moment, as if to say, *You are here*?[13] When the mind looks too closely at reality, it starts seeing things that aren't there. It becomes spellbound, transfixed:

---

12. Stefan Holander hypothesizes that Stevens "may have intuited a similarity in structure between metaphor and chiasmus" (214), especially in lines like these, which verbalize (in an almost negative capacity) the "vital, arrogant, fatal, dominant X" (*CPP* 257).

13. See also Eleanor Cook comparing St. Paul's enigma ("through a glass darkly") to Stevens's reversal here of "beautiful enigma" (*Poetry* 16).

We seek

The poem of pure reality, untouched
By trope or deviation, straight to the word,
Straight to the transfixing object, to the object

At the exactest point at which it is itself,
Transfixing by being purely what it is. . . .

(CPP 402)

The oxymoronic "trans-fix[ed]"—itself surrounding "the object // At the exactest point at which it is itself"—implies the repetition-with-inversion form of the chiasmus: fixed = repetition; trans = inversion. Is the "itself"-ness of the object something tangible in the world or is it the materiality of language—straight to the word, as it were? Or is the "exactest point" the moment of crossing in the middle? And what, exactly, is this e-X-actest point between the two moments of transf-IX-ing, for a section IX that is about to cross into a section X? We respond as if the enigma could be resolved, but it may in the end lead more to the transverse shades of figural shapes than to answers: "It may be a shade that traverses / A dust, a force that traverses a shade" (CPP 417).

Once we get the sense that Stevens is always playing with those supposedly incidental markers on the page, it is difficult not to see a manner of winking in some of his other longer poems. "Things of August" places its X between the calligraphic acts of writing and the real time of composition:

Writing and reading the rigid inscription.

X

The mornings grow silent, the never-tiring wonder.

(CPP 422)

Not to be outdone, "Thirteen Ways of Looking at a Blackbird" brings the X alongside the circle, marking that space between the spatially abstract and the sensually pleasurable:

It marked the edge
Of one of many circles.

X

At the sight of blackbirds
Flying in a green light,
Even the bawds of euphony
Would cry out sharply.

(CPP 76)[14]

Canto XXVI of "The Man with the Blue Guitar" speaks of the "giant that fought / Against the murderous alphabet" (*CPP* 147). It is a confounding phrase in a confounding canto. Explaining this phrasing to his friend Hi Simons, Stevens conjures what would play out to be quite a few time-travel movie plots generations later. One often thinks back to the past—"And you may ask yourself, 'Well, how did I get here?'" as David Byrne tells us (with apologies for recycling the past allusion)—and one often imagines alternative paths to one's life—"Footfalls echo in the memory / Down the passage which we did not take / Towards the door we never opened / Into the rose-garden," as T. S. Eliot recounts ("Burnt Norton" in *Four Quartets*). Stevens asks that we go back to the past to imagine the new life and become "so completely transformed" by the imagining that we are left with a great nostalgia for the actual world we already have. "It was not," he writes, "so much a remote land's end as something that changed its identity, denied its familiar intelligence (fought against its thoughts and dreams, as if these were an alphabet with which it could not spell out its riddle). With every transformation, with the fluctuations between reality and imagination and the inescapable and frequent returns to reality, a mountainous music always seemed to be passing away" (August 10, 1940; *Letters* 364). Stevens's explanation illuminates the uncanny feeling of losing something still at hand. The simile conjures a language of infancy, but, rather than a hollowness in spoken sounds, we have a graphic alphabet unable even to spell out its own riddle. The poem will thematically locate these impossibilities in the generally fraught tension between imagination and reality—a common path for Stevens—but behind whatever reality or imagination the words desire to isolate will always lie the foot falls of language. The opening couplet of Canto XXVI shows these letters, a part of the scripted system, washing apart:

---

14. In a letter to Henry Church, Stevens clarifies his objective in this part: "What was intended by X," he writes, "was that the bawds of euphony would suddenly cease to be academic and express themselves sharply: naturally, with pleasure, etc." (qtd. in Furia and Roth 69).

> The **world washed** in his imagination,
> The **world was a sh**ore, whether sound or form. . . .
>
> (emphasis my own)

Stevens called a specific canto of "The Man with the Blue Guitar" (*CPP* 135–51; hereafter cited with the canto number) "a series of antitheses" but the description could aptly apply to the whole of the poem. The great antithesis, once again, is between reality and the imagination. Vendler summarizes, "At one extreme is the joyful domination of the world, where the poet plays with reality as if it were a toy" and "[a]t the other extreme . . . is the moment when the mind is annihilated by nature" (*On Extended* 128, 129).[15] These two metaphysical forces are related to the gravitational pulls of the moon (imagination) and sun (reality), especially in canto VII where the moon "is a sea"—or Stevens's "C."

Although Stevens denied the specific connection to Pablo Picasso's Blue Period classic *The Old Guitarist* (1903–04), the artist and the color can't help but saturate the poem. In this way, the work—with or without the "pretense" to do so—does go beyond the confines of a purely semantic poetry to touch on the phonic vibrations of music and the visualizations of art. Midway through the poem, Picasso's framing of art as a "hoard / Of destructions" gives way to the "harvest moon" of song (XV).[16] Given its early reappearance, this would also be a blue moon. That color—associated by Stevens often with the imagination—conjures both sadness and a contemporary musical genre. It is called the "The amorist Adjective aflame . . ." (XIII), recalling both the erotic "blue" and the burning hot center of a fire. We meet the guitarist, "[a] shearsman of sorts," in the first canto but there is no lyric "I." This "I" appears densely in the second canto, where, despite its later conjuring of the sun and moon, here declaims "I cannot bring a world quite round"—paronomastically aligning its failure to summon a planet with its inability to smooth the edges of a world to get it to conform to whatever metaphysical universe one would want to

---

15. Though no fan of paraphrase, Stevens explains to Renato Poggioli in a July 12, 1953 letter that the "general intention of the *Blue Guitar* was to say a few things that I felt impelled to say 1. about reality; 2. about the imagination; 3. their inter-relations; and 4. principally, my attitude toward each of these things. This is the general scope of the poem, which is confined to the area of poetry and makes no pretense of going beyond that area" (*Letters* 788).

16. Cook (*Against* 120) identifies it as the 1908 hit "Shine on, shine on, harvest moon" (Jack Norworth lyrics; Nora Bayes music).

put it in. This "I" then disappears for the next four cantos, perhaps pulled into space by the counterforce of gravity; the lines, though, still exhibit a (mostly detached) lyric voice. This voice, in a discursive moment, laments, "Ah, but to play man number one," or what we might read visually—as in the canto headings—as the numerical "I."[17]

The middle of the poem introduces first the Stevensian X and then the apostrophic O, which will both come together toward the poem's conclusion. The "ex" in canto XVIII acts as a negation of reality[18]:

> . . . Or as daylight comes,

> Like light in a mirroring of cliffs,
> Rising upward from a sea of ex.
> *(CPP* 143)

Al Filreis sees the "sea of ex" as "negat[ing] the negation of intelligible language in the poem," adding that the canto is "a dream of the sort that defies the term 'dream' ('to call it a dream' is the best we can do)" (18). One might see, or rather hear, "a c of x" here, in what, with all of its riddles, has apparently become Stevens's murderous alphabet. Two cantos later, a lonely Stevens shifts to the O, apostrophizing to the "Good air, my only friend" (XX).[19] A little while later, he invokes two voices—one heavenly,

---

17. When isolated, the columnar figures don't always fare well. Section X, a not-so-subtle denunciation of celebrity celebrations, revels in its double vertical ls. Its opening, mocking more than the litter of a parade, declares, "Raise the reddest columns. **Toll a bell** / And clap the **hollows full** of tin" (my emphasis). After a few more offerings ("wills" "all" "roll"), the speaker ruminates on the possibility of tipping the vertical columns ("Lean from the steeple"; "The touch that topples men and rock"). The metaphorical columns return in section XIV a little better off, as "First one beam, then another, then / A thousand are radiant in the sky." The single candle replaces the more baroque German chandelier: "Even at noon / It glistens in essential dark." It is a measure of unity, two vertical lines coming together as one, a multi-layered I.

18. In a series of annotations to the poem for Hi Simons, Stevens writes, "The imagination takes us out of (Ex) reality into a pure irreality. One has this sense of irreality often in the presence of morning light on cliffs which then rise from a sea that has ceased to be real and is therefore a sea of Ex" (*Letters* 360). Another approach might note the aubade-like setting and its own post-erotically charged letter concatenation.

19. "I apostrophize the air and call it friend, my only friend. But it is only air. What I need is a true belief, a true brother, friendlier than the air. The imagination (poor pale guitar) is not that. But the air, the mere joie de vivre, may be" (*Letters* 793).

the other earthly—in the otherworldly back-and-forth of apostrophe. The explanations to all of the previous unanswered meditations, he writes, are:

> . . . like a duet
> With the undertaker: a voice in the clouds,
>
> Another on earth, the one a voice
> Of ether, the other smelling of drink,
>
> The voice of ether prevailing, the swell
> Of the undertaker's song in the snow
>
> Apostrophizing wreaths. . . . (XXIII)

Contrary to most apostrophic expectations, the ethereal voice prevails, but is it really that other voice from beyond returning a call or is it just the reverberations of the undertaker's song? Either way, the "[a]postrophizing wreaths" offer a wink at the salutatory Os on those stones in the snow. A little later on, Canto XXIX has us overhearing the speaker reading a Review in the cathedral. "The shapes are wrong and the sounds are false," he tells us, calling the "bells" in another line overrun by double lls, "the bellowing of bulls." If the punning on "papal bull" doesn't lead to revelation, it does carry over into the cock-and-bull achievement of the following canto—where else but number XXX?

This canto introduces Stevens's industrial suburb "Oxidia" and his reconstruction of the modern man, called the "old fantoche," as if he were a marionette controlled by the strings on the wooden cross of the puppeteer.[20] "Man, when regarded for a sufficient length of time, as an object of study, assumes the appearance of a property," Stevens writes, continuing: "We go back to an ancestor who is abstract . . . [,] that is to say unreal, finds it a simple matter to hang his coat upon the wind, like an actor who has been strutting and seeking to increase his importance through centuries, whom we find, suddenly and at last, actually and presently, to be an employee of the Oxidia Electric Light & Power Company" (*Letters* 791). One is tempted to say that there is no mythical backbone to this modern man. What ages earlier could have been Prometheus bringing humankind light is now recast as a man connecting electric cables to light the suburbs. Canto XXX continues:

---

20. Stevens: "fantoche is used rather arbitrary for a fantastic actor, poet, who seizes on the realism of a cross-piece on a pole (the way the nightingale, I suppose, pressed its breast against the cruel thorn)" (*Letters* 362).

At last, in spite of his manner, his eye

A-cock at the cross-piece on a pole
Supporting heavy cables, slung

Through Oxidia, banal suburb,
One-half of all its installments paid.

Dew-dapper clapper-traps, blazing
From crusty stacks above the machines.

Ecce, Oxidia is the seed
Dropped out of this amber-embed pod,

Oxidia is the soot of fire,
Oxidia is Oympia.

With Olympia no longer possible in this world, the "dingier" Oxidia becomes the new "paradise."[21] Beyond this grasping at modern sufficiency, the name, quite bullishly, brings together Stevens's O and X four times in eight lines. The worker with his "eye / A-cock" attaches semicircles of a dangling cable through the cross-piece X of the telephone pole—*chiasmus* from the Greek letter *chi* but also the verbal form "to place crosswise." Toward the end of the canto, the speaker turns to exclaim, in an almost phonetic recurrence: "Ecce, Oxidia," *behold modern existence.* The quasi-apostrophe gestures, of course, toward Pontius Pilate's *ecce homo* and perhaps also Friedrich Nietzsche. The performance is odd—someone clearly alone, yet knowing he has an audience who will listen.

How does one recreate a modern sense of human possibility, Stevens wants to ask, even if there are still strings attached? In the opening canto, the guitarist's audience demands that he strum their reality with his fingers:

And then they said then, "But play, you must,
A tune beyond us, yet ourselves,

A tune upon the blue guitar
Of things exactly as they are." (I)

---

21. Stevens writes, "If I am to 'evolve a man' in Oxidia and if Oxidia is the only possible Olympia, in any real sense, then Oxidia is that from which Olympia must come. . . . The dingier the life, the more lustrous the paradise. But, if the only paradise must be here and now, Oxidia is Olympia" (*Letters* 788–89).

The early pun on "a tune" / "attune" will resonate throughout the poem, and even though we still have thirty-two cantos to try to circle around the tensions between reality and the imagination, the audience already has a sense of the relationship between sounds and self-identity, of how one is constituted by the chiastic shape of apostrophe.

Hiding in much of Stevens's verse is the "IX"—how the "I" of the lyric speaker comes to be at that exactest point of the crossing. In this regard, Stevens's "The Creations of Sound" seems to play with what has become an embodied figure of chiasmus. Published first in 1944, the poem begins with a logical dismissal of an unnamed poet X: "If the poetry of *X* was music" (which it is not), then we would not know "That X is an obstruction." But, inversely, since we do know that X is an obstruction, then his poetry is not music. Some scholars tend to read Stevens's critique of this kind of obstruction as a romantic gesture (following Emerson), while others tend to understand it as an antiromantic stance. In criticizing the unnamed poet for overshadowing his words with too much personality, Stevens finds this poet to be "Too exactly himself" (*CPP* 274). By contrast, he hopes to offer a detached poetic self ("A being of sound" from whom one reflectively collects oneself) and a poetics of peculiarity, which "make[s] the visible a little hard // To see" (*CPP* 275). The stanza break right before "To see" adds a hesitation to the voice and seemingly clouds our hermeneutic visibility a little further; it makes the visible not tangibly "a little hard" but "a little hard [pause] to see." One might even hear a common Stevens pun in this set-off phrase: to C. One tends to read the arithmetic variable "X" in this poem as a hypothetical rival. (A few scholars, following Harold Bloom [151], presume the poet to be none other than T. S. Eliot—which is interesting, given Eliot's strictures against artists expressing their personality but perhaps not so surprising given the very public figure Eliot had by then become.)[22] But given this poem's critique of poetic presence, to correlate the variable with an individual is to miss the point. As Susan Stewart significantly notes, "Spontaneity belongs to the particulars of sounds, not to the gestures of human beings" (89). Edward Ragg similarly sees this spectral poet as "undeniably a verbal creation" but one whose " 'sound' is not oral" (122).

"Tell X that speech is not dirty silence / Clarified. It is silence made still dirtier," the speaker explains, drawing us into the poetic glass darkly (*CPP* 275). What happens in the (non?)clarifying conceptual and phonetic space between "dirty silence" and "silence made still dirtier"? Ironically, the

----

22. In a letter from 1950, Stevens writes, "After all, Eliot and I are dead opposites" (*Letters* 677).

figure of chiasmus always seems to turn inward and to get away from the dictates of the lyric subject, but it is the very sense of this lyric subject that is continually called into question by the sounds he supposedly makes. This is not the only poem in which Stevens's lyric voice seems caught in the crossroads between self and sound, yet it is one of the places where the chiastic connection is made most explicit. The ambiguous subject-predicate relationship of the title seems, on the one hand, to insist that we create sound, and, on the other hand, that we are sound's creations and only possible because it exists outside us. "Sound" is noise, but it also connotes qualities associated with wholeness, firmness, and proper logic. We are sound bodies. Unlike poet X who cannot understand the complicated subjectiviz-ing relationship between self and sound, Stevens's speaker encourages us to

> . . . eke out the mind
> On peculiar horns, themselves eked out
> By the spontaneous particulars of sound.
>
> We do not say ourselves like that in poems.
> We say ourselves in syllables that rise
> From the floor, rising in speech we do not speak.
>
> (*CPP* 275)

X is not simply an unnamed poetic rival but moreover also a gesture toward chiasmus and the shape and sound of a letter which echoes throughout the poem: "Too e*X*-actly himself," "a secondary e*X*-positor," "Through any e*X*-ag-geration" (*CPP* 274–75; emphases added). Even the wonderful "eke"s are visually and phonetically close to this X. But how do we make sense of the figure of chiasmus, which is "more than an imitation for the ear"? Like the sound echo, this "separate author, a different poet" who comes out of the self, is doubled back: "From him, we collect." We move from the peculiar to the particular, "peculiar" as linked here etymologically to the Latin for "property" (*peculium*), which itself is derived from the word for cattle (*pecu*) (*CPP* 275). The peculiar horn is a musical horn, but it is also an animal horn—itself an accretion, like the detached "self" of the poet. It is an imperative to embrace nonlinearity, the unknown, to hearing what we did not think we had uttered. Ideas, a poetics, and even subjectivity itself are derived from this chance concatenation of letters. It is the speech and then the echo returning, in a chiastic manner, to form who we are. This is different, for Stevens, than the poststructuralist sense that we are beings constructed ideologically through language. For Stevens, there is a creative freedom in such arbitrary constructions of sound, in not being ourselves or who we have come to believe that we are.

"The Creations of Sound" is not the only time that Stevens figures the self out of sound, and it is not the only time he does so through chiastic shapes.[23] Section II of "An Ordinary Evening in New Haven," for example, gives us "transparencies of sound, // Sounding in transparent dwellings of the self" (*CPP* 397). The effect is both terrifying and liberating, flowery and evil. In another of Stevens's monumental poems, "Esthétique du Mal," the speaker relates, "It is a declaration, a primitive ECS-tasy, / Truth's favors sonorously EX-hibited," right before the turn to section X (*CPP* 283; emphases added). Even the title of this poem crosses its sounds, constructing the poet's name in speech he didn't speak:

Figure 2.3. The crossing of sounds. *Source:* Created by the author.

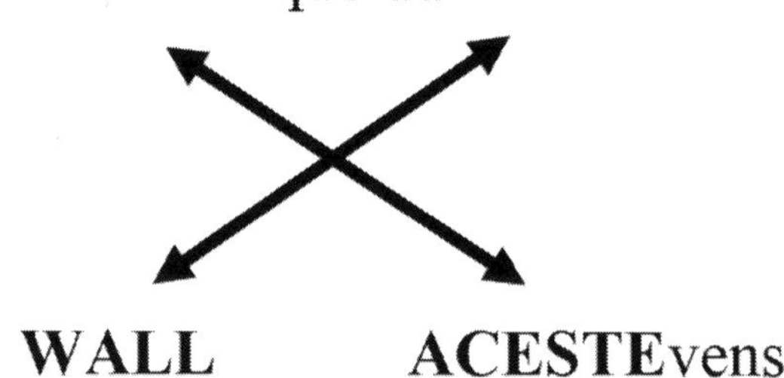

As an instance of multilingual paronomasia (in the Dutch of Stevens's ancestry, the first *e* in his family name is actually pronounced like the French *é*), this somehow feels less threatening, but is it—and are *we*, in the end—as the poem poses in section XIV after moving from the sun to the moon, merely "a logic not to be distinguished / From lunacy" (*CPP* 286)?[24]

What would it mean to have a name come out of the chiastic shape of apostrophe, emerging from the sounds beyond the end of the mind?

---

23. See Bruhn and Keyser in their discussion of different poems of Stevens. Bruhn writes, "chiastic 'reversals of words' and other language forms help to engender the poems that contain them and thereby function as 'the progenitor' of Stevens himself as a poet" (203); and Keyser notes that "people, or better still, personages [are] composed out of words" (235).

24. I am indebted to Bart Eeckhout for eking out the peculiar horns of the Dutch pronunciation.

The sounds of "Of Mere Being," often thought to be one of Stevens's final poems,[25] might resonate with one more than another. The poem crosses back to some of the themes of his earliest verse: reckoning with those spaces of reality not encased by the imagination. It opens:

> The palm at the end of the mind,
> Beyond the last thought, rises
> In the bronze door,
>
> A gold-feathered bird
> Sings in the palm, without human meaning. . . .
>
> (*CPP* 476)

You are not there and then realize years later in those moments when you choose to play, that you have been summoned—not by someone but by the golden feathers of language itself, by "A poem like a missal found / In the mud, a missal for that young man, / That scholar hungriest for that book" ("The Man with the Blue Guitar" XXIV). You have become this avid hunger, simply being mere.

---

25. Eeckhout cautions against this assumption. As he phrases it, the poem "taps so well into the critical nostalgia for teleological narratives that it is presented time and again as Stevens's final text, though it is really of uncertain date" (31).

The embodied curves of the imagination poke through reason's linearity in the last of Stevens's "Six Significant Landscapes": "Rationalists, wearing square hats, / Think, in square rooms . . . / They confine themselves / To right-angled triangles." But "[i]f they tried rhomboids, / Cones, waving lines, ellipses— / As, for example, the ellipse of the half-moon— / Rationalists would wear sombreros." The rounded edge of reality, however much it lives for Stevens in its own imagination, can help temper whatever hat one feels one needs to wear. It is neither an abstract reality nor the unearthly imagination that is so constrained in Elizabeth Bishop's "Exchanging Hats," but the possibility afforded by gendered costuming. Addressing those "[u]nfunny uncles who insist / in trying on a lady's hat," she remarks: "—oh, even if the joke falls flat, / we share your slight transvestite twist // in spite of our embarrassment. / Costume and custom are complex."[26] What happens, though, for a poet when dressing in another's clothes means always conjuring someone or something that isn't there?

---

26. Bishop, *The Complete Poems 1927–1979*, 200.

Chapter 3

Elizabeth Bishop

"O falling fire and piercing cry"

> . . . he rushes in circles in the fallen leaves
>
> —Bishop, "Five Flights Up"[1]

With its twenty sides, the Cirque d'Hiver, located in the 11th arrondisse-ment of Paris, is more icosagon than circle. Curves notwithstanding, this "winter circus," a locus for the artistic imagination for over a century and a half, gives rise to one of Elizabeth Bishop's quirkier poems, an early one and the first of many to be published in *The New Yorker*. She called it "the little poem about the toy horse (*One Art* 86), but it yet has a darker side.[2] It is not until the twentieth line of her "Cirque d'Hiver" that one realizes the mostly descriptive lyrical voice has a person behind it. The mechanical toy she had been describing: a "little circus horse" with "a little dancer on his back"

> . . . canters three steps, then he makes a bow,
> canters again, bows on one knee,
> canters, then clicks and stops, and looks at me.

---

1. *The Complete Poems 1927–1979*, 181. Unless otherwise indicated, all poetic citations from Bishop are from this edition.

2. The poem was originally titled "Spleen"—a nod to Charles Baudelaire (Millier, *Elizabeth*, 142).

With the key turned, the horse is forced to meander across the floor. The dancer on its back has turned her back to the speaker who judges the horse, rather than the dancer, "more intelligent by far." "Facing each other rather desperately," the speaker tells us, "his eye is like a star." If the scene is fantastic, the poet doesn't mind hiding it: the horse's "mane and tail are straight from [the surrealist artist Giorgio de] Chirico."[3] Lavish though they are, they hide a terrifying fragility: "the little pole / that pierces both her body and her soul // and goes through his." But rather than wallowing in what Bishop, at another time, called an "emotion too far exceed[ing] its cause,"[4] the horse and speaker unite, in the end, simply to "stare and say, 'Well, we have come this far.'"

The shrug is typical of Bishop, who, like the horse with its "formal, melancholy soul," moves without a pretension of art. Formal, yes, but the gait is often unexpected, even with such metrical dressage. The rhyme scheme of each of the five stanzas is ABCBB with the first and last B-rhyme being the same word (e.g., stanza one's toy-back-hair-black-back). But Bishop teases one's expectations. The fourth line of the fourth stanza in the block quotation I cited ("canters again, bows on one knee") features two bucking choriambs, pulling against the poem's mostly trotting iambic meter. Further upsetting the reins, the following line rhymes "me" with the earlier "key" (as opposed to repeating the previous word), as if someone needed to call attention to some inherent relationship between the two. In this same stanza, the end-words of the first and third lines (the unrhyming ones) are "below" and "bow," which the eye sees as a rhyme until the ear recognizes that the horse is vertically curtsying (*bou*) rather than horizontally turning in an arc (*bō*)—an unrealized alternative movement for this circuitous winter playroom of verse.

Like apostrophic rhetoric or the poetic arts generally (or, for that matter, any number of nonpoetic items), "the mechanical toy, / . . . with real white hair" lives between the real and the manufactured. As if to reinforce how cultural conceptions of beauty and authenticity are always already caught up in a material marketplace (as I will explore more fully in a different context in chapter 6), the second stanza repeats the phrase "spray of artificial roses," which adorns the dancer. Say it once, and it's communication; twice, and it's an advertisement. The horse, though, seems

---

3. Georges Seurat's unfinished painting *Le Cirque* (1890–91) offers a two-dimensional view of the original scene, frozen in time.

4. "The Map," *The Complete Poems*, 3.

to be more aware of these mediating contexts than the dancer on its back, or at least that is how the speaker is animating it. The horse comes to life: his eyes, earlier "glossy black" are now "like a star," and through a bit of ventriloquism the speaker gives the horse a voice, one which, if we follow the poem's logic, speaks the words as she speaks them. The final line of the poem has this mechanical horse and speaker reaching the same conclusion: "well, we have come this far." The unsaid *so we might as well keep on going* feels a bit ironic at this point, given the poem is about to conclude, but it does signal a bit of existential hopefulness if not so much enthusiasm for life's circus. But one still wonders, if the key the horse cannot reach is needed to animate it, what would be the key that animates the speaker, the "me"? In a sense, what is the impetus that allows for her to have gone this far? And what will it take for her to undertake another step?

$$* \quad * \quad *$$

Of course, the mechanical toy of "Cirque d'Hiver" doesn't speak. The words are projected from a mostly hidden lyric speaker addressing another. As Victoria Harrison compellingly argues, Bishop's "construction of subjectivities . . . are at their core relational" (9).[5] She can piece together a sense of self by navigating other subjects. The domesticated circus scene offers an address, perhaps, to the horse that isn't there, to another cultural era ("well, we have come this far"), to the reader listening in, to the poet herself.

Notwithstanding the instance of crafted lyric expression in the final stanza of "The Armadillo," with which I opened this book ("*O Falling Fire*"), it is generally not easy to find classical instances of poetic apostrophe or any of its rhetorical cousins in a poet so predisposed to disowning emotion. When they do appear, they are notable.

. . . he is preoccupied,

Looking for something, something, something.
Poor bird, he is obsessed!

("Sandpiper" 131)

---

5. Harrison approaches what she calls Bishop's "intimacy" through a lens of American pragmatism mixed with gender and cultural theory. Psychological and sociological relational theories do not always account for "the unbalanced power and gender relations inherent in such 'comingling'" (213 n.13). McCabe's *Elizabeth Bishop: Her Poetics of Loss* (especially chapter 3) explores how Bishop's longing for another constitutes a self-identity.

Thankfully, Bishop is writing about her sandpiper and not about this author. No mechanical key seems necessary for the sandpiper, who runs "in a state of controlled panic," writing with his feet as the million-year-old tide washes his constructed page away: "a sheet / of interrupting water comes and goes / and glazes over his dark and brittle feet." Before the waves wash over them, the sandpiper's footprints resemble arrows, pointing the wrong way. In a draft version of the poem, Bishop drew such a footprint toward the margin of the page. In another draft of the same poem, that footprint doodle was turned into a circular pie, cut eight ways, almost like its own token of trivial pursuit.[6] Generally overlooked by us, Bishop's sandpiper watches his own toes, or, rather, as she writes in the poem, he watches "the spaces of sand between them."

The graphic representation of the footprint, so present on the poet's draft page, has been washed away by subsequent drafts, editorial demands, and cultural expectations of the printed verse form, which, as it were, needed to toe the line. But as evinced by the manuscript drafts, poetic texts, unlike the sandpiper's footprints, leave traces of their past movements. Looking at these draft pages, one can see more fully how the visual image is always already in the mind's eye of the poet, even, as I argue in this chapter, for the oral address. If the last two centuries have taught a certain reading public to romanticize the finality of the poetic artifact rather than the journey taken to get there (my own close reading practices cast me as more guilty than most), the last couple decades might have recalibrated the aura of handwritten texts. In my looming Dickinson chapter, I will discuss what Betsy Erkkila called "The Emily Dickinson Wars" regarding how one ought to treat the essentially graphic nature of Dickinson's manuscript variations.[7]

---

6. Two drafts of "Sandpiper," Elizabeth Bishop Papers, Vassar College Library Special Collections, box 73, folder 4. Bishop liked to doodle, though perhaps not as much as most. The Vassar College Library Special Collections include her manuscript drawings of a jukebox and slot machine, the former featured on the cover of Alice Quinn's edition of Bishop's *Uncollected Poems*.

7. For the most part, Dickinson's poems, unlike Bishop's, do not exist in a printed, published form. Although questions exist as to whether Dickinson considered certain individual poems "completed"—whatever that might have meant for her then (and us now)—Bishop's published oeuvre leaves much less doubt about finality. See also Christina Pugh on the relationship between the recent critical revisiting of the Dickinson and Bishop manuscripts, and her warning about some of the politically reactionary dangers that might come with co-opting Bishop's "finished" lyric voice. The aura surrounding the manuscript connects to notions of immanence or "presence," and can leave the poetic text tied to cultural expectations of the gendered body. It is a way of framing the specifically

The critical debates surrounding those Dickinson manuscript pages feel more like a day at the beach when compared to the controversies surrounding those of Bishop. But let us hide those in the umbrellaed shade of a note.[8]

*　*　*

Because of a memorably unplaceable exclamation of "*oh!*" (160), Bishop's "In the Waiting Room" reverses the measure of mastery that the speaker of "Cirque d'Hiver" was able to attain with an address to (or alongside) a mechanical horse in her familiar, domestic space:

> Suddenly, from inside,
> came an *oh!* of pain
> —Aunt Consuelo's voice—
> not very loud or long.

Simply speaking, "In the Waiting Room" dramatizes a young girl's trip with her aunt to a dentist's office. But the young girl remains in the waiting

female poet in an exclusionary manner (as Bishop would have seen it), even if other poets would embrace the manuscript text as a form of radical alterity. Pugh writes, "If we let graphic considerations replace or displace voice when we read lyric poetry, or the manuscripts of lyric poets, we do so at the peril of poetry itself—not because we thereby flout the poets' intentions, or because voice restores some chimerical sense of presence; but instead because the 'finish' of a carefully crafted voice—whether formal or otherwise—allows for a necessary abstraction from the immanence of the body and its matter, an abstraction that is necessary for the creation of text itself" (287).

8. In part, at stake is whether the façade of the perfect poetic artifact should be forsaken in favor of recognizing the often accidental and at times sloppy journey it took to get there. But there are also ethical considerations of viewing a writer unclothed, as it were. Reviewing Alice Quinn's edited collection *Edgar Allan Poe & The Juke-Box*, Helen Vendler called the uncollected poems, drafts, and fragments "maimed and stunted siblings" of Bishop's work, and she suggested that the subtitle instead be "Repudiated Poems" ("Art of Losing" 37, 33). Still, what is one to do with the often-striking poems—as many of the essays collected in Cleghorn, Hicok, and Travisano's *Elizabeth Bishop in the Twenty-First Century: Reading the New Editions* (2012) make apparent—that Bishop had not (or, importantly, not yet) published? The essays in this collection generally push back on Vendler's judgment. As they make clear, the questions involved in such a process of collecting the uncollected are much more complicated than whether or not one should publish a poet's unpublished work.

room, outside what one imagines to be the (paternalistic) inner room of the action, remains, as it were, before the law. There, following a moment of confidence "(I could read)," she has an uncanny moment of shared female community that neither she (dramatized at almost age seven[!]) nor readers (whose purported job it is to do so) can quite understand. It is an unusual setting for a poem, perhaps even more so for the epiphanic moment that soon occurs, and language ("I didn't know any word for it") can't quite capture what is happening. "In one way," Jeredith Merrin writes, "the language of this poem seems to suggest that one can make the terrifying and strange normal and orderly by putting ordinary words in ordinary places. In another way, it suggests (by its halting, anxious flatness and its flashes of menacing imagery) that just beneath the individual attempt at rational arrangement or domestication is intractable otherness, ready to erupt" (*Enabling* 58). At first, the poem appears not so much to offer an instance of a specifically graphic "O" but rather an investment in that apostrophic space between the "you" and the "I."

The turning point occurs early in the poem, when, while reading a copy of *National Geographic* in the titular room, the young speaker hears "an *oh!* of pain," a pang most readers attribute to the aunt, presumably under the drill. There, in the office beyond the waiting room, one makes involuntary sounds without a content other than their own agonized, reactive performance. *Open your mouth but don't speak*, one is told. But this initially disembodied sounding of "*oh!*" is made ambiguously from the "inside." Is this the inside of the dentist's room where her aunt is being treated or is it the inside of herself? Bishop writes,

> . . . What took me
> completely by surprise
> was that it was *me*:
> my voice, in my mouth. (160)

Later in the poem, during a more comprehensible moment, the speaker tells us that she "overhear[d] / a cry of pain." Helen Vendler, as do most scholars, attributes the earlier poetic disconnection to a moment of vertigo the child feels after hearing the voice of the aunt (*Part of Nature* 347). It is as if a young Bishop, hearing the phonemic cry as a summons, is impelled to fashion her own mouth accordingly, shaping it into the O she will utter. Here, in a manner the speaker can't quite yet understand, a shared closeness, a shared womanhood navigates that valley between addresser and addressee.[9] But the origin of the cry—the irruption of language paralleling the volcanic eruption the girl sees in the *National Geographic*—is far from certain. Focusing on "the problem of determining the place from which this voice originates" (185), becomes a metacritical concern for Lee Edelman, who pushes back against the (understandable) critical desire for such closure: "It is a cry that cries out against any attempt to clarify its confusions because it is a female cry—a cry of the female—that recognizes the attempts to clarify it as attempts to put it in its place. It is an '*oh!*' that refuses to be readily deciphered because it knows that if it is read it must always be read as a cipher—as a zero, a void, or a figure in some predetermined social text" (196). Julia Kristeva would have seen it as a semiotic eruption. In a draft version of the poem, Bishop, for her part, contemplated the phrase "senseless waves of sound."[10]

At another time, Jacques Derrida might have called the more-than-graphic distinction between *o* and *oh* the "*sameness* which is not *identical*."[11] Clarifying the general relationship between the two, Barbara Johnson notes that the "O," which carries with it the long years of poetic ritual, is usually seen as "pure vocative," and the "oh" as "pure subjectivity"; the first gives us the illusion that the "you" is created; the second gives us an illusion of the "I" (*World* 187).[12] *But oh! that deep romantic chasm. . . .* Along and against these senses, Bishop's "*oh!*" navigates the unresolvable space between the subjectivity inherent in a discursive moment and the conjuring fantasy of the vocative address, precisely because its origin is unclear. As "I" becomes

---

9. Kalstone connects the poem to Bishop's story "The Country Mouse," where the young child in the waiting room "felt *I, I, I,* and looked at the three strangers in panic. I was *one* of them, too, inside my scabby body and wheezing lungs" (qtd. in Kalstone *Becoming* 245). The poetic reminiscence, in Kalstone's view, "pulls the [earlier] episode taut and transforms it from a vague initiation into a fearful recognition of her link to the suffering women" (245).

10. Draft 2, page 3, Elizabeth Bishop Papers, Vassar College Library Special Collections, box 58, folder 14.

11. The translated phrasing—taken out of context—is from *On Grammatology*.

12. In an earlier draft of the poem Bishop considered "an <u>Ooh</u> of pain" [draft four, page 2]. I imagine this altered tenor would be mouthed and understood differently with different enunciations of personal pain. It is as if the violence of it all could not be so confined to a singular meaning.

"you" becomes "I" becomes "you" becomes "one of them" becomes "it" and then "I" again, one wonders whether one is addressing or being addressed:

> But I felt: you are an I . . .
> you are one of them
> Why should you be one, too?
> I scarcely dared to look
> to see what it was I was.

What ought to be the "you" and what ought to be the "I" can even become confused in a manuscript draft, which renders the third line above as "why should I be one, too?"[13] It is a minor twitch—an "I" simply addressing itself in the second-person—but, given the ungrounded context of subjectivity here, it is notable.

Readers have been confounded by Bishop's (or the young dramatized Bishop's) insistence on details—like "the *National Geographic*, February, 1918"—that it gets wrong. Either intentionally or not, Bishop conflated in her memory different issues of the magazine but would still keep the single date, even after checking the reference. It is as if the different graphics connected by what a printer's space would allow could not but go together in this cratered experience reified into an enameled textual artifact. Voila—poem! The result, even in this most personal sounding of Bishop's work, is a performance of objectivity, distancing the poetic inside from the real outside. In subsequent drafts of the poem, the speaker distances herself at certain moments from the personal description more and more such that the phrase "Their breasts terrified me" became "frightened me" to the final subject-less "were horrifying" (Marshall 208). But the uncanny body is where the two—inside and outside—cannot be separated.[14] "Then I was back in it," she tells us at the end, the "in it" of reality ("Worcester, Massachusetts, / the fifth / of February, 1918") uncannily being "Outside" the isolated lyric moment.

The explosive epiphanic instant—whatever it is (after many years of

---

13. Elizabeth Bishop Papers, Vassar College Library Special Collections, box 58, folder 14.

14. "Perhaps the foreign would not feel so unsettling," Robert Dale Parker speculates, "if it were not intensified with the feminine, which unnerves the little girl by its blend of the unfamiliarly frank (nakedness) with the eerily familiar (the bodies that nakedness exposes)" (138).

pedagogically domesticating myself to it, I am still not exactly sure)—is presaged earlier in the poem by the graphic images of the volcano in the *National Geographic*: "the photographs: / the inside of a volcano, / black, and full of ashes; / then it was spilling over / in rivulets of fire." Earlier drafts of the poem made explicit the connections between the circular fissures of the volcano and that of the tooth cavity: the "cry of pain that might / ~~get worse~~, and fill the crater" (draft 2, page 3) or the description of the Alaskan volcano, Mount Katmai as "the largest active crater / in the world" (draft 4).[15] Such is the fear that lurks in the dark behind the waiting room door. But the unknown blacknesses of the poem (the volcano, the room that "was sliding / beneath a big black wave") cannot be disentangled from images of colonial legacies, which intrude on the formerly comfortable space: "Babies with pointed heads / wound round and round with string; / black, naked women with necks / wound round and round with wire / like the necks of light bulbs. / Their breasts were horrifying."[16] Michael Abraham writes, "Blackness serves as an inscrutability that masks the capacity for magnificent violence, a violence which is desired as a kind of catharsis to cut through the suspensions by which Bishop constructs the mood of the scene" (n.p.).[17] The dramatized young speaker cannot or will not engage with the racialized images ("I read it right straight through. / I was too shy to stop"), but her muffled reaction, as far as she can understand, seems to result from a nascent sexuality rather than any colonial awareness. Her attempts to make connections, as a young poet might, through graphic similes ("like the necks of light bulbs") brings a metaphorical light to the darkened scenes but cannot enlighten her ostensible obliviousness to the violent geopolitical contexts, always in the background of a domesticated whiteness. The girl (and I imagine most of Bishop's early readers) would not be aware of her own poetic—and problematically so—attempts to assimilate another culture to the vectors of her own understanding. The poem, accordingly, navigates between a sense of control the young speaker

---

15. Elizabeth Bishop Papers, Vassar College Library Special Collections, box 58, folder 14.

16. Bishop's nightmarish poem of bodily decline, "Faustina, or Rock Roses," connects once again the breast to the light bulb, but causally rather than metaphorically: "Meanwhile the eighty-watt bulb / betrays us all" (72).

17. See also Stephen Gould Axelrod, "Bishop, History, and Politics"; Jacqueline Vaught Brogan, "Mapping Elizabeth Bishop's 'Brazil, January 1, 1502'"; and Bethany Hicok, "Bishop's Brazilian Politics."

wishes she had and an experience that cannot be captured in words: "I didn't know any / word for it—how 'unlikely' "—the ethical window of an antisimile that points to the unpredictable weightiness of it all.[18] It is an odd existential middle ground to be for a poet who is accused on the one hand of being too distantly objective, and, more recently, on the other hand, of being too lyrically centered.[19] It is the space of the waiting room, for one yet to be called into service.

*   *   *

Teeth, volcanos, necklaces, lightbulbs, "the round, turning world": it would be a stretch to claim that the circular figures and fissures of "In the Waiting Room" engender the specific "*oh!* of pain" however much those protuberant round shapes resemble each other in the speaker's unconscious mind. It is the image of the breasts, though—against that of the "dead man slung on

---

18. James Longenbach notes that the "child realizes for the first time that selfhood is an arbitrary social construction, that experience as it comes to her has no coherent order or meaning." Distinguishing the child's realization from Bishop's poetics, he clarifies that the poet "does not embody this realization in a poem that is 'consequently' incoherent or arbitrary: she remains perfectly comfortable with a simple narrative, aware that its shape is, like all systems of meaning, arbitrary but nevertheless useful" (113).

19. More than a generation ago, Susan McCabe importantly rejected the critical tendency to see Bishop as a modernist able to "record objectively immediate experience" (xii). Bishop is a poet of the personal, if not the confessional. Her poetry, in McCabe's phrasing, "dismantles the notion of the traditional self as it confesses to a disunified self" (xvi). Victoria Harrison quotes some of Eavan Boland's words on this point: Bishop's "earth is not represented as a dramatized figment of her consciousness. Instead, she celebrates the separateness, the awesome detachment of the exterior universe" (77; qtd. in Harrison 2). Here, Boland distinguishes Bishop from the romantic poet who would subsume the external within the self. That the exterior universe is detached, does not, for Boland, mean Bishop is not conditioned through it. Finally, as Lynn Keller argues, "Bishop appears to be trying, in Modernist fashion, to see external things truly, while in fact what she scrutinizes is herself" (100). Bishop's poems with an absent or muted "I," which seem to be about capturing the material thing or event are, in the end, as Harrison contends, a mode of Bishop's relational subjectivity. Astoundingly, Gillian White does a lot of work (unnecessary, in my view, though compelling) recovering Bishop's reputation from her Salem accusers. White explores the "[a]mbience of lyric shame . . . especially as it circles about and gets projected onto the work, critical reception" of Bishop and others (4). For her, critics who reduce Bishop to "mainstream 'lyric' " miss the poet's "more radical nature. The result is a Bishop canon held to exemplify post-Romantic lyric understood both as an imaginative net over 'reality' and also . . . as an achieved personal expression—views she pointedly rejected. While Bishop used the term 'lyric,' [she] . . . wrote poems that resist modes of lyric reading that came to overwhelm the term" (96).

a pole"—that explicitly mark the speaker's connection to a shared sense of womanhood: "those awful hanging breasts— / [which] held us all together / or made us all just one."

Although not so explicit as the midcentury *Histoire d'O*, Bishop makes the connection between the breast and the O shape of the mouth more apparent in "O Breath," the final poem in Bishop's short grouping "Four Poems." The four poems, about the often-failed attempts of lovers to communicate, play a bit on the sonnet form. The first poem "Conversation" focuses on the lover's "tone of voice" (76) and the hope that language can conjure more than the empty pleading of the speaker. For lovers, as for poets, finding the appropriate word, the right rhetoric of seduction, can mean success. But even when that right word is found, the manner that it exits the mouth can change everything. If only language (be it onomatopoeia or prayer or apostrophe) had such magical abilities to map name onto meaning:

> And then there is no choice,
> and then there is no sense;
>
> until a name
> and all its connotation are the same.

The fourth poem in the sequence, the sensual, mysterious, corporeal Anglo-Saxon mock-up "O Breath" shows the very bodily underskin of language:

> Beneath that loved   and celebrated breast,
> silent, bored really   blindly veined. . . .
> Equivocal, but what we have in common's   bound to be
>   there. . . . (79)

The voiced opening demands that we hear "breath" in "breast"; they move together at each inhalation and exhalation, both involuntarily. The harmony, though, is not always there when the breast is not your own. Here, the breathing is attended to with a caesura, as if the line itself needed to wait for the next gasp of inspiration. The silent voice in the middle of the lines operates within what Marilyn May Lombardi calls a "rib cage of words" (33). Lombardi and Megan Marshall (114) both note the similarities between the poetic act and Bishop's debilitating asthma: "the poem's gasping, halting rhythms and labored caesura mimic the wheezing lungs

---

20. The broken lines give "the agonies of asthma visible shape" (34).

of a restless asthmatic trying to expel the suffocating air" (Lombardi 33).[20] Lombardi reads these struggles with breath and voicing alongside the mid-century social obstacles facing the female poet.

It is an unusual poem—more about resignation than passion, and certainly not quite what one would imagine from the apostrophic title, which seems to call out to join a whole overromanticized poetic tradition. Oddly, the poem's specificities lead the speaker into universality, or at least a hope for one, as the intimate moment is grasped, yet not permanently—a recurring sentiment in Bishop. Her meditation in language—this talking through something—becomes its own lyric conjuring of sorts—desire, writ small. One is left with questions. Will the sexual act, with its own involuntary breaths, voiced hesitations, and erotic ohs follow? No choice, no sense in the sounds, but the understanding that the name and connotation of a voiced oh might finally be the same. Bishop plays with the sounds and hesitations of words, here, at the end. "Equivocal" is balanced on the next line with "equivalent," though the evasive meanings on each side of each caesura are not commensurate. Holding out hope for "a separate peace," the speaker contemplates various proximities: "beneath / within if never with." However interlocked their bodies, the lovers can't quite come together in the romantic certainty of a harmonious preposition. Nevertheless, the sounds of the words across each separated hemistich echo some connection: "**peace** [pause] ben**eath**" . . . "**with**in [pause] if never **with**."

Jonathan Ellis understands the lengthy caesurae as "figurative space[s] between intimacy and strangeness" (50). Lombardi sees them in relation to "the barely endurable proximity of the loved one's body, [which] awaken[s] a longing for still-deeper contact that may not be achieved" (35). For her, the possibility of the two lovers connecting is also frustrated by the social expectations of the time. "[T]he difficulty and restraint associated with breathing and speaking in the poem," she writes, suggest "the ongoing constraints the poet labors under as a woman and a lesbian bound to leading a life of surface conformity and concealed depths" (34). If much of the early (and still influential) criticism of Bishop followed Adrienne Rich's assertion that Bishop was a poet who "kept sexuality at a measured and chiseled distance in her poems" (36), a lot of the recent critical work has endeavored to reframe Bishop's seemingly disinterested voice as a political locus of repressed desire.[21] "Both the literary establishment and those

---

21. McCabe sees Bishop as "particularly engaged, if often covertly, by the difficulties involved in gender definitions and labels" (xvi–xvii). "O Breath," in this model, "seems to reinscribe a traditional romantic paradigm while it also invites us to laud female

feminist critics intent on constructing a female tradition have privileged in Bishop's poetry an aesthetic and metaphysic that her poetry does not entirely support and, therefore, have underestimated the subversive features of her practice" (247), Lois Cucullu writes. Even Rich would eventually let up a bit in order to recognize the political angles of Bishop. Part of the early difficulty stemmed from Bishop's antagonism toward being viewed primarily as a "female poet" or toward being included in anthologies of women poets. "I felt it was a lot of nonsense, separating the sexes," she related in a conversation with George Starbuck, adding that she "suppose[d] this feeling came from feminist principles, perhaps stronger than I was aware of."[22] Like her close friend James Merrill, she wanted to keep her private life private.[23] However conspicuous it might feel now, one would be hard-pressed to argue against the sense that, compared to many of her contemporaries, most of Bishop's intimacy hides in her verse. Still, in poems like "O Breath," which breathes "Beneath that loved and celebrated breast," it is difficult to ignore, especially as it exhales a measure of desire in a quasi-apostrophic form.

*　*　*

Two of the three poems separating "O Breath" and "The Shampoo," the final poem in the collection *A Cold Spring*, are second-person addresses, each playing

---

sexuality" (McCabe 112). Brogan reads "A Miracle for Breakfast" as a repressed story of sexual desire; the "we" of the opening line signals that the poem is secretly an aubade—two lovers having woken up together ("An Almost"). Merrin connects the poet's poetic form to her sexuality: "Bishop's gaiety or delight in the possibilities of change is in turn inextricable from her gayness: her questioning of gender boundaries . . . and the exploration (however oblique and shrouded) of the pleasures and anxieties of same-sex love" ("Elizabeth" 154). In "Bishop's 'Wiring Fused': 'Bone Key' and 'Pleasure Seas,'" Angus Cleghorn explores how Bishop's time in Florida "prompted her to write less emotionally evasive and more frankly erotic poems—even if these poems remained unpublished" ("Introduction" Cleghorn, Hicok, and Travisano, eds., 4). See also Diehl and Goldensohn (especially Chapter 3).

22. Conversation with George Starbuck, reprinted in Schwartz and Estes, eds., 322; originally published in *Ploughshares* 3, numbers 3 and 4 (1977), 11–29.

23. Noting the hermit's exclamation ("Love should be put into action") that seemingly comes out of nowhere in Bishop's "Chemin de Fer" (Complete 8), Merrill makes the wonderful point that the parallel railroad tracks of "Chemin de Fer" are two Marvellian lovers who can never meet ("Afterward" 253).

with the distance between the speaker and whom she is addressing. The first, "Letter to N.Y.," is dedicated to Louise Crane, at whose hands Bishop suffered an early heartbreak. The poet implores, "In your next letter I wish you'd say / where you are going and what you are doing" (80). That the poem is specifically characterized as a letter is a reminder of its deferred presence, its graphically belated address to the receiver. The speaker/dramatized-letter-writer even has the moxie to invite the terms of how she—soon to be the absent voice of her own words—will be addressed in the future correspondence. Although undedicated, the following poem in the collection, "Argument," is similarly about the temporal ("days") and spatial ("distance") separation between two former lovers—this time, Bishop's companion, Marjorie Stevens. The "you" that centers each poem about a former love is necessarily absent, and although not apostrophic, the address to each absent "you" need necessarily take a graphic form; yet it can't be an O of completion or summoning, however much the speaker pines. A wicked multilayered pun in "Argument" on "some hideous calendar / 'Complements of Never & Forever, Inc.'" offers three senses of the never/forever togetherness of lovers: the homophonic "compliments of" as free, a measure of courtesy; "compliments" as praise; and "complements" as a harmony. The abbreviated "incorporated" at the very end—a marker of a consumer marketplace forever now mediating modern love—suggests one final pun on "ink"—the material, graphic form within which a past argument could be memorialized.

But it is the final poem in the collection—about Bishop's subsequent lover, Lota de Macedo Soares—that is most germane for my own critical endeavor. "The Shampoo" brings together images of the natural world and the older female body, as Bishop, in a tender gesture, offers to wash her lover's hair, "battered and shiny like the moon." McCabe sees Bishop "searching for a vision of the female body that conforms more closely to her vision of the natural" but not in a renaissance or romantic sense (78). It is a love poem that, in Bonnie Costello's words, "challenges the courtly convention . . . which recognizes as lovable only what is youthful or immutable" (75). It is a love poem, as Bishop found out following its numerous publication rejections, that challenges even more than that:[24]

> The still explosions on the rocks,
> the lichens, grow
> by spreading, gray, concentric shocks.

---

24. See Marshall, 110–12.

The lichens, organisms that grow by latching on, are oxymoronically called "still explosions." Like the streaks in Lota's hair, they are gray (the poem was originally called "Gray Hair" or "Gray Hairs"), and they multiply with what Bishop terms "concentric shocks." Working through the math of algebraic curves during her time at Vassar, Bishop sketched such concentric circles, which are "similar," as she notes, "but not con-focal."

Figure 3.1. Geometry sketches from lecture at Vassar College, page 6. *Source:* Elizabeth Bishop Papers, Vassar College Library Special Collections, box 71, folder 2.

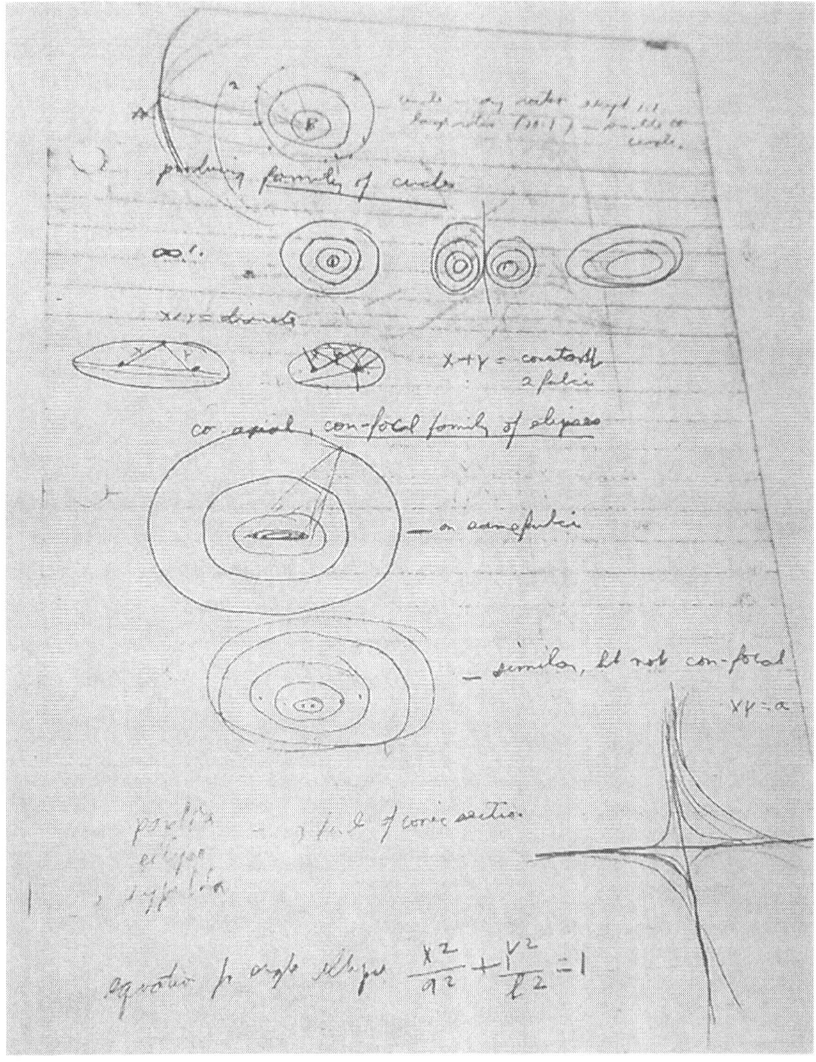

"Similar but not con-focal" would not be an inapt phrasing to describe her circular relationships with others or her almosting-it poetics. The spreading concentric shocks, waves of tumescent circles, feel as though they could reach the rings of the cosmos: "They have arranged / to meet the rings around the moon, although / within our memories they have not changed. . . ." Given the sensual context of the poem, it is difficult not to read these radiating circles as also describing orgasms.[25] In the final stanza, Bishop questions why her lover (metonymically through her hair) is leaving so soon. The hair is straight, but so is the departure path. A circular path, on the other hand, would, as in an aubade with a hopeful future ending, have the lover return. Instead of watching her lover depart, the speaker turns to address her: "—Come, let me wash it in this big tin basin, / battered and shiny like the moon." In a lover's hands, the reflective basin can bring the heavens to the earth. In a draft version of the poem, Bishop contemplated beginning the penultimate line "—Well, let me. . . ."[26] The final version, "Come," on the other hand resituates what might have been an imagined "you"—as in "Letter to N.Y." or "Argument"—as someone who could be successfully conjured by the poet's address.

*   *   *

Bishop published her "Three Sonnets for the Eyes" in *Con Spirito*, the Vassar literary magazine she helped create. It is a puzzling and terrifying series of poems. Bishop scholars haven't really known what to do with it or how to talk about it, usually dismissing it as a piece of juvenilia or simply noting its Hopkins-esque influence. Vendler calls the triad "tortured and baroque" (*Ocean* 243), and Linda Anderson sees it "stag[ing]—in baroque fashion—the drama of vision," warning that "[b]ehind or beyond the multiplying effects of vision is the fear of an abyss" (130). Brett Millier notes its "wit . . . delivered with such detachment and irony that the tone can be nasty, the effect vaguely disgusting" (50). Bishop herself confessed that "the idea behind [the first] sonnet is not a very pretty one," but more interestingly added that, like Hopkins, she wants "to portray[. . .] not a thought,

---

25. Diana Collecott notes how, in a letter to Vita Sackville-West, Virginia Woolf reduces the "forbidden" name Orlando to "O—o" (34; *Letters* 335). See Collecott 33–39 on "O" as a sign of female sexuality.

26. Draft 6, Elizabeth Bishop Papers, Vassar College Library Special Collections, box 57, folder 6.

but a mind thinking" (*One Art* 11, 12).[27] Her aesthetic self-diagnosis here could describe her career output.

The first sonnet is the only one of the three that's titled, punningly so, as "Tidal Basin." The extended conceit has eye sockets becoming tidal basins in which thoughts, like the tide, ebb and flow. "How blind / Are eyes . . . / [leaving] their vacant truths" says the withdrawing water (223). The emptying in the opening gives way to a replenishment in the sestet, where "Soon it all the awful socket'll flesh to health . . . / And see / Thine eyes new-sphéred, held whole, shine to thee!" In the third sonnet, the sockets become nests sheltering the eyes, now called "soft shining birds in the skull." But after the turn, a simile from the first sonnet ("like angel eyes / on the old gravestones" returns, and the speaker, still addressing the "you," imagines a future without her. "[Once] you are dead," she shares, ". . . I'll / Look in lost upon those neatest nests of bone / Where steel-coiled springs have lashed out, fly-wheels flown." The organic or natural quality of the nests and eyes are lost in this jack-in-the-box description of a body after death. On the back of a draft page of this poem, Bishop drew her own flywheels—circular mechanical devices used to store energy—making the disembodied, automaton-esque horrific scene even less palatable. Behind the sketch, she also scribbled a list of notes, the first of which is Endymion—possibly an allusion to John Keats's work—or more generally to the mythological shepherd in love with Selene, the Moon—she who could guide the tidal basin of the opening sonnet. As some accounts relate, Endymion kept his beautiful eyes open for her to gaze at, even in his legendary eternal slumber.

The one extant draft of the poem shows changes Bishop considered but that never made it into the final copy. Part of the unfamiliar baroque diction and syntax includes the short syllables Bishop elided in order to preserve the rigid meter (to uproot becomes "t'uproot"). One of the more awkward elisions—intended to be excised by Bishop but still remaining in the published version—broke "thought't" across a parenthetical:

> Evening overwhelms,
> We thought ~~(I knew we)~~'t fortunately covers
> With lashes, lids of reticence, these eyes those lovers.

---

27. The second quotation Bishop cites directly from M. W. Croll, "The Baroque Style in Prose." On a copy of *Con Spirito* sent to Louise Bradley on November 6, 1933, Bishop wrote that "Most of this is terrible—a last gasp—but I thought you might like to see it." (Elizabeth Bishop and Louise Bradley Collection, 1924–1979, at the Wylie House Museum, Indiana University Libraries; [https://archives.iu.edu/html/VAD3254.html.])

Figure 3.2. Reverse sheet of the final poem in "Three Sonnets for the Eyes." *Source:* Elizabeth Bishop Papers, Vassar College Library Special Collections, box 56, folder 3.

As confusing as they are, the lines seem to insist that, like the eyelid, the evening, however coy, can offer a measure of cover. It is unclear if the parenthetical was an earlier alternative phrase that made it into the typed copy (*I knew we thought it fortunately covers*) or an intentionally dramatized rethinking within the poem—Bishop portraying not a thought, but a mind thinking. As is, though, it visually splits "wet" in two with its own emoji-like eyelash, a serendipitous coincidence(?) from the nebulous realms of the typewritten tidal basin.

This is not the only watery phonetic play of the poem, which cannot help but splash across different tonal registers and addresses in its two quasi-apostrophic exclamations with possible sexual overtones—one ("Oh wait!") commencing the turn of the first sonnet, the other beckoning eye contact in the opening of the second:

> They all kept looking at each other's eyes.
> Look, here I am, in here! you're warm—oh look again!

As Culler illuminates about Baudelaire's sonnet (discussed in the previous chapter), each "oh" might very well be a pun on "eau," here washed ashore by its own wave of lunacy.

*　*　*

Toward the end of Bishop's "Sestina," "the little moons" of an almanac "fall down like tears" and marvelously water the flowerbed of the child's picture (123). Behind the flowerbed, the child had drawn "a rigid house / and a winding pathway" (123)—an apt description of the recursively spiraling sestina form itself. By their very formal nature, sestinas exude circularity. Villanelles do too.

Bishop's villanelle "One Art" famously aestheticizes loss, which was an all-too-prominent theme in Bishop's life.[28] The poem asks us to understand "losing" as an artform, and accordingly brings together the odd rhyming analog "master" and "disaster" in its refrains, setting the frightening fickleness of life against the desired mastery of artistic representation (178). For Joanne Feit Diehl, the "mastery sought over loss in love is closely related to poetic control. . . . 'One Art' presents a series of losses as if to reassure both its author and its reader that control is possible—[an] ironic gesture that forces upon us the tallying of experience cast in the guise of reassurance" (96).[29] Bishop navigates between the idealized oneness of art and the zero of loss, and she is quite playful with the curvature of her refrains. For example, "to be lost that their loss is no disaster" becomes "to travel. None of these will bring disaster" becomes "I miss them, but it wasn't a disaster." In a sense, Bishop formally loses her way as she goes, such that, at the end, whether out of "forgetfulness" or boredom or poetic constraint, she must force herself to acknowledge the predetermined conclusion:

> —Even losing you (the joking voice, a gesture
> I love) I shan't have lied. It's evident
> the art of losing's not too hard to master
> though it may look like (Write it!) like disaster.

---

28. Bishop's father died when she was an infant, and her mother was institutionalized. Her longtime partner Lota de Macedo Soares committed suicide about a decade before the publication of *Geography III*, where the last instantiation of "One Art" finally found its home. Susan McCabe, through a psychoanalytic lens, stresses the autobiographical nature of this poem.

29. Diehl and Mutlu Blasing stress the connection between life and art. Blasing writes, "the art of writing and the art of losing are one, and the requirements of the form serve to render loss certain from the start" (*American* 111–12). Unlike most other critics, Doreski stresses the mastery, writing, "This encapsulated lesson is for the master alone; unlike the free, gestural 'And look!' designed to deflect attention from the self, the parenthetical injunction maps a course for only one" (15). Anne Colwell considers the contrary impulses. "In the earlier drafts of this stanza," she writes, "Bishop struggled with the desire to say and unsay, to say two things at once, both admitting to the truth of the argument that the villanelle has established and admitting to the evasion of the truth that the tone has insisted on" (178).

"Write it!" the final line exhorts, and she did, over and over again. Bishop revised this poem considerably through the years, finally settling on the formally intricate villanelle form.[30] "The play of 'twos' within it—two rivers, two cities, the lost lover not being 'two' anymore" Millier reasons, "suggests that the villanelle is a form appropriate to the content" (508). Even when she had the form, though, just what she was trying to say, as was the habit of her words, wouldn't sit still. Bishop toyed with a more confessional sounding "I'm writing lies now" before the sentiment finally settled into the final antiquated wink "I shan't have lied." More interesting, perhaps, is that through successive drafts she kept going back and forth between "Say it" and "Write it"—each a graphic representation of a vocative imperative to the self, but one an exhortation toward script, the other toward voice (unless colloquially taken). In a draft, Bishop also considered including the resigned "oh" of surrender ("Oh, go on"; "Oh write it") at the very end.[31] One takes the apostrophe ironically, as it is a turn to address something that, as even the speaker seems to acknowledge, will not reappear. The specific imperative to write is tied perhaps to a romantic notion of literary authorship, connecting the spectral past with the present and the present with a ghostly future. Bishop clipped and saved part of a 1968 interview with John Berryman in the *Harvard Advocate*, who quotes an anecdote of Johan Georg Hamann by way of Søren Kierkegaard: "There are voices, and the first voice says, 'Write!' and the second voice says, 'For whom?' I think that's marvellous; he doesn't question the imperative, you see that. And the first voice says, 'For the dead whom thou didst love'; again the second voice doesn't question it; instead it says, 'Will they read me?' And the first voice says, 'Aye, for they return as posterity.' "[32] Beyond the pressures of literary posterity and the poet's "joking voice," the "you" in the final stanza acts as a shield, concealing all the people Bishop had lost—most notably her recent partner Alice Methfessel (who, like a poetic refrain would soon return).[33] The "you" also feels as if it doubles back on the "I," which, after lines

---

30. There are well over a dozen known versions, some untitled, others with different titles. One draft connects the lyric speech act with discovery or self-discovery ("I really / want to introduce myself"); another inserts a vocal act of resignation ("oh no") in the final lines (See Millier 506–16, *passim*).

31. Draft 10 of the poem in the Elizabeth Bishop Papers, Vassar College Library Special Collections, box 60, folder 2.

32. Elizabeth Bishop Papers, Vassar College Library Special Collections, box 75, folder 1.

33. See Marshall 273–77.

and lines dedicated to loss, now feels empty. The final refrain has the poet addressing herself with what seems to be a joking voice, demanding that she—forgetful, tired, lost—still complete the circle.[34] We might understand this hesitation psychologically as a lyric speaker unwilling to deal with loss or meta-poetically as a wonderful commentary on the tedium and expectation (and possibly hopelessness) of the villanelle form. It is a victory of sorts—completion—but is this suggestive of a personal (rather than poetic) mastery over the psychological and somatic or a more modest desire just to see things end? However one understands these final lines, they gesture toward the sense that lyric subjectivities—rather, that our very identities—are constructed and reconstructed over and over through the slowly changing refrains of experience mediated by the voiced possibilities of language.

*   *   *

During the winter of 1935–36, *le temps juste avant la guerre*, Bishop was in Paris. Her poem "Paris, 7 A.M." was written later that year, just after Hitler's armies occupied the Rhineland, and it was published in 1937. The first stanza begins:

> I make a trip to each clock in the apartment:
> Some hands point histrionically one way
> And some point others, from the ignorant faces.
> Time is an Etoile; the hours diverge
> So much that days are journeys round the suburbs,
> Circles surrounding stars, overlapping circles.
> The short, half-tone scale of winter weathers
> Is a spread pigeon's wing.
> Winter lives under a pigeon's wing, a dead wing with damp
>   feathers. (26)

---

34. Colwell writes, "This duality that Bishop works so hard to achieve in draft after draft . . . she finally finds in one word, 'shan't.' This word, with its overformal stiffness, its anachronistic sound, its school-marmish precision, says both 'I'm lying' and 'I'm not lying'" (178). "The whole stanza is in danger of breaking apart, and breaking down," J. D. McClatchy writes, adding that "[i]n this last line the poet's voice literally cracks. The villanelle—that strictest and most intractable of verse forms—can barely control the grief, yet helps the poet keep her balance . . ." (145). Then, "when 'disaster' finally comes it sounds with a shocking finality" (145).

The poem brings the speaker into the shadow of the upcoming war, which hangs metaphorically over the city in the half-tone winter grays of a pigeon's wing. Through the architectural turns of the city, the speaker attempts to process this dreadful uncertainty about the future. While the poem delves in and out of the speaker's present, past, and imagined future, it strangely only uses the word "I" once—as the initial word of the poem. The clocks are in disarray, and time is more than metaphorically out of joint. The speaker personifies the clock's faces and hands, understanding them to be "histrionically" gesturing. Given that the title of the poem ought to set each clock accurately, as Thomas Travisano notes, "it is the observer . . . who finds the clocks' hands histrionic" (43).[35] The ramifying hour leads the speaker to see time itself as a star, an image that is then mapped onto the cityscape. David Kalstone reminds us of the circular layout of many Paris avenues, which Bishop would have seen outside her apartment window (*Five* 45). Those familiar with Paris will also recognize the Place de l'Étoile (now renamed "Place Charles de Gaulle"), around which twelve streets, including the Avenue des Champs-Élysées, meet, as though at the center of a clock face. The Champs-Élysées and the Arc de Triomphe (which stands in the middle of the square) are war memorials—the Champs-Élysées, named after the mythological Elysian Fields, and the Arc de Triomphe, itself often encircled with famished pigeons, memorialize those who died in the French Revolution and Napoleonic Wars. Because, when viewed from above, the intersection resembles a clock, the remark that "the hours diverge / So much that days are journeys round the suburbs" feels more like a guide to navigate the urban space than a mere passing reference.[36] The circular paths of the hour and minute hands, as well as the labyrinthine nature of the city itself create "overlapping circles," but here such intersections might ominously resemble those territories claimed by different European powers, say the overlapping circles in two national memories of Alsace-Lorraine.

The speaker commands herself discursively (or turns to command her audience) to "Look down into the courtyard," reminding us (and herself)

---

35. Why did Bishop throw the clock out the window? To flee time. Sigh. Bishop's "Trouvée" ("Oh, why should a *hen* / have been run over / on West 4th Street / in the middle of summer?" [150]) could be read as a poetic answer to the kindergarten tease *why did the chicken cross the road?* "How did she get there? Where was she going?" If not merely to tickle the funny bones of five-year olds . . . *why, indeed?*

36. Given the tonal echoes throughout and the almost gradual changes in voice, one might also be reminded of another twelve-part circle: the chromatic scale.

that she is not in a poetically "timeless" or "universal" poetic place but really *here, now*. The metaphorical pigeons of stanza one return as literal birds atop the mansard roofs and beside the ornamental but threatening urns. The sight will soon force her circular memory, in a fascinatingly ambiguous phrasing, into something "like introspection":

> It is like introspection
> To stare inside, or retrospection,
> A star inside a rectangle, a recollection:
> This hollow square could easily have been there.
> —The childish snow-forts, built in flashier winters,
> Could have reached these proportions and been houses;
> The mighty snow-forts, four, five, stories high,
> Withstanding spring as sand-forts do the tide,
> Their walls, their shape, could not dissolve and die,
> Only be overlapping in a strong chain, turned to stone,
> And grayed and yellowed now like these.

How mesmerizing this almost-simile is at the heart of this poem—that looking into the traces of your own mind is like trying to look into someone else's apartment. The spatial simile (akin to the concentric circles of inner identity) is rethought temporally as a "retrospection" and then spatio-temporally as a "recollection." These internal attempts to get at the meaning of the scene also aptly describe the concentric circles of repeated sounds ("stare," "star," "square"), as Eleanor Cook notes (*Against* 46). Is the "hollow square"—a conjuring of absence—a memory that can't be reconciled with the speaker's present thoughts? Is it the speaker's lapsed perception? Her apartment? An empty Parisian street in winter? A reference to an empty space across the way describing something that is no longer there? In a lighthearted moment, such retrospection teases the speaker into a memory of her New England winters, brighter in the back of her mind than what she is seeing now. The future still looms, though, and even those "flashier" memories circle back to the anxieties of the present and eerily foreshadow the games of war that the adults will play:

> Where is the ammunition, the piled-up balls
> With the star-splintered hearts of ice?
> This sky is no carrier-warrior-pigeon
> Escaping endless intersecting circles.

> It is a dead one, or the sky from which a dead one fell.
> The urns have caught his ashes or his feathers.
> When did the star dissolve, or was it captured
> By the sequence of squares and squares and circles, circles?
> Can the clocks say; is it there below,
> About to tumble in snow?

Expanding and then half-rejecting her own metaphor, the speaker concludes that the sky is not the messenger-hero of a wartime carrier-pigeon, but a dead one. Syntactically, the lines become confused; the metaphorical sky, as it were, is turned upside-down, and the pigeon seems to fall from its own metaphor. Like tokens atop a board game, the shapes of squares and circles move to surround and capture the stars. Finally, at the end, we come back to the opening clock, which now has a deceptive face. Like in the villanelle, we must wonder whether time is really moving or whether we, like the speaker, are just frozen in a singular lyric sensibility. "Where is the ammunition, the piled-up balls / with the star-splintered hearts of ice?" She might as well have been asking *Mais où sont les neiges d'antan*! This invocation of absence voices desire, but it is one that runs down from the hills of yesteryear. It is within this failure of speech to conjure, this resignation of language, that something like the lyric voice emerges. Adding a temporal dimension grounded in the sign to the presumed "now" of the vocative would mean that apostrophe cannot be understood only in its immediacy but rather, to turn a phrase, must somehow also be recollected in tranquility. The delay, the hesitation, the turning away from oneself enacted by the calling out in graphic form allows, quite purposefully, another generation to hear what could not, at the time, always be heard. The poet and the reader may each utter the apostrophe anew, and in turn constitute and reconstitute a voice—be it that of François Villon or Bishop or me or you—but that invocation must linger as a voice unheard perhaps for centuries, enduring in the potential of the written sign to circle back. Thankfully, there is no zero on the analog clock. The clock will always return to 1. Then again, as Bishop warns, history ought not be subject to its own lived retrospection. At least that's the hope of the monument—perhaps more the poetic one than the marble one: to remember so that time (oh time!) can move along to warmer places.

One of Bishop's short unpublished poems, "For M.B.S., buried in Nova Scotia," elegizes the poet's aunt and caretaker, Maud Bulmer Shepherdson, a considerable influence on Bishop's early career. The opening offers a direct address: "Yes, you are dead now and live / only there, in a little, slightly tip-tilted graveyard / where all of your childhood's Christmas trees are forgathered / with the present they meant to give. . . ."[37] It is unclear whether Maud is surrounded by what were the pines of her youth or if these are memories of Christmas trees mulched into the ground. Whatever gift they meant to bring or might still bring to the poet will not be a now of presence. James Merrill's terrifyingly hopeful poem "Christmas Tree" is one of his last. With "the end beginning," it is almost a self-elegy, told through the eyes of the tree, cut down and dressed, if not addressed, for the holiday. Ornaments including a Model T, "BUD and BEA (The children's names) in clownlike capitals" adorn the tree, and "in shadow behind . . . a primitive IV / To keep the show going."[38] Given the setting, bud and bee sound almost perverse. And how is one to read the ★ at the top of the poem, which lingers on the page, unspoken? It is almost as if Merrill were saying that, at the heart of a voice fading into oblivion, there lies a star, vividly, graphically ever-burning.

---

37. Bishop, *Edgar Allan Poe & The Juke-Box*, 98. The poem, for Charles Berger, "masterfully backgathers so many elements of the elegiac tradition—but then refuses to bequeath itself to the reader as a present, by remaining unpublished" (45). See his "Bishop's Buried Elegies."

38. Merrill, *Collected Poems*, 866.

Chapter 4

James Merrill

"Breath after breath, harsh O's of oxygen—"

The owlet umlaut peeps and hoots
Above the open vowel.

—Merrill, "Lost in Translation"[1]

Safe from Bishop's fire balloons, James Merrill's öwlet can lose itself, for a time, in its own graphic materiality. The line comes toward the end of the long, intricately pieced-together poem, which sets a quest to find a Rainer Maria Rilke translation of Paul Valéry's "Palme" against a childhood memory about spending a summer alone with his sitter, "Mademoiselle." They played with marionettes and constructed a jigsaw puzzle of the mythological "East"; his father, Charles Merrill of Merrill Lynch, was well on his way to his second divorce.[2] Behind the many frames of the many puzzles the young boy cannot understand—where are his parents? when will the jigsaw arrive in the mail? why does Mademoiselle live between two languages? ("Patience, chéri. Geduld, mein Schatz")—lies the mystery of Rilke's missing translation, eventually found, as the poem's German epigraph attests: *Diese Tage, die leer*

---

1. *Collected Poems*, 148. Unless otherwise indicated, all quotations form Merrill's poems are from this edition.

2. "When he died," as Merrill recounts in "The Broken Home," "There were already several chilled wives / In sable orbit—rings, cars, permanent waves / We'd felt him warming up for a green bride" (197).

der scheinen / und wertlos für das All, / haben Wurzeln zwischen den Steinen / und trinken dort überall." [These days that seem empty / and worthless to the universe / have roots between the stones / and drink there everywhere.] Following, as such, the childhood experience waits for decades under the stones of memory. But that is not why we are here. Patience dans l'azur!

One can count two umlaut owlets (or is it umlauts owlet?) epigraphing this puzzled lyric. Like the poets explored in this study (as I have been arguing), Merrill can get productively lost in the shapes of letters. He shared this especially with his close confidant, Elizabeth Bishop, to whom he dedicated (in English) his wonderfully quirky poem "The Victor Dog," about Nipper—the dog (currently retired) who used to sit and spin on RCA Victor records. Bishop and Merrill had similar poetic appetites.[3] Their conversational tones weren't hampered by their senses of craft, and their tempered "I"s embraced a lyric discretion that was becoming more and more uncommon in their contemporaries. As a result, they were often (misguidedly so, as others saw it) considered too absent or uncaring, too modernist. Timothy Materer traces the criticisms of Merrill to significant "early review[er]s of his work . . . who considered him too controlled and impersonal to write moving poetry" ("James" 123).[4] More patient readers would soon be able to recognize the human depth of what Merrill called his "chronicles of love and loss," even if he would always avoid fabricating a more consumable form of American sentimentality. But it—the pain of life and love—was always there. "[T]he form that [Merrill's] self-examination takes—a questioning of

---

3. Merrill's elegiac poem "Overdue Pilgrimage to Nova Scotia" offers a later meditation on Bishop's influence. W. S. Merwin calls it "an elegy not only for her but for what she comes to signify, a world that is departing: "Part of a scene that with its views and warblers, / And at its own grave pace, but in your footsteps / —Never more imminent the brink, more sheer— / Is making up its mind to disappear" (Merrill, *Collected Poems* 667). Many articles and book-length studies examine Bishop's relationship with Merrill. Timothy Materer ("Mirrored Lives") recounts their interactions and poetic affinities, Luke Carson considers their aesthetics of manners, and Deborah Forbes sees them both as poetic inheritors of John Keats (151–89).

4. See, for example, James Dickey, "James Merrill" in *Babel to Byzantium*, Farrar, Straus & Giroux, 1968, 97–100. Materer shows how, in poem after poem, Merrill's "emotional power" does not come at the expense of his "mastery of form" ("James" 124). The later poems especially "address the ravages of AIDS on Merrill's friends and the poet himself, and question the pursuit of love when it involves the risk of death" (124). See also Reena Sastri, who compellingly illustrates the contours of Merrill's social awareness and responsibility.

his own language and perceptions," Langdon Hammer writes, "derives from Bishop, for whom self-questioning was a trademark device. Her poetry was richly personal, but she shied away from Confessional poetry's bold self-dramatizations and . . . its claims to public authority" (276).[5] In a letter Bishop sent Merrill, cited by Lois Cucullu, the older poet wrote:

> (Something happened to my i iii i letter *I* last n'ght—oh dear, do you suppose 't 's because *I* use 't so much? How awfully revealing.)[6]

Whimsical, yes. But there was a material point, too, if not a double-eyed umlaut, to Bshop's often shrouded I.

Merrill's final collection, *A Scattering of Salts*, was published posthumously; throughout, its "I" is on the verge of vanishing. It is the one word conspicuously absent from his poem "b o d y":

> Look closely at the letters. Can you see,
> entering (stage right), then floating full,
> then heading off—so soon—
> how like a little kohl-rimmed moon
> o plots her course from b to d
>
> —as y, unanswered, knocks at the stage door?
> Looked at too long, words fail,
> phase out. Ask, now that body shines
> no longer, by what light you learn these lines
> and what the b and d stood for. (646)

What happens when the words we use to understand our world suddenly lose all sense because their letters are too saturated with meaning? As if they were four actors on the stage of life, the letters "b" "o" "d" and "y" perform, but never long enough. "b" we might take as "birth," "d" as "death"—the lines of existence, between which the circle of life "o" moves.

---

5. Like Bishop, Merrill kept his sexuality at arm's length. It was always there, just not as public as many now would have desired it to be. See Piotr K. Gwiazda, for the influence and confluence of W. H. Auden's sexuality.

6. March 31, 1971; Elizabeth Bishop Collection, Vassar College Library; quoted in Cucullu, 246.

Its movement from one line to another reminds Merrill of the phases of the moon and then to a maquillaged face ready to perform. In the final line, we are asked to answer *the* riddle of existence: "y" or "why" (which stands outside the lines of life) offers a final pun, but the joke is on us—we who are conjured by the verse—as we try to listen for an answer (*what does it all mean?*) that will never come. Just as the moon phases out, words fail, but the failure of this word—"body"—carries with it grave consequences. "Can you see . . . ?" the first line asks. Can U C? An unfinished circle of a letter tips over, as a body on stage. And what about all those pregnant Os and double OOs (look, so soon, moon, door, looked, too long, stood), which vie for the theatrical spotlight? Underlying all this harmless fun with word puzzles and games lies a glimpse into the dark recesses of our staged being and the failure of lettered attempts to fend off the vaudeville hook in that unseen hand behind the curtain. What does one lose when one looks too closely at letters? (It is not only the antiformalist who seeks this answer!) One does not have to know Merrill well to know that his figuration was always more trope than body—"the figure turned around" (267) as he called it in "Matinées." It is false to claim, though, as some readers of his have done, that the two, for him, are distinct. He is not an obviously plaintive poet, but pain does hide in the shadows of his well-polished penumbras.

If the movement of o from b to d constitutes our lives, the simple letters "I" and "O"—a line and a circle—become in the staggering poem "Syrinx" a binary of being and oblivion. Coming to terms with a friend's diagnosis and treatment—the cure, as the pedestrian saying goes, is worse than the illness—Merrill looks back to the myth of the nymph Syrinx. Pursued by the god Pan and terrified by his sexual advances, she flees to the waters and cries out for help. Her cry, its own apostrophic conjuring of sorts, is heard and she is transformed into water reeds, which Pan, ever the lecher, eventually fashions into his panpipes—also called syrinx today.[7] As a reed, Syrinx trembles, her movement dependent on the volition of the wind. No hands with which to write, no voice with which to speak, her only mark can come as the illiterate's X of crossed reeds. The tragicomedic pun of the poem sounds in what Stephen Yenser calls a "muffled solfeggio" (185): "Who puts his mouth to me / Draws out the scale of love and dread— / O ramify, sole antidote!" (Merrill, 355). If one slows one's enunciation, the sounds morph into the musical scale: d—O—ra—mi—fy—sol—le—ti—do. There is the hope, as with the vocalization of an apostrophe, that one

---

7. Syrinx is also the name for a dangerous watery build-up in the spinal cord.

can somehow will a state of affairs into the wounds of the world. But here, the speaker lacks the godlike power of the artist, captured in another of Merrill's poems, "The Doodler," whose titular speaker can call out: "Emerge, O sunbursts, garlands, creatures, men, / Ever more lifelike out of the white void!" (99). Here, alas, the scales always seem to balance more toward dread.

One celebrates natural proliferation perhaps too often in readings of poetry. Yet it is such proliferation, such ramification that the "fatal growths / Proliferating by metastasis / Rooted their total in the gliding stream" bring. The word "rooted"—itself answering the call to "O ramify!"—then leads to the poetically unexpected formula of a "square root" (something cut down by its own number). This "formula, not relevant any more," gives us (surprisingly) an almost perfectly iambic line:

$$\text{Like } \sqrt{\left(\frac{x}{y}\right)^n} = \text{I}$$

—Or equals zero, one forgets—

The y standing for you, dear friend, at least
Until that hour he reaches for me, then

Leaves me cold, the great god Pain. . . .

Does the formula equate to "one" or the "I" no longer with a voice? No matter, it might have been zero after all. One forgets. Once again, what appears to be harmless fun with letter puzzles and word games betrays a glimpse into the dark hollows of being. That simple sign of number/letters—I and O, the line and the circle that even cavemen drew, the basis of binary computer code today (on and off, on and off . . . dancing repeatedly to OO)—determines here the difference between life and death. The variable X of the equation above, we know from line 6 ("Illiterate—X my mark"), is the speaker. The Y—attached at the hip but separated by a bar—stands for "you." If we take the "S" and the "R" from "square root" and add them to the letters in the equation (X, Y, N, I), we are left with an anagram for "syrinx"—another metamorphosis, another transformation. Caught in its own airstream, the poem concludes with a circular compass:

> Or stop the four winds racing overhead
>   Nought
>   Waste   Eased
>   Sought

How are we to read the wood-winds of these final lines? Linearly? Moving from the zero of "nought" to a hopeful "sought"? *Nought, waste, eased, sought?* Normally, one would voice the directions as "Nought, sought, eased, waste," but this would compel a break in the poetic line and a jeté through the page. Rather than a circle or an "S," we would invoke the winds as a cross, perhaps more charitable than the earlier "Christian weeds," for they blow us between one and zero, between nothingness and possibility, between our wasting bodies and whatever can alleviate the pain.

A *Scattering of Salts*, described by Hammer as "about a dream of rescue from the mortal danger that at times was all around [Merrill]" (800), is bookended by two companion poems. "A Downward Look" inaugurates the collection and "An Upward Look" closes it. The first makes a whole geographic terrestriality out of the body of a speaker in a bath ("Over protuberances, faults, / A delta thicket, glide" (589). Its companion, the final poem of Merrill's final collection, begins with a classic poetic apostrophe—generally something one would imagine Merrill only offering up ironically.[8] But this time, in what W. S. Merwin calls "the end of more than a book,"[9] it feels different:

> O heart green acre   sown with salt
> by the departing   occupier
>
> lay down your gallant   spears of wheat
> Salt of the earth   each stellar pinch

---

8. The sonnet sequence "Days of 1971" recalls a car trip Merrill took through Europe with his former lover, Strato Mouflouzélis ("Strato, each year's poem / Says goodbye to you" [137]). Along the way, they stay with some of Merrill's friends, including Stephen Yenser. Strato would "stagger forth to find us talking. Not still about poetry! Alas . . ." Merrill could ventriloquize. The car ride becomes a metaphor for writing, and, at the heart of the poem, Merrill dryly apostrophizes about a novel he has been writing: "O book of hours, those last / Illuminated castles built / In air, O chariot-motif // Bearing down a margin good as gilt / Past fields of ever purer leaf / Its burning rubric, to get nowhere fast . . ." (136). "Burning rubber" becomes "burning rubric" as the inspirational chariot tears through the pages of metaphorical land, its gilded margins very different than that of verse.

9. Merwin: "While I was reading [the final collection] and trying to persuade myself that what all this amounted to was merely a timely apprehension of mortality, word came of [Merrill's] sudden death. Heart. Viewed from afterward, the immediate cause of death seems to have been prefigured in the poems, however skeptical one may be, or may try to be, about such notions. Tropes and asides all through this new book seem to be pointing to something of the sort, nowhere more directly than in the final poem. . . ."

<blockquote>

flung in blind   defiance backwards
now take its toll. . . .   (674)

</blockquote>

The bath that was sown with salt to alleviate bodily pains now covers the body. Merrill's once-verdant heart—with a secondary connotation of youthful romantic (but also poetic) inexperience—has been so scorched by the former love so as not to yield a harvest again. The apostrophe is not simply a call to a wounded soldier. It hearkens back to a whole poetic tradition that Merrill finds himself at the end of. The gaps in each line recall some of the earliest verse forms in English—that of the Anglo-Saxons. Merrill, naturally, is looser with the alliterative form, his poetic skin, perhaps, made droopier by the bath. Vendler (*Ocean* 135–39) sees the pseudo-Anglo-Saxon caesurae as typifying the ailing Merrill's need to pause for breath. "[H]alves of a clue" he tells us, in his own enigmatic words. And then

<blockquote>

Up from his quieted

quarry the lover   colder and wiser
hauling himself   finds the world turning

</blockquote>

Part planetary rotation, part exhaustion from the bath, the exit creates a minor terrestrial disturbance in the embodied cosmic sphere.

O is a symbol that performs for Merrill, and his fascination with it does not end with the lyric form (but that will have to be a novel approach for another day).[10] Beyond the invocation or the excited utterance, beyond nothingness, Merrill—as he did in "b o d y"—turns often to the circular shape of the moon or the face or the metaphorical seasonal cycle, whose archetypical histories are continually informing his verse. On one hand,

---

10. We see the "O" occupy a shorthand for the narrator's older half-brother Orson (or "Orestes") in Merrill's *The (Diblos) Notebook*, a novel about writing a novel, which includes excised words and pages, not to mention an upside-down paragraph, as though he were really capturing the process of writing during his time in Greece. In a notable passage, for example, a crossed-out half revision ("dark blue" changed to "indigo") fortuitously gives Merrill enough creative Oxygen to arrive at "blind I go." He writes, "Holding my hand for comfort / inhale this gas / made by the cricket's voice / acting on ~~dark bl~~ indigo oxygen / blind I go!" (*Collected Novels and Plays*, 335). All of this is not to challenge the special place apostrophe might hold for the lyric, but simply to see how this orbiting grapheme might land on other worlds.

the circle gestures toward rejuvenation but on the other, especially in his later poems, they signal the final movement toward the end. "Family Week at Oracle Ranch" chronicles the poet's visit to see his friend and former partner, David Jackson. The poem is in twelve parts, as if mirroring the twelve-step program or the hours on a clockface that would, as carefully planned, divide each segment of the day. Each part is four stanzas long, the first and final lines of the stanza rhyming—thus, as it were, completing the circle. The presumption with any oracle (from the Latin "to speak") is that the gods would take the time to turn away from their godly affairs to tell some people what is in store for them. Seeing, though, how often the gods invested themselves in the affairs of humankind (usually for their own political or personal machinations), such condescension is not unimaginable. When Merrill arrives at "Oracle Ranch," a modern rehabilitation center in what is feasibly Arizona, he is struck by a different sort of condescension. The group circles he describes ("Ken had us break the circle and repair / To 'a safe place in the room'" [657]), provide more counsel (however clichéd) than forecasts, but the threat of a possible relapsed future—a return to zero—still lingers overhead. Initially, Merrill seems to be poking fun at the unaware earnestness of the "new age" scene—what Hammer calls a mix of "hallmark-style sentimentality and cynical realism" (757). The psychother-apeutic gods of old ("Underwear made to order in Vienna") are nowhere to be found, replaced here by the wonders of Benetton ("stone-washed, one size fits all")—an apt wink at both the stanza form and Merrill's own conversational tone—and a brochure featuring a "wide-angle moonscape, lawns and pool."

Although the healing circle might be reminiscent of the séances those in Merrill's circle were familiar with—other manners of apostrophic sum-moning—he is reluctant at first to engage with the counselors, or as he calls them in a stutter "deadpan panels." The poet's vocabulary (and emotions) are reduced to the seven words allowed in the circle: "AFRAID / HURT, LONELY, etc." On other occasions, the poet has been asked to do more with less—say with the six words allowed in the sestina—but the reticence here is cutting. The poet learns "Not to say / 'Your silence hurt me,' / Rather, 'When you said nothing I felt hurt.' / No blame, that way" (654). Interestingly, in calling attention to the things that would not be spoken (AIDS diagnoses among friends[11] or what "family" entailed to a discriminatory public), the

---

11. See Gurganus, Materer ("James Merrill's Late Poetry"), McClatchy ("Monsters"), and Hammer (especially Chapters 16–18).

modified lines bring the turn of address inward, to the wounded subject rather than the "you" who would not respond. Memories of the past ("In great waves it's coming back") and future apprehensions ("In a flash I saw // My future") circle around. Merrill is asked to envision "home"—that locus so central to his earliest scripts.[12] The word itself, of course, cannot conjure Merrill's childhood home, but it can call up a whole nest of memories in the poet's imagination: "Years have begun to flow // Unhindered down my face. Why? / Because nobody's there." Emptiness, it seems, is the only thing that can be conjured.

If poetic apostrophe is about holding on, Oracle Ranch is about letting go: "Let go / Of the dead dog, the lost toy" (658), the "GUILT" from an insignificant moment half a century ago. After being castigated for thinking himself "terminally unique"—a frightening paronomasia, given Merrill's diagnosis—the speaker wonders "if it were all like the moon," thereby circling back, or poetically "recover[ing]" the commercialized image from the poem's opening. The final lines expand the simile and seem to imply that recovery (amounting to "self-forgiveness") is more a tidal ebb and flow of falling down and standing up than ever being re-composed. The speaker, in a self-address, writes, "Ask how the co-dependent moon, another night, / Feels when the light drains wholly from her face. / Ask what that cold comfort means to her." The self-effacing co-dependency, a cycle of need between the moon and the sun or the moon and earth—orbs in the sky, forever pulling at each other—leads in Helen Vendler's words to "a rueful acknowledgement of the elementary nature of feeling, no matter how elaborate its eventual transmutation into art" (*Ocean* 206). Personified here, but un-addressed, the moon occasions the speaker's own final silence. Rather than the earlier consumer-mediated "moonscape" of the brochure, the mesmerizing shape of this final moon and its hints at a lifetime of circularity—however eye-rolling such cheesy humanistic tropes seem to be—constitute a meaningful lyric moment, despite any sense of nothingness that might lie at its center.

---

12. Merrill grew up in Southampton, New York, in a mansion designed by Stanford White and colloquially known as the "Orchard." Although he made homes across the country and the globe—Stonington, Connecticut; Key West, Florida; Athens, Greece—the Orchard was always the locus of "The Broken Home"—as he titled one of his more notable poems about his familiar upbringing. In this poem, another one of his sonnet sequences, he casts his parents' relationship as "Always that same old story— / Father Time and Mother Earth, / A marriage on the rocks" (198).

Linked to each other etymologically (κύκλος), the circle and the ring seem to go together for Merrill. As Andrea Mariani expounds, rings "signify the transmission of a heritage, the reification of a promise . . . The ring can be priceless, not so much because of its stone setting, but because it belongs to a dynasty and represents the stratification of a family history . . ." (63). The ancestral meaning of the ring surfaces in "The Emerald," the heart-warming second part of the modern diptych katabasis "Up and Down," which takes Merrill and his mother down in the bowels of the earth to a bank vault. She wears a bracelet from her deceased ex-husband, she wears a bracelet from another lifetime. Merrill writes,

> No rhinestone now, no dilute amethyst,
> But of the first water, linking star to pang,
> Teardrop to fire, my father's kisses hang
> In lipless concentration around her wrist. (342)

If the absent person speaks, he does so through a lipless voice, a reified kiss turned into a band. The mother wants to pass along, if not a similar history, then a similar familial sentiment, also hardened into a thing. She wants to give her son a ring, for when he marries, for his bride. Of course, Merrill—as both he and his mother know but cannot voice—will never take a bride, but the awkwardness of the failed gift is alleviated once Merrill, who doesn't want to sound, as he phrases it, "theatrical" (342), softly slips the ring back, completing a circle of return if not inheritance. All the while, prosodic puns on feet pattering and the underground room—a hermetic "stanza"—show that the possibilities of a heritage exist as much in the graphic voicing of a poetic line as in the tokens of a familial one: "*The little feet that patter here are metrical.*"

An altogether different Rhine-stone, Richard Wagner's *Ring Cycle* was an early influence on Merrill, who recounts his first trip to the *Ring* in "Matinées."[13] It would soon become a lifelong delight. He returns to Valhalla many years later for a major New York City event—"Four operas in

---

13. "Matinées" explores connections between the opera space and a sexuality that hides behind the curtain. As he phrases it in the poem, "The love scene (often cut)" (269). Although she does not specifically discuss Merrill, Monica Pearl's "The Opera Closet" details the relationship between the opera space and homosexuality for ambivalent writers who deflected discussion of the latter onto the former.

one week, for the first time / Since 1939." The history of that unbearable year returns, as do kinder, familiar faces, not seen for decades ("That man across the aisle . . . / Was once my classmate, or a year behind me. / Alone, in black, in front of him, Maxine . . . / It's like the *Our Town* cemetery scene!" (611). Midway through the poem, he begins thinking about his own three rings, which, like the operas, are all being worn at once—in Merrill's case, for the first time: "Of their three givers one is underground, / One far off, one here listening" ("The *Ring* Cycle" 613). One ring seems to have been inherited from his father Charles. Even if the father didn't end up encircling Merrill in a prison of fire, their relationship, to say the least, was complicated. (*Das ist kein Mann!* would ring differently from Charles's mouth.)[14] A second ring comes from a former partner and the third from his current companion. Luckily for the poet, sharing his fingers doesn't mean chancing Brünnhilde's wrath.

The three rings he wears carry the weight of more than their material substances. They have been robbed from the natural earth and unnaturally processed through the "sweatshops of Nibelheim / That worry nature into jewelry, / Orbits of power . . ." (613). In this context, Brünnhilde's immolation and the destruction of Valhalla correspond to a growing sense of impending global doom in the Atomic Age, a leitmotif (forgive me—in 2025, that feels a careless phrasing) across Merrill's later work. "We have long evenings to absorb together," he writes of his fellow operagoers, "Before the world ends." If there were any doubt that faceless corporations were ravaging the earth like the Nibelungs ravaged the Rhinegold, the third section of the poem makes the parallel explicit: "The very industries whose 'major funding' / Underwrote the production continue to plunder / The planet's wealth . . ." (612).

These same anxieties of an apocalyptic world loom throughout Merrill's great epic work of disembodied voices, *The Changing Light at Sandover*, which chronicles half a lifetime of experiences with the Ouija board, and which also returns at times to Wagner's *Ring*[15]:

---

14. Merrill's memories of his parents' responses to his gendered performances and sexuality are described in his 1993 memoir *A Different Person* (in *Collected Prose*).

15. Alison Lurie's *Familiar Spirits* recounts her supernatural time with Merrill and Jackson. Timothy Materer's archivally researched *James Merrill's Apocalypse* explores the Cold War history in the background of *Sandover*, and Lee Zimmerman's "Against Apocalypse" sees the epic poem as an antiapocalyptic response to the dangers of nuclear war.

> *Götterdämmerung.* From a long ago
> Matinee—the flooded Rhine, Valhalla
> In flames, my thirteenth birthday—one spark floating
> Through the darkened house had come to rest
> Upon a mind so pitifully green
> As only now, years later to ignite. . . .
> The heartstrings' leitmotif outsoared the fire. . . .
> How to rid Earth, for Heaven's sake, of power
> Without both turning to a funeral pyre? (*Sandover* 56)

If the twilight of the gods meant entrusting the care of Earth to humans, we would have to admit that we haven't done such a great job, more so in Merrill's time than in Wagner's, more so in our time than Merrill's. Before *Sandover* took its epic proportions, though, Merrill teased the specter of the other world in shorter lyrics, the first: "Voices from the Other World":

> Presently at our touch the teacup stirred,
> Then circled lazily about
> From A to Z. The first voice heard
> (If they are voices, these mute spellers-out). . . . (*Collected Poems* 112)

The connection to poetic apostrophe is palpable: a voice calling out to someone who isn't there, with the hope (and here expectation) that they would magically answer. And they did . . . ish. As it turns out, the spirits like to talk but, aside perhaps from an occasional haunting "Ooooooooooooooo," the ghostwriters make their apostrophes in graphic form ("mute spellers-out"), alphabetically signaling in the capital letters of the Ouija board: "PERSEVERE."

At first, Merrill's appetite for the spirit world, at least as confessed in "Voices," was less anxious, less obsessive. The ghosts, accordingly, grow lonely: "New voices come, / Dictate addresses, begging us to write." They want the earthly vessels to "OBEY" and warn of doom "[i]n ways that so exhilarate / We are sleeping sound of late." But rather than heed the ghostly decrees and warnings, Merrill has "grown nonchalant / Towards the other world." He and his summoning partner are less stirred "by those [ghosts] clamoring overhead, / Obsessed or piteous, for a commitment / We still have wit to postpone . . ." (113). Seeing the disquietude of the spirit world and "the cold reflections of the dead," Merrill's life had "never seemed more full, more real" (113). Hammer (214) traces the experience to

Merrill's first time at the Ouija with his classmate, Frederick Buechner. It would later become Merrill's household routine with Jackson. "Two crucial subjects—the supernatural and Merrill's domestic relationship with Jackson—enter his poetry here, and do so in tandem," Hammer writes, and "[l]ike a mirror, it showed them to themselves, and it added meaning to their daily life together" (215).[16] There is an echo also, in the block quotation, of Yeats's sentiment in "The Second Coming" that "The best lack all conviction, while the worst / Are full of passionate intensity" (187).[17] But while Yeats's version—a not-so dispassionate proclamation of dispassion—is (intentionally) rhetorically dishonest, Merrill seems to be shrugging in earnest, thereby willing a different sort of ethical knot to many readers of his time and to their inheritors today. Not everyone has the privilege of talking and smoking on the cleared table; not everyone is able to ignore voices calling out for help. Years later, more poetically conscientious that time and wit do not exonerate one from a commitment, Merrill would begin again to listen to the pleas from more than the spirit world.

Sandover collects three of Merrill's very long poems—*The Book of Ephraim* (1976), *Mirabell's Books of Number* (1978), and *Scripts for the Pageant* (1980)—along with a newer poetic "Coda: The Higher Keys." At over 550 pages, *Sandover* tells the decades-long (or possibly millennia-long) story of Merrill's and Jackson's Ouija conjuring. Merrill ("JM") acted as the transcriber and Jackson ("DJ") as the medium, and they used an overturned teacup ("WE ARE ALL BROUGHT TOGETHER BY THE CUP" [73]) as the planchet.[18] The epic trilogy (plus the belated Vorabend) recounts their summoning of deceased friends, historical figures, invented

---

16. By the time of *Sandover*, Judith Moffett writes, Merrill was "no longer masked in that armored, defensive sense at all; by this point masking and passion had ceased to be the foci of his concern" (13).

17. "Causes / Were always lost—on us," Merrill later recounts (*Sandover* 14). Still, he kept a poetic pied-à-terre in Yeats's spirituality and mystical aesthetics: "as it happened I had been half trying / To make sense of *A Vision* / When our friend [Ephraim] dropped his bombshell: POOR OLD YEATS / STILL SIMPLIFYING" (*Sandover* 14). Toward the end of *Sandover*, Merrill could inquire of the spirit of the great Irish poet, "From your present viewpoint, Mr Yeats, / Was our instruction of a piece with yours?" (481). For more on Yeats's influence, see Bauer.

18. It should be noted that readers seem divided over whether Merrill really believed he was communing with spirits or if the whole enterprise was an (elaborate) method of stimulating the writing process.

spirit guides—including Ephraim (a two-thousand-year-old Greek Jew), Mirabell (a bat-angel-peacock)—and, among others, the recently departed W. H. Auden and Athenian socialite Maria Mitsotáki who would both soon kibbitz the party. *Sandover* is filled on one hand with grand cosmic visions, and on the other hand with the day-to-day domestic life on Water Street in Connecticut: "What do you do?" Merrill and Jackson ask, to which the spirit replies, "READ BUFF MY NAILS DO CROSSWORDS JUST LIKE LIFE / THOSE YEARS WITH WYSTAN ONCE A BACKSTREET WIFE" (106). The spirits had, like Merrill in his time, a great propensity for iambic rhyme. Even with such attentiveness to the faculties of the ear, though, all of the summoning and mis-summoning back and forth was graphic. And with that alphabetic medium, comes—as it does with any experience rec-ollected in the tranquility of print—the possibility of misplay: "IM NOT CNOFUSDE GODDAM THIS TYPEWRITAR" (*Sandover* 103). The form of *Sandover* mirrors the visual layout of the Ouija board. The first part of the trilogy, like an abecedarian, is organized according to the alphabet, the second according to the numbers from 0 to 9, and the final part is divided into "Yes," "&," and "No." Everything a spirit could want.

The "O" section of *The Book of Ephraim* begins with Merrill thinking of his time in Athens with his former partner Strato Mouflouzélis. The oval of a mirror converging through the window with the light of the circular moon, gets the spirits stirring:

> O's of mildest light glance through the years . . .
> Moonglow starts from scratches as my oval
> Cheval-glass tilting earthward by itself . . .
> Converges with lamplight ten winters back.
> Strato squats within the brilliant zero. . . . (50)

Whereas Bishop's "O Breath" left her breathless, here, instead, Merrill's opening vacancy leaves the night gasping. A couple lines later, Ephraim appears and responds to Merrill with his own quasi-apostrophe: "O MY DEAR HES IN / HIS 1ST MANS LIFE WHAT WD U HAVE HIM DO" (50). Portending our text message textual culture, Ephraim often spks in abbr. (The data plans of the spirit world have not yet caught up to ours.)[19]

---

19. The second of Merrill's "Eight Bits," referring to a subway sign, promises: "IF U CN RD THS / u cn gt a gd jb w hi pa!" before warning us to "Think twice when letters disappear / Into Commodity's black hole—" (*Collected Poems* 538).

Half a foot in desire and the other in memory, Merrill confesses that "We've wanted / Consuming passions; these refine instead." Ephraim, in turn—never one to miss a paronomastic refinement—conveys to Merrill that his regret and wit "MERRILY GLOW ON."

Toward the end of *Ephraim*, the spirits have quieted. The poem ends with "Z"—the section beginning at "Zero hour." Heaps of transcripts (to the slight dismay of Jackson) adorn the house in Stonington. "Letters scrawled by my own hand unable / To keep pace with the tempest in the cup— / These old love-letters from the other world," Merrill acknowledges (91). Linking the two poems, *Mirabell's Books of Number* begins with the love-letter of the tennis court: zero or 0. "Oh, very well then," it starts in a resigned moment of simple domesticity, "Let us broach the matter / Of the new wallpaper in Stonington" (97). The spirits soon return: "O JIM WE LEARN U HERE" (107). These spirits of *Mirabell* are far more perplexing than the familiar Ephraim. They are also more demanding. In Book One, we (as did Merrill) learn that they need

> POEMS OF SCIENCE THE WEORK FINISHT IS BUT A
>   PROLOGUE
> ABSOLUTES ARE NOW NEEDED YOU MUST MAKE
>   GOD OF SCIENCE
> TELL OF POWER MANS IGNORANCE FEARES THE
>   POWER WE ARE
> THAT FEAR STOPS PARADISE WE SPEAK FROM WITHIN
>   THE ATOM (113).

"So much for preface" (112). In today's text-message speak, one would ask the spirits to stop yelling. In their defense, though, they only have the capitals on the board with which to communicate. Besides, as they tell Merrill, they are not evil, just impatient. Their divine force, as they eventually reveal, is symbolized by the "twin zeroes" or the double O: "WE ARE ETERNITY WE ARE 00 BEYOND THE NINE / THOSE STAGES ARE OUR LAB & YR DEAD FRIENDS OUR WORKERS. . . ." (116). The 00 sign, as Yenser (252) explains, becomes a measure of infinity and the source of birth (as in the oo of oogenesis) in the middle of what will become the b00k of *Sandover*: "Central to this b00k / Are lenses, the twin zeroes" (174). What would it mean for Merrill to connect the 00 to measures of control inherent in the apostrophic act? It is as if he is being summoned by larger forces at the moment he thinks he is summoning them. The double circles, it seems, have been performing, directing the events of Merrill's life even before he meets them.[20] That is, if one believes in fate. Experiences have a way of resolving themselves into the stories we like to tell. Or, as the spirits repeat throughout the epic, "NO ACCIDENT" (187, *passim*). The same holds true for words and phrases spit out by ghosts over time. I guess for critical pieces, too.

One of these preordained moments, for Merrill, was a trip he and Jackson took to Avebury, a five-thousand-year-old circular stone monument near Stonehenge in England. The site, as it is believed to have originally existed, consisted of a large circle of stones with two smaller circles within. (Remnants of the inner circles still remain.) Merrill and Jackson's trip there is recounted in the opening book of *Mirabell*:

> Within a "greater circle" (the whole myth
> Dwarfed by its grass-green skyline) stand
> Two lesser, not quite tangent O's
> Plotted monolith by monolith
>
> Two lenses now, whose once outrippling arcs
> Draw things back into focus. . . . (112)

After the initial stanzaic aside above, Merrill drops a sonnet into the mix to close out the book. But, as the three other parentheticals contained in this initial one make evident, the graphic parenthetical is more than a b00kmark. "These enclosed parentheses, Evans Lansing Smith writes, "form a chiasmus of turnings and reversals, thus (()()()), which figure the enclosure of the 'two lesser' stone circles within the 'greater circle' of monoliths demarcating Avebury's perimeter (lenses within lenses of a primordial telescope)" (174).

The spirits get the final words of *Mirabell*, orthographically recentering their demands around the letter O—doubled in their imperative, spotlighted in the center of God: "LOOK! LOOK INTO THE RED EYE OF YOUR GOD!" (276). But before they can issue their commands, Merrill is able to circle back one last time to his own O at the beginning of the book. As Yenser notes, this comes by way of a final homophone. As the lines convey, he knows that his existential bill has come due: "Birdlife, leafplay, rockface, waterglow / Lending us their being, till the given / Moment comes to render what we *owe*" (275; emphasis my own).

Toward the closing section of the final poem of the trilogy, *Scripts for the Pageant*, the divine character known as "God B" guides the teacup in

---

20. See Yenser 247–80.

a quincunxed X across the Ouija board, before the mirror through which the spirits are conjured finally breaks (it had had a good run):

> Is it the mark
> That cancels, or the letter-writer's kiss?
> The X
> Of the illiterate? (493–94)

"No pulsing zeroes, no ascent," Merrill tells us. But the spirits persist. "LOOK ALIVE! MUCH TO DO! THE SUMMER TO GET UNDER WRAPS!" they write, before offering an ambiguous farewell pun. "AU RESERVOIR!" (507), they say, rather than the expected *au revoir*, dropping "serve" into a phonetic invocation of surplus—*O reservoir* (507). Robert Polito notes the real "Grief and impoverishment that DJ and JM feel after they break the mirror that returns Auden and Maria to earth" (6). Time might cure this "pure ache . . . If there were time in Heaven, or these dead / Weren't so addicted to the loving cup" (*Sandover* 510). But the friends, habitués are "gone . . . / Left without a trace UNLESS THIS (M) / WHITE HOLE WE CARRY HEDGEWARD STANDS FOR THEM" (510). As the arced M signals, they are remembered on the texts of the circular stone.

Returning to the shorter lyric works, we find that one emblematic stone Merrill carried was an Ibis, associated with his departed father. "I bought it with / A check my father wrote before his death," he tells us in "The Will," another of Merrill's sonnet sequences (*Collected Poems* 394). The ibis, Materer reminds us, is the iconic bird of Thoth, the Egyptian god of writing. In Merrill's orthographic hands, it also encores as an "I"-*bis* (the pronoun and an adverb used for French addresses). Both signified and signifier are apparently on Merrill's unconscious mind, because he dreams of a hotel in Paris,

> Its front door, Roman-numeralled,
> Still said, "I" in white-on-emerald.
>
> Some humbler way into the edifice
> Was chalked just legibly "I*bis*." (392)

The dreamlike "I," as it did in "Syrinx" navigates between subjectivity ("one façade he seemed to know") and a numeric counter, here, showing Merrill which detour to take. The poem begins earlier when a trinity of three strangers enter Merrill's house in Connecticut, tasked with getting him to sign a will. He is distracted by his work on a manuscript, unable to remember where he is going: "I have wrapped in jeans / With manuscript on either side for wadding / Something I'm carrying to a . . . to a wedding . . ." (392). He is on his way to the ritual by way of his mother's house in Georgia. With him, he carries the funerary Ibis, intended as a wedding gift, wrapped in the draft manuscript of a novel. He is still distracted in the taxi ride from the airport, perhaps by phrases that would make their way into this very poem. (The "dog days" of this summer join with the dogwoods they drive through to form the realization "O dogwood days.") He thinks he might paint the wooden base of the Ibis with flowers and quench its thirst with an "Abstraction of a river, eau de Nil / Arrested by the powerful curving bill." Like Baudelaire's swan's apostrophe "Eau, quand donc pleuvras-tu?" (illumed by Culler and discussed in my chapter on Stevens), Merrill's "eau de Nil," or water from the Nile, puns on *water of nothing*, another empty sign of the apostrophic O.

While playing bridge with his mother's friends, he suddenly remembers that he left his bag and Ibis in the cab. "When he lost the bird, it was an act of dispossession, relieving him of one sign of the 'untold means' at his disposal," Hammer writes (534). "U DID WELL JM TO DISINHERIT / YR SELF & FRIENDS OF THAT STONE BIRD" (395), the spirit Ephraim feels obliged to relate. It was more a "burden" than any measure of wedding gift. One might say (or even epigraph a book with the lost sentiment) that "It [is] not the present but the thought that counts" (392), but it's probably not a great habit to pass along looted trinkets to friends. Ephraim reminds Merrill of the item's curse—that it caused a temporary bout with paralysis and is currently doing the same to the taxi driver's sister. Ephraim, as it turns out, has been jealous of Merrill's questioning and lack of faith in the spirit's artistic tutelage and communicates as much:

> WITHOUT SO MANY DAVIDS TO COMBAT
> MY GIANT DESIGNS UPON YR ART MON CHER
> SHRINK TO THIS TOPSYTURVY WILLOWARE
> IGLOO WALTZING WITH THE ALPHABET (396)

The teacup planchet has become an ornamental igloo, simply dancing across the Ouija board rather than offering any deeper revelation. With (yet another) David complicating the spirit's plan, Merrill has become paralyzed with writer's block at his desk and is unable to write this very same poem he is describing. But that incongruity seems to trigger a revelation. "My word!" he exclaims, both idiomatically and literally, as his manuscript and Ibis have finally been unearthed. Another sense of "will" surfaces, as Materer shows, when "the other world as will and idea . . . drive Merrill to take on the deferred task of prophecy" (75). With this revitalized poetic energy, the once-lost novel will soon become *The Book of Ephraim* and, years later, the epic *Sandover*.

Beyond Reflection: Messages in Coda

High on its own throne of royal state, but at the other end of the length spectrum from *Sandover*, the villanelle exalted sits. Existing between prophetic knowledge (the knowledge of how things will end) and the juggernaut of time (an all-too-hasty nineteen lines before this end comes), the villanelle can be a terrifying exercise. W. H. Auden's teases with the knowledge of decay:

> Time can say nothing but I told you so,
> Time only knows the price we have to pay;
> If I could tell you, I would let you know. (314)

It is not enough for Time to reign supreme. Like a sibling who divined the wrong turn you were inevitably going to end up taking, Time won't let you forget it—the refrain repeating over and again, "I told you so . . . I told you so."[21] In Sylvia Plath's hands, the refrains' forced repetitions rhetorically capture a spurned lover's fixation and apocalyptic solipsism:

> I shut my eyes and all the world drops dead,
> I lift my lids and all is born again.
> (I think I made you up inside my head). (50)

Her "I" worries that the addressed "you" isn't real, and the stanzas themselves seem to spiral out of control, moving from the vivid colors of a dance to lovemaking to a biblically apocalyptic end. At the center of it all is the

---

21. It is a common refrain in Auden, for whom even the clocks of a city could call out "O let not time deceive you / You cannot conquer time" ("As I Walked Out One Evening" 134). Interestingly, in this instance, the apostrophe would be projected from the addressee (who is present) rather than a speaking, anthropomorphized Time.

apostrophic belief or fear that words themselves can create a reality. Marilyn Hacker's "Villanelle" metaphorically plays the formality of raveling and unraveling refrains against lovers separating and coming back together again.

> Every day our bodies separate,
> exploded torn and dazed.
> Not understanding what we celebrate. . . .

No matter. Whatever is to come will come, even if we rage and rage.[22] Merrill, for his dive into this ornamentally circular pool in his aptly titled villanelle "Dead Center," will choose to pair his metonymic pen with the stars of an ambiguous "Then":

> Upon reflection, as I dip my pen
> Tonight, forth ripple messages in code.
> In Now's black waters burn the stars of Then.
>
> Seen from the embankment, marble men
> Sleep upside down, bat-wise, the sleep bestowed
> Upon reflection. As I dip my pen. . . . (540)

Like Bishop, Merrill will be playful with his forms, allowing different syntactical continuities to bend the semantic arc of each refrain. Yet neither the conversational tone nor the illuminating stars—once taken as future premonitions—is able to clarify the widening ripples of the code. Is the "Then" of line three (the second refrain) a past *then* or the *then* that is soon approaching? We know, when searching the night sky for stars lightyears away, that these black waters burn with the past *then* of their interstellar lives. But could the poet also be proleptically anticipating the determinate future—something the villanelle seems to relish? For that matter, are these burning stars of Then being quenched by or fueling the Now? And does the reflection of the opening phrase bring the past into the present or is it merely a mirroring of the present? At stake is merely one's freedom in an eschatological scheme. These black waters might also allude to the poet's inkwell, another sort of upside-down reflection, already conjuring its own end with the pen dip of the opening stanza. The poem continues:

---

22. Merrill: "But really—rage?" ("Losing the Marbles" 572).

> As I dip my pen
>
> Thinking how others, deeper into Zen,
> Blew on immediacy until it glowed,
> In Now's black waters burn the stars of Then. . . . (540)

The Stevens-esque attempt to get at the cold, ignorant nothingness of immediate experience brings us (wink-wink) "deeper into Zen." The immediacy that Merrill is blowing on, though, feels more like the end of a cigarette—its smoke-rings masking the "Breath after breath, harsh O's of oxygen / Never deciphered." Reduced to its elemental sign O (here acting on the one hand as poetic inspiration and on the other as the basic element necessary for human life), the code remains uncracked or, rather, "never deciphered." "Cipher" (as I will explore a bit further in the Dickinson chapter) is etymologically related to the word "zero," which in turn, comes from the word zephyr, a reminder of Earth's gentle breath after breath.[23] Merrill, as he recalls it here in his "then" of memory, is ten years old: 1 0—the line and the circle once again framing the being and nothingness through which this poet moves. But like Bishop, who danced in that lyric circus between one and zero, Merrill is able to look through whatever hoop was necessary to seek out the wealth that emptiness could hide.

Finally, it is not the vocative O but the resigned "Ah," which signals the turn to the apostrophic address to Memory itself at the end:

> Ah then
>
> Leap, Memory, supreme equestrienne,
> Through hoops of fire, circuits you overload!
> Beyond reflection, as I dip my pen
> In Now's black waters burn the stars of Then.

Memory is what constitutes our subjectivity: we *are* because we know who we once were and who we might become—our past and future *then*s. What

---

23. Alex Bellos writes, in a book that has nothing to do with Merrill but with a title (*Here's Looking at Euclid*) he would have enjoyed: "From zephyr came 'zero' but also the Portuguese word *chifre*, which means [Devil] horns, and the English word 'cipher,' meaning code. . . . Indian philosophy embraced the concept of nothingness just as Indian math embraced the concept of zero. The conceptual leap that led to the invention of zero happened in a culture that accepted the void as the essence of the universe. . . . The circle, 0, was chosen because it portrays the cyclical movements of the face of heaven. Zero means nothing, and it means eternity" (81, 92–93).

would it mean, though, given the repeated refrains of the villanelle form, to turn to address "Memory," an addressee tied as much—and never more so than in a villanelle—to foreknowledge as to recollection? Constituted somewhere in the blazing horseplay between the graphic and vocative, Merrill's lyric subjectivity is invoked in this multitemporal "Now"—not a magically isolated time outside history but one with a necessary past and longed-for future. Thus, the memory at the close of stanza one (that *then*) then returns, brazenly leaping through the double-oo "hoops of fire" to get back through the overloaded rings of the mind to conjure where it once was and where it might be going.

As I have been arguing, Merrill's poetic hoops of fire need not make everything feel as though a human, with his loves and losses, were not standing behind the curtain.[24] The final part, the tenth, of Merrill's late poem "Nine Lives" has him returning to the spirits of the Ouija board. "There is a moment comedies beget," he writes,

> When escapade and hubbub die away,
> Vows are renewed, masks dropped. . . .
> It's then the connoisseur of your bouquet . . .
> Will shed, O Happiness, a furtive tear. . . .
>
> To all, sweet dreams. The teacup-stirring eddy
> Is spent. We've dropped our masks, renewed our vows
> To letters, to the lives that letters house. . . . (600–01)

Throughout this book, I have been searching for the varied lives that the letter O houses. Knowing Merrill, it is hard not to see him winking at the centuries-old poetic pressure that went into allowing this supposed authentic, immediate address, "O Happiness." But one need not choose between the clichéd mechanics of apostrophe as figure and the desire to call out to something that is or will soon no longer be there. The tear, however furtive, is real, even if the speaker tries not to reveal it. Making a vow to letters does not mean forsaking the lives that these letters house, even if that house will always remain on one stage or another.

---

24. Midway through his "The *Ring* Cycle," Brünnhilde confronts Siegfried. "That is to say," Merrill recalibrates, "Two singers have been patiently rehearsed / So that their tones and attitudes convey / Outrage and injured innocence. . . . / Who'll joke at supper side by side, now hate / So plausibly that one old stagehand cries" (612). Artifice—yes, but the tug is powerful. Even an old stagehand who has seen this acted out many times before can't help but lose himself in the moment.

Merrill's ominously outmoded formula boiled down to one or zero (one forgets). Context is important. At another time, his ghostly friend would "mark . . . time back and forth from One / To Zero: a pavane / Andante in an alley of green oaks."[25] *The dance puzzling Emily Dickinson appears blushingly on a young girl's face: "The Rose did caper on her cheek—[.]"*[26] *It wasn't until a second rose came into sight that Dickinson gathered what was what:*

> *A Vest that like her Boddice, danced—*
> *To the immortal tune—*
> *Till those two troubled—little Clocks*
> *Ticked softly into one.*

The youthful crush, pulling from the long garden of poetic metaphor, can make two dance like one. But what of the lone eye watching them, what if the zero, alone, was ample enough?

---

25. Merrill, *Sandover*, 159.
26. Dickinson, F200; J208; M118.

Chapter 5

Emily Dickinson

"An Ampler Zero"

Starting with nothing.

"The Zeroes," Dickinson writes:

>   . . . taught Us – Phosphorus –
> We learned to like the Fire
> By handling Glaciers – when a Boy –
> And Tinder – guessed – by power
>
> Of Opposite – to equal Ought –
> Eclipses – Suns – imply –
> Paralysis – our Primer dumb
> Unto Vitality – (F284; J689; M366)[1]

---

1. Unless otherwise noted, quotations are taken from the Reading Edition of R.W. Franklin, *The Poems of Emily Dickinson* (Harvard UP, 1998). For convenience, I cite Franklin's number (F) along with Thomas H. Johnson's number (J), followed by the poem's page in Cristanne Miller's new edition, *Emily Dickinson's Poems As She Preserved Them* (M). I also note the first line of the poem (as printed in Franklin's Reading Edition) when the number alone feels inadequate to the sense a person wrote the lines, even if she left them untitled. Any variants cited come from the Emily Dickinson Archive (https://www.edickinson.org/), which uses Franklin's variant letter designations from the three-volume Variorum Edition of *The Poems of Emily Dickinson* (Harvard UP, 1998). Quotations from Dickinson's letters (L) are taken from and numbered according to *The Letters of Emily Dickinson*, Volumes 1–3, edited by Thomas H. Johnson and Theodora Ward (Harvard UP, 1958). Generally, I do not normalize Dickinson's spelling and use of apostrophe (the other "apostrophe"), which she sometimes uses to pluralize or when substituting "it's" for "its."

In what could be a primer to a lecture on structuralism or poststructuralism (although this epistemological sentiment goes back thousands of years), Dickinson tells us that one learns what isn't there or isn't there yet by the presence of its opposite. There must be heat (phosphorus) because there is cold (zero degrees); there must be fire (tinder) because one has handled glaciers. In an optimistically reversed outlook, it is the eclipse that engenders knowledge of the sun, without one seeing the radiance of its light, and, finally, even this speaker's present moment of inertia means that there exists vitality in a future elsewhere. The "dumb" primer is contrasted with the initial sense of how one learns this all, but it also ties the final hopefulness to the possibilities of the written text, even if the only writing at present is a rote repetition of what one currently has access.

Other Dickinson poems about knowledge transmission, even those more self-assured ones from the pedagogical side, also stress its indirect, nonlinear nature. "Tell all the truth but tell it slant" (F1263; J1129; M563) – ironically, itself one of Dickinson's more accessible poems – favors the incline or the staircase[2] or the circumlocution ("Success in Circuit lies"), as if truth were a castle to be sieged. It is not through slow revelation or rerouting, though, that the Zeroes of F284 teach but rather through a logic of negative intu-ition: *if there is an X, there must also be a ~X.* Thus, the "power / . . . Of Opposite," as the poem reveals, pivoting in the nonspace between the two stanzas. But where X and ~X would give us a mathematical nothingness, a zero of "nought," Dickinson's opposites leave a remainder of "ought" (a something) – that surplus knowledge of what still lies beyond what is immediately accessible. The circular character of zero, an Indian symbol, as Alex Bellos writes (not about Dickinson), "was chosen because it portrays the cyclical movements of the face of heaven. Zero means nothing, and it means eternity" (93). It is an empty sign of presence. As a concept, zero was unknown to Greek and Roman mathematicians, for their philosophies could not accommodate a void, and it was refused by medieval Europeans, most likely because of its link to the supposed heretical Arab world. In modernity, however, it is indispensable. "The place value system" – either theoretically

---

2. Helen Vendler (*Dickinson* 432) points out that "gradually"–an alternative adverb Dickinson considers to modify "dazzle" is etymologically linked to *gradus*–the Latin word for "stair-step." One also sees that similar step shape in the visual depiction of the lightning and (without speculating about graphic intentionality) in the Zs of dazzle and overabundance of alliterative Ss.

in decimal columns or practically, say, on an abacus – "requires the concept of a placeholder for instances where there is no quantity in a given column or position" (Bellos 78). Dickinson's "zero," as Mutlu Blasing articulates it, "is neither presence, since it signifies nothing, nor absence, since it is both a number and a word; rather, it proposes a system of delineating and designating presence and absence" (186).[3] " 'Nothing,' " Dickinson herself tells us, "is the force / That renovates the World – " (F1611; J1563; M728).[4]

Over the last generation, Dickinson scholarship has been heavily invested in how readers today ought to approach her poetic alternatives – whether these are different phrasal possibilities she considered on a manuscript page and/or different versions of the same poem kept in her room or sent to different friends and family members. *If there is a Dickinson "text" here, there must be its opposite somewhere else.* To be sure, this has become a Dickinsonian lesson about how we might otherwise understand textuality.[5] An earlier variant of "The Zeroes taught," for a moment eclipsing the one I quoted earlier, offers different lines for the first half of the second stanza: "Of Opposite – to balance Odd– / If White – a Red – must be!" (F284A). The white and red seem without difficulty to mirror the colors of the opening ice and fire. The more curious part of this alternative offers an odd substitutive equivalence: "equal[ing] Ought" for "balanc[ing] Odd." The earlier phrasing, itself a countenance of opposites (even-ing what's odd), returns us to a scale (or scaling) of Zero. "Odd," oddly but not unusually so for Dickinson, occupies its own line on this earlier manuscript page. Whether this is accidental or

---

3. Blasing continues, "[b]oth a letter and a number, the cipher *O* is the key to writing and to counting–both indeed guarded by the Father, the Logos *and* the Banker, who backs symbolic transactions and who himself counts in order to teach the uncountable" (*American* 187). (The patriarchal references are to Dickinson's "I never lost as much but twice–" [F39; J49; M57].) I will further consider Dickinson's sense of the "cipher" later in this chapter.

4. "I'm nobody!" (F260; J288; M128), she relates in another poem, and there is indeed much ado about nothing. Domhnall Mitchell tells us that "doing and saying nothing is what she has to say" (*Monarch* 7), and Sharon Cameron sees Dickinson's verse as "resonant with the presence of what has been given up" (*Lyric* 78).

5. Jerome McGann notes that the variants force "the reader to make a series of recursive shifts in the course of reading. We keep turning back to re-read and reconsider the textual options–to 'better see' what the print conventions of poetry work to keep us from seeing" ("Visible Language" 49). I will return to the critical conversation over Dickinson's variants toward the end of this chapter.

not, or meaningful or not, occupies another slice of the recent Dickinsonian critical pie, as do her calligraphic habits.[6] The handwriting on the earlier manuscript page (serendipitously for my purposes) scribbles "odd" as almost three zeroes (see figure 5.1). At what point, we might ask, does an oddity of circles, oddly alone on a line, become poetically meaningful?[7]

Returning from the ifs of this odd meta-critical circumlocution, I would argue that even the second version of the poem (even in print) is mindful of the visual shape of its zeroes, which take the form of celestial spheres – one blocking the other out in a rare coincidence of elliptical orbits. This hidden

Figure 5.1. Emily Dickinson F284A. *Source:* Emily Dickinson Archive. Used with permission.

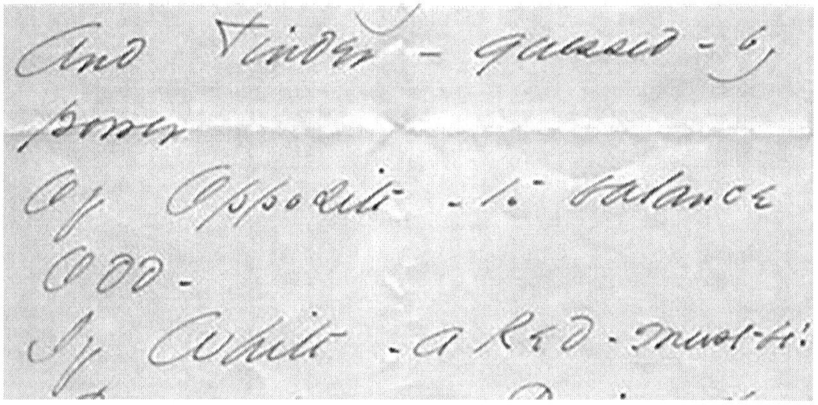

6. Betsy Erkkila summarizes: "Are the line breaks in Dickinson's poems 'intentional visual strategies' as [Susan] Howe has argued or merely matters of 'arbitrary convenience' as R. W. Franklin has argued? Are Dickinson's letters 'literary' letters as [Mabel Loomis] Todd suggested, 'letter-poems' as [Ellen Louise] Hart and [Martha Nell] Smith have argued, 'prose-formatted poems' as [William] Shurr claims, or, as some might argue, simply letters" ("Emily Dickinson Wars" 20). Critiquing Dickinson's editors who "claimed to know the difference" between poems and letters, Virginia Jackson argues that there is "not a difference in genre but a difference between us and everyone else, between personal and personified address" (*Dickinson's Misery* 124, 125). This notwithstanding, Jackson's index still manages to divide Dickinson's letters and poems into two distinct categories. I will return to these critical conversations toward the end of this chapter.

7. Her handwritten "odd" consistently appears as three circles in her other work. One (slight) exception can be found in one of the three existing versions of "Of all the Sounds despatched abroad" where the two Ds of "odd" in the line "in some odd fashion of its own" (F334; J321; M146) are drawn with more of a backbone.

sun generating heat in a manner the speaker of the poem can only anticipate is joined in its thermogenesis by the more terrestrial phosphorus. Easing our famine at her lexicon, the element of phosphorus, as Dickinson knew, is from the Greek for "light-bringing." It "burns in common air with great rapidity; and in oxygen gas, with the greatest vehemence. Even at the common temperature, it combines with oxygen, undergoing a slow combustion and emitting a luminous vapor. It was originally obtained from urine; but it is now manufactured from bones, which consist in part of phosphate of lime" (Webster 1828). Though not yet a neighbor of Oxygen on the periodic table Dmitri Mendeleev would put together soon after Dickinson wrote her poem, phosphorus was known to be combustible in Oxygen (or "O," as its abbreviation had become standardized by the time she was writing). This was not the only poem in which Dickinson, who studied chemistry at Amherst Academy and Mount Holyoke, would link phosphorus (or its bone-mine) to a figuration of zero.

In one of Dickinson's rare published poems, "A narrow Fellow in the Grass" (F1096, J986, M489),[8] the fear of a snake brings an utter disembodied coldness, akin almost to Wallace Stevens's later chilling lines that conclude his "The Snow Man": "And, nothing himself, beholds / Nothing that is not there and the nothing that is" (*CPP* 8). The extra biting coldness in Dickinson comes again by way of opposites. She is not in Stevens's winter and not in Stevens's snow. Her serpentine encounters occur when the sun is at its peak ("more than once at noon"), most likely in the lush summer grass:

> But never met this Fellow
> Attended or alone
> Without a tighter Breathing
> And Zero at the Bone.

---

8. Dickinson was not pleased with one of the printings of this poem, ostensibly because of an editorial decision out of her reach, which added a question mark at the end of the third line. In a letter to Thomas Higginson, she related, "Lest you meet my Snake and suppose I deceive it was robbed of me–defeated too of the third line by the punctuation. The third and fourth were one–I had told you I did not print–I feared you might think me ostensible" (L316). More partial to the possibilities of cultural mediation, Martha Nell Smith–though not specifically absolving Dickinson's specific editor–contends, "In disfiguring poems or letters, editors reproduce their own versions as mediations for readers. . . . [S]uch mediations are part of a reading dynamic" (*Rowing* 8).

In other Dickinson poems, the pseudo-zero of noon like that of midnight (the number before one on the clock) acts as a time of transition – from a nothing to a something, a nought to an ought. Here, though, the zenithed sun and vertical clock hands that come to mind – themselves as if in shock – are contrasted with the snake's circuitous movement on the ground. The oxygen intake (understandably) tightens, as the zero surges through the constricting bloodstream into the bone.

Noting the indeterminacy of Dickinson's verse amid our own anachronistic critical lenses, Domhnall Mitchell writes that "zero can be thought of as the instigation of an incremental sequence . . . or as the lens, the perspective, with and from which things are retroactively understood" ("Introduction" 720).[9] Although Dickinson does not link breath to phosphorus here, she does make the connection explicit in another of her more recognized poems, which, once again, pivots on a somethingness of zero:

> More life – went out – when He went
> Than Ordinary Breath –
> Lit with a finer Phosphor –
> Requiring in the Quench –
>
> A Power of Renowned Cold,
> The climate of the Grave
> A temperature just adequate
> So Anthracite, to live –
>
> For some – an Ampler Zero –
> A Frost more needle keen
> Is necessary, to reduce
> The Ethiop within. . . . (F415; J422; M163)[10]

In contrast to the "Others – [who] extinguish easier," the subject of Dickinson's elegy who is "Lit with a finer Phosphor" cannot be extinguished but with "A Power of Renowned Cold." Dickinson plays with this notion of a degree-zero coldness in her phrasing of "an Ampler Zero" – a zero not of nothingness, but of such power as to reduce the metonymic African heat burning, as she phrases it, within each person, but burning hotter within some more than others.

---

9. He goes on to compare the contour of Dickinson's zero to an Edvard Munch mouth scream and female genitalia.

10. I have not retained Dickinson's spelling of "nescessary."

Ironically, Dickinson here uses "ample" as bountiful – a bountiful zero – but there is also the simple sense of sufficiency, a zero of enough-ness. It is this ampleness of zero – the hopeful critical circling around something we know is there that interests me most. To borrow and twist a phrase of hers, my chapter is an attempt to find out "what puzzled us– / Without the lexicon!" (F264; J246; M130) . . . or maybe with just a little lexicon. In this eclipsed light, it is hard not to take Dickinson's "Ampler Zero" as a precursor of sorts to Wallace Stevens's modernist poetics of "what will suffice."[11]

Dickinson's verse is riddled with – and one doesn't use the colloquial term lightly – meaningful circular forms, which at times, however infrequently, intersect with apostrophic turns of address. Putting aside temporarily, her frequent second-person addresses, severe poetic turns, and her epistolary-poetic forms themselves (or genre, as some of her readers would have it), which each echo part of what is stake in poetic apostrophe, I want to focus for a moment on how she figures and refigures the circular shapes of her natural world. Moons, suns, clockfaces, eyes, rings, wheels, diadems, arcs – these are all common images in her works (as in most verse for thousands of years). But behind the more common symbolic suggestions of these forms, often lies a nuanced exploration of its material shape.

The shape of eyes, for example, in "Like Eyes that looked" (F693; J458; M335) can morph between the zeroes of nothingness and infinity:

> Like Eyes that looked on Wastes –
> Incredulous of Ought
> But Blank – and steady Wilderness –
> Diversified by Night –
>
> Just Infinites of Nought –
> As far as it could see –
> So looked the face I looked upon –
> So looked itself – on Me – . . .

As much as they do thematically, the lines formally play with the idea of a mirror, as in the anaphora of lines seven and eight, which mirror each other. Line 7 mirrors "looked" internally – the word repeated also above and below, hiding its own visual eyes in the double oo of the word. But, as we can see in the intentionally misplaced or delayed rhyme from line two ending line five, something is slightly off. Judith Farr reads the poem

---

11. The phrase, central to Stevens's poetics, comes from his poem "Of Modern Poetry" (*CPP* 218).

as "explor[ing] the fear and joy that characterized Dickinson's memorable [Sapphic] relationship with her sister-in-law," Susan Huntington Gilbert (167). Connecting homosexual love first to the symbolic figure of a circle (102–3) and then to the trope of a mirror, an "exercise in narcissism, the worship and service of one's own body in the body of another" (161), Farr understands the sorrowful lines as essentially the two "would be" queens looking at each other. I tend to understand them as a single speaker, looking into a mirror, seeing oneself as an other (while, perhaps, imagining a lover). Either way, the eyes looking into the mirror or would-be mirror see themselves as wastes, blank, uninhabited. The connection between "ought" and "nought" is made explicitly: if one eye were a circular zero of "nought," two zeroes together would form the sign of infinity, but this would be "Infinites of Nought" rather than an ample infinitude.

In a terrifyingly humorous poem like "A Clock stopped" (F259; J287; M127), Dickinson relocates the circular figure to the intricate details of a Swiss-like clockface:

> A Clock stopped –
> Not the Mantel's –
> Geneva's farthest skill
> Can't put the puppet bowing –
> That just now dangled still –
>
> An awe came on the Trinket!
> The Figures hunched – with pain –
> Then quivered out of Decimals –
> Into Degreeless noon –
>
> It will not stir for Doctor's –
> This Pendulum of snow –
> This Shopman importunes it –
> While cool – concernless No –
>
> Nods from the Gilded pointers –
> Nods from the Seconds slim –
> Decades of Arrogance between
> The Dial life –
> And Him –

The figurines of a cuckoo clock ironically come to life, anthropomorphized in the poem, just as the clock breaks at noon. Despite this poetic empowerment, nothing – not the skilled Swiss, not a doctor, not a shopman – can fix the clock. Helen Vendler sees Dickinson's imagination here as much less humorous than I do and at "its most agitated." She writes, "As [Dickinson] contemplates the corpse – having watched its quivering death agony – she wants to convey both the exquisite workmanship of the body and its inert cold rectangular shape on the deathbed, its loss of all voluntary self-positioning, its indifference to the commercial world importuning it to resume its function, and its refusal to concede to the ministrations of doctors and 'stir' once again" (*Dickinson* 89–90). At the heart of the poem sits "Degreeless noon" – not just zero degrees, a temperature that can go even lower, but rather the absolute zero of a frozen death. "Degree" puns on the segments of a circle: each hour gets its own thirty degrees on the clockface. At noon, with both hands held high, as if in a gesture of surrender, the clock stands at degree zero.[12] The shopman cannot "tune" the clock, so he "importunes" it. The clock, "cool concernless," and not warmed by the mantel, refuses. Its "No," as Vendler makes the point, generates the phonetic openings of the two following lines "Nods from the . . ." – ironically gesturing "yes" – and it is tied to the intricate inner workings of the "Pendulum of sNOw" and mirrored earlier by "Degreeless NOON." I am not quite sure what to make of the poem's "decimals" and "decades" – two nods to a base-ten system – underlying the duodecimal dial. I am also not quite sure to whom the final "Him" refers. Grammatically, it could be the shopman; thematically, the puppet. It is hard not to think of the divine clockmaker here, too, and His metaphorical distance from the "dial life" of His earthly trinkets. This cosmic joke of existence, in Dickinson's hands, can get dark pretty fast, but its etymological punning can also be quite amusing. "Dial" derives from the Latin for day or "*dies*" – another Dickinsonian pun – and it is related to the root "to shine" (hence the connection to the sun-dial – that which derives meaning from the absence of light) and the *rota dialis*, or "daily wheel."[13]

---

12. Noon, rather than the expected midnight, is often the time of numbness for Dickinson. The bells in "It was not death" (F355; J510; M187) "Put out their Tongues, for Noon." There, death would at least provide an ought, a something, but the causeless despair is a degree zero of feeling. On "degree," see also Webster, 1845, 230.

13. Dickinson takes up this trope in other poems, such as "This slow Day" (F1198; J1120; M555), which begins: "This slow Day" moved along– / I heard it's axles go."

The wheel – another significant circular form for this poet – can point to autumn or a hummingbird[14] or, as in "The Outer – from the Inner" (F450; J451; M225), a more metaphorical sense of privacy:

The fine – unvarying Axis
That regulates the Wheel –
Though Spokes – spin – more conspicuous
And fling a dust – the while.

The poem's overarching premise is that one's inner identity (or "mood") determines how one appears to others on the outside.[15] As it phrases things in a circular proportionality, "The Outer – from the Inner / Derives its magnitude." In the second stanza (quoted above), Dickinson plays with the paradox of the wheel.[16] Viewed from the side, the wheel's axis looks like a point. While it controls the whole mechanism of the wheel, it doesn't look like it is moving (close up, it spins). The circle's blustering diameters – the spokes or spokesmen – get all the credit, but that's beside the point. In the final two stanzas, Dickinson more solemnly reframes the poem's premise in terms of an artistic canvas (the inner paints what is outer). A pun on "Arterial Canvas" – the blood behind the work or the embodied representation ties it all to the art-erial (or artistic) process. There is a disjunction between whatever is underlying the creative imagination ("the inner Brand") and what "Its Picture publishes." There must be some symmetry, though, between these two spheres, because in the mysterious final lines, Dickinson suggests that the only way to get at the inner is through reflection: "The Star's whole secret – in the Lake– / Eyes were not meant to know." But there is another circular parallel here at the end: the terrestrial eyes reflecting whatever inner phosphorus burns in the star.

---

14. In "The name–of it–is 'Autumn'" (F465; J656; M233), Dickinson likens the botanical colors of the season to "Vermillion Wheels." In "A Route of Evanescence" (F1489; J1463; M618), she writes of the "revolving Wheel" of the hummingbird.

15. Rather than center itself on the synchrony of inner and outer lives, Dickinson's "When Bells stop ringing" (F601; J633; M274) focuses on the teleological relationship between wheels and circumference: "When Cogs–stop–that's Circumference– / The Ultimate–of Wheels." One cannot help smirking at the stopped "stop" enclosed as it is in the final line. That it parallels the stopped "Church" of the first line might make us rethink for a moment just what is being rung.

16. T.S. Eliot has fun with it too, albeit toward a different spiritual end, in *Burnt Norton*.

17. One can get carried away thinking through all of Dickinson's circular figures–her "Infinities of Nought," which can be just as agonizing as optimistic. Following some unidentified event, "'Twas like a Maelstrom" (F425; J414; M169) offers three terrifying

Eyes, clocks, and circadian wheels notwithstanding,[17] the most auratic of Dickinson's circular forms in both her verse and critical history seems to be her enigmatic "circumference," which, like F450, is also based on the relationship between circular insides and outsides and the space that frames the difference. "My business is circumference" (L268), Dickinson writes in an 1862 letter to Thomas Wentworth Higginson, before labeling herself the only kangaroo – off-balanced with its two os at the end – among the beauty.[18] The word appears over a dozen times in her verse and, when we expand to its circa-cousins – circuit ("going-around"), circumvent ("coming around"), circumspect ("looking around"), circumscribe ("writing around"), circumstance (what is "standing around"), etc. – it is even more frequent. Many of Dickinson's readers have a clearer sense than I do of what the word means for Dickinson, even if their various senses seldom overlap. It is seen as a boundary (either traversable or untraversable), a navigable path in itself, and a vantage point – its own critical range expanding with time and interest: it has now been connected to the romantic sublime,[19] New England praying circles,[20]

---

nightmares, each revolving around a circular form. The first is the feeling of being caught in the narrowing vortex of a maelstrom (from "malen" "stroom" or grinding wheel). The second continues as if the speaker were being tortured in the Paws (or hands) of a Goblin, who is playing with the speaker as if winding a clock. The final nightmare has the speaker being led to the gallows. Such a circular noose returns in a terrifying poem about a suicide, which opens "He scanned it–Staggered– / Dropped the Loop" (F994; J1062; M456). Still torturous, two of Dickinson's poems about a mousing cat also take the circular form in their poetic paws. The cat's eyes widen ("increased to balls") to a metaphorical three dimensions in "She sights a bird" (F351; J507; M185). A companion poem, "The Whole of it came not at once" (F485; J762; M241), has the cat "Murder[ing] by degrees."

18. In other letters to Higginson and the Hollands, her business is "to love" or "to sing." Compare this business of circumference with Dickinson's near-dismissal of the divine in "I got so I could take [hear] his name" (F292; J293; M137) where she refers to her "Business–with the cloud" or with the poet's detective energies ("My business is, to find!") in search of her "priceless Hay" (the heart of whom she is addressing) in "I cautious, scanned my little life–" (F175; J178; M102).

19. In his reading of Dickinson as a poet of the romantic sublime, Gary Lee Stonum writes, " 'circumference' honorifically names the poetic or more precisely the mathetic idea . . . that which through its native powers the mind has been able to grasp" (133).

20. Victoria N. Morgan ties Dickinson's symbolic representations of circles and circumferences to the maternal, hymnal "practices of the praying circle" (173). For her, circumference "serves as a symbol of a divine power that can be traced but not contained" (175). Dickinson's acerbic dismissal of such social gatherings in "What Soft–Cherubic Creatures–" (F675; J401; M418) would seem to push back on Morgan's reading.

feminist critique,[21] the figuration of influence,[22] Antipodean contexts for American literature,[23] and Eastern philosophy.[24] William Sherwood, one of the earliest critics to treat the term as a deeper Dickinsonian thematic, saw it as an "extension of the figure from mortal consciousness into the immortal sphere" (220; qtd. in Giles 11). Other early critics, such as David T. Porter, Albert J. Gelpi, Robert Gillespie, and Zacharias Thundyil follow Sherwood in linking Dickinson's circumference to a transcendental, romantic, and explicitly Emersonian world. Gelpi sees circumference as "signif[ying] ecstasy in its expansiveness, in its self-contained wholeness, in its self-ordered coherence" (123), while, for Gillespie, who understands Dickinson as a "conventionally religious poet" (258), circumference "swells out to encompass time and space. Circumference is her image for the powerful, totally absorbed, circumscribed experience" (256).[25] An Emersonian poetical metaphysics infuses the word for Thomas Johnson, for whom circumference means "a projection of [Dickinson's] imagination into all relationships of man, nature and spirit" (140).

Although Audrey Rodgers and David Estes agree that circumference is related to Dickinson's "function as an artist" (Rodgers 16), they are more circumspect in always assuming an optimistic reading. For Rodgers, circumference designates "the boundary that separates that which she could perceive and that which lay beyond the horizon-beyond-reach – the limit of human understanding" (22). In the end, though, this epistemological limit does find romantic "achievement . . . in the inner world of the artist" (16).[26] Rather

---

21. The opening line of "Circumference thou Bride of Awe" (F1636; J1620; M648) might recall Keats's "bride of quietness"–the ambiguous opening of his "Ode on a Grecian Urn"–where it is uncertain if the "of" of "Bride of Awe" is one of possession or identity. It is clear, though, that Dickinson's speaker is addressing circumference herself, the unambiguously gendered bride. The "de-mastering" circularity of the figure, according to Lissa Holloway-Attaway's Kristevan approach, implies a "resistance to linearity [which] allows [Dickinson] to de-structure the hierarchical, biased, and binary codes of the patriarchal formula for success" (183–84).

22. Annette Gilson reads Dickinson's circumference alongside John Ashbery's "Clepsydra." Circumference, in her words, "functions as a kind of emblem for the movement in much of her work from the expectable, quotidian world to the bizarre or otherworldly" (489).

23. See Giles, " 'The Earth reversed her Hemispheres': Dickinson's Global Antipodality."

24. Yanbin Kang offers a transcultural perspective based on Chinese philosophy, and Midori Andō traces the parallel influence of the idea of circumference on modern Japanese faith.

25. "The world of spirit," Gillespie writes, "is the world of meaning" (255). Contra to any materialist understanding of circumference, he sees it in an Emersonian vein as "a limitless expansion away, a radiation in all directions, with her at its center" (255).

26. Rodgers references Charles Anderson who sees Dickinson as "radiating outward toward infinity from the center of poetic experience" (qtd. in Rodgers 16–17).

than being a radiating center of transcendental knowledge, Dickinson, for Estes is able to center herself as a poet in the middle of the circle by finding where the diameters of intersect (212). Laura Gribbin argues convincingly against transcendental understandings, even those that recognize human limits to knowledge. For her, Dickinson's liminal figuring of circumference offers "a powerful critique of Romanticism" (4).[27] It is "not the means to a sublime end but is at once the source and terminus of poetic discourse, marking the perimeter beyond which language, thought, and 'awe' cannot penetrate" (2). Instead, it becomes the experienced if not completely understandable "space within a circle where life is lived, pain is felt, and death is observed" (2). Reading Dickinson against an Emersonian poetical metaphysics, Gribbin sees the Amherst poet as rejecting the idea "that humankind can transcend material reality to become 'past or particle of God'" (1; quoting Emerson's "Nature"). Still, such an imagination becomes "a potent poetic source" (13).

Fortunately, it is difficult to find a rigid consistency to circumference across Dickinson's verse. In "The Poets light but lamps" (F930; J883; M436) circumference is presented as a marker of poetic influence. The poem tells us that "Each Age [is] a Lens / Disseminating their / Circumference." Poets perish but their work – if vital – continues on, expanding outward in the next age, as if it were the light of a lamp. In another poem, circumference is presented not as an enduring vital force but as the journey of an aimless, evanescent existence.[28] Dickinson's "From Cocoon forth a Butterfly" (F610; J354; M300) compares the figure to the "miscellaneous Enterprise" of an insect's life.[29] The butterfly "To Nowhere – seemed to go / In purposeless Circumference– / As 'twere a Tropic Show." "Tropic" connects the warm, colorful climates metaphorically painted onto the butterfly wing to poetic troping, each a show in its own way. The journey of life might be purposeless, but it is difficult not to understand it here, however anachronistically, as if

---

27. "Circumference is not simply a defense mechanism designed to protect the self," she writes. "It is also an offensive strategy that blocks the acquisitive, appropriative, and omnipotent urge of the Romantic 'I'" (4).

28. "Behind Me–dips Eternity" (F743; J721; M373) portrays one's existence, "the Term between" Eternity and Immortality, as a type of circumference.

29. Compare this poem to the Icarus-like butterfly-lovers of "Two Butterflies went out at noon" (F571; J533; M610) who "espied Circumference / And caught a ride with him." They flew too far through circumference that "Gravitation missed them" and they were pulled into the sun. In an earlier alternative version (or a different poem with the same initial line, composed and fascicled fifteen years earlier), circumference is replaced with firmament: "Then stepped straight through the Firmament / And rested, on a Beam–" (M260).

she meant it in a twentieth-century French Existentialist sense. Poets – and those who write about them – like to exaggerate the peaks of being, but it is often the smaller moments, like a butterfly flitting by, that seem to endow a life with meaning. The moment of existence writ small, for Dickinson, often overshadows the bigger metaphysical ideas, even something akin to the wholeness of circumference. In "An ignorance a Sunset" (F669; J552; M317), circumference itself can be decayed by a sublime evening moment. Dickinson also plays with other figures for circumference – such as the "orchard for a dome" in "Some keep the sabbath" (F236; J324; M115) or the webbed "Arc of White" in "A Spider sewed at Night" (F1163; J1138; M705) – as well as other meaningful spatial positionings.[30]

Even though Percy Shelley would remind us in his *Defence of Poetry* that "[p]oetry is at once the centre and circumference of knowledge" (656), Dickinson's readers still seem either to want to peek over the perimeter of circumference or otherwise look to what hides in the center. Some see this inside (akin to how Dickinson often writes about "circuit") as constraining, while others, like Gribbin, extol the center as the space of lived experience. In a letter to Elizabeth Holland (1884), Dickinson writes, "All grows strangely emphatic, and I think if I should see you again, I sh'd begin every sentence with 'I say unto you –' The Bible dealt with the Centre, not the Circumference –" (L850). In "Each life converges to some Centre" (F724; J680; M362), the movement toward the center means the attainment of an ultimate goal. Jay Leyda and Vivian Pollak both write of Dickinson's "omitted center."[31] In Pollak's phrasing, "One has the sense of an omitted center – of a single traumatic narrative or of many traumatic narratives pressing against the language and needing to be recovered" ("Introduction" 6). Similarly, in her monumental *Lyric Time*, Sharon Cameron talks about "an absent or invisible order that is invoked as 'Immortality' or alluded to as Centre" (1). Cameron's centering of the center aligns well with logocentric critique, the deconstructive decentering of its time. Decentering the center, yet again, Elisa New critiques the Romantic leaning of Dickinson's earlier critics who "take as axiomatic that Dickinson seeks a kind of timeless

---

30. Is the corner of "I saw my Life a Loaded Gun" (F764; J754; M354) a figure for circumference because it is around the center of the room or dissimilar to circumference because of its unrounded edge?

31. Weisbuch and Orzeck cite Jay Leyda, who writes of Dickinson's "omitted center" in *The Years and Hours of Emily Dickinson*, 2 volumes, Yale UP, 1960 (qtd. in Weisbuch and Orzeck 2).

transcendental signified" through the "pursuit of an elusive center" (3, 4). New sees Dickinson, instead, situated "more riskily, on the circumference" because so much of her greatest poetry happens . . . when furthest from its own center" (4).[32] As New cautions, the danger remains of taking circumference as Dickinson's (and our) own centering figure, thereby risking "the Devil's transgressions, his imitations of God from the vantage point of circumference" (24). Given that both the centripetal and centrifugal forces pulling at Dickinson's circumference can make sense given its individual poetic context, I tend to like the idea of wandering around her center, which typifies her periphrastic choices and the similarly periphrastic process of reading her in our own time.

While the focus for scholars studying Dickinson's circumference seems to be whether it is Emersonian or anti-Emersonian (and the literary tradition of an ample nation that comes with it), other questions abound. *Is what is inside it what matters or what is outside it? Is the center (as we tend to see a circle) actually inside the circumference or, in a Calvinist sense, is it what is all around, without limit? If it is the latter, do we have access to it? If it is the former, can we do more than circle around it? Where is Dickinson's speaker or Dickinson herself, and from where are we reading and thinking about this all? Does circumference (unlike that of a circle, mathematically speaking) have a width or is it simply a limit without extension in space?*[33] Because Dickinson is more often a poet exploring an idea rather than constantly pontificating

---

32. Despite returning to the circle's circumference, New finds Kierkegaard a better model than Emerson for Dickinson's "hard wandering": "Emerson's thrust of self-reliance will give way to Kierkegaardian instability" (10). New turns to Dickinson's "It always felt to me–a wrong" (F521; J597; M255), where Dickinson pities Moses, who is left on the circumference of Canaan, as it were. For different reasons, Mutlu Blasing also sees Dickinson as a centrifugal poet. Dickinson's poetic variants demonstrate "that she proceeded not by getting closer to some blueprint and controlling her inflections but by moving farther away from a center. Thus the line between logic and illogic, between the legal and the illegal production of meaning, and between the spoken Logos and the written 'logarithm' becomes the very axis Dickinson's poems spin on" (*American* 180).

33. Mathematicians and (some) sophomoric undergraduates seeking a neat poster to hang in their dorm rooms will occasionally turn to a visual representation of what is called the Mandelbrot set (undiscovered in Dickinson's time). One of the many odd features of this fractal set is that its circumference differs depending on whether one measures it from within (inside the boundary) or without (outside the boundary), an inconsistency that ought to be a mathematical impossibility. This is because a mathematical circumference is a limit without extension.

about it, many of these questions will be answered differently poem to poem or even within a poem. But a poem like "She staked Her Feathers – Gained an Arc – " (F853; J798; M392) might show us a little how the questions come together (and waft apart):

> She staked Her Feathers – Gained an Arc –
> Debated – Rose again –
> This time – beyond the estimate
> Of Envy, or of Men –
>
> And now, among Circumference –
> Her steady Boat be seen –
> At home – among the Billows – As
> The bough where she was born –

In its triumphant feminist assertiveness, it is hard not to understand the third-person narratee as a figure for Dickinson (who often be-feathers herself). Her public act of "stak[ing]" is an unexpected image, given her well-known proclivity for privacy – this notwithstanding the frequency to which she writes to public figures – but it does mark her claim to a certain (poetic, one imagines) ground. This grounding, however, would seem to not be terrestrial, as the narratee rises into another sphere by gaining arcs, as if martyred debate were the method by which one completes the circle. Having achieved this boundary, she is now not only out of sight but more-over away from the estimation – what can be understood and perhaps more importantly judged – of what is here a very male public sphere.

The "Billows" of circumference – waves generating arcs around a center of impact – can suggest a measure of freedom at one moment and a threat at the next. In the lighthearted "A Single Clover Plank" (F1297; J1343; M571), a bee seeks sanctuary from a storm between the firmament of the sky and the firmament of the ground. This dangerous, billowing circum-ference ends up menacing the bee until a leaf of the clover plant, an "idly swaying plank," provides a temporary refuge. The clover is "Responsible to nought." It is outside any ethical obligations (plants, as far as we can tell, haven't yet read their Kant) or, alternatively, it *is* responsible to the "nought" – the empty space of a circumference delineated as the in-between two firmaments. It is a "harrowing" event for the bee, as Dickinson puns on the earth-shattering "harrow," who is saved not by circumference but by the clover plank – another joke likening the relief of a clover leaf to a piece of discarded driftwood, like Ishmael's coffin.

"A Coffin – is a small Domain" (F890; J943; M424), Dickinson tells us in a bitter poem, comparing the material containment after death to the boundlessness of an afterlife Paradise. In the second stanza, the coffin becomes a grave "restrict[ing] Breadth" – a gasping pun – yet it is "ampler" than the embodied, divine Sun and terrain it shines upon. The knowledge of the afterlife can't comfort the grieving friend; instead, it brings "Circumference without Relief." It is the infinitude of the circumferent grief – no estimate, no end – that won't allow the closure that even a coffin could bestow. Still, even in this immeasurable sea, Dickinson can revel in the unrestrained possibilities of language. For the reader who takes communion in her breadth/breath pun, her promise of "Repose" – being able to rest, as if a horizontal corpse – might help ease one off one's otherwise inconsolable feet.

Around the corner from Dickinson's circumference lies "circuit." In a poem like "He put the belt around my life" (F330; J273; M144), "circuit," which will, in another poem, be linked to success, becomes here like a prison:

> He put the Belt around my life –
> I heard the Buckle snap –
> And turned away, imperial,
> My Lifetime folding up –
> . . . Henceforth – a Dedicated sort –
> A Member of the Cloud –

The striking sadomasochistic opening depends on a visceral disjunction – confusing life with an actual waist (or, more horrifyingly, neck) or otherwise metaphorizing what reads as a very tangible, very violent belt. The rest of the first stanza confirms that the buckle snaps closed (rather than snaps broken), as the speaker seems numbed to her new "dedicated" place as "Member of the Cloud." The pun on "Dedicated" – on the one hand devoted, on the other allocated to – underscores the coerced nature of the attached arrangement. The poem compares a life committed to God to the confinement of a domestic household, whose tedium becomes apparent in the second stanza:

> Yet not too far to come at call –
> And do the little Toils
> That make the Circuit of the Rest –
> And deal occasional smiles. . . .

The belt's constricting ring is matched in this stanza by the formalities of domestic obligation – here, the "Circuit of the Rest," as if life (however

privileged, as one would see it now) amounted tediously to closing the circle.[34] Midway through the stanza, there is an odd spatial displacement. The
speaker ought to be in the metaphorical sky, but the neighbors who come
to visit are the "lives that stoop to notice mine" – an (unwelcome) gesture
reminiscent of divine condescension – rather than the reverse from someone
who must have short-circuited her gold-star membership in the cloud.

The tedious cell of existence is again likened to a circuit, but perhaps
more optimistically or at least more realistically in "A Prison gets to be a
friend" (F456; J652; M229). If, early on in life, the possibilities of circumference seem endless in a promising way, the poem seems to suggest that when
one is older one gives up such hope "For something passiver – Content" and
gives up splashing in the pools for something simpler: "a Demurer Circuit
/ A Geometric Joy – ." This poem, like many, many others plays upon the
horizontal and vertical lines we have access to – diameters of sorts – somehow connected to, but still far away from circumference.[35] "We come to
look with gratitude," she writes, possibly punning on gratus/gradus, "For
the appointed Beam" – light coming through the oubliette of heaven. "[T]
he Planks– / That answer to Our feet –" offer a poetically resonating linear
walkway. There is room to move, even in this prison. We have no ability
to escape our circuited lives, so we might as well appreciate what we have.
Although the poem concludes with cynicism toward undelivered promises
of heaven ("If That – indeed – redeem – "), Dickinson is still able to find
ampleness in the arc she calls "the narrow Round."

---

34. The feeling recalls the "Blank to Blank / Threadless Way" and "Mechanic feet" of
F484 (J761; M241) and the iambic second stanza of the more familiar "After great pain"
(F372; J341; M198). Here is the latter: "The Feet, mechanical, go round– / A Wooden
way / Of Ground, or Air, or Ought– / Regardless grown, / A Quartz contentment, like
a stone–." In F372, the numbness is tied to inertia in the poetic process ("The Feet")
and pencil writing ("A Wooden way"; "the Hour of Lead"), and the poet once again
figures things through a metaphorical clock ("A Quartz contentment"; "the Hour of
Lead") and (what one takes to mean) the zero-degree coldness at the end.

35. The horizon of "The Road was lit" (F1474; J1450; M614) is illuminated by "magic
perpendiculars," and "On a columnar self" (F740; J789; M371) exalts the unbending,
unround "Rectitude" of the immovable columnar self (perhaps a refence to poetic columns also). "The Angle of a Landscape" (F578; J375; M264) teases out various linear
forms in the field of vision: coffin, chimney steeple, finger, ample crack. Rather than
being naturally opposed to the circle, the linear, diameter lines form the angular joint
that allows for the round arc of circumference.

The relationship between Dickinson's "circumference" and "circuit" isn't always certain. If circumference designates a perimeter (accessible or inaccessible, finite or infinite), "circuit" usually means the literal or metaphorical movement around something. Sometimes the two seem to overlap, other times one overtakes the other.[36] In "I should have been too glad" (F283; J313; M346), various circular forms are at play amid a circumlocution that winds up saying (perhaps part sarcastically, part earnestly) that it is better that things weren't too easy because then the reward wouldn't have been as good: "Defeat whets Victory" as, ahem, "they say." Here, circuit is once more a limited part of circumference. But if things had been otherwise, Dickinson wonders:

> I should have been too glad, I see –
> Too lifted – for the scant degree
> Of Life's penurious Round –
> My little Circuit would have shamed
> This new Circumference – have blamed –
> The homelier time behind –

Punning again on degree as a division of a circle, Dickinson calls out the cycle of life for being greedy about sharing its curve. Noting that Dickinson's whole poetic enterprise depends on such amplitude, Gribbin optimistically writes, "This circumference, as the domain of poetry, must be protected from the homogenizing influence of eternity" (12). Dickinson gives voice or, rather, presence, to the earthly form of such a homogenizing influence in the next stanza when the first stanza's circuit turns into prayer:

---

36. I am less confident than Audrey Rodgers in the ability always to distinguish between the two. Rodgers writes, "Dickinson does not use the term to suggest a bounded enclosure. The narrow circle of experience she called 'circuit'" (17). Cynthia Hallen explores the complicated relationship between the two, noting when they appear synonymous or when "circuit" is being treated as something like "circumlocution." Usually circumference–with all its majesty–has the wider scope, but sometimes the more terrestrial circuit wins the day. "The Brain–is wider than the sky–" (F598; J632; M273) offers a metaphorical contrast between the two, favoring the metaphorically inestimable space of the (thought of) smaller and contained brain. Still, if one were to understand the circumference as the inner space of thought, the hierarchy would be reversed.

> I should have been too saved – I see –
> Too rescued – Fear too dim to me
> That I could spell the Prayer
> I knew so perfect – yesterday –
> That Scalding One – Sabachthani –
> Recited fluent – here –

The lines invoke Christ's words from Psalm 22, when he directly addresses God, asking why he has been abandoned: *Eli, Eli, Lama Sabachthani? My God, my God, why hast Thou forsaken me?* The apostrophe, originally a moment of supposed pure Presence (Christ talking to God – so with even more flavoring on the Presence), loses a bit of its lustre in iteration. Here, Dickinson offers an iteration of an iteration, referencing the verse prayer in verse.[37] The apostrophic act of prayer, the turn away from the world to address God, recreates that gesture of the initial apostrophe – what, as considered in my introduction, Jonathan Culler identified as a discursive speech act rather than narrative representation. But Dickinson does something interesting here, in referencing her own speech act of "yesterday." The initial lines of the first three stanzas of the poem all end "I see –" while the fourth and final stanza concludes its initial line with "they say –." One is a personal (lyric, if you will) present moment invoking sight (even if we understand "see" as "understand"), and the other is a pedestrian generality (like a verse, repeated by rote). One is about what can be seen (again, even if this is offered idiomatically), the other about what is said. For prayer to "work" (I have been told), it must be uttered aloud or mutedly – though phonetically – articulated in the mind. Hence apostrophe, hence presence. Dickinson's stanza, though, in the block quotation above, moves back and forth between prayer as utterance and prayer as text. "Spell[ing]" the prayer means offering it as an incantation, but it also means graphically

---

37. Dickinson is at her most dismissive of prayer in "Prayer is the little implement" (F623; J437; M306), where prayer is shown to be an apostrophic failure: "Where Presence – is denied them – / [Men] fling their Speech" toward God's anthropomorphic ear, but it is unlikely he hears or listens. Dickinson is also quite dismissive of prayer in "At least – to pray" (F377; J502; M200) and "Of Course – I prayed" (F581; J376; M265), but less so in "My period had come for Prayer" (F525; J564; M289). In this last poem, the inability to find an anthropomorphic God leaves Dickinson in silent worship, if not prayer itself. Even there, though, she cannot help but get carried away by the wonderful capriciousness of language and unpredictability of verse form: "prayer" phonetically turns into God's "Vast Prairies of Air," which though "Unbroken" in Calvinist spirit are broken by a stanzaic turn.

spelling it out on a page. She claims she knew it perfectly yesterday (as if that were the day that needed it most), which seems to imply that it isn't known as perfectly today. She deictically notes which prayer ("That . . . one"), but then in naming it on the page claims that she has "recited" it "here"—again on the page, and fluently so. However, its textual rather than vocative presence means that we cannot hear what Dickinson has immortalized as a claim of prayer until we read it ourselves, thereby performing, even mutedly in our minds, an absent poet's words.

The final stanza of the poem reiterates the central idea of living within the circuit and yet having an appetite for circumference. Beggars, Dickinson tells us, can appreciate banquets best, and it is thirsting that "vitalizes Wine." In spite of all the sheepish "Kingdom of the Poor" rhetoric, the poem seems to give way in the final, bitter line, which, almost begging, states, "Faith bleats to understand." In the manuscript for F283C, Dickinson thought about changing the line to "Faith faints to understand." The playful anagrammatic possibility gives way in the other versions to "bleats," which shears at the 23rd Psalm. "Bleats" is a meaningless utterance, yet one that vocalizes an almost bodily need—here, to understand what feels like a forsaking. In another variant of the poem (283B), part of a letter sent to Sue and signed "Emily," Dickinson places "Faith" in quotation marks.

Compared to the rest of the script, the "to" pushed toward the margin of the penultimate line looks to be under erasure. It would be as if anthropomorphized Faith were itself bleating "understand." And yet, such preaching

Figure 5.2. Emily Dickinson F283B. *Source:* Emily Dickinson Archive. Used with permission.

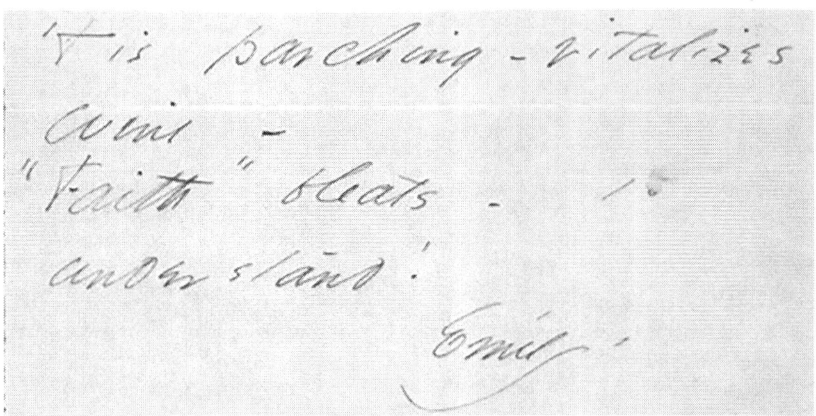

from the vantage point of knowledge is not within Faith's ken. Wandering around in circles, Faith attempts to understand the circuit of one's life, the divine plan, but it can only endure and, in doing so, moan. Perhaps the life of suffering makes one value heaven more or perhaps one ought to question whether such faith without understanding is worth it in the end.

Before jumping along the circle to Dickinson's apostrophic addresses, I wanted briefly to touch on two poems which also link circumference to an idea of presence. "At Half past Three" (F1099; J1084; M491) tracks the clock time of an early morning, beginning with a bird singing hesitatingly, at first, and then being the unmatched voice in the sky. The final stanza concludes:

> At Half past Seven
> Element nor implement be seen
> And Place was where the Presence was
> Circumference between

With the bird gone as day approaches, circumference is shown to spatially occupy the temporal gap between the earlier musical "Presence" and the empty "Place" it is now. As Gribbin underscores it, Dickinson is "not concerned with experiencing the sublime but with the effect of its absence on the imaginative process" (14). Each stanza begins "At half past" (not something-thirty) as if the clock hand were already in the place between – circumference – for a speaker called away from the window for an unknown reason at the hour.

Dickinson opens another poem, a very enigmatic one: "Crisis is a Hair / Toward which forces creep" (F1067; J889; M478). Thinness and slowness are invoked but toward what end? Whether an event turns into a crisis or not may depend on something as delicate or inadvertent as a hair. The second stanza, "Nicely balancing" between life and death, invokes a suspension of breath (the word in the same place as "hair" was in the first stanza), perhaps punning on the phrase a "hair's breadth" and making us wonder whether averting a crisis entails escaping by this idiomatic means[38]:

---

38. The pun on a "hair's breath" (without the "d"), would connect the spatial idiom to a moment of embodied terror. Dickinson uses the embodied idiom "by a hair" to full effect in "That after Horror" (F243; J286; M129), a poem which anthropomorphizes "Conjecture's presence."

> To suspend the Breath
> Is the most we can
> Ignorant is it Life of Death
> Nicely balancing –

Against the expected even-line rhymes, "Breath" and "Death" oddly rhyme in the first and third lines of this stanza. The rest of the poem continues to explore the smallest instances of time and space, before taking a peculiar turn:

> Let an instant push
> Or an Atom press
> Or a Circle hesitate
> In Circumference
>
> It may jolt the Hand
> That adjusts the Hair
> That secures Eternity
> From presenting – Here –

The pressure from infinitesimal time (the instant) or infinitesimal space (the Atom) parallel the opening hair and the creeping forces. In the concluding lines, Eternity is kept away from the present stage, called "– Here –" as if this conspicuously isolated word were like an X on a map at a mall. Yet this deictic gesture of presence is now what has become eternalized. The lines between these two infinities – one moving inward toward the atomic, the other outward to eternity – similarly unsettle, just as they do in another poem of hers.[39] If we were to understand "hand" once more as indicating a clockface, the puzzling "circle . . . in circumference" might be read as a clock pendulum. Any slight adjustment to this hair, balancing life, could trigger the crisis – "Eternity" or, less euphemistically, death, which would "present" as absence. The poem notes not just the circular pendulum within its circumferent arc but moreover its "hesitat[ion]" – that instant it reaches

---

39. A comparable scene is staged in "The Admirations–and Contempts"–of time" (F830; J906; M409). Here, the speaker is positioned between curved lenses, which become spatial markers of the infinities of time: the "Convex–and Concave Witness" of eternity. Dickinson's linguistically convex pun on "contempt" and con-temps (against-time) cannot be overlooked.

its limit and has to turn back. "Hesitate," derived from *haesito*, as Dickinson's dictionary noted, relates to a stammer in speech: words turned into phonemes, coming out wrong (Webster 1845, 410). Just as "crisis," with a pen's push, can turn into "circle," so, by a hair's breadth, can "Hand" turn into "Hair" turn into "Here." Understanding cannot be isolated from the lyric hesitations and missteps of poetic language that constitute it.

If my search for Dickinson's ampler zero has circled around but not located a center to her apostrophic gestures, I would say that this is not entirely my fault. Faith Barrett writes, "Dickinson rarely uses the figure [of dramatic apostrophe] and uses the apostrophe to a reading public only ironically; her work might seem like an improbable place to look for ideas about the relationship between the lyric and the public speaking circuit" (92, fn10).[40] The difficulty is not that Dickinson isn't concerned with notions of "presence" or with lyric addresses or unexpected turns or breathing life into absent beings or having the dead speak,[41] but that they rarely come together as one would expect. As she might have said it herself, "I know the Whole – obscures the Part / The fraction – that appeased the Heart."

Dickinson makes use of address more often than the specifically apostrophic address. Most of these are to an unspecified "you" – as in the unknown but painfully tangible "you" of "I cannot live with you" (F706; J640; M343), the impersonal "you" of "You'll find – it when you try to die" (F441; J610; M221), or even the "you" who is a nobody of "I'm nobody! Who are you?" (F260; J288; M128). But there are other addresses, too, including to a goblin, a letter, the month of March, and, as delightfully penned through a fly's letter, to a bee.[42] Dickinson also won't hesitate in employing an address only to dismiss

---

40. For Barrett, these historical contexts show that Dickinson "disrupts [John Stuart] Mill's model" of lyric address (70). She writes that Dickinson's "work illuminates changes in the stances of the lyric self, changes which result in part from the crisis of a nation divided by war" (68). Noting the "lack of reciprocity in the scene of the lyric address" (72), Barrett turns to Dickinson's F519 (J441; M254) ("This is my letter to the World / That never wrote to Me") to "emphasize the oxymoronic status of the lyric as 'written utterance'" (70). See also Bryan C. Short, who traces Dickinson's knowledge of rhetorical forms and then examines different aspects of her rhetorical apostrophe.

41. The most famous of the last instance would have to be Dickinson's "I heard a Fly buzz – when I died" (F591; J465; M270), which also features the textbook example of onomatopoeia (a speech act, unifying word and thing as "presence").

42. "The Soul has bandaged moments" (F360; J512; M190); "Going to Him [Her/ them]! Happy letter!" (F277; J494; M529); "Dear March – Come in" (F1320; J1320; M577); "Bee! I'm expecting you!" (F983; J1035; M453).

the person it is summoning: "Art thou the thing I wanted? / Begone" (F1311; J1282; M574). Very often, what is at stake in such an address is troped in the very same poem. For instance, the address to a generalized but absent "you" of "You know that Portrait in the Moon" (F676; J504; M418) comes along with an extended anthropomorphizing of the moon, as if breathing life into one depended on breathing life into the other.

It is difficult to ignore the relationship between the epistolary form and apostrophe.[43] Although he doesn't name the trope, Martin Orzeck's words fit some of Dickinson's correspondence well: "Dickinson conceived of letter writing as an imaginative exercise through which the writer might project herself into the absent one's presence for the duration of her discourse" ("Dickinson's Letters" 137). Dickinson's private letters can also be seen as types of unheard utterances with addressees, even considering her contemporary culture of letter exchange that was more public (passed letters were recited aloud to others) than it generally is now. The epistolary form that informed Dickinson's verse itself can also be thought of (and has) as a type of address. Within this form, one will find textual addresses (within poems) and extra-textual ones—addresses to her contemporary readership who didn't actually read her work, to her actual circle of friends who did, and, possibly, to a century and a half of readers since her posthumous publication. In addition, recent Dickinsonian criticism has addressed how her poetic addresses were much more political than either ideas of lyric privacy or images of a woman self-secluding in her room would suggest.[44]

---

43. This relationship would carry over to Dickinsonian poetics as well. Against the more common scholarly practice of trying to understand how Dickinson's poems influenced her letter writing, Cindy MacKenzie seeks to "determine the extent to which fundamental elements of Dickinson's poetics emerge from and are inflected by the properties of epistolary" (13).

44. Barrett reads Dickinson's work, however "skeptically and tentatively" it may be, as a manner of apostrophic address to the nation (67). Shira Wolosky makes the point that one is taught to read Dickinson as a private poet to the detriment of her public engagement. She writes, "Dickinson's relationship to audience is . . . deeply inscribed in her acts of writing" and idea of herself as a poet, even without publication ("Public" 130 n. 23). Andrea Brady is more cautious in celebrating the poet in this regard. Brady finds the "wound" of slavery in Dickinson's poetic gaps, but does not see the poet's radical poetics mirroring a radical progressivism: the "oblique poems about the Civil War . . . [show] no sympathy to enslaved people" (177; 173). On this topic, see also Wolosky, *Emily Dickinson: A Voice of War* (Yale UP, 1984), Miller's *Reading in Time*, and Pollak's edited collection *A Historical Guide to Emily Dickinson*.

Most of Dickinson's semiapostrophic "O"s are written as "Oh"s—textually represented realizations, which turn and perform (what we would see today as) a lyric presence sometimes, though not always, with an address to the absent other. We see this "Oh" in "One Year ago—jots what?" (F301; J296; M142)—a stunning poem, that varies stanza length as it jumps between pentameter and dimeter, iambs and spondees, medial caesura and unexpectedly enjambed lines. The poem begins in pseudo-narrative form and right away loses itself. *What does one year ago mean?* she asks, playing on the double-sense of "jot" to draw her own poetic scribbling about its possible meaning into the picture. The first stanza gets similarly frustrated by her own hermeneutic inabilities. She stops and starts, asks questions and apostrophizes to God to "spell the word!" she can't, thereby connecting divine incantation, where saying means doing, to graphic writing. At first, she thinks that "Grace" might be the magical word, but rejects that in favor of "Glory," which still isn't the perfect word but, instead, an ample one: "That—will do." In the one extant manuscript version, Dickinson wonderfully considers replacing "That—will do" with "'Twas just you." In doing so, she highlights "external" to the poem the poem's own cautious acts of poetic spelling and makes a search for poetic ampleness its own paratextual form. Across the next two stanzas, she projects "Such anniversary"—etymologically, *annus-versus*, the "turning" of the year—into a circumference of sorts, an imagined, eternal future and actual past. The future time together she calls a banquet and admits that she didn't know the past feast together would only come one (metaphorical) time:

> I tasted—careless—then—
> I did not know the Wine
> Came once a World—Did you?
> Oh, had you told me so—
> This Thirst would blister—easier—now—
> You said it hurt you—most—
> Mine—was an Acorn's Breast—
> And could not know how fondness grew
> In Shaggier Vest—. . .

After comparing hurts (*"I miss you more"* . . . *"No, I miss you more"* . . .), she offers as an odd metaphor her and (presumably) his respective chests. (His is hairy and hers is small, rounded, and possibly armored, like an acorn.) She admits that had he pursued her a year earlier they would have met "eye to eye." Was it because she was still a child ("No Acorn – then"), she wonders, before connecting inspiration to the mouth taking in air: "We breathed– / Then dropped the Air." In the final stanza, she claims with certainty that she is old enough now and wonders how soon they will be able to reunite. *Will it be one more year or ten*, she asks? Faced with the choice, she opts for "None," cutting out the "1" from "10" and leaving 0.[45]

I am still circling.

*   *   *

I like to imagine the look on Emily Dickinson's face, seeing my agonized attempts to make this chapter whole. I am in trouble.

The very un-lyric sounding Dickinson poem Ralph Franklin numbers as 240 and lineates into two quatrains begins:

> Bound a Trouble – and Lives will bear it –
> Circumscription – enables Wo –
> Still to anticipate – Were no limit –
> Who were sufficient to Misery? (F240; J269; M371)

On the whole, the poem is an address of sorts – someone speaking to an unnamed and un-present other or, otherwise, more circumspectly to herself, but without the signature turn of the apostrophic address. The more one circles around the language, the message – if never straightforward – seems to clear its path. Unbounded trouble is unbearable.[46] Set or find its limit, and people, as

---

45. Mutlu Blasing calls attention to Dickinson's playful seriousness with how one and zero make ten. F646 (J545; M326) begins: "'Tis One by One–the Father counts– / And then a Tract between / Set Cypherless–to teach the Eye / The Value of it's Ten–. . . ." Blasing writes, "According to such binary logic, One + o = 10, and the poet's business is properly a 'logarithm' (Logos + rhythm)–a lettering and an accounting, an engraving and a rhythm. The *O* that is a letter and a number connect the two systems; it is the quintessential cipher *and* a gap, a blank, a 'cypherless' 'tract.' It adds nothing to 'One' ('1' and "I"), infuses a self-contained presence with absence, and liberates it to create the word" (*American* 187).

46. The apparent endlessness of unbounded pain is taken up in "Pain–expands the Time–" (F833; J967; M410), where Dickinson accuses pain of expanding the "Minute circumference / Of a single Brain." There might be a pun, here, on minute (as small) and minute (as a small segment of a clock hour). Gribbin sees the poem as "challeng[ing] autonomy of time by naming circumference, which marks the limits of perception, as its

she says, will be able to bear it. It is not the binding of, say, Isaac, but rather a covenant that pain will eventually come to an end. The ambiguous second line at first seems to suggest its opposite: the act of circumscription causes woe; but, given the context here, the line more readily echoes the first: the closing off of circumscription allows for woe to be endured.[47] Trouble becomes woe becomes the more enigmatic, more indiscernible "misery." The proportions among the three aren't immediately apparent. Are these parallel sentiments of grief or a circular wave of agony emanating outward in circumferential vastness as much as it spirals inward in inexplicability?

One circumscribes a space (drawing a circle around something) rather than a temporal span, but trouble sometimes demands a chronological constraint. This appears in the "anticipat[ion]" of line three. In addition to the sense of delimiting, circumscription, for Dickinson, also meant "writing round" (Webster 1845, 147), as if articulating something in writing—even something so powerful as woe—and having it bound, as one would a book, becomes part of the process of enduring. The imperative mood continues in the second stanza, with the advice about articulation morphing into the vocative:

> State it to the Ages—to a cipher—
> And it will ache contented on—
> Sing, at it's pain, as any Workman—
> Notching the fall of the even Sun—

Read literally, the suggestion to "state it to the ages" follows the reading that the written poetic statement stands beyond its own immediacy: *ages after Dickinson stated this sentiment, I am still able to encounter it.* The line, playing off a more colloquial sense, could also be a bit of a throwaway: *go sound your clichéd pain toward the heavens because no one else is listening.* This

---

arbiter" (9). The second stanza translates the infinite temporality to a matter of density, where, in contracting time, Pain brings "Gammuts of Eternities" into a single moment. Another poem, "Pain—has an Element of Blank—" (F760; J650; M352) similarly depicts pain's "Infinite" without a past or future or generally any awareness of its cause. In a sort of reversal, "Time feels so vast that were it not" (F858; J802; M394) makes sure to distinguish between the *feeling* of time and the actual infinites surrounding it: "I fear me this Circumference / Engross my Finity— // To His exclusion, who prepare / By Processes of Size / For the Stupendous Vision / Of His Diameters."

47. Miller conjectures that Dickinson may have preferred the spelling of "wo" because she was either influenced by Shakespearean texts or "to emphasize the long *o*" (*Emily Dickinson's Poems*, 21).

latter sense complicatedly echoes the odd suggestion complementing this fifth line – that one ought to express the woe to a cipher.[48] One encounters that word – cipher – much more regularly today in its noun form (as a code to be de-ciphered): "an intertexture of letters" or "a disguised manner of writing," as Webster's dictionary reminds us (1845, 146). It also reminds us of an additional sense: "In arithmetic, an Arabian or Oriental character, of this form, 0, which, standing by itself, expresses nothing, but increases or diminishes the value of other figures, according to its position." The word derives from the Arabic *ṣifr*, meaning "zero" – the concept itself derived from the Sanskrit term for void: *śūnya*. The byzantine (or, rather non-Byzantine) history of the mathematical concept I briefly discussed at the beginning of this chapter, of course, was not so much on Dickinson's radar. But *cipher*'s derivation and link to the sign and concept of zero was. Tell of your woe to a cipher, the line tells us. State it to a nobody or to "the World," a lyric addressee who isn't there. It is a call, of sorts, to apostrophize. Without the closing off of this cipher's circle, misery reigns.

If the poem were grammatically consistent, the three instances of "it" in the second stanza would refer to "trouble" or "woe" or "misery." This, though, would anthropomorphize the woe, and the second and third

---

48. The quantifying of woe arises in one of Dickinson's early poems, "Low at my problem bending" (F99; J69; M71), which embraces the slippage of "figure" between the bodily and the mathematical. As "figure" turns into "baffled fingers," the reader is made aware that the problem might be connected to a form of writer's block. In a variant (F99A), Dickinson considered substituting "My Ciphers steal away" for "My fingers file away," pointedly calling her own poetic works "ciphers." The sense that, as ciphers, they need to be decoded carries over into the "baffled fingers" (though, at this moment in the poem, it is Dickinson who remains baffled). Years later, Dickinson would again bring "baffle" together with "cipher" in her "My Cocoon tightens" (F1107; J1099; M494). The speaker of that poem, still wrapped tightly in her cocoon, must hope for the future life as a butterfly. In the meantime, she "must baffle at the Hint / And cipher at the Sign / And make much blunder, if at last / I take the clue divine–."

Sandra Gilbert and Susan Gubar connect the sign of the cypher specifically to the female poet: "Even if they had not studied her legend, literary women like Anne Finch, bemoaning the double bind in which mutually dependent images of angel and monster had left them, must have gotten the message Lilith incarnates: a life of feminine submission, of 'contemplative purity,' is a life of silence, a life that has no pen and no story, while a life of female rebellion, of 'significant action,' is a life that must be silenced, a life whose monstrous pen tells a terrible story. Either way, the images on the surface of the looking glass, into which the female artist peers in search of her *self*, warn her that she is or must be a 'Cypher,' framed and framed up, indited and indicted" (36).

instances of "it" would become the suffering body, contented and yet aching with and then pained by the knowledge of its own circumscription. It is a more interesting reading, perhaps, but one likely overshadowed by a simpler version where "it" has now become the poem's unsummoned "I" or her lingering words. The simile concluding the poem posits a connection between the circumscription of woe and the daily grind of the workman, counting down the hours to, presumably, the known date of liberation. The "even" of the cropped *evening* sun provides a balance or equilibrium that could only be dreamt of earlier. The workman's material notches signify by erasure; the scratches feel "real," unlike the circular void of Dickinson's cipher. They are also linear, having a beginning and an end in a way her zeroes – and most of her verse – never can. Nonetheless, it is hard not to see her circular *nothing* still hiding in the "notching" of the workman's day, regardless of how private it once may have been.

Circumscribing woe – drawing a circle around it – means being able to quantify it. An alternative version of the poem or possibly a poem beginning with the same line, makes the algebraic connection a little more explicit:

> Bound – a trouble –
> And lives can bear it!
> Limit – how deep a bleeding go!
> So – many – drops – of vital scarlet –
> Deal with the soul
> As with Algebra! (F240A; M105)

Dickinson could not imagine how deep the sanguine counting of trouble's blood – now in the hands of Excel spreadsheets, cognitive scientists, higher ed administrators with MBAs, and very soon AI – would go into the body, but the dehumanizing overtone remains, even if, here, it becomes a measure of pacification. Another possibility Dickinson considered was replacing "anticipate" with the more speculative (but also mathematical) term "conjecture." Dickinson moreover hazarded ending her first stanza with the possibility: "Who could begin on Misery?" (240B) rather than the "Who were sufficient to Misery?" Ending on misery is another story, as it is worth noting that in the above version (F240A) "Misery" has been excised. The alternative possibilities expand the closed circumference of the poem but, in turn, meta-poetically undermine its boundedness, thereby eroding the presumed lyric immediacy. The romantic sense of the vision – the picture of what all the counting leads to – can become lost because of this unbounded possibility or what, in another instance, Dickinson calls "the Instead" (F697; J462; M338).

That frighteningly enigmatic poem, which seesaws on the "the Instead" concludes with an actual apostrophic turn (something missing in F240):

> But – the Instead – the Pinching fear
> That Something – it did do – or dare –
> Offend the Vision – and it flee –
> And They no more remember me –
> Nor ever turn to tell me why –
> Oh, Master, This is Misery –

Here, misery is invoked, but the apostrophic address is to "Master," and the tone is reminiscent of Dickinson's much-debated "Master Letters." Misery is addressed directly, though, in another poem, "On the World you colored" (F1203; J1171; M556), which Virginia Jackson expands into its own cultural-historical universe. In a very abbreviated form, her intervention (already discussed in my book's introduction) boils down to the (misguided) critical contention that "Now we think that lyric poetry is what Emily Dickinson wrote" (*Dickinson's Misery* 233), whereas, according to Jackson, Dickinson is better read through "the nineteenth-century poetics of misery, or lyric sentimentalism"

---

49. Jackson writes, "Dickinson's writing is immersed in female sentimental lyricism, and especially in the discourse of vicarious feeling . . . that developed around that genre" (212). Such verse, specifically coming from the hands of female poets, becomes more derided through the century due to "a more general unease with the inevitable proximity between personal and testimony in the lyric and especially with the difficulty of distinguishing between them" (217). In the end, "Dickinson's emphasis on the material trace of written (and unwritten) intention may itself be traced past the modern idealization of Dickinson's lyric voice to a moment at which the gendered (that is, bodily) cost of such an idealization was very much at issue" (220). Once again, a lot of the critical disagreement depends on how one understands the nebulous term "lyric." For Melanie Hubbard who understands the lyric as an antitotalitarian thinking-through, "Dickinson's fugitive productions in the scraps take the lyric's logic, its refusal of totality and metaphysic, to its extreme by drawing attention to a thought's materiality in time" (27). Cristanne Miller calls our attention to the "focus on the dynamics of sound, form, and thought in Dickinson's poetry in ways that mark it as distinctly lyric, as understood by her immediate predecessors and contemporaries, and on patterns of her borrowing or adoption of popular poetic forms, modes, and idioms" (*Reading* 17). Against most twentieth- and twenty-first-century notions, the "nineteenth-century American definitions of and references to 'lyric' rarely mention subjectivity, address, or temporality. . . . Instead . . . they tended to understand the lyric in relation to song" (21). Noting the very different poetic voices one finds across Dickinson's oeuvre, Domhnall Mitchell writes, "Dickinson's work is pervaded with other voices and vocabularies, which suggests that it comes closer to Bakhtin's definition of the dialogic imagination" (*Monarch* 229).

(209).[49] Rather than harmonize the experiential moment with the scene of writing, as a Wordsworthian poetics would encourage, Dickinson's "Misery" becomes the name for the "difference between what is seen and what is felt, between a powerful personification and what underlies it" (207). In Jackson's self-professed retrospective view, "the strangely amputated corporation [of writer and reader] addressed as 'Misery' . . . is the best word for Dickinson's equivocal emphasis on the implicit historicity of textual intention, a pathos of transmission that has been realized beyond her wildest dreams" (207–8).[50]

Alas, my circles seem to be going one way, and Dickinson's apostrophe another. The speaker of F240 doesn't address misery. She approaches without reaching it, via the ample arc of "sufficiency," the closing off of something with an imperfect tie, because there is no other way to stop the blood loss. But her question in line four is not about a what but about a whom ("Who is sufficient to Misery?"), as if misery itself were demanding an embodied sufficiency. Here, though, she tracks how a bounded trouble could still expand to a circumscribed woe to whatever border could be sufficient for misery: concentric circles of protection, fortifications around moats around castles. In a later poem, sufficiency gets its own ring:

> He outstripped Time with but a Bout,
> He outstripped Stars and Sun
> And then, unjaded, challenged God
> In presence of the Throne –
>
> And He and He in mighty List
> Unto this present, run,
> The larger Glory for the less
> A just sufficient Ring. (F1111; J865; M496)

One ought not challenge God until one builds up a decent track record. Defeating Time is a good start; besting the Stars and then the Sun helps too. Only then might one be ready for the high-stakes cosmological derby. Using one's horse sense, one pieces together an equine track, where some of Dickinson's capital-lettered words (not by any means uncommon to her)

---

50. "[A]rtistic representation," Jackson continues, "cannot be extricated from the determining pain of personal experience; the subject of Dickinson's poem cannot . . . put . . . grief behind her. Instead midnight collapses into dawn, suffering into representation, morbid reaction into diurnal action, and self into text: 'Misery, how fair'" (218). Dickinson's "literature of misery" is thereby based on the "division . . . of the self from itself" (223).

might be understood as proper nouns – names of horses. "Outstripped" means to surpass but also to outrun; "jade" originally denoted a "tired horse"; a "bout" is a contest, and it also means a turn or circuit or rotation; finally, the mighty "list" – a catalogue of entrants amid a litany of racing terms – can also indicate an incline, like a boat turning, which is necessary when circling a curved track (Webster 1845, 579, 471, 101). The body must lean in, in order to keep going or it won't be able to follow the narrow round. The sufficiency found at the end of this poem does not appear to meet its Icarian aspirations. The danger of moving too far beyond circumference is that one might lose the inner track. What running one does for Glory might, in the end, not matter. Instead, Dickinson seems to suggest that it all might depend more on what track we are running on, and sometimes running in circles is ample enough.

To circle back to the poetic fragment at the outer perimeter of my Interlude (Fragment A879), the rider longs not for a horse that would outstrip all the others but, instead, one that could move at the circumferent velocity of nature. To know something is not to move beyond it, but to move alongside. Marta Werner notes the parallel between this fragment and another:

Did you ever
read one of
her Poems back-
ward, because
the plunge from
the front over-
turned you?
I sometimes [often] [many times] have –
A something
overtakes the
Mind – (A851)[51]

---

51. The fragment contains possible variations at the end. The concluding lines might be rendered more faithfully as:

I   sometimes
    often have–
    many times have–
A   something
overtakes   the
Mind– (A851)

Even Dickinson's lines have curves. Consider how different the fragment is as scripted versus how it usually appears recirculated in the hands of a critical text: "Did you ever read one of her Poems backward, because the plunge from the front overturned you? I sometimes . . . have – A something overtakes the mind." What happens in that space after "have –" – as if its dash were a diving board into the unknown? Beyond dramatizing how one gets lost in the sounds and hesitations of one's own words, the fragment draws attention to the semiotic "plunge" into what William Watkin, illuminating the caverns of Agamben's logopoiesis, calls the "abyss" of verse ("The / Turn" 60). The inspiration to consider the effects of lineation could not be more apparent,[52] even if the question remains as to what constitutes Dickinson's line. Does Werner's reproduction of Dickinson's fragment abide by the poet's intention, or does it follow a contemporary lyric reading practice, and when, for that matter, does such a distinction matter? Such questions find themselves at the junction of two critical impasses. The first asks if we ought (and, if so, how we might) differentiate Dickinson's poetic forms from her supposedly nonpoetic ones when there is much overlap, even if Dickinson

---

52. Consider, for a moment, a poem like "You constituted Time" (F488; J765; M243):

> You constituted Time–
> I deemed Eternity
> A Revelation of Yourself
> 'Twas therefore Deity
>
> The Absolute–removed
> The Relative away–
> That I unto Himself adjust
> My slow idolatry–

The poem is about the worship of another person (God doesn't usually need to be revealed as "Deity"), which, by the second stanza, seems to need some adjustment. What that is, however, doesn't quite reveal itself. The near anagrammatic connection between *revela[-tion]* and *relative* might point to Dickinson's relative, Sue. What the poem is trying to say, though, is complicated by its equivocal linear relations–what Cristanne Miller calls Dickinson's "syntactic doubling" in service of the poet's feminist project of "disruption" (*A Poet's Grammar* 37, 16). Are we to read an implied stop or an enjambed turn after "Eternity" and/or after "removed"? Is it: *You constituted the time that I deemed eternity. A revelation of Yourself was therefore Deity?* Or is it: *You constituted time. I deemed that eternity was a revelation of Yourself . . . ?* Is it: *the Absolute was removed; the relative was away?* Or is it: *The Absolute got rid of the relative?* Dickinson reveled in such zero-at-the-bone ambiguities.

(and scholarly indexes) can unproblematically distinguish between the two.[53] The second concerns how we ought to reproduce Dickinson's works. Should we follow her musical ear or lineate the graphic signs as they appear on the page? And, if we choose the latter, we must ask to what extent do her calligraphic practices and orthographic choices matter? Following the earlier remarks of Susan Howe and Martha Nell Smith, much recent Dickinson scholarship – such as that from Jerome McGann – favors adhering to the graphic actualities of the manuscript page.[54] Other scholars, such as Cristanne Miller and Domhnall Mitchell, though approaching the matter in different

---

53. Miller urges a bit of restraint in this regard: "There is also a lyric grace in several of Dickinson's metered prose messages, aphorisms, and textual fragments that might well lead readers to call them 'poems' or to classify them as occupying an intergenre borderland. As the same time, much great prose has lyrical qualities, as do most of Dickinson's letters, but that does not make them poems" (*Emily Dickinson's Poems*, 11). Dickinson, for her part, famously contrasts poetry (as "possibility") and prose in "I dwell in Possibility" (F466; J657; M233) and writes metaphorically of the paternally confining nature of prose in "They shut me up in Prose" (F445; J613; M223).

54. Susan Howe and Martha Nell Smith are two of the earliest advocates for retaining the calligraphic and orthographic materiality of Dickinson's manuscript pages. "Letters are sounds we see," Howe writes (*The Birth-Mark* 139), before cautioning us about ignoring "what gets lost in any typeface": "Retrace one sweeping S, a, or C, and you will know how sure [Dickinson's] touch was/is. Shapes and letters pun on and play with each other. Messages are delivered by marks" ("Some Notes on Visual Intentionality in Emily Dickinson," 11–13; qtd. in Smith, *Rowing* 62). Seeing the printed poems found in collections as a "collaborative process" among transcribers, editors, and publishers, Smith argues that Dickinson's "chirographic 'publication'" was "a consciously designed alternative mode of textual reproduction and distribution" (*Rowing* 1–2). Jerome McGann has become one of the strongest voices for maintaining and interpreting the graphic sense of Dickinson's page–what McGann calls her "Visible Language." In *Black Riders*, he stresses that her work was "not written for a print medium, even though it was written in an age of print . . . therefore we must accommodate our typographical conventions to her work, not the other way around" (38). It "does no good to argue . . . that these odd lineations are unintentional–the result of Dickinson finding herself at the right edge of the page, and so folding her lines over," McGann writes, distinguishing lineation from metrical units, adding that the "manuscripts show that she could preserve the integrity of the metrical unit if she wanted" (28). Looking at the flip sides of some of Dickinson's verse fragments, Melanie Hubbard argues that "Dickinson's verse is so entwined with its paper, and even the previous writing on the paper, that it defies print" (33). In the end, Dickinson, makes us see "reading as a material encounter, a struggle with the potential obstacle to consciousness of the embodiedness of letters" (28). The graphic appetite extends beyond what had been traditionally treated as poems to Dickinson's letters. Ellen Louise Hart argues that "print editions of the letters limit our understanding of their prosody and nuanced meanings" ("Alliteration" 235). "[T]he relationship between poetry and prose is so complex in

ways, follow R. W. Franklin in understanding the calligraphic subtleties as generally accidental and mostly inconsequential.[55]

Maintaining fidelity to Dickinson's graphic space in A851, Werner, for her part, recaptures a prose thought written down and lineated by the necessity of a margin closing fast. Beyond any (non)distinction between poetry and prose that one may hope to draw, Dickinson undermines the romantic sense of an organic poetic order or causality or eschatology – one line naturally following from another toward a necessary end. Here in Fragment A851, referring to an unnamed poet, she offers what in the twenty-first century has become a common creative writing exercise: flipping a poem upside-down to make the related experience even more poetically uncanny. In Dickinson's hands, however, the exercise is necessitated not by a 101-course instructor needing to illustrate a point about the space of verse but because the drop from line to line was so overwhelming that she was "over- / turned." It is tempting, at this moment, to begin reading every Dickinson poem backward but, in lieu of that exercise, I turn to consider another poem that is difficult to make head or tail of.

> I saw no Way – The Heavens were stitched –
> I felt the Columns close –

Dickinson's writing," she maintains, "that lineating poetry but not prose sets up artificial genre distinctions" (49). To combat this, Hart advocates for "diplomatic transcriptions" (72), which would additionally lineate Dickinson's prose. Similarly, McGann exhorts us to print all the texts as they appear, because "Dickinson's writing, particularly in the letters, continually erodes the distinction" between poetry and prose (46).

55. Cristanne Miller, though not opposed to the "expanded pleasure" of critical readings deriving from access to the manuscript pages, cautions against the "demand" that one necessarily always address them and their orthographic features ("The Sound" 222–23). She reminds us that in the nineteenth-century US "readers tended to perceive poetry aurally more than visually and poets wrote more for the ear than the eye" (202). Although mindful of the importance of Dickinson's variants, grammatical idiosyncrasies, and syntactical irregularities, Miller contends that "Dickinson's art does not consist primarily or substantively in the visual irregularities of her handwritten texts and that, as a mid-nineteenth-century poet, she is unlikely to have constructed poetry along these lines" (218). Perhaps no one has been more rigorous in his quantitative analysis of the question than Domhnall Mitchell, who has the patience to measure, to the millimeter, the right-hand marginal space of the manuscript lines in order to examine "the extent to which levels of meaning are or are not lost for particular poems when they are transposed from the author's handwritten originals to printed translations" ("Revising" 705). Against Howe's and Smith's sense of Dickinson's "proleptic textual radicalism" (706), Mitchell contends that most of the words split between lines "seem largely accidental" and are not "deliberately manipulated for semantic purposes" (710). Although he won't go so far as to suggest the

> The Earth reversed her Hemispheres –
> I touched the Universe –
>
> And back it slid – and I alone –
> A Speck upon a Ball –
> Went out upon Circumference –
> Beyond the Dip of Bell – (F633; J378; M320)[56]

Access to the heavens – initially, described as though through a curtain-esque door, then through a more classical architectural entrance – has been closed. The poem feels more like an inside-out switcheroo than a north/south east/ west hemispheric reversal (as earth's polarity apparently does every three hundred thousand years), which ends up casting the speaker away from the terrestrial such that she "touched the Universe." Some readings have her then falling back, but it is the universe that flinches, leaving the speaker in the free, terrifying sublimity of circumference.[57] Vendler sees an existential theater: once the heavens have been closed off, Dickinson becomes "the

----

possibility that McGann is reading ahistorically (!), Mitchell does call the calligraphic matters "formal deviations interpreted as significant by twentieth-century readers and then imposed upon the nineteenth century as fully deliberate graphic experiments" (732). "Almost any feature of Dickinson's manuscripts can be interpreted to suggest a proleptic concern with the semantic potential of the poem's visual properties–its line and word breaks as well as its punctuation" (711). While he acknowledges some linear stoppages are deliberate even if there's no general rule for their determination, he still maintains that the primary cause of her prose lineation is "a combination of arbitrary factors: the size of the page, for example, and the length of Dickinson's words as they are written on the page" (715). In the end, he concludes, "respecting Dickinson's wishes involves more than the exact reproduction of her line arrangements" (719).

56. The speaker of "It was not Death" (F355; J510; M187), a poem thematically related to F633, is similarly ungrounded in a metaphorical space, yet not out of reach of the Bells, which "Put out their tongues, for Noon." Still within its circumference of sound, the speaker floats, as if at sea, hoping for a "Report of Land" not to reverse her theological "Despair" but rather to "justify" it.

57. From the vantage point of the universe, it wouldn't matter if Dickinson's speaker were above the earth looking down at it or below the earth looking up, not because the hemispheres have been reversed, but because there is no up or down from the vantage point of space. One generally reads Dickinson's bell as metonymic of institutionalized religion. Its "dip" is an apt description of both the bell's shape (one sense of the word suggests curve or arc) and movement (the bell's clapper follows a circumferent arc, like a pendulum). To be *beyond* this dip rather than inside its arc, the speaker would have to be on the earth, under the bell or otherwise the bell would have to be swinging upside down. But this, I imagine, is neither here nor there.

agent of her own enlightenment" (*Dickinson's* 277). Cameron sees Dickinson flinging language "into the reaches of the unknown in the apparent hope that it might civilize what it finds there" (*Lyric* 9). Elisa New, reversing Cameron's hemispheres, sees this as "a poem of chastised circumference," where the sin of knowledge "delivers Dickinson into a religious originality, and isolation, which the poem's tone tells us terrifies" (13, 14).

The poem takes up a hemisphere, as it were, of the first sheet of Fascicle 31 – one of forty little hand-crafted poetic booklets Dickinson assembled, as their own poetic universes. "[T]o read the poems in the fascicles, Cameron writes, "is to see that the contextual sense of Dickinson is not the canonical sense" (*Choosing* 19).[58] In order "[t]o make a booklet," Miller writes, Dickinson "stacked folded sheets of copied poems on top of one another, poked holes through the stack at the folded edges, and then bound them together with string" (*Emily Dickinson's Poems*, 1). Taken together, the fascicles give us a new sense of how one might "bound a trouble." Dickinson was years into her informal fascicle binding when she drafted, for the first time, "I Saw No Way." It is possible that her bookmaking processes amusingly informed what would otherwise seem to be a mostly terrifying poem. The second compounded "verse" form (re-versed, uni-verse) in two lines might ring a bell. However much these two words dip in different poetic directions (one, a "turning-back," the other, a "turning-into-one"), each points to the process of arranging a poetic volume. The "Stich[ing]" of the heavens – "hem"ispheres, if you will – would not be unlike the stitching of the fascicle booklets, themselves closing the verse "columns" on a moment turned into graphic form.

*   *   *

. . . the plunge from
the front over-
turned you? . . . (A851)

Coda of silence

Not unexpectedly, Dickinson writes on both sides of her fascicle pages, continuing a long poem or copying another in. At times, the trace

---

58. The fascicles, for Cameron, gesture toward indeterminacy and collectivity. Their form ties directly into the matter of Dickinson's variants (different versions of a poem and different possibilities for word choices within a poem). Cameron argues that Dickinson chose not to choose among her variants, thereby leaving her poetic texts open to possibility. "The difficulty in enforcing a limit to the poems turns into a kind of limitlessness," she writes, adding that "it is impossible to say where the text ends because the variants extend the text's identity in ways that make it seem potentially limitless" (6). Contra Cameron, Melanie Hubbard contends that not all variants are necessarily about choosing ("The Word"). See also Alexandra Socarides, who explores how the fascicle form works against the idea of the lyric.

of each poetic hemisphere bleeds scantily through the sheet, a shadow of its former self reversed on the other side. One of these fascicle poems is " 'Tis so appalling" (F341; J281; M179), which connects sight, knowledge, and death to some unnamed horror – "it." "It" might be "seeing death" or "knowing death" or another of the overburdened words in the poem, such as "ghost," "torment," "woe," or "dread." Unlike the reader who circles around this "it," the speaker knows what it is: "we, who know, / Stop hoping, now – " for what would seem to read as some manner of religious salvation. Those not in the know are shown prayer, which isn't presented in a performative sense but almost like a text Dickinson contemptuously passes around. The knowledge, however merciless, allows for an existential freedom: "It sets the Fright at liberty– / And Terror's free– / Gay, Ghastly, Holiday!" It was the earlier not-knowing that seized hold: "Suspense kept sawing so – ." (The play on sawing-seeing has a lot of work to do to crack a smile in this terrifying image of suspense severing the body in two.) Despite a tone which seems to descend from the other earthly hemisphere, the poem is oddly similar to an earlier poem of Dickinson: " 'Tis so much joy!" (F170; J172; M98). The earlier poem is more about taking a (possibly romantic?) risk: whatever the result, it's better to know, and heavenly things might just await. In one of fifteen (!) exclamatory phrasings, " 'Tis so much joy" tells us that "to know the worst, is sweet!" Here, however, in the untethered hopelessness of F341, "To know the worst, leaves no dread more – ." Daneen Wardrop connects the back-and-forth motion of the poem's dreadful sawing to "the dichotomy at the core of Gothicism: *appalling exhilaration*" and "the psychological fact that what can scare the most remains what is closest" (144).[59] Attentive to the very bodily graphic form of the fascicle, she writes, "[t]he handwriting squirms on the page. The dashes so uniform and nearly regulatory in Johnson's print editions become less like scaffolding. In the manuscripts the dash instead seems to destabilize the lines, goring and tossing language about" (143). Here is how " 'Tis so appalling" looks in the middle of Fascicle 16:

---

59. Paula Bennett and Betsy Erkkila ("Dickinson and the Art . . .") both see the poem in a Civil War context and the "terror of a world in which Death is the only 'Truth,' and hopelessness, the only way to deal with fear" (Bennett 127). Bennett understands the poem as a response to the death of a family friend, Frazar Stearn, the son of the Amherst College president. In the end, the poem ". . . reminds us that the human limits of pain are set at that point when one has nothing left to lose, and everything ceases to matter, life included" (125). See also Cameron on this poem, in her lyric (*Lyric* 98–100) and fascicle (*Choosing* 144–46) modes.

Figure 5.3. Emily Dickinson F341 (recto side) in Fascicle 16. *Source:* Emily Dickinson Archive. Used with permission.

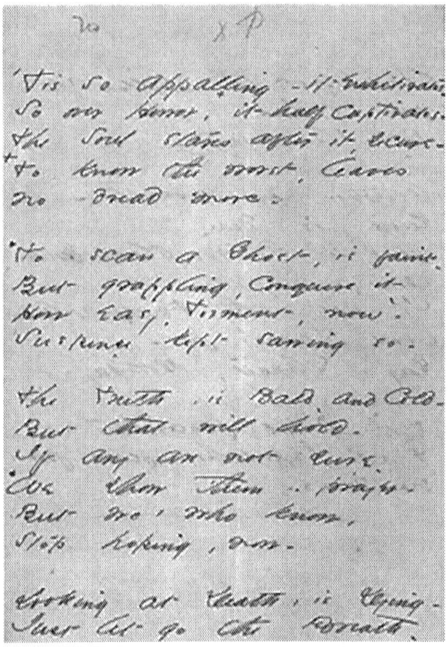

Figure 5.4. Emily Dickinson F341 (verso side) in Fascicle 16. *Source:* Emily Dickinson Archive. Used with permission.

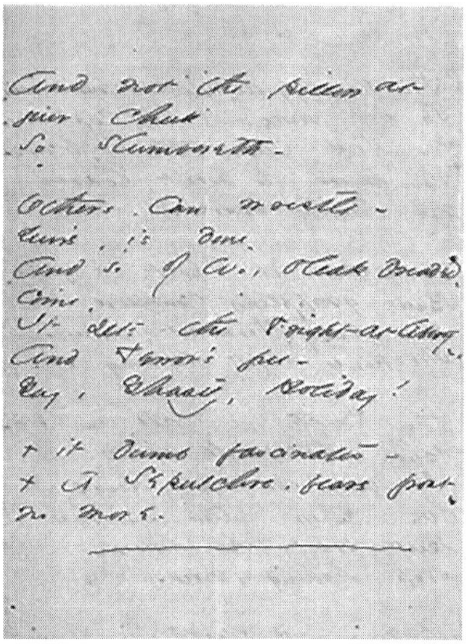

On the outer side of each page, one can see the same two pin holes used to bind this poem to others in the fascicle. On the verso side, above the line drawn across the bottom of the page, one can see the two variations Dickinson considered for the first stanza: the first a hemistich for line two, the second a complete alternative for line four. The ampersandish plus-signs on the recto side signal where the alternatives would be substituted. (*Which did Dickinson intend? The suspense keeps sawing so.*) Finally, between and around each of the written lines, one can see the faint images of the other side of the page. Wardrop notes the page break after "Just let go the Breath" – "an instance in which the physical rendering of the poem on the page underscores the activity endorsed" (146). At what point, as one exhilarated and captivated reader might wonder, does the material page frame how a poem ought to be understood?[60] A close-up of the manuscript page might push this question further.

Across from "No dread more –" in figure 5.5, one can see a reversed "Others can"; its "wrestle –" hiding backward beneath "dread more." Read-

____

60. Both Smith and McGann trace Dickinson's attention to the materiality of the fascicle page to 1861 and fascicle 9 when she "[d]ecided to use her textpage as a scene for dramatic interplays between En a poetics of the eye and a poetics of the ear" (McGann "Visible Language" 41).

Figure 5.5. Close-up of Emily Dickinson F341 (recto side) in Fascicle 16. *Source:* Emily Dickinson Archive. Used with permission.

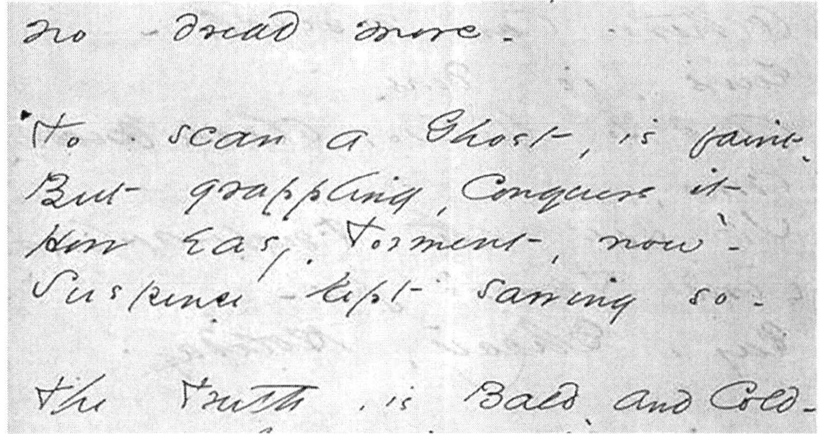

ing between the lines of the first two stanzas, one sees "Yours, is done—" floating in reverse just atop the line "To scan a ghost, is faint—." In an 1876 Letter to Thomas Higginson, Dickinson writes, "Nature is a Haunted House—but Art—a House that tries to be haunted" (L459A). Fascicle 16 gives us written script as a haunting, a ghost one sees of oneself. I am not so bold as to suggest that the phrase "Scan a ghost" on the recto refers to the yet-to-be-written ink on the verso, which was to be copied onto the fascicle page from a now nonextant draft, but just for a spell I do want to dwell in this possibility, a fairer house than our usual critical prose. Here, we might ask, what exactly is happening in this liminal, circumferent space between the two sides of the same page?[61]

---

61. Christine Jacobson, the associate curator of modern books and manuscripts at Harvard University's Houghton Library, which is in possession of Fascicle 16, believes "'Tis so appalling" was written on embossed laid stationer's paper—the specific stationer yet to be identified. In an email correspondence, Jacobson noted that due to the "chain lines and embossment we can reasonably conclude the paper is of very good quality. Therefore, the bleeding on to the back of the page likely has more to do with the ink . . ." and added that this was "not an aspect unique to the digitized copy." I am curious under what circumstances such a hermeneutic gamble—finding meaning in the ghostly trace of one's former writing—would leave a faint (but viable) impression. Assuming one does not find a letter where the poet says *I was writing a poem and saw my words on the reverse page and then changed what I had to say*, when would this haunted act of reading—to revisit a word from Dickinson—"captivate"? Perhaps there is zero chance, but a zero to the bone.

Leaving others to wrestle in that ring, I want to grapple with one other mutinous moment. The final stanza, as it is reproduced in most editions, is six lines long. Its re-composition, however, as seen in figure 5.4, is seven lines:

> Others, can wrestle –
> Yours, is done –
> And so of Wo, bleak dreaded –
> Come,
> It sets the Fright at liberty –
> And Terror's free –
> Gay, Ghastly, Holiday!

The stanza pivots on this apostrophic address (*to woe? to dread? to one-self?*) – "Come."[62] We do not hear it [pause] come. What ought one do with a metrical line that in the manuscript appears over two scripted lines? Do we make meaning out of something that, in McGann's words, "might appear to be a mere shift in her handwriting or in her copying habits" ("Emily Dickinson's Visible Language" 41)? Miller importantly cautions us to tread lightly with our hermeneutic assumptions about manuscript lineation: "to present all Dickinson's run-on rows of script as though they were poetic lines ignores her repeated and typical indication that she has a more deliberate sense of the line" (*Emily Dickinson's Poems*, 21). Dickinson "marked poetic lines by beginning with a capital letter written flush with the left margin" (15). A cursory scan cannot determine if the "C" of "Come" is the lower-case "c" of the poem's "can" or the upper-case "C" of its "Cold." Either way, it does uncannily stop the iambic clip-clop of the poetic line and visually present itself, as though it were calling memento mori from the grave.

One thinks one looks into Dickinson's verse and sees her infinites of nought, but then one wonders whether one is merely looking into a mirror. Am I reading her or standing in the middle of a circle I can no longer see beyond?[63] My wheel is in the dark. With apologies for the unseemly segue, I turn to one final Dickinson poem:

---

62. Wardrop also notes this odd position of the word, but arrives at a different finish, one that "demands a line to itself in the fascicle. As a one-word line it proclaims its potency, a plenary word that plays on the erotic expectation as well as suspenseful *dénouement*" (145).

63. Uneasy with the convenient proximity between her own interests and Dickinson's vast space of poetic possibility, Susan Howe discloses, "I often worry that I may be

My Wheel is in the dark!
I cannot see a spoke
Yet know its dripping feet
Go round and round.

Some with new – stately feet –
Pass royal through the gate –
Flinging the problem back
At you and I! (F61; J10; M49)

It is an early poem, one which meanders to tell us that we don't always know where we are going, but there's a place for us at the end or, more darkly, the very end. The speaker's wheel conjures the paddleboat: its diameter-spokes, moving in circuits, keep her moving; its dripping feet act as a reminder of a specifically poetic vehicle. The turn at the end addresses an absent somebody – either a specific one she had in mind or a more general readership. The difference over 160 years later is, for the most part, neither here nor there. Instead, it is the earlier jest of a dripping language, still splashing whatever circumference one has drawn around it that now pokes at me. "I cannot see a spoke."[64] Of course, no one can see what another person spoke, even atop the wagon tongue, especially if that other person were alone, shouting out to someone who wasn't there. Only when it is visible on the page will it last, however wet its feet.

---

imposing my particular obsessions on her" (*Birth-Mark* 155). Howe is not alone in this concern. Both Cristanne Miller (notably in *Emily Dickinson: A Poet's Grammar*) and Martha Nell Smith call attention to the importance of the reader's involvement in Dickinson's poetic bouts of knowing and not-knowing. According to Smith, Dickinson is "conscious of the inevitability of the reader involved in such play" that might not have been intended (*Rowing* 13). Readers are "well aware that some omissions, both foisted on the written record and inherent in the dynamics of language itself, can never be closed" (40). Ultimately, Smith sees "manipulations of texts [as] transformations, opportunities for Emily Dickinson and her readers to exert control over expression by remaking supposedly fixed utterances and thereby challenge conventional authorities in a constructive way" ("The Poet as Cartoonist" 72).

64. Dickinson similarly plays upon the sound and material senses of "ring" in "Dare you see a Soul" (F401; J365; M214): "Least Village, boasts it's Blacksmith– / Whose Anvil's even ring / Stands symbol for the finer Forge / That soundless tugs–within–."

The Dickinsonian "void of mystery . . . changes its appearance as the reader's various approaches create this or that origin," David T. Porter offers.[65] There is a vanity to reading, to imposing one's own sense of the world on what one sees, all the while pretending one is not there. "The Show is not the Show / But they that go—" Dickinson reveals the secret.[66] Pathos might be real, but its charm is artifice. There is a market for faces painted with pain. But why watch these theatrical faces when emotional authenticity is more easily seen in the menagerie of an audience reaction? Surely, though, it is an authentic emotion—maybe hate, maybe love—that impels a singer-songwriter to take her spot on stage? Surely, this emotion, this "oh!" of surprise has the same depth night after night, performance after performance. Or does the staged "oh!" ever lose its spotlighted vigor the hundredth time she sings about it, her own hat strategically dipped below one eye?

---

65. Porter, *Dickinson: The Modern Idiom* 187.
66. Dickinson, F1270; J1206; M565.

Chapter 6

Carly Simon

"[Oh] you had me several years ago"

A careful ear will catch a slight difference between Carly Simon's studio recording of "You're So Vain" and how the lyrics are generally disseminated.[1] "Oh you had me several years ago when I was still quite naïve," she sings on the wonderfully titled *No Secrets* album, adding an "Oh" to the liminal space between lines. The moment becomes a cousin of sorts to poetry's apostrophic performances. Sometimes heard, sometimes "overheard," songs, as I will explore in this chapter, very often play with the expectations of lyric address. But perhaps this and other lyric acts needn't be so romanticized. They are, after all, as embroiled as every other text in a discursive marketplace, and, like these texts, have their own marketable façades. I would quote more at this time, but I am not sure I am permitted. Let me backtrack.

With (real) apologies, this chapter has begun with one eye in the mirror, and it will continue down the crooked path of this funhouse.[2] I reprint three figures here. Figure 6.1 is a conventional permissions request form, filled out on or about 2010; Figure 6.2 is an automated email from a publisher/distribution company, deferring, for a *minimum* of three weeks, the previous address; and figure 6.3 is a (mostly) human response to the initial request. These three figures are authentic. As can be typical, the email correspondence above began before the form in figure 6.1 was completed, and it continued well after the date in figure 6.3.

---

1. See, for example, Simon's website: https://www.carlysimon.com/youre-so-vain.

2. See Ben-Merre, "I'm So Vain."

Figure 6.1. Permissions request form. *Source*: Screenshot courtesy of the author.

Pub Title	Author	Publisher	Format	Price	Territory	Print Run	Pub Date
I?m so vain, I bet I think this song is about myself: Carly Simon and the Problematic ?I?	David Ben-Merre	deGruyter	Academic Publication	40.0	university libraries	250	TBD

Publication Description	This will be for an academic article in the collection entitled Metalepsis in Popular Culture, edited by Karin Kukkonen and Sonja Klimek. I do not stand to gain financially from this publication. The print run will be 250 copies which are marketed to university libraries. (I do not know the price of the volume. The amount entered below is an estimate.)
Additional Titles/Writers	n/a

Song Title	""You're So Vain""
Writer	Carly Simon
Lyric Text	"You're so vain / You probably think this song is about you"

Figure 6.2. Automated email response to permissions request. *Source*: Screenshot courtesy of the author.

From: Hal Leonard Permissions [mailto:permissions@halleonard.com]
Sent: Fri 7/9/2010 3:08 PM
To: Ben-Merre, David N
Subject: Hal Leonard Permission Request Confirmation - PR0159085

Thank you for your request.

Please be advised that we request a *minimum* of 3 weeks to process permission requests, due to the high volume of requests we receive daily.

If you have any questions, please see our Frequently Asked Questions page, or email us at permissions@halleonard.com. Be sure to reference the tracking number in any correspondence to us.

Permission Request Submission

Date Submitted:	July 9, 2010
Tracking Number:	PR0159085
Request Type:	Lyric Usage

Figure 6.3. Email correspondence from Hal Leonard Corporation. *Source*: Screenshot courtesy of the author.

RE: **You're So Vain**

Dear Mr. Ben-Merre:

Thank you for your request dated July 9, 2010.

Before we can consider your request to reprint a lyric excerpt of the above mentioned composition in your publication, please provide all of the following additional information:

- Publication date (approximate is acceptable)
- A complete list of all songs (with writer names) that will be quoted in the publication
- The excerpt as it is to appear in your publication, including one page before and after the excerpt

I look forward to hearing from you.

Sincerely,

Permissions Administrator
Business Affairs
Hal Leonard Corporation

Those who have been here before know the exhausting efforts it takes sometimes to secure permissions—this, after one has thought one has already moved along to the aura of the next gavotte. At the time, I hoped to explore an underlying deictic incongruity in Carly Simon's 1972 hit song "You're So Vain" in order to consider metaleptic features of pop music in general, specifically rhetorical effects of immersion and authenticity.[3] Part of the charm was due to the vortical excitement of paradox, the other part was

---

3. The original essay spent a fair amount of energy tracking how many scholars felt as though they still needed to justify their work on popular music in some academic circles. In a sense, much of this earlier scholarship had to contend with an institutionalized vanity, which, though in different guises, boiled down to the assertion that popular music just wasn't serious "Art." As if flaunting a line from Carly Simon's song ("Well, you're where you should be all the time"), the serious study of popular music entered university courses. As David Hesmondhalgh and Keith Negus wrote in 2002, "The pioneers of popular music analysis spent many years having to justify paying serious attention to a cultural form and medium of communication which was often dismissed for its association with entertainment and pleasure. But now university courses and units in popular music are proliferating, and the study of popular music is an established, though still relatively marginal, academic area" (1). As it happened, with the turn to cultural studies in the humanities, it only made sense to study the popular art form that had the most impact on mediating subjectivities. The emerging field brought together the sounds of music—often studied by musicologists—with the historical, social, and political frameworks mediating those sounds. As Richard Middleton summarizes, "To locate

that "Rock music," as Stephanie Burt writes, "brings with it a far stronger claim . . . to convey immediate authentic feeling, than any claims U.S. or U.K. poets can now make" ("O Secret" 202–3). As you know, Simon's song is a perfect enactment of a spurned woman not wanting to give her "vain" former lover the time of day even in the testimonial that decries him. She spends the length of the song describing in detail the degree of her former lover's vanity, a man who, as she puts it (and he seemingly would), "had [her] several years ago." He is affluent and voyaging, full of moxie and charm, intrigue and deceitfulness. While his rhetoric in the end might not be real, he certainly possesses the pecuniary means to back up his voracious appetite. His worst attribute seems to be his sense of entitlement—that the whole world, the eclipsing sun included, revolves around him. The absurdly comical extent of his self-centeredness comes through in the opening stanza, where we are shown how his gaze remains fixated solely upon himself—one eye hides behind his hat, as the other watches himself dance. To twist the lyrics of another song: he only has eyes for himself.

The chorus introduces both the singer, who happens to be one of this man's former lovers, and one of the most famous refrains of popular music:

> You're so vain
> You probably think this song is about you
> Don't you don't you don't you?

In total, counting this chorus which is repeated four times in the song, there are sixty-nine instances of "you" or "your" or "you're" or "yourself." Nine of these instances occur in the first eight lines of the song, and it

---

music's meaning in its objectively constituted sound-patterns, regardless of its cultural contexts, social and emotional effects, and the bodily movements which accompany and perhaps generate it, is in origin part of a broader Transcendentalizing tendency within post-Enlightenment bourgeois aesthetics . . . an ontology which would exclude the secular life-processes of the pop song" (4–5). The work of early cultural critics of popular music—such as Simon Frith, Charles Hamm, Middleton, John Shepherd, Philip Tagg, and others, who had been publishing during the 1970s and 1980s—would soon be joined by that of Susan McClary and Sheila Whiteley among others, who each added much needed gender critiques, and that of Robert Walser stressing the importance of cultural contexts. The importance today of studying popular music within the classroom has led to an outpouring of critical books and anthologies by scholars such as Frith, Middleton, Georgina Born, David Brackett, Reebee Garofalo, David Hesmondhalgh, Allan F. Moore, Keith Negus, Roy Shuker, Sarah Thornton, and Peter Wicke.

is not until line fifteen that we get a line without a "you." On top of all this, we hear the lines "You're so vain" a total of fifteen times, including the times the back-up singers chime in. (They, too, *know*.) The "you're/your" homonym—indistinguishable in speech but for context—brings together an ontological proposition with the subject of ownership—that "being," in a sense, means being possessed, here, by a vain lover who can think only of his own gratification. On the one hand, the repeated "you-you-you" of these lines mirrors the "me-me-me" of the lover's self-entitlement. On the other hand, though, the repetitiveness rhetorically presents a singer who cannot seem to get over being the spurned lover. But the second-person address of the famous chorus complicates things. "You're so vain / You probably think this song is about you," the singer accuses her former lover, referencing him as listener, and thereby both conflating and denying any conflation between real and lyrical worlds. Through these seemingly incompatible lyrics, lis- teners are put in the awkward position of being asked to believe that the absent person to whom the song is being addressed is not the person to whom the song is being addressed.[4]

In introducing this famous incongruity, the opening lines of the cho- rus also name the instrument and medium of discourse—"this song," an irony espousing that, in order to point outward, we must look inward. Whether or not her former lover is also a part of the song becomes the lyrical paradox, which depends upon how a shifting "you" changes or does not change in the course of the singer's utterance. "You" and "I" and "this" are deictics, Émile Benveniste would remind us, words that need a vocative presence and/or a gestural pointing in order to have any meaning because they have no referent outside the particular speech act in which they occur.[5] "[T]he instances of the use of *I*," he writes,

> do not constitute a class of reference since there is no "object" definable as *I* to which these instances can refer in identical fashion. Each *I* has its own reference and corresponds each

---

4. Barbara Johnson notes a similar moment in the line "I write this   not for you" from Adrienne Rich's "To a Poet," a poem itself in the shadow of John Keats's "When I have Fears That I May Cease to Be." "In saying 'I write this   not for you,'" Johnson reasons, "it is almost as though Rich is excluding as addressee anyone who could conceivably be reading this poem" ("Apostrophe" 37).

5. They are analogous to Otto Jespersen's linguistic "shifters." The term comes up across Jespersen's work, but see, for example, *Language*, 123–24.

> time to a unique being who is set up as such . . . What then
> is the reality to which *I* or *you* refers? It is solely a "reality of
> discourse." . . . *I* signifies "the person who is uttering the present
> instance of the discourse containing *I*." (218)

Simon's chorus references the "you" five or six times, with the conceit that one "you" should no longer be understood as another "you" . . . if you take the singer at her word, that is. Earlier, she condemned her lover for "[giving] away the things he loved." Here, we have the singer trying to "give away" the "you" she might once have loved. The absurdity of it all comes out in the final lines "Don't you? Don't you? Don't you?" where we don't know whether the "you" is the "you" the singer is addressing or the "you" the singer isn't addressing, as though having both at once were now a real possibility.

The vanity of the lover, who seemed always to have "one eye in the mirror," gets reproduced as a type of vanity in the singer who hopes to control each referential instance of the "you." The trick of the song is that the "I" assumes the previous role of the lover—the "you"—who sang a song of courtship offstage ("Well you said that we made such a pretty pair / And that you would never leave"). His song, as we learn, was all along never really about her. She becomes vain, in a sense, because she is acting "in vain," seemingly still for the only man who wouldn't care why he is being addressed, only that he is. He is more interested in the "I"; she, in the "you." Neither the song nor its singer can invoke an actual *you*—the *you* has left and will not return—so it has to do one better, invoking time and again a rhetoric of the "you." The vanity of the singer comes with the attempt at memorializing not only her past engagement (which we see in the obsessively repeated instances of "you"), but also herself, still injured by a past event she cannot seem to move beyond. That would be the case were it not all a staged performance.[6]

What makes much popular music, and this song especially, metaleptic and not just naturalistic is the ability for it to step outside its own frame by naming it and, as we hear in Carly Simon's song, by naming listeners and

---

6. In her memoir *Boys in the Trees*, Simon reveals the lyrics to a verse that did not end up in the final song. This verse, shifting the entire agency of the song, ends with the line: "Maybe that's why I have tried to dismiss you, tried to dismiss you" (255). The exclusion keeps the language more about victimization, despite, as I argue, the rhetorical authority of the songwriter to control the story.

singers too.[7] This in turn grounds the song in a familiar reality, which is what seems to sell popular music so well. Where the "you" in poems creates an impression of immediacy, Simon's creates a pretense of "authenticity"—what the novelist Tom McCarthy characterizes as an "age-old Western fetish" (8). No longer do we have a lyric speaker pretending not to know that her words are being overheard, but, instead, we have someone who feels very close by sharing her story. As Jahan Ramazani explains, quoting Charles O. Hartman, "a song is its performance. . . . [I]t exists for its audience at a pace which is set, not by the person experiencing the song, but by the performer" (191; quoting Hartman, 102). Conversely, written lyric poetry, unlike song performance, is actualized or ventriloquized by a reader in a way that decenters the actual poet's voice. Also apparently quite marketable, as Grant Packard and Jonah Berger point out, is this vocalized gesture of "you," which generally invokes more communal agency in song than Simon's track and the history tied to it in the cultural marketplace seem to do.[8]

Metaleptic acts are about taking control by authorizing the levels of discourse. So are apostrophic ones. Lauren Berlant writes, "The condition of projected possibility, of a hearing that cannot take place in the terms of its enunciation ('you' are not here, 'you' are eternally belated to the conversation

---

7. Most scholars distinguish narrative metalepsis from tropological metalepsis. (For an approach that considers their paradoxical temporal commonality, see Ben-Merre, *Figures*.) In Gérard Genette's terms, narrative metalepsis entails "[t]he transition from one narrative level to another . . . consist[ing] precisely of introducing into one situation, by means of a discourse, the knowledge of another situation" (234). There is a level of comfort in narrative borders; they delineate the scopes of stories, allowing us to feel at home in our knowledge of insides and outsides, real and make-believe. A metaleptic gesture, on the other hand, allows extradiegetic narrators (those outside the narrative frame) and readers to be thrown into a diegetic world (the fictional universe of the story) and diegetic characters to be cast off into an extradiegetic space. Characters would be able to see themselves not as people but as characters, as though they were readers of the novels of which they are a part. The effect is reversed on actual readers to a palpable degree. "The most troubling thing about metalepsis," Genette writes, "indeed lies in this unacceptable and insistent hypothesis, that the extra-diegetic is perhaps always diegetic, and that the narrator and his narratees—you and I—perhaps belong to some narrative" (236). This echoes the threat of prosopopoeia, following the apostrophic act. As de Man writes, "by making the death speak, the symmetrical structure of the trope implies, by the same token, that the living are struck dumb, frozen in their own death" (*Rhetoric* 78).

8. Packard and Berger see second-person pronouns as "help[ing to] shape cultural success" (397) in a marketplace, because they "invite audiences to imagine a personal 'you' who is the recipient of their own attention" (398).

with you that I am imagining) creates a fake present moment of intersubjectivity in which, nonetheless, a performance of address can take place" (25). With the ability to voice comes the ability to address; but with the ability to apostrophize comes the knowledge that there won't be a response. An apostrophe is a gesture of inclusivity without giving the addressed a voice. It is Narcissus and Echo at once. We see this in Simon's song, as the presumptive addressee is shut out of the circuit of communication. If "taking hold of (telling) by changing level" (Genette 235 n.51)—getting to tell the story—is the metaleptic power of narrative form, then the power of apostrophic address, going by the name of "vanity," is precisely what is at stake in Simon's enigmatic song. Accordingly, this "you" of her song mirrors the "I" of the singer or more general lyric speaker, and both represent a sort of vanity: the addressed lover, because he seems always to be looking at himself, and the singer, because she hopes to control each shifting instance of "you," as though the "you" has become—and must always remain—part of *her* song. It is a copyrighting of the "you" in perpetuity.

Deflecting the mystery of the song's much-debated "real-world" addressee, I hinted at the time that the "you" was actually the "I"—a very different sense of what my niece insists I write now as *iCarly*. Now, amid this otherworldly desire to make a public culture one's own, I would have to add that my own "I" ought to be thrown into the ego of that shifting "you." Vanity is contagious. In the end, I was not given permission to quote the lyrics in full. I did, however, get a half serious footnote out of the whole experience: "As international property laws, which do not allow me to quote more than 4 lines of the song, make clear, the singer-songwriter Carly Simon is very much in charge of her words" (79 fn18). What began in either resentment or vanity turned out to be a not-as-witty-as-one-hoped attempt to make light of the whole situation. In retrospect, from a very different place now, the situation feels not so much about a junior faculty member hoping for a much-needed helping hand (he was still quite naïve) but rather a glimpse into how a mass-mediated cultural artifact actually operates in a modern consumer marketplace with its own rules about circulation.

Article I, Section 8 of the *U.S. Constitution* grants Congress the power "to promote the Progress of Science and useful Arts, by securing for limited Times to Authors and Inventors the exclusive Right to their respective Writings and Discoveries." At the time, copyrights were seen as protections for an "author" (~5.5 billion Google hits today) or what is now called a "content creator" (only 185 million Google hits, but growing), and intended to incentivize creative production and distribution. Over a century earlier in Europe, though, they had the function of facilitating state regulation. "Before becoming goods caught up in a circuit of ownership," discourse, as per Michel Foucault, was a "gesture fraught with risks" (212). Writers could be linked to their words. Foucault's seminal "What is an Author?" refigures the essentialized humanistic author—a romantic invention—as an author function. Rather than being a genius in a transcendental realm, the author or, more accurately, the notion of it, *does* something: "we could say that in a civilization like our own there are a certain number of discourses endowed with the 'author function' while others [a private letter, a contract] are deprived of it. . . . The author function is therefore characteristic of the mode of existence, circulation, and functioning of certain discourses within a society" (211). Modernity has the author "play[ing] the role of the regulator of the fictive, a role quite characteristic of our era of industrial and bourgeois society, of individualism and private property" (222).

In the United States, copyrights are governed by the congressional Copyright Act of 1976 (a far-reaching revision to the one in existence for most of the twentieth century) and subsequent amendments. Intended to protect original expression (not ideas or information), the Act grants copyright protections to artists and their estates for fifty years after their death. It also provides for a "fair use" exception, as Robert Spoo writes, "permit[ting] users other than the copyright owner to copy protected expression without the owner's consent, if such copying is done in a reasonable manner and for a legitimate purpose" (183).[9] "Fair use," Matthew Bunker explains, "is one of the key statutory limits on the monopoly power of copyright owners. It is intended to allow some reasonable scope of borrowing to encourage the dissemination of copyrighted works, even against the copyright holder's

---

9. As Chapman Distinguished Professor at the University of Tulsa College of Law and a former English professor and editor of the *James Joyce Quarterly*, Robert Spoo has been an ally of scholars pursuing fair-use claims. Spoo's article traces copyright infringement cases mainly dealing with unpublished works, which, until a 1992 revision to 1976 Act, were generally considered private property—not copyrighted but also not subject to fair-use exceptions. An update to Title 17 §107 of the U.S. Code ensures that "the fact that a work is unpublished shall not itself bar a finding of fair use if such finding is made upon consideration of [the four] factors." At the time of Spoo's article, he hoped to shift some of the onus of asserting fair use to more timid publishers ("a weak link in the fair use chain" [199]), who were fearful of invoking that right. For Spoo, the copyright law's supralegal purpose is in "fostering a climate of mutual tolerance and understanding among authors, heirs, scholars, and other members of the copyright ecosystem" (198).

wishes" (4).[10] As amended, the 1976 Act lists possible fair uses including "criticism, comment, news reporting, teaching (including multiple copies for classroom use), scholarship, or research," which, though relevant to a claim, are not dispositive.[11] Title 17 §107 of the current U.S. Code lists the fair use limitations on copyright exclusivity:

> In determining whether the use made of a work in any particular case is a fair use the factors to be considered shall include-
>
> (1) the purpose and character of the use, including whether such use is of a commercial nature or is for nonprofit educational purposes;
>
> (2) the nature of the copyrighted work;
>
> (3) the amount and substantiality of the portion used in relation to the copyrighted work as a whole; and
>
> (4) the effect of the use upon the potential market for or value of the copyrighted work.[12]

When considering fair use, courts take these four factors into account together with what is termed the "transformative use" doctrine, which considers, as Bunker summarizes, "if the borrowed work is deployed for a different purpose (say, scholarly analysis) than that for which it was created" (6).[13] The first factor tends to support scholarly uses of copyrighted material, which, as far as things go, have minimal financial gain.[14] The second factor

---

10. Too strict a monopoly, as a federal court held, "would stifle the very creativity which that law is designed to foster" (qtd. in Bunker 4).

11. For an explanation of the value to having a scholarly exception to copyright exclusivity, see Bezanson and Miller: "Scholarship was driven in law by a felt need to encourage its dissemination and by a sense that its product was common property, its production a common good, and its availability a common necessity" ("Abstract").

12.See https://uscode.house.gov/browse/prelim@title17/chapter1&edition=prelim.

13. "Transformative use," Bunker writes, "is a sort of value-added borrowing that emphasizes adding new meaning or message to the borrowed work or, in some cases, the use of the work in a different functional context" (2). This doctrine has become central to how courts now determine fair-use decisions. The transformative doctrine came out of the Supreme Court's decision in *Campbell v. Acuff-Rose Music, Inc,* where 2 Live Crew's parody of Roy Orbison's "Oh, Pretty Woman" was found to be fair use.

14. A nonnegligible amount of intellectual or academic capital, however, does attach. Bunker writes, "Of course, even purely 'nonprofit' scholarship can have an economic or pecuniary motivation that is less direct than, say, the payment of book royalties. Published scholarship can result in the granting of tenure, promotions, raises, and even the possibility of lateral moves to other institutions at a higher salary" (5).

has to do with whether the copyrighted work is fictional or not, with the presumption that more protection is bestowed on the former, due to its creative nature. What, we might ask, is the "nature" of Carly Simon's song, with its sing-songwriter flair of authenticity? Does pointing outward to a real "you" in the world make it more or less fictional? As is often the case, the philosophical questions asked of literary works (or, rather, asked by literary works) undermine jurisprudential borders. We will see who will win out in the end. *Won't we, won't we, won't we?* (I will come back to these questions in a bit, with the assumption that their nature would change given the social, cultural, or legal contexts they find themselves in.) The third factor when considering fair use is the amount of material borrowed. This goes beyond a quantifiable proportion of the original work. A photograph or artwork, for instance, might need to be reproduced in its entirety for scholarly purposes, while "even relatively small borrowings can be ruled unfair if a qualitatively important portion of a work—sometimes referred to as the 'heart of the work'—is taken" (Bunker 7). Under this rubric, it would seem one would be able to quote Carly Simon's song in its entirety but for the famous line, even though that is the one imprinted on the ethos of American culture. The final factor courts consider when determining fair use is whether the borrowed work is likely to act as a substitute for the original in a commercial market. Thankfully, one would be hard-pressed, even in overselling a project to one's editor, to make the case that a scholarly chapter about a popular song would compete in a marketplace with that song. The vagueness of these gray areas creates flexibility for the courts but leaves practice hard to understand and predict. Even what counts as "transformative use" is not altogether clear. Noting T. S. Eliot's famous "Tradition and the Individual Talent," which "is anathema to the essentially Romantic myth of sovereign selfhood that sustains our faith in original expression," Spoo notes that "it is concretely arguable that, far from being a mere exception to genuine creativity, transformative use is the unacknowledged condition of *all* expression" (199).

If so far I have sounded a little whimsically aggrieved, I should clarify that I am more curious about this intersection of the law and literature, especially as it relates to, what is here, the context of a very unusual mode of address. I myself have profited (though not so much economically) from both the fair use doctrine and the Copyright Act of 1976, simply by signing below.

> By their signature, the Author(s) warrant(s) that the article specified above in no way infringes upon any copyright or proprietary

rights of others, and is in no way libellous or unlawful, and hereby transfers the copyright to this article to Walter de Gruyter, effective immediately. The copyright transfer covers the exclusive rights to reproduce and distribute the article, including reprints, photographic reproductions, microform, on-line, electronic database, videodisks, or any other reproductions of a similar nature, and translations.

However, the Author(s) reserve(s):

1. All proprietary rights other than copyrights, such as patent rights.

2. The right to use all or part of this article in future works of their own published more than two years after the original publication in the above-named work and to grant or refuse permission to third parties to republish all or part of the article or translations thereof. To republish whole articles, such third parties must also obtain written permission from Walter de Gruyter.

However, Walter de Gruyter alone may grant rights concerning the work as a whole.

This Agreement must be signed by the Author. In cases of multiple authorship, this agreement must be signed by at least one of the Authors, who agrees to inform the other(s):

___10/30/2010___	___David Ben-Merre___
Date	Author's Signature

It is a little stunning that the curves of a signed name under words can secure the rights to other words but that, apparently, is where capital has brought human language to us today. Normally, this de Gruyter block quotation, lifted directly from the signed contract, would appear or be referenced in this book's paratextual acknowledgment section. But I wanted to make the point, again, that such mediating factors of the cultural and critical marketplace are always in the background of discursive production, even if they are pushed to that background and little acknowledged.

If, beyond the exhaustively irritating instances of self-reference, the visual appearance of this chapter so far does not resemble the visual appearances of the other chapters in this book, that is partly by design. Whatever idealized version of a poem or song one has, it is always already conditioned by a very unromantic, sociohistorical (economic) mediating structure. (One gets the sense that poetic apostrophes would be more successful in their summoning if poetic lobbyists were to prod congress to pass an attendant act.) Beyond attributions of authority and beyond acknowledgments of property-status, the name of the author, for Foucault, can invoke a whole slew of suggestions. Conversely, the lack of a name creates its own air of mystery, not to be ignored. He writes, "We now ask of each poetic or fictional text: From where does it come, who wrote it, when, under what circumstances, or beginning with what design? . . . And if a text should be discovered in a state of anonymity—whether as a consequence of an accident or the author's explicit wish—the game becomes one of rediscovering the author. Since literary anonymity is not tolerable, we can accept it only in the guise of an enigma" (213). The same seems to be the case for Carly Simon's anonymous "you." Questions about the self-references or paradoxes in the song have generally given way to the more popular quest to find out who this "you" *really* is. This speaks as much to a (very American) celebrity culture as it does to how supposedly private lyric spaces are mediated by the discourse of the public sphere. Since the song's release many have sought the identity of Carly Simon's elusive "you," as if the whole thing were a riddle poem or—to borrow a phrase from the song—a race at Saratoga and everyone were searching for an inside tip. It has become a cult question of postmodern proportions which wonderfully captures (while also missing) the point of the whole enterprise. The motivation, for fans and music critics alike, seems to be in pinning down a "you" who cannot be successfully pinned down, thereby disregarding the words of the song which claim the identity lies elsewhere. Accordingly, the song has received a type of market immortality based upon the fact that the celebrity has no name. While my own interest in this song's quasi-apostrophes is not tied to the biographical "you," the figure behind the address has become a very big part of the song's cultural reception.

While apostrophes cannot make something that is not there present, Simon's simple address has conjured a whole slew of countering presences. And the mythology of this "you" has far outpaced its illogicality. The biggest candidate has been the actor Warren Beatty, followed closely by the singer Mick Jagger—both notorious for their sexual exploits. "The narcissistic movie star" (Beatty), Greg Haymes writes, is an "obvious choice" as is the singer (Jagger) who happened to sing backup vocals on the record. In response to an interview question by *The Washington Post* in 1983, asking if the mystery man were indeed the movie star, Simon answered that "it certainly sounds like it was about Warren Beatty. He certainly thought it was about him—he called me and said thanks for the song" ("Carlysimon.com"). One might say he has acted out the part. This, though, once again, shows what is so odd about Simon's address—that anyone vain enough to claim to be the "you" would, by association, fit the model. Simon would subsequently deny that the song is about either Beatty or Jagger, only to then partially deny her denial. James Taylor, Simon's onetime husband, has also received consideration, as have Kris Kristofferson, Jack Nicholson, and Cat Stevens, each reputedly a former love interest. Even Oprah Winfrey (playfully suggested by Simon herself), as Haymes reports, and the tongue-in-cheek dark horse Mark Felt have been suggested. Though a lark, the parallel with Felt is rather telling about perceived differences between historical anonymity and literary anonymity across cultural spaces. Does it really matter, in the end, who "you" is? Does it matter what Simon says?

Apparently so because that is where the cultural market resides. If one wondered how much capital one could get out of a lyric moment, Simon's memoir, conveniently published between versions of my own chapter, would offer a glimpse. Because the song had so imprinted itself on a social consciousness, the mysterious "you" became an expedient way to market the memoir. But this strategy had an ironic effect, shifting the attention in what is ostensibly even more of an ego-driven genre than the lyric from the "I" to the "you." A review in *The Guardian* crowed, "No need for a review, folks: it was Warren Beatty." This wasn't quite correct. Using a baseball metaphor, Simon identified him as one of the men referenced by the song. She wrote, "And no, the song is not just about one person. Let's just say Warren Beatty played second base in this particular infield, which he knows so well, but as for who manned first and third—ask the shortstop. In all seriousness, the subjects of the first and third verses don't know that this song is also about them, so it would be inappropriate and a rude awakening to disclose their identities until they, them (vain) selves, were notified" (254). Beyond a great number of *I-told-you-so*s across the globe, what would it matter, to the specific *lyric* sense of the song—the sense that maintains its viability in the openness of deictic anonymity—if she had named Beatty as the unknown paramour? Or, to ask the question on a social level, is it to say that because Beatty has been identified, all other men are now exonerated from any blame? There is an odd yet persuasive sense that the celebrity-hunting afterlife has really nothing to do with what is at stake—socially or lyrically—in the song, and yet that is where the attention seems to lie. Too often, though, such a celebrity reveal seems to function as a socially desired act of alibi-ing all others, misdirecting the attention away from deep-seeded, gender-based structural inequalities.

On a related note, we might ask if the public imagination has to reframe the story in terms of a normative heterosexual coupling, what it would mean to de-couple the "I" and the "you" from any publicly known bodies? Such a queer approach would already have been anticipated by Eve Kosofsky Sedgwick's essay (with apologies for predictable bridges), "Paranoid Reading and Reparative Reading; or, You're So Paranoid, You Probably Think This Introduction Is About You." In reversing the expected critical etiology of the literary object, Sedgwick chooses a title we have already been taught to process in order to explain a theory. I am now (inadequately) using this paranoid theory to explain the ever-shifting figuration behind Simon's title. It is the very same anticipatory tautology of the song. (And this is to say nothing of the paranoia inherent in rehearsing for oneself, at the very least, fair-use guidelines, based on the vain assumption that someone will be watching.) In the essay, Sedgwick reminds us of Leo Bersani's understanding of a paranoiac mindset to be a "doubling of presence," an "I" becoming a "you."[15] What, we might ask, does it say about a social culture when this "you" is almost inevitably turned into a "he," decontextualizing for one's own purposes, as I have been doing, crucial scenes of address?

I began this chapter by noting a slight variation between the written lyrics and recorded performance of "You're So Vain." In the recorded version on *No Secrets*, Simon, in what sounds like a moment of rhythmic ardor, draws the final syllable from the chorus's "don't you" into the opening of the next verse: "Oh you had me several years ago." The ever-so-slight modulation into the "oh" connects these two instances of "you" so they are not so awkwardly buttressed against each other. But it is also a moment, like those other sounds of pop music—the "oohs" and "ahs" and "yeahs" and "babys"—that smack of presence, especially because they don't often

---

15. Bersani, 188; qtd. in Sedgwick 6. In prefacing a collection of queer readings, each turning away from the earlier "deontological project of 'ought'" (2), Sedgwick hoped, at the time, to move the discussion from the "hermeneutics of suspicion" to reparative reading, asking what knowledge is *doing* rather than whether it is true. "[W]hat seems less settled," she writes, "is any predetermined idea about what makes the queerness of a queer reading" (2). See also Kurnick's recent reassessment of Sedgwick's piece in light of the "method wars."

make it onto the written score. This rhetoric of variation, this rhetoric of the moment, is a media affordance that gives pop music its authenticity and pushes us, in "You're So Vain," to mistake the discarded lover rescuing a sense of agency from her situation for the singer-songwriter Carly Simon.

The "authenticity" of performed song is irrevocably tied to the presence of a speech act. One is still able, in writing, to describe a vainglorious "you," but it loses its tonal luster a bit. This notwithstanding, one might wonder whether the supposed presence inherent in the performance is more about immediacy and voice or whether it is the result of a mass-mediated persona? One thinks of the "I" as less shifty than the "you"—that the "I" who set the words down on the page is still the "I" who utters them later. What happens to notions of authenticity with every cover of the song, or when someone tries in vain to sing it at karaoke? Or, for that matter, what happens when an audience sings the lines from the floor of the amphitheater alongside the lyricist singing them from the stage?[16] Is it still really about Warren Beatty or Kris Kristofferson? Or, does the deictic end up invoking a new, yet fleeting, mysterious presence that has little to do with a private "I"? If the performance depends upon iterability, does this very same iterability not defeat the expectations of performative authenticity?

"[W]hat appears as spontaneity is in fact carefully planned out in advance with machinelike precision . . . [as a] more or less feeble rehashing of basic formulas," Theodor Adorno writes ("Perennial" 123). He is speaking specifically of jazz, and he is not one of its most judicious listeners. On the whole, he did not care for the popular culture industry, calling it "the swarming forms of the banal" ("On the Fetish" 274). The problem was the mass-mediated form—in terms of both production and consumption.[17] His critique was leveled at the fascistic tendencies always at play in mass culture, where, as Richard Middleton writes, "social control of music's meaning and function has become absolute, musical form a reified reflection of manipulative social structures" (*Studying* 35). Modernist, avant-garde art, on the other hand, embodied for Adorno an authentic type of "negative knowledge," because it could not be so easily consumed, its dialectical pressures not so

---

16. Songs, as per Mark Booth, are "also said somehow in extension by us, and we are drawn into the state, the pose, the attitude, the self offered by the song" (15; qtd. in Burt "What" 436).

17. Simon Frith calls the popular song "a mass-produced music which carries a critique of its own means of production" (qtd. in Hesmondhalgh and Negus 6); Michael Hoover and Lisa Stokes understand the tension in terms of a dialectic between "cultural pessimists" like Adorno and "cultural populists." See also Charles Hamm, *Putting Popular Music in its Place*, and Elizabeth Eva Leach, "Vicars of 'Wannabe'. . . ."

easily resolved ("Reconciliation" 160). That Adorno did not recognize that the mass-circulated popular art form was historically mediated and thus part of the dialectical process should have gone without saying. His own tendency to romanticize modernism as having an inherent oppositional force in its form might also have undergone its own dialectical examination.[18] But, more importantly, and beyond dialectics (!), he also couldn't recognize some pretty good music. Still, he is right (at times) to caution us about romantic notions of performance we may have acquired.

"Despite the passage of some pop music styles since the 1970s through various aesthetics of irony and self-destruction," Middleton writes, "the discourse of authenticity within music culture still holds much of its critical primacy, as dismissive response to turn-of-the-century 'manufactured pop' and 'corporate hegemony' makes clear" (*Voicing* 203).[19] Authenticity

---

18. The musical wing of "subcultural studies"—following the work of Dick Hebdige in *Subculture* (specifically regarding punk), Sheila Whiteley in *The Space Between the Notes* and Barry Shank in *Dissonant Identities* (rock), and Tricia Rose in *Black Noise* (rap)—insists that pop music forms an oppositional style, able to critique the cultural narratives of the dominant or "mainstream" class. With apologies to each and every one of my friends, literatures of resistance, as Sarah Thornton argues, are not any more or less outside the cultural marketplace. Such "oppositional" narratives are produced, marketed, sold, and consumed just like any other product of the culture, especially when authenticity is packaged alongside. "The weakness of 'consumptionism,'" Middleton writes, "is its assumption . . . that the listeners are completely free to use and interpret music as they wish—an assumption which, commonly, goes on to link freedom with 'resistance' (to the bland homogeneity attributed to the received meanings of commercial cultural provision" (*Reading* 9). See also Angela McRobbie, "Settling Accounts with Subcultures: A Feminist Critique" and Gary Clarke, "Defending Ski-Jumpers: A Critique of Theories of Youth Subcultures," in Frith *et al.*, eds., 55–67, 68–80.

19. The question of "authenticity" seems to come up in every discussion of popular music, even for those who seek to shift the discussion of it to the audience, like Simon Frith or Sarah Rubidge, or those, like Georgina Born and David Hesmondhalgh who argue that it "has been consigned to the intellectual dustheap" (qtd. in Middleton *Voicing* 30). As Allan Moore writes, "'Authentic.' 'Real.' 'Honest.' 'Truthful.' 'With Integrity.' 'Actual.' 'Genuine.' 'Essential.' 'Sincere.' Of all the value terms employed in music discourse, these are perhaps the most loaded" (131). For more on authenticity, see Simon Frith, "'The Magic that Can Set You Free': The Ideology of Folk and the Myth of the Rock Community," *Popular Music* 1 (1981): 159–68; "Playing with Real Feeling—Jazz and Suburbia" in *Music for Pleasure*, 45–63; Sarah Rubidge, "Does Authenticity Matter? The Case for and against Authenticity in the Performing Arts," in *Analysing Performance: A Critical Reader*, edited by Patrick Campbell (Manchester UP, 1996), 219–33; Reebee Garofalo, "How Autonomous Is Relative: Popular Music, the Social Formation and Cultural Struggle," *Popular Music* 6, no. 1 (1987); Elizabeth Eva Leach, "Vicars"; Richard Middleton, *Voicing*, 199–246; and Allan Moore, "Authenticity as Authentication," in Moore, *Critical Essays*, 131–45.

is marketable. One so easily mistakes the rhetoric of confession for confession—even (I have been told) in a confessional booth—and mistakes an "Oh" of performance for genuine feeling, even at its hundredth iteration. Authenticity sells because it fits in seamlessly with that individualistic narrative of neoliberalism or late capitalism or whatever name one wants to give it. It is a narrative we like, even if, in the end, we have been trained to do so. Pop music helps sell this narrative and this narrative helps sell pop music. This is not to say that songwriters are liars or their performances insincere: only that "authenticity" wholesales very well in a sociocultural marketplace. Nowhere is this more notable than in the personae of the singer-songwriters and what David Brackett calls their "sound[s] of autobiography."[20] Brackett notes how Carole King, Joni Mitchell, James Taylor, and Carly Simon "released influential albums between 1970 and 1972 that were recognized as introducing a new 'introspective,' 'intimate' quality into 'rock' music . . . And their lyrics were heard as somehow referring to their own lives: Critics frequently introduced biographical elements into articles and reviews as important information that might explain the meaning of the songs . . ." (237–38). The music journalist Chuck Klosterman illuminates the irony behind this autobiographical imperative:

> If a musical entity aspires to unconditional greatness—be it a song, a band, or an entire aesthetic—it has to be grounded in some kind of espoused reality. And I'm pretty sure pop music is the only artistic idiom where this is true . . . in film, literature, television, painting, and sculpture, and just about everything else that's viewed as artistic, 'greatness' is derived from how creative something is; in modern pop music, greatness is derived from how creative something *isn't*. (259)[21]

---

20. For Brackett, the songs and persona of David Bowie would be an example of a nonauthentic or ironic aesthetic. Brackett writes of "Bowie's unabashed acknowledgement that his performances present him as an actor playing a part. This apparent distance from his persona places him at the opposite end of the authenticity spectrum from singer-songwriters, who had made self-revelation the cornerstone of their art" ("I Have No Message Whatsoever," in Brackett, 276–82).

21. He continues: "From what I can tell, 'real' translates as 'great.' Rock writers see those two words as synonyms. [Kurt] Cobain wore a flannel shirt, which is what normal people in Seattle wear, so he was real (and therefore great)" (261).

Klosterman calls this aspiring toward reality "The Carly Simon Principle." For him, it all comes down to "replicating sincerity," "forc[ing] our understanding of what a song is supposed to mean into its notes and lyrics" (263, 260). What is "outside" moves "inside." This critical sentiment comes across metaphorically in a wonderful passage from Simon's song: "I had some dreams they were clouds in my coffee. . . ." In her memoir, she attributes the line to her friend and piano player, Billy Mernit, who, from an airplane seat, saw the reflection of clouds wafting across the top of her coffee cup. It is an unexpected silhouette of a reverie, what is outside moving inside. It is an artistically invigorating type of vanity, the turning inward. It is the alleged centripetal space of the lyric, which certainly always pointed more outward than critical vectors had allowed.

As I have argued, the introspective authenticity typical of the singer-songwriter's lyric (popular in popular music) is a type of vanity because it focuses attention on the individual in the guise of focusing attention on the song. While most popular songs do not reproduce the metaleptic paradox at the center of Simon's lyrics, they do reenact a type of quasi-apostrophe by gesturing as though they were turning outward. Part of that is the desire to have someone else listening when we call out. There is a warmth to this sense of address, to the space not only of "being there," but of being there with you.

If, through this chapter, I have meant to suggest that, on one level at least, it feels ridiculous to argue (from privileged positions) about lyric/antilyric, voice/antivoice, performance/script when the ground of aesthetic representation is mediated by legal institutions, themselves mediated by nebulous power currents of discursive systems, this does not mean one ought not to continue, even if a court says I am not able to shift into the "you" of someone else's song. Whatever sense of vanity attaches to control over proprietary rights does not diminish the crucial humility of communal feeling. Mediated representations of pain and loss—perhaps genuine, perhaps not—ramify authenticity; they are "real" in the sense that they are relatable for any number of yous. Deictic words without concrete references do not remain empty, and inauthentic representations—*oh*, whatever that might mean—are not necessarily in vain.

"(I was on chorus all through school—even in college, but don't let that get out). I suppose painting taught me as much about the ways to look, to see, as music did about the ways to hear and listen,"[22] *Terrance Hayes confesses in an interview, performing the private (or very private) sphere, knowing full well his secret will out. If authenticity is not a function of lyrical gestures and not a function of vocal performance but rather what one is taught to read in the residue of each scene, how is one supposed to reassess the mass mediated expectation filling the auditorium even before the spotlight is turned on for the guest speaker, even before he has reached the stage door? "I am so / fucking vain I cannot believe anyone / is threatened by me," he professes on a rooftop in "New York Poem."*[23] *His ambiguous utterance comes before he starts to list his contranyms—"how 'cleave' and 'cleave' are the same word / looking in opposite directions." If words can't even see eye to eye, what hope is there for the individual who is asked to perform, often in ways not asked of others?*

22. Terrece Hayes, qtd. in Rowell, 1070.

23. *How to Be Drawn*, 10.

Chapter 7

Terrance Hayes

"A Perfect Circle"

Qual è 'l geomètra che tutto s'affige
per misurar lo cerchio, e non ritrova,
pensando, quel principio ond'elli indige,

tal era io a quella vista nova:
veder voleva come si convene
l'imago al cerchio e come vi s'indova

—Dante, *Paradiso* Canto XXXIII ll. 133–38

I began an obsessive regimen of drawing
Peanuts. (Charlie Brown began with an O)

—Terrance Hayes, "The Blue Terrance"[1]

The catalogue to the 1999 National Gallery exhibition of Rembrandt's self-portraits elaborates on the faint enigmatic half circles behind the painter's brazen visage in *Self-Portrait with Two Circles* (c.1665–69): "One of the more plausible arguments links the circles to a well-known *topos* from the theory of art, namely the ability to draw a circle freehand as evidence of consummate artistic skill. Because of its closed form, the circle was associated with perfection and eternity, and was therefore ideal as a symbol of artistic excellence."[2] Among the reasonable symbolic associations offered by art historians for the

---

1. *Wind in a Box*, 65.
2. Christopher White and Quentin Buvelot, eds., *Rembrandt by Himself,* 220.

circles, the editors reference a possible artistic precursor, relating how Giotto (c.1266–1337), when asked by one of the pope's emissaries to demonstrate his artistic skill for a possible paint job the pope had in mind (an early CV of sorts), simply drew a circle freehand. The messenger couldn't understand the effort, but the brilliance was thus demonstrated to the pope. Viewed from afar, even a child can pick out a circle's shape, but at the microscopic level little deformities emerge: the arc bends too slowly or too quickly or its width ventures just slightly too far in either direction. A high-tech printer might fare better, but still to no avail. The pixelated ink just cannot bend with the less than atomic precision of the mathematically ideal circle of the mind. It is a mythological impossibility—this, the perfect circle, toward which artists may strive. That, of course, thankfully doesn't stop attempts at a Kandinsky circle or a Rembrandt eye, which, in their own ways, hope to break down the visible world into its visual turns.

"I can imitate the spheres of the model's body," Terrance Hayes writes, and he means it, much more than most who do not have his artistic eye and hand to match.[3] His "How to Draw a Perfect Circle" follows his own "Self-Portrait as the Mind of a Camera" in the *A Circling Mind* section of *How to be Drawn*, a collection title that plays upon subjective and objective artistic senses of "draw/drawn" with a wink at the magnetism of desire.[4] It also suggests the difficult position of modeling for a social culture that insists on how certain individuals ought to be drawn. "I can imitate the spheres of the model's body," he continues,

<blockquote>

                    her head,
Her mouth, the chin she rests at the bend of her elbow
But nothing tells me how to make the pupils spiral

From her gaze.

</blockquote>

The stanza break dramatizes the poetic abyss between subject and object, threatening more than the poem's attempts to connect the eye to the world. The incommensurability between the sight line of the gaze and the circular pairs of eyes navigating it presage the poet's later attempts to make sense of the world, to square its rounded edges. In the Dante quotation epigraphing

---

3. The complete poem is listed in my book's Appendix B.

4. Hayes, *How to Be Drawn*, 90, line 1. Subsequent parenthetical references will note the line number.

this chapter, to which I will return at the end, the problem is posed metaphorically as the classical geometrical attempt to square the circle. The collection's cover art was drawn by Hayes himself, a self-portrait with its own imperfect circle and half-circle of headphones. One of the headphones is out of view, but we know—we must know—its circular half hides behind the head's circular irises and pupils and nostrils and chin. With the artist's hands out of the picture, the stare is inescapable. Like the entire collection, this is a man looking at himself. And at us who aren't there, looking at him looking at us.

From his semi-successful poetic attempts to recast the model as a figure of shapes, Hayes drifts to the literal edges of vision but one that feels like a whole metaphysics: "Everything the eye sees enters a circle, / The world is connected to a circle" (l. 4) and soon after, "The shape inside the circle / Is a circle" (ll. 6–7). Accustomed as we are to the rectangular borders around us (books, TVs, most artistic wall hangings), Hayes's speaker reminds us that everything in our immediate vision is framed by the circular contours of the eye. "The eye is the first circle," Ralph Waldo Emerson memorably writes, articulating a vision for cyclical existence, adding that "the horizon which it forms is the second; and throughout nature this primary figure is repeated without end."[5] The circularity of life and of history matches the circularity of the natural world. He continues, outlining a natural theology without outlines:

> It is the highest emblem in the cipher of the world. St. Augustine described the nature of God as a circle whose centre was everywhere, and its circumference nowhere. We are all our lifetime reading the copious sense of this first of forms. One moral we have already deduced, in considering the circular or compensatory character of every human action. . . . Our life is an apprenticeship to the truth, that around every circle another can be drawn; that there is no end in nature, but every end is a beginning; that there is always another dawn risen on mid-noon, and under every deep a lower deep opens. (403)

---

5. These opening lines follow the poetic epigraph, which, naturally, centers the essay ("Nature centres into balls . . ."). The philosopher does not shy away from his own rhetorical exclamations ("O, what truths profound and executable only in ages and orbs are supposed in the announcement of every truth!" [408]) and apostrophes, including one in which he proleptically conjures a future audience addressing himself: "And thus, O circular philosopher, I hear some reader exclaim . . ." (411).

Unlike Emerson, Hayes is not the all-seeing center, although he is necessarily the centering lyric presence. He is ambivalent about his own romantically transcendental leaning, noting in his "Self-Portrait" the magnitude of perspective: "Not even two eyes in the same head see the same thing." It often feels as if Hayes's own two poetic eyes want to move in different directions. Even his hemistich phrasing of a "world connected to a circle" piles two metaphorical circles atop each other to connect to the line's other half: "breath spools from the nostrils" ("How to" l. 5). The word "spools"—itself visually hiding two circular eyes or nostrils in its center—recalls the earlier failed attempt to capture the "pupils spiral[ing]."[6] Is this spooling breath emanating from the model he has been studying or is it his own exhalation? Or, at this moment, does each intimate breath open onto the other? The sexually suggestive lines then turn meditative again before he offers a foreboding metaphor, grounding the hunger: "the egg fallen outside the nest the serpent circles / Rests in the serpent's gaze the way my gaze rests on the model" (ll. 7–8). This will come back later. As if it were part of the act of love making, the hand wants to follow the eye in Hayes's blind contour drawing, reaching for something it cannot altogether possess. This blind contour technique gives a name for the feeling that Hayes—or any artist, really—doesn't actually know where he or she is going and can only see the whole picture, complete with its wanderings outside the canvas, after being informed that it is time to put down the brush.

Throughout this poem, Hayes plays with the material and symbolic reverberations of the circular O. Like in Dickinson, Hayes's circle feels a metaphor for the poetic, that temptation of unattainable lyric wholeness. And like for Dickinson, one feels Hayes is more invested in the circumference, that unpredictable journey around the perfect circle, than in whatever prophetic truth the circle, at its center, would conceal. "At the center of God," he teases a bit later in the poem, "looms an O" (l. 28), the graphic clarification leaving one still yearning for revelation, and perhaps feeling more threatened by the double o in "looms" than by a god reduced to a child's shape. The meditative movement—here between letters and gods,

---

6. One might be reminded here of Ellen Gallagher's images of spiraling locks and deeply evacuated eyes from "Wiglette," part of her DeLuxe collection (2004–05), an influence on Hayes's poem "Wigphrastic"—also from *How to be Drawn*. See: https://www.moma.org/wp/inside_out/wp-content/uploads/2012/02/Ellen-Gallagher-DeLuxe.jpg?_ga=2.132913678.1039278854.1680550917-802747082.1680550917.

earlier between models and snakes—keeps ramifying throughout the poem, circles within circles, like layers of an onion—"the best symbol of the O" (l. 40)—which makes an appearance later on. In a phrasing that might illuminate Hayes's aesthetic, the speaker tells us, "Everything is connected / By a line curling and canceling itself" (ll. 10–11). These words, though, again connote unease, someone being watched, hunted: "the eye tracks the subject" (l. 9). This unanticipated, looping line of connection cycles back to the snake, now likened to the ouroboros and then to the autosarcophagy of a self-destructive mind. And then, suddenly, everything turns violent. But let me pause for a moment before getting there—something, sadly, the hardened poetic mind and its unavoidable place at the nexus of a very violent American history won't let us do.

Hayes is a poet characterized by what he calls a "schizophrenic aesthetic,"[7] which tends to mean, for some of his strongest readers like Christopher Spaide and Calista McRae, lyric ambivalence, playful juxtaposition, formal experimentation, and exploration rather than statement.[8] Describing such nonlinear (or circular) poetics, Hayes offers: "I'm not just interested in beginning-middle-end stories, or stories that have a clear moral or inspirational point" (Koo 67). Elizabeth Alexander detects "intricate galaxies inside his head," William M. Ramsey, in a wonderful phrasing, sees him as "imbalanced by destabilizing, galactic-scale assaults on self-coherence," and Hayes, for his part, claims he is "often a STRANGER to [him]self."[9] For many of his readers, this means a rejection of lyric subjectivity, but that is a position Hayes, in his ambivalence, is critically hesitant to adopt. As McRae writes, Hayes is "interested in the ways one is connected to others . . . and in how one can represent these partial, shifting connections in a genre

---

7. Casper 180 (see also Koo 64 and Simpson 134).

8. Christopher Spaide calls this a "constitutional ambivalence" (237), and he sees Hayes as "ever dedicated to multiple choice" (251). Calista McRae, in her study likening lyric poetry to stand-up comedy (two modes of "performing the self" [9]), notes Hayes's "comic indeterminacy" (121), where delight (of sounds, language, puns, unexpected turns) exceeds the immediate cause. He has "a comically wayward and uncertain mind" (117), "a wandering subjectivity" (122), whereby his "scattershot effects seem to move outwards from—and in excess of—a poem's meaning; there is something centrifugal, something that declines to be tacked down to meaning" (129). Robert N. Casper sees Hayes as "a man who dares to make connections where it seems there is only difference" (180).

9. Alexander qtd. in Burt "Galaxies"; Ramsey, 128–29; Hayes, "Line 1," 810.

that continues to be seen as solipsistic, asocial, sealed off" (139–40). He is a considerable example of how poetic experimentation, polyphony, and immediate and diachronous historical/communal connections need not be opposed to a (falsely) romanticized idea of lyric subjectivity.[10]

Formally, Hayes calls himself "a kind of poetry slut," noting how he "want[s] to sleep with all forms, all styles, all schools, but . . . [is] committed to none of them" (Simpson 135). The final words-under-erasure of his *Light-head* collection (a "Scene Deleted Under the Emperor's Order") ventriloquize the final words of a decapitated prophet: "I have no form because / I have no allegiance / to form" (93). Another way to say this might be that Hayes is a mercenary for all forms (hence the emperor's displeasure)—committed for the moment, but willing to leap to another continent when called upon to fight. As he makes clear in an interview, one of his collection titles, *Wind in a Box*, directly invokes this pseudo-paradoxical freedom within form—one very importantly not isolated from an American racialized context: "The box represents form, and then the wind is the spirit you breathe into it, the imagination, how it moves around in that space and takes its shape but still possesses its own freedom of movement" (Koo 73).[11] Or, as he relates to Stephanie Burt for a *New York Times* profile, "If you can breakdance, that's cool. . . . If you can breakdance in a straitjacket, that's even better" ("Galaxies"). Such sentiments notwithstanding, Hayes does not immediately subscribe to the easy rhetoric of "poetic freedom," as formal constraints for him push back (in positive ways) against what he thinks he might want to say. Hayes's wrestling with and within form would include his distinctive

---

10. Attendant to this ambivalence, McRae writes, "Hayes's interest in what cannot be reduced to a single coherent interpretation suffuses his flourishes of sound and image, his highly controlled long poems that seem to invite and foil lyric readings" (23).

11. Henry Louis Gates Jr. turns to Hayes's poem "The Blue Seuss" from this collection to articulate the historically encumbered racialized context of this cultural metaphor (xxvii–xxviii). "For me," Gates writes, "the black box is also a powerful metaphor for the circumscribed universe of being within which people of African descent were forced to attempt to construct a new identity after emerging on this side of the Atlantic after the horrors of the Middle Passage. . . . [B]ut it also is a resonant metaphor for the social and cultural world that they created within this circumscribed space . . ." (xvi). Andrea Brady sees the constraint in/around/adopted/rejected by Hayes as "the *condition* of freedom and an indispensable tool of poetic invention" (17). Her project interrogates the poetry-as-"bondage" metaphor adopted in vastly differing ways by poets over the centuries and then recontextualized within actual and incommensurate global histories. How, she asks, "can attending to actual bondage and resistance help us to track a different history of lyric poetry, one that does not map its liberation from formal constraints on to the emancipation of the individual under liberal democracy?" (4).

takes on classical forms—such as his ghazal or villanelle or much-discussed "Sonnet," which repeats fourteen times the line "We sliced the watermelon into smiles"[12]—and adventures with his own invented forms, including his anagram poems based on newspaper word games,[13] poems based on the Japanese *pecha kucha* presentation format,[14] and what is called the "Golden Shovel" form, titled after the "original" poetic form he created.

---

12. On the page, though not necessarily in oral performance, the towers of fourteen identical words form continuous vertical chasms, almost like visual caesurae of melon slicing. Similarly attentive to the sonnet's graphic space, Anthony Reed sees it as an example of "concrete poetry." Although he calls it "inscrutab[le]" (34) and understands it as "cancel[ing] its own referentiality, yielding a poetics of unsaying and incomplete resignification" (33), he does end up remarking quite a bit on its referential and paronomastic overtones. The menacing smile, he notes, "link[s] the threats of violence to the legacy of minstrelsy that governs some aspects of black public life" (35). He also calls attention to the near similitude between "smile" and "simile," noting how the extra "i" puns on the absence of the expected lyric "I," which is lost between sliced fruit and facial expression. It is "an effaced sign of the poet's presence" (36). Spaide reads the sonnet as a "defiance of genre conventions, and refusal to turn" (231). Similar to the repetitive blues stanza, the "unwavering line plays out the historical persistence of those racist formations, along with the other Western hand-me-down, the sonnet" (232). More generally, Hayes vacillates between the lyric "I" and the plural pronoun "we" of the Black Arts Movement: "not timeless or universal but immediate and affirmatively black" (243), "one voice inherited from the tradition and one voice speaking in opposition" (254). Jess Cotton sees Hayes's general playfulness with the sonnet form as more subversive: "Hayes moves the sonnet outwards from this reductive, all-absorbing white interiority" such that "the reader is prompted to conceptualize an unending complexity of black interiority, which they cannot reach . . ." (547). Noting the second-person address of many of the sonnets in Hayes's *American Sonnets*, she reads the collection as "deliver[ing] a whiplash to white liberalism, as it carves out a definition of lyric privacy against 'what is inward, is absorbed'" (546–47; internal quotation from *American Sonnets* 15). Returning readers to the moment of performance—here specifically a reader reading this poem aloud—Metta Sáma questions how one ought to declaim a poem of the same fourteen lines. Though visually and literally the same, the lines can't help but be transformed on reading.

13. Hayes describes the compositional method for these "A Gram of &s" poems: they are "based on the daily word game found in the puzzle section of many syndicated newspapers. I end each line with one of the eleven words derived from the title word" (*Hip* 91). Regular puzzle rules apply. So "e x a m p l e," for example, makes use of the end words: lamp, palm, maple, peel, lame, apex, exam, male-[dictions], plea, axle, and leap. Hayes has expressed some regret at occasionally losing himself in the form: "Those anagram poems in the second book were all an effort to trick myself into a space that wasn't concerned with anything other than the poems" (Koo 73).

14. The *pecha kucha* poems and variations are based on the ephemeral "Japanese business presentation format wherein a presenter narrates or riffs on twenty images connected to a single theme for twenty seconds at a time" (*Lighthead* 94).

Now the basis for its own anthology, Hayes's "The Golden Shovel" constructs a poem around Gwendolyn Brooks's famous "We Real Cool," as if Brooks's work were a Sapphic fragment in want of reconstruction.[15] Hayes's title comes from the name of the pool hall in the epigraph to Brooks's poem. He takes each of the twenty-four words of the original poem as the end-word starting point for each of his twenty-four lines, which are then reconstructed around these words. This times two, as his poem is divided into two parts, each twenty-four lines, divided by a decade in time. Much more than what Sianne Ngai would characterize as a "gimmick," the form shows how the possibilities of one voice in a loose tradition might give rise to another. Even in this "post"-whatever world, we—some much more than others—still need to grapple with pain that cannot be immediately explained away by market forces. "We / die soon," Brooks's poem ends with finality. In Hayes's hands, the paper-machéd lines become: "That night we / got down on our knees in my room. *If I should die / before I wake*, Da said to me, *it will be too soon*" (*Lighthead* 7). Inverting the classical apostrophic act of prayer, the father turns away from God to address the son, pressed by the fears and promises of that day. They are a "we" but a "we" that cannot always bulwark the world around them.

Spaide sees Hayes's lyric "we" not only as communal in the moment but moreover as "playfully collaborative" with different cultural traditions (254). Rachel Galvin sees such metaphorical collaboration as (a nonpejorative) "poetic cannibalism," which "seeks to overturn the matrix of power under-girding notions of literary primacy and to cultivate compositional procedures based in radical mixing" ("Poetry" 24).[16] A collaborative aesthetic as such challenges the myth of lyric subjectivity for Galvin. Here, she seems to be speaking directly to the fiction of a "closed" text, not so much to Hayes's more nuanced lyric meditativeness. "Homage and lineage are inscribed directly into Hayes's poems," she writes, "so that the reader cannot read one without

---

15. *The Golden Shovel Anthology: New Poems Honoring Gwendolyn Brooks*, edited by Peter Kahn, Ravi Shankar, and Terrence Hayes, U of Arkansas P, 2017.

16. Referencing Roberto Schwartz's attack on "'coordinates' of authorship, influence, and originality" (*Misplaced Ideas*, 6; qtd. in Galvin 26) and Françoise Meltzer's *Hot Property*, Galvin hopes to decolonize the romantic ideal of authorship, noting how poets like Hayes ". . . deliberately play upon the anxiety associated with plagiarism, which is linked to the notion of a sovereign textual subject: a subject that 'purports to double mimetically the authoritative and self-contained subjectivity of the author' or what has been commonly called the lyric 'I'" (29; quoting Meltzer, 4). See also Galvin, "This Song . . ." where Hayes and others critique mimicry as a negative colonial patrimony.

the other" (36).[17] His two epigraphs to *Wind in a Box* ("I tell a story of bodies that change"—attributed to Ovid and DJ Spooky—and Whitman's "I contain multitudes" [xi]) reveal as much. "[A]ll of us be / floundering interiors" (*Wind* 19), Hayes writes in "The Blue Baraka," one of a series of "blue" poems, written in the idioms of memorable voices.[18] Along with Amiri Baraka, the collection includes blue poems in the manner of J. L. Borges, David Bowie, Etheridge Knight, and Dr. Seuss, among others. One is tempted to call these pseudo dramatic monologues, but even what one might call Hayes's lyric mode is masked and manifold, which comes out in his own three blue poems titled "The Blue Terrance." This is not, of course, to deny the "intricate galaxies" of Hayes's idiosyncratic "voice"—even if it is a voice of juxtaposition, even if he is a self-proclaimed "poetry slut" with "no allegiance to form." In interviews, he offers an analogy to Prince (the artist formerly known as "The Artist Formerly Known as Prince"). Hearing Prince doing falsetto, he argues, one still knows it is Prince: "Voice is there whatever you do, why bother trying to tie it down" (Simpson 136). It is not just the diachronic weight of tradition(s) in all its abundance and baggage that intersects his poems, but also the supposedly different realms of "high" and "low" cultural texts, which Hayes jumps between effortlessly. Everything is connected. Or at least that is what the lyric mind—or the mind on the lyric—wants to believe and says as much, as if uttering those words were enough to convince itself of the perfect circle of its worth.

"Everything is connected." Pause. Line break. *Line break.* "Everything is connected / By a line curling" (ll. 10–11), "How to Draw a Perfect Circle" tells us, as the end of the line curls back to the start of the next. Yet it doesn't do so boustrophedonically, because a poet can't follow the rules of blind contour drawing. The hand has to come up again, leave the page and come back to the left margin, so as to start anew. Poetic syntax makes us jump or dangerously fall between the connections, not saunter, as one gets to do in prose. Suddenly, as if falling between these lines, the speaker loses

---

17. Lisa M. Steinman sees Hayes's ambivalent responses (a poetry of "inconclusion" rather than "inclusion" [219]) to poetic precursors, notably Wallace Stevens, as almost apostrophic addresses, calling out the "unfeeling distance from or unexcused ignorance of the everyday realities of the lives of actual African Americans" (218).

18. Noting the enormous influence of Baraka on contemporary African American poets, Emily Ruth Rutter understands Hayes to be "ventriloquiz[ing] Baraka's voice and empathiz[ing] with his critique of America's caste system" (336). Spaide, on the other hand, sees Hayes's response to Baraka's influence as more ambivalent (244–48).

the model, loses the Emersonian meditations on metaphysical circularity, loses the O of the egg, and plummets into the violent opening of the fifth stanza: "A man circling a railway underpass before attacking a policeman." "Orpheus dragged long silences around with him," Hayes writes elsewhere ("Line 1" 810). This line breathes such a long silence. If a bridge were to give us the classical metaphor of connection or the metaphor for metaphor itself (a "bearing across"), here we are all too abruptly tossed to the underpass, under the bridge, under the metaphor, to a very literal, dangerous world, however much it might poetically circle back to connect. One was warned, perhaps, with the earlier threat of the "serpent's gaze," but there is really no preparing for this turn. The scene disappears for two stanzas, then returns more forcefully—the descriptions spiraling inward—then hovers, reappears again, until it dissipates while lingering until the end. But before Hayes circles back to it, he returns to the roundness of the model's body. He, in his own words, has "to let [him]self be carried away" (l. 14), meaning it aesthetically as much as libidinally. "There are as many curves / As there are jewels of matrimony," he writes, carrying himself away metaphorically from the circular wedding ring to spherical pearls—possible jewels of the soon-to-be sexualized clam—to "sleeping ovaries," which are "like the heads of riders bunched in a tunnel" (l. 18). The dormant ovaries, one presumes, are awakened in the mind of the poet by the wedding ritual, but they also circle back to the earlier defenseless "egg fallen outside the nest." Here, though, the simile ends with the tunnel—another type of bridge, another underpass—a possible womb, cradling the future. Everything is connected.

The tunnel leads the speaker to think of subway doors (round ones, naturally) opening and closing: they "imitate an O." The shadows of the outward, urban traffic move inward to the body and its circulation. "In the blood the O spirals its helix of defects, genetic shadows" (l. 20), he writes, punning on type-O blood and the circular, spooling structure of DNA. The Os loom in blood. The reference to the genetic is not just about something—some recipe of the body—circling back, but moreover about trying to understand the linearity of cause and effect. And thus he returns to the stabbing and homicide in the underpass. "There are no instructions," Hayes writes, "for identifying loved ones who go crazy" (l. 21):

> When one morning a black man stabs a black transit cop in
> the face
> And the cop, bleeding from his eye, kills the assailant, no one
> traveling

> To the subway sees it quickly enough to make a camera phone
>   witness. (ll. 22–24)

A note at the end of the collection directs the reader to Hayes's website (he likes to provide contexts, references, and inspirations outside the presumed organic whole of the poem on the page). There are three links on his website to the poem, the reference all-too real. The July 4, 2012 *NY Post* and *Daily News*, respectively, headline the story as "MTA cop stabbed in eye, attacker killed at Queens LIRR station" and "Lunatic slashes MTA cop in the eye, but officer kills deranged suspect in holiday horror outside LIRR station in Queens." A day later, the news had crossed the Atlantic, with the *Daily Mail* captioning the story as "Iraq vet-turned-officer risks losing his eye after being stabbed by crazed attacker before shooting him dead on the scene."[19] Lunatic, deranged, crazed—such an overabundance of synonyms, none of which can capture the visceral irrationality of the act or the moment or the consciousness behind it. Hayes choses "crazy" for his own ventriloquized line. "Lunatic" would have connected better with the O of the moon, but, perhaps, not everything is always about poetic harmony. Unlike the blind contour drawing, there are sometimes serious consequences of a mind not knowing what the hand is doing. Here is how the *Daily News* described the horrifying event:

> Bleeding from his eye, an MTA police officer took aim at a knife-wielding cop-hater who had just stabbed him—and then fired four times as the man lunged at him again.
>
> Despite his pain and impaired vision, three of the bullets found their mark—killing the deranged suspect and ending a holiday horror outside an LIRR station in Queens.
>
> Officer John Barnett, who has served in Afghanistan with the Navy Reserves, was then rushed into surgery at Jamaica Hospital with a "devastating" wound. . . .

---

19. *NY Post* (July 4, 2012), https://nypost.com/2012/07/04/mta-cop-stabbed-in-eye-attacker-killed-at-queens-lirr-station/; *Daily News* (July 4, 2012), https://www.nydailynews.com/new-york/mta-stabbed-face-violent-confrontation-queens-long-island-railroad-station-article-1.1107703; *Daily Mail* (July 5, 2012), https://www.dailymail.co.uk/news/article-2169042/Officer-risks-losing-eye-stabbed-knife-wielding-attacker-shooting-dead-scene.html.

Five hours later, Barnett, 45, was out of the operating room, where surgeons found the knife went in just below his eyelid and could have penetrated his brain.

The blade nearly severed his eyeball and he could still lose it. Chances he will recover his sight in his left eye are slim, MTA officials said.

Barnett, a 13-year veteran, was attacked without warning while talking to a taxi dispatcher outside the Sutphin Blvd. station in Jamaica. Out of nowhere, Bronx troublemaker Edgar Owens made "a bee-line" for him while carrying a gravity knife down at his side, a source said.

He started slashing and caught Barnett on the eye with the blade, officials said. The cop—who had never fired his weapon on duty before—backed into the street and barked at Owens: "Police! Don't move!"

Owens just kept coming at Barnett—who fired his gun four times, hitting the suspect in the jaw, chest and hip. The attacker died instantly. . . .

Authorities said the attack was completely unprovoked; one source said it could have been "suicide by cop." . . .

Jahan Ramazani writes of "the difference between poetry's often slow, layered, and indirect way of telling the news and much of what is found in the newspaper" (69). Unlike poetry—"long memoried [and] built out of vast transnational storehouses of figure, rhythm, and sound" (103)—the news is immediate but quickly forgotten. With the extratextual gesture, Hayes blends the two modes, bringing the urgency behind a newspaper's reportage into an unrelenting cultural memory. The first time Hayes tests this horrific event in the poem, he does so in one line of disembodied, indistinct language ("a man"; "a policeman"). When he returns to it soon after, it takes up three lines, and, while the language is still general, he provides salient details: "attack" becomes "stabbed"; "man" becomes the slain "assailant" (etymologically "to leap at"); and the policeman (now "cop") is "bleeding from his eye."

The OED tells us that the English "O," by way of Rome and Greece, derived from the Phoenician/Hebraic letter ʻayin, meaning "eye." The Phoenician alphabet transcribed the Hebraic form (ע), as the now familiar circle. O-mega and o-micron, like the circus bicycle called the penny-farthing, coexisted in Greece for some time until the omega horseshoed, an incomplete ending but, perhaps with its podium, more stable. Like the alphabetic center of God, at the center of Cop looms an O. Terrifyingly, this moment in Hayes's poem both connotes the power center of the civilian police force and the wound in the policeman who was attacked. We also now learn the race of the policeman and assailant—something the reader might have been taught to anticipate from the initial poetic leap to the assault, given US history and how sociocultural texts teach everyone to read the books of poets like Hayes by their covers.

"How does one change the valences of the burdens of black writing in a society where people presume to know in advance what one will say?" Anthony Reed asks, interrogating the role "poetry [can] play in changing the terms of racialization? In short, the question is not whether one can be a poet and not be black but whether one can be both black and a poet in a situation where race seems to frame what one will say in advance" (21). The pressure on Black writers is double, Reed notes, conjuring W. E. B. Du Bois: to perform as a writer and as a Black subject—each galaxy of interiority always already mediated by social texts. This is not to argue that the subject positions are incongruous for many if not most Black writers, but rather to reiterate that only certain individuals are pressured with this false choice.[20] Such goes to the heart of racism, and, though the concerns are sui generis, they feel akin to the point Simone de Beauvoir memorably makes about sexism in *The Second Sex*. Current criticism like Reed's shows how contemporary Black poetics is attentive to but desiring to move beyond the stalemates of earlier debates. But there need not be an easy reconciliation here. The "prevailing tendency to approach black literature exclusively through thematics of race of the social narrowly conceived," Reed compellingly argues, "is one factor that has persistently led to the exclusion of black experimental writers from genealogies of presumptively white avant-garde writing, on the grounds that its concerns seem insufficiently 'universal'" (6–7). Accordingly, "celebration," while warranted and unavoidable, "justifies the tacit maintenance of racial boundaries and a hierarchical structure that encodes the normative 'same' as white, heterosexual, male, and bourgeois" (23). Celebration and

---

20. How one ought to position oneself critically and aesthetically in this space has been debated by Black writers for generations. I previously wrote about Langston Hughes and George Schuyler's debate, and its staged and unstaged recurrences with Ralph Ellison and Amiri Baraka, and between Haki Madhubuti (Don L. Lee) and Blyden Jackson in *Figures of Time* (especially 148–54). The most immediate earlier poetic context for Hayes would be the very different lyric and anti-lyric aesthetics of Robert Hayden and Amiri Baraka.

the heroics of cultural "subversion" seem to go hand-in-hand.[21] For some, this duo means a real undermining of institutional power—a hopeful sense that a radical poetics does more in this world than it is often seen as really capable of—while others see this as a simple ruse of real power, not really outside any systems of subjugation (only pretending to be). Either way, as Reed maintains, it is a compelling and worthwhile narrative but one that must be conscious of fetishizing Black poets and poetics, reading into each a politics and nonindividuated or not-enough-individualized identity. He uses the phrase "racialized reading" to describe such prescriptive accounts of Black aesthetics, and it is indeed a *reading* practice (essentially a parallel to what Jackson and Prins call "lyricization").[22]

Working against such problematic categorizations, Reed's "postlyric" designation of Black experimental writing includes "both the formally innovative writing practices of black writers and the ways such writing transforms our understandings of race" (9). It is a two-way subversive space without being "subversive"—meaning it is productive-of-the-self rather than being reactionary.[23] He writes, "As a deconstruction of the possible, black experimental writing promotes dissensus with the calculable present, an aesthetic break that anticipates new forms of community. The political value of black experimental writing, therefore, does not lie in its advocacy or its themes but its commitment to the 'aesthetic break' where consensus slips away and new thinking breaks through" (22). Reed's poetics is celebratory in its own right, but with a twist that recognizes the subject-building, productive space

---

21. The nuances among the various un-lyric modes and modes of reading are sometimes difficult to grasp. Jess Cotton's intervention argues for less ambivalence in Hayes. She coins the term "lyric reconstruction" to describe what she sees as Hayes's subversive "black subjectivity." While she acknowledges that Hayes embraces the term "lyric" (532), he, along with other African American poets, "reorient[s] poetry's history towards an unforeclosed future" (525) and makes "lyric unrecognizable to itself" (550). [She very consciously uses the term Black.]

22. He writes, "racialized reading provides a selective, occasionally prescriptive account of the project of black aesthetics as one of rejoinder, protest, or commentary, figuring black writing as reactive rather than productive" (8).

23. "Black experimental writing," he argues, "occasions a reconsideration of a more radical literary politics that are not rooted in the biography or politics of the author or in the determinant political situation to which the work 'responds.' It also announces a challenge—and opportunity—to disarticulate race as a pseudo-ontological category from the ethico-political obligations thought to derive from race as a 'lived experience.'" Literature is not a reflection of social life but "a mode of *self-production*" (5–6; emphasis in original).

of experimental language. As to the pressures on Hayes specifically, McRae sees the poet as "pulled between the impulse to document the effects of the institutionalized racism lived with each day, and the impulse to resist the burden of always being responsible for documenting what one lives with each day" (134). It is a tall order—not only on the page but in life, and it is not asked of everyone. How should readers reconcile as much for a poet who, according to himself, is "just interested in being present," when every instance of "presence" is mediated but also ought to include the irreducibility of individual being?[24] McRae turns to Kevin Quashie's critique of how Black subjectivity is disseminated culturally and his vital insistence on "the wild copiousness of the interior" (104; qtd. in McRae 123). She hopes to find Hayes's lyric subjectivity—"an inner life not strictly defined by public resistance, not wholly separate from publicness, not wholly understood" (144)—in his ambivalence, "sheer formal extravagance" (118), and "comically wayward and uncertain mind" (117). In this regard, Hayes's ambivalence—a meditativeness that always seems to be contemplating these questions critics argue about—ought not be confused with forsaking a racial identity or with an apathy toward commitment. It is simply what remains in the surplus of language. Quashie's and McRae's "inner life" feels a lot like how readers have understood and/or created and/or applied the term "lyric," which might, in the end, be more about a type of existential hopefulness than genre. Without lyric reading, one ends up saying the same thing over and over again about certain poets, bound to how history has become textualized, which, although crucial to understanding their work, can miss so much else inhabiting the vast intersections of their galaxies.

Many poets and critics who are part of this discussion are wary of abandoning the term lyric, even if it is to be prefixed, suffixed, or otherwise refashioned for the twenty-first century. Although he is not discussing Hayes specifically, Kamran Javadizadeh asks how we ought to approach poets who want to "retain the intimacy allowed by the lyric tradition without replicating its pernicious political effects," notably its "form of white innocence" (477). He quotes Claudia Rankine who asks, "How do you keep the intimacy of the language that is afforded the first person in the meditative introspective lyric, and yet make it democratic and aware of its political investments?" (477; Rankine, "The Art" 157). One must also not be blind to the privileged

---

24. Quoted in Burt, "Galaxies." The full quotation from Hayes is: "I'm just interested in being present, not in being representative of anything." Hayes, according to Burt, "works to escape not the African-American identity but the demand that he (or anyone) express that identity in the same way all the time."

scene of the academic institution (and even those with altruistic intentions engaging within it), where critical marketability allows for such discussions to take place in protected chapters of a scholarly book. One must ask how and with what access such a professional reader participates in the dissemination of the spectacle of critical engagement.

No one, Hayes writes, sees the Black cop bleeding from his eye or the Black assailant dead on the ground "quickly enough to make a camera phone witness" (l. 24). Beyond signaling that there are all-too-many unwritten histories of such encounters, Hayes's turn toward the mass-mediated spectacle of witnessing in the twenty-first century captures the initial impulses of those who would be on the scene. Is it about documentation or about something else entirely? With no such technologically anthropomorphized witness, "The scene must be carried on the tongue, it must be carried / On the news into the future where it will distract the eyes working / Lines into paper" (ll. 25–27). Etymologically "draw away" with a modern connotation of confusion, "distract" is an intriguing word choice for this dramatized moment. The scene of the assault, transmitted orally, finds the poet at his desk, and draws him away from his ostensible linear task. Like a pest, it keeps biting at him in his protected space, his unharmed eyes rather than his hand working the lines. "This," he writes, in the future beyond the future registered, "is what blind contour drawing conjures in me" (l. 27). What is the "This," here, I wonder. Is it the assault? the news of the assault? the poetic distraction? Or is it the realization of it all—the hand carrying the news of the tongue, distracting the eyes working the lines?

The looming O in God is then contrasted with the zero of the devil's justice, which leads the speaker to think about other deadly spheres: a fighter's helmet, a war drum, a clenched fist, a gun barrel, ruined eggs, and finally a skull, which rounds out the lot. Previewing the funeral of the assailant, which is still to come in the poem, the speaker thinks about the strain on someone lifting something. "The lifter bends like a broken O" (l. 31), he says—the shape mirroring the body, its brokenness metaphorically mirroring the earlier "loved ones who go crazy." It isn't the body lowered into the hole that seems to elicit a response from the pallbearers and onlookers, but rather the *weight* of the body. It "can make anyone say *Oh*," we're told (l. 32). "Omen," concludes the speaker's temporary meditation in this part, "begins with an O" (l. 33). If, by omen, one thinks that we are about to glimpse into the future, the speaker flips the other way, contrarily pulling himself and us into a past moment when an unnamed boy—possibly himself—ventures a backflip. The "onlookers" watching the spectacle, as if the double-o in their name comprised their staring eyes, "called him crazy" (l. 35). The double-o returns a line later in a moon which isn't there but which is replaced in a domestic scene by paper plate and an innocuous plastic knife. Before the moment can continue in the imagination, though, the speaker relates that "[a]n assailant is a man with history," as if a backflip in the past, like an O spiral of DNA, could later explain an unexplainable event.

The ambiguous "His mother" in the following line leaves us unsure if we are now back in the past or, more likely, in the present, at the undisclosed home of the assailant's mother, preparing for his funeral. The onion—two os, one heading the word, the second buried deep inside it—"is the best symbol of the O" (l. 40). Sliced open, it becomes dangerous, as if an atom were split. "[A] volatile gas stings / The slicer's eyes" (ll. 41–42) until they begin to tear, clouding the world.[25] The speaker describes this "soft-edged world" as a "blur of blooms," again playing with those double oo-eyes, which now see the coffin buoyed by those same flowers. Sounds and letters recur, as if precariously circling around the scene. "The onion is pungent," the speaker tells us, echoing the sound; "its scent infects the air," he adds "scent" a partial anagram of "infects." The smell circles the room, invading the nostrils of the pallbearers and mourners, who

> . . . watch each other,
>
> They watch the pastor's ambivalence, they wait for the doors
>   to open,
> They wait for the appearance of the wounded one-eyed victim
> And his advocates, strangers who do not consider the assailant's
>   funeral
>
> Appeasement. Before that day the officer had never fired his gun
> In the line of duty. He was chatting with a cabdriver
> Beneath the tracks when my cousin circled him holding a knife.
>
> The wound caused no brain damage though his eyeball was
>   severed. (ll. 45–52)

In each instance of retelling the event, Hayes circles closer and closer to the personal. Here, the assailant is named his cousin, connecting the assailant to the "young boy [he] had not seen in years," the mad one doing

---

25. It is difficult not to see the olfactory echo of Gwendolyn Brooks's "onion fumes" of "kitchenette building" in these lines.

backflips and holding a plastic knife, the one onlookers called "crazy." The lyric wholeness—the poem building itself out of language's roots and capricious paths—feels incommensurate with the event being related. Still, the expectations of this cultural language differ from those of the *Daily News*. For McRae, who "explor[es] how a frequently comic mode responds to the excruciating" (23), Hayes's "sheer formal extravagance . . . stave[s] off the pain of remembering or acknowledging something bitter" (118). How is one to make artistic connections, given the circumstances, the poem seems to want to ask over and again, unafraid of failing as long as it keeps circling. The "policeman" turned "cop" is now the "wounded one-eyed victim"; he shows up at the funeral with a group curiously called his "advocates." One pictures a legion of other police officers and imagines they are there to make sure the mourners aren't allowed to mourn too deeply.

———·↓———If this were Mad Magazine™, the "Fold-in" would begin here ——↓———

The word "avocado" has an interesting and controversial etymological history. It comes from the Aztec word "ahuacatl," which was re-adopted as the Spanish word "avocado," because it was close to the more familiar sixteenth-century word for lawyer (or advocate). (The word for lawyer is now "abogado.") For a time, until very recently, there was some confusion as to the literal meaning of the Aztec word, which had been linked to "testicles"—another wrinkled globularity. The thought was that the word for the fruit derived from the word for the genitalia. It turns out that the Aztec descriptions of testicles using the word "ahuacatl" were already metaphorical, already part of a poetic system. (The name of the fruit never derived from testicles.)

Hayes's poem "The Avocado" begins:

> "In 1971, drunk on the sweet, sweet juice of revolution,
> a crew of us marched into the president's office with a list
> of demands," the black man tells us at the February luncheon,
> and I'm pretending I haven't heard this one before as I eye
> black tortillas on a red plate beside a big green bowl
> of guacamole made from the whipped, battered remains
> of several harmless former avocados.
>
> (*Lighthead* 27)

The scene imagines a young, presumably Black man listening (not for the first time) to an older man recount his vibrant advocacy during the civil rights movement. The red, black, and green of the snack tray are reminders of the Pan-African flag, designed by Marcus Garvey, but the young man (the lyric speaker of the poem) seems even bored with that recognition, exhibiting what Douglas Jones calls "a general apathy toward, if not vexation with, nominal commemorations of African Americans and their cultural, political, and social achievements" (47). It is February, Black History Month. The speaker thinks the avocado is an apt symbol for an abolitionist flag. It can move stone, or, as he puts it, "The roots of the avocado tree / can raise pavement" (27). But for this man of a younger generation, who thinks of "the money-colored flesh of the avocado" (27), even this revolutionary sentiment is not to be romanticized outside a market economy. The poem jumps between the older man's enumeration of his demands from forty years earlier—which grow more absurd the longer down the list he gets—and the speaker's odd factual interjections (not vocalized) about avocados. The speaker zones out between demand #1 (reparations) and demand #3 ("more boulevards named for the Reverend Dr. Martin Luther King Jr." [27]), but it's possible his subconscious picks up on #2 because his avocado fact, dangling in the poem between the two other demands, notes that the avocado is *second* to olives in oil content. It is unclear where the speaker's head is because the poem next jumps to demand #21—"a Harriet Tubman statue on the mall!" The speaker loses the man's exact words in his own avocado metaphors, in his hunger for more than snacks, and in his appetite for the young woman sitting beside him. On cue, "Brother man is weeping now." Poetically, one might imagine they are crocodile tears, perhaps to match the once-named "alligator pear" of the avocado, but, given the history, the tears are real however iterable the performance. That doesn't stop the speaker's light accusation that "every time [he] hear[s] this story it's the one telling the story / that's the hero" (28). It is an accusation, though, that also might be leveled at the speaker himself, who, one gathers, will be retelling the story of this day, marketable as it is. Both his narrative eye-rolling at being inconvenienced in the twenty-first century and the tales of the twentieth century, which grow taller every year, are offered for different rhetorical effects. But what is at stake in the latter comes through the speaker's safeguarded apathy. "Hush now," Harriet Tubman enters the speaker's thoughts, consoling "some starved, stammering slave" but also gently chastening the speaker. Unlike both the speaker and the older man—each, in his own way, unable to listen—Tubman is granted the final space if not the concluding word, as she "lift[s] her head to listen for something no one but her could hear" (28).

Noting the older man's "inability to capture the [speaker's] attention," Douglas Jones sees "dissatisfaction with the [older] critique as both redress and narrative reclamation of race-based crimes and injustices throughout American history" (47). He reads Hayes's "The Avocado" as "ultimately reject[ing] narratives of historical continuity and temporal compression" (43); while the past is esteemed, "now is not then" (50).[26] What does it mean to be an advocate now, the poem asks? For Jones, it means "encourag[ing] new conceptual horizons with which to reconceive and thus inhabit our postslavery present—and such openings, it seems, might be the best we can hope for" (43). The poem also seems to weigh in metaphorically on the place of that supposedly distant and individualistic lyric voice. For one, the speaker's apathy at what he seems to be taking as the tired ritual of the month is presented as anything but heroic. His immediate motivations—a better lunch and a night with the young woman—do not seem to evoke urgent readerly sympathy. Hiding behind this speaker's own words, though, is a yearning for community. This, again, comes across through the metaphorical avocado. One of the speaker's factoids reminds us that avocados are "high in monosaturates" (27), which, if what I remember is correct, are the "good" fats, the ones that lower the "bad" cholesterol. Health benefits aside, I am interested in the linguistic ingredients of that chosen word—"mono" and "saturated," which feel an apt metaphor for the thoroughly inundated solitariness of the lyric. What might seem a safe castle of subjectivity surrounded by a moat, however, begins to show cracks throughout the poem. The speaker warns of the danger of an overripe avocado—one left to its own devices for too long—"causing internal molds and breakdown," and he relates that "[m]any isolated avocado trees fail to fruit from lack of pollination" (28). While this last detail is again sexual or procreative in nature and could be taken as self-interested, the overall ambivalence regarding the

---

26. Jones's intervention comes as a chapter in Soyica Diggs Colbert's *Psychic Hold of Slavery*, which probes the continuities and discontinuities "between slavery and antiblack domination in general" in order to understand "how the primary psychic rubric of loss becomes a discursive device that animates contemporary relationships with slavery as a traumatic historical object" (3). The "persistence of antiblack violence in the present," she argues, "necessitates attending to that violence as the recurrence of not the thing itself but a nation-shaping psychic dynamic" (14). Because the slave past is "fundamentally oblique and mystifying," Jones reads Hayes's poem as a suggestion to "abandon slavery as the source for current and future forms of black political belonging and social affiliation" (48, 49).

dangers of a solitary lyric mind or individualistic motivation does undercut the flippant nature of the speaker, as it seems to gesture toward the greater need within the lyric for community. Or maybe that is just Hayes, here, playing devil's advocate.

It feels sometimes a wonder how Hayes is ever able to get a linear poem down on the page (despite how narratively circular it may be) because each node, be it a single letter or word, seems to want to jut out for him in multiple cultural or linguistic directions. After the description of the funeral, Hayes wonders how a man without an eye could weep, which makes him think of Odyssey's bout with the Cyclops. Fears then turn inward, and, with a syllepsis, he worries that anyone could wake up one day, "lose his mind or his vision" (l. 57), and walk the streets naked and shouting. Needless to say, and the speaker doesn't say it, the responses to mental health breakdowns, especially those in public, are not color blind. He worries about being murdered or arrested: the double OO returning as handcuffs, likened to the sign for infinity, in this context, ironically meaning "*unboundedness.*" Each is possible to draw with the blind contour technique.

The difference between the two-dimensional surface puns and the three-dimensional life behind them comes to the fore when he compares a bullet hole to its trajectory through the body. He writes,

> Though the bullet exits a perfect hole it does not leave perfect
>   holes
> In the body. A wound is a cell and portal. Without it the
>   blood runs
> With no outlet. (ll. 61–63)

Both "cell" and "portal" are offered as metaphors for a wound, a spatial marker of a past event. If "portal" brings us back to the earlier doors of the subway car, a temporarily claustrophobic space but one that moves—"cell," despite its dynamic nature, feels more restricting. There is a loneliness to it, a feeling confined to its own body, just out of reach but not out of earshot. It is the simile John Stuart Mill uses to describe the (lyric) poem: "the lament of a prisoner in a solitary cell, ourselves listening, unseen, in the next."[27] Hayes connects more explicitly the bodily cell with the space of incarceration in his book on Etheridge Knight, which includes Hayes's drawing of his own cellular history—complete with corporal maternal and paternal ancestry parts, loves, strangers, hopes, fuckups, and teachers—as though the biological body itself, *pace* Lamarck, would ingest its sociocultural surroundings (*To Float* 3).

Returning again to the blind contour drawing, Hayes relates that "it is not possible to give your subject // A disconnected gaze" (ll. 66–67), the final phrase mischievously dispatched to another stanza. The literal and idiomatic senses of disconnection, though, begin to weigh heavily on these lines, which contrast the artist's eye separated from his hand and the Cyclops's eye separated from his body. The world, Hayes declares, "comes full circle" (l. 71). After paying poetic fealty to some of the cycles of life—the hours, harvests, life itself—and circular body parts, the model from the opening reappears to "pull a button loose on her jeans and step out of them" (l. 75), as if the whole poem occurred in the seconds between her undressing. Where does one start? With the eyes usually. After the model appears, like a mermaid from the sea, time seems to have disappeared, leaving the speaker (and us) in this confused lyric moment. Hayes writes,

> I found myself
> In the dark, I found myself entering her body like a delicate shell
> Or soft pill, like this curved thumb of mine against her lips.
>
> (ll. 76–78)

We are either metaphorically still in the art space—with Hayes's fine tip marker or pencil in hand, his thumb up against his own eye to scale out the model's circles—or hours later, celebrating the day with an intimate moment. It is hard to ignore the Dante-esque allusion in these lines and, once they're spotted, it's difficult not to see Hayes, throughout, spiraling forth from the great epic work. Hayes's circle poem is Dante-esque in its tercets but, charitably, not nearly as long. Perhaps its eighty-one lines (three times three times three times three . . . or nine squared) is a wink at Dante's nine circles. It does, after all, have its inexactly corresponding limbs of limbo and lust, anger, heresy, and beyond. To twist a line of *Paradiso* ("Ne

---

27. He writes specifically of the sorrowful song of a "mountaineer in exile" ("What is Poetry" in *Essays*, 14)—a reference forgotten in other incarnations ("Thoughts . . .") of this essay; "What is Poetry?" *Monthly Repository*, VII (January 1833).

l'altra piccioletta luce ride / quello avvocato de' tempi cristiani" [*Paradiso* X 118–19]), Dante has become that great advocate of Hayes's light.[28] And suddenly, Hayes emerges: "I found myself / In the dark . . ." (ll. 76–77), a narrative reversal of the unforgettable opening of the *Divine Comedy*, but with a different type of paradisiacal reward.

As Dante, toward the very end of his poem, is beginning to comprehend the three concentric circles of Christian divinity, he speaks of one of the mythological paths of geometry:

Qual è 'l geomètra che tutto s'affige
per misurar lo cerchio, e non ritrova,
pensando, quel principio ond'elli indige,

tal era io a quella vista nova:
veder voleva come si convene
l'imago al cerchio e come vi s'indova

[As the geometer his mind applies
To square the circle, nor for all his wit
Finds the right formula, howe'er he tries.

Even such was I at that new apparition;
I wished to see how the image to the circle
Conformed itself, and how it there finds place;]
(Canto XXXIII, ll. 133–38)

When Dante was writing (and for many centuries afterward), this classical problem of squaring the circle—here, as a metaphor for trying to reconcile the human and divine Christ—was still thought to be solvable.[29]

---

28. "Within that other little light is smiling / The advocate of the Christian centuries." Translation is Henry Wadsworth Longfellow's, courtesy of Dartmouth's Dante Lab (https://dantelab.dartmouth.edu/). Robert Hollander's note on the website states that Dante is most likely describing the influence of Orosius on St. Augustine.

29. For a metaphorical reading of this in the context of Dante's concluding stanzas, see Ronald B. Herzman and Gary W. Towsley, "Squaring the Circle: 'Paradiso' 33 and the Poetics of Geometry," *Traditio*, 49: 95–125.

For millennia, this impossible undertaking, believed to have originated with Anaxagoras, had mathematicians attempting to construct a square with the same area of a given circle using only a compass and straightedge. It was not until the late nineteenth century that Ferdinand von Lindemann proved that, because pi was a transcendental number, a circle could never be so squared. By then, idiomatically speaking, the phrase "squaring the circle" had come to mean a fruitless endeavor, rather like drawing that perfect circle. But this still seems to be the hope of Hayes's poem—turning a fluid movement into straight lines—even though he knows the blind contour will always veer off when he wants it to return home. "How to Draw . . ." is a poem of circles, Os, turns, exclamations, and loss, but one that doesn't seem able or willing to apostrophize in the classical sense. The poetic ritual doesn't fit the day. The poem concludes, not a hemistich too long:

> You must look without looking to make the perfect circle.
> The line, the mind must be a blind continuous liquid
> Until the drawing is complete.

I imagine a similar demand in one drawing Hayes's gaze, which spirals inward as much as it spirals out. You just have to keep moving until you run out of room.

Etymology could have done worse than letting prosody (pros-ōidé ["ode"], "toward song" Gr.) join the world un-twinned from prose ("direct" / "straight-forward" Lat.). If, in the metaverse of 21C, one were still able to offer a light metaphorical banality, one might do worse than to call linearity prose, and circularity lyric. "Do not depend on speech to be felt" Hayes says in his "Ars Poetica for the Ones Like Us," before turning to Orpheus' failure. Sadly, it is the prosaic condition of all lyric. The poem has Hayes Scheherazading: "I like the story about the man who talks / God into letting him live until he is done / With his masterwork." To sing is to stay the mortal hand for the thousandth and second night. But this is only if the divine apostrophe succeeds. Or do we all have it backward—that the only reason to remain is so that one can sing another night? If a lifeline tossed below Orpheus is not an option, a measure of recovery might still be found in giving oneself up to another: "It is evening that lets us, / For an instant, be possessed by someone else."[30] Sometimes that possession happens—in a Dantesque fashion, dispossessed from a Dantesque space—alone, alone, / Alone above a raging sea.

---

30. *How to Be Drawn*, 95–96.

Epilogue: Every Þrose has its thorn

On Poison, the Cure, and other
Pharmacological Prickles; Or, Why are you so far away?

And the wind, a voiceless thorn,
goes over the details,
making a soft promise
to take our breath away.

—Anthony Hecht, "Crows in Winter"[1]

Want to be careful. Enough stuff here to chloroform you. Test: turns
blue litmus paper red. Chloroform. Overdose of laudanum. Sleeping
draughts. Lovephiltres. Paragoric poppysyrup bad for cough. Clogs the
pores or the phlegm. Poisons the only cures. Remedy where you least
expect it. Clever of nature.

—James Joyce, *Ulysses*[2]

Taking Jacques Derrida to task for misreading Jacques Lacan's mistaken
readers' reading *as* Lacan's reading of Edgar Allan Poe's "Purloined Letter,"
Barbara Johnson returns to the scene of the crime—the very first word of
Derrida's interlocution, itself purloined from Baudelaire: "Ils le remercient
pour les grandes vérités qu'il vient de proclamer,—car ils ont découvert (o
verificateurs de ce qui ne peut être vérifié!) que tout ce qu'il a énoncé est
absolument vrai. . . ." ("The Purveyor" 31). Johnson translates Derrida's

---

1. Hecht, *The Transparent Man*, 65.
2. Joyce, *Ulysses*, 69 (U5.480–84).

transposition of Baudelaire: "They thank him for the grand truths he has just proclaimed,—for they have discovered (o verifier of what cannot be verified!) that everything he said was absolutely true . . ." ("The Frame" 478). In his reframing, Derrida suggests that the "him" of Baudelaire's fictive truth (Baudelaire, of course, was never so kind as to repay his influence forward) applies equally as well to Lacan, hence the parallel with Poe's erstwhile Minister. It is a tidy little hermeneutic circle. "The evils of Lacan's analysis of Poe," Johnson notes, "are thus located less in the letter of the text than in the gullible readers, the '*braves gens*' who are taken in by it. Lacan's ills are really *ils*" (478). So much can go wrong with hermeneutic jury-rigging. An el is pulled from Lacan's ills, and his *I* becomes a *they*. It is a remedy for lyric expectations (o versifier of what cannot be versified!), in which the signature that is an organic, intentional, individualized "Lacan" gives way to a multitude, erroneously (as Johnson charges Derrida) reduced to a new singular voice, a new purveyor of truth.

As you know, the title of this epilogue (which, alas, most likely does more work than its body), is distilled from Jacques Derrida's apothecary, "Plato's Pharmacy": "There is no such thing as a harmless remedy. The *pharmakon* can never be simply beneficial" (*Dissemination* 102). Long story short, Plato, who thought speech was closer to truth than writing (and told us as much in writing), referred to writing as a pharmakon, a drug that could either mean a poison or a cure, depending on the context.[3] Regarding writing, that context for Plato most likely meant poison, but Derrida, as was customary for him in the waiting room, wasn't so sure.[4]

---

3. Johnson, in a footnote (!) to her translation of Derrida, likens the role of the *pharmakon* to the *supplément* of *Of Grammatology* (Derrida, *Dissemination*, 96 n.43).

4. But let us resolve this in a supplemental note, dividing ourselves vertically before continuing in the linear horizontal. As the story goes, the Egyptian lunar deity Theuth (Thoth) one day found himself in a sharing mood. As the god of writing, science, magic, and art (among other things), he admittedly had much to share. He approached King Thamus (whose cv also lists as a demigod) and offered up the craft of writing—back then, no doubt, still on the down-low. As Plato scripts it, Theuth says, "Here, O king, is a branch of learning that will make the people of Egypt wiser and improve their memories: my discovery provides a recipe [*pharmakon*] for memory and wisdom" (*Phaedrus*, page 157; 274E). Presaging thousands of years of good will between philosophers and artists, King Thamus replied that those who create are not qualified to offer ethical opinions on the consequences of their creations. If men learn about writing, he countered, "it will implant forgetfulness in their souls: they will cease to exercise memory because they rely on that which is written, call things to remembrance no longer from within themselves, but by means of external marks" (275A). If I remember correctly, this meant men would

The 1980s offered what, to many now, seems like a fad of deconstruction: aspiring undergraduates learned it; aspiring graduates unlearned it. But ours are small circles. Deconstruction (as far as I know) hasn't made it onto VH1's *I Love the '80s*. In my own view, it was never so threatening to reason or truth as detractors make it out to be, however much "our" seemingly commonsensical Enlightenment ideas were to be mediated by language or gaps in philosophy itself. Still (at risk of generalizing), liberal humanists and conservatives joined to accuse its practitioners, as Barbara Johnson explains, of being "radical nihilist[s] . . . [who] undermined the foundations of Western values," and many on the left saw those same practitioners as "closet conservative[s] . . . den[ying] . . . history and . . . refus[ing] . . . politics" ("Poison or Remedy" 358).[5] Light of actual touch, but awe-striking and fatal, as Anthony Hecht's murderous crows—to borrow a flock—would have it.

Following the "de Man affair," as Johnson would quip, deconstructors would be "getting a taste of our own *pharmakon*" (357), and they did, for years—a whole new industry.[6] For most academics, it—whatever it was—was over. This, such that in 2022 someone could pen in *The Chronicle of Higher*

---

have semblance, not wisdom. Plato's mouthpiece, Socrates, then summarizes, "anyone who leaves behind him a written manual, and likewise anyone who takes it over from him . . . must be exceedingly simple-minded" (158; 275C).

In a wonderfully quirky moment, Socrates claims that "if you ask [written words] anything about what they say . . . they go on telling you the same thing forever" (158; 275D). This, despite also "drift[ing] all over the place" (158; 275E). As Derrida understands it, one of the words that doesn't seem to be telling him the same thing forever is "pharmakon": "The common translation of *pharmakon* by *remedy* [remède]—a beneficent drug—is not, of course, inaccurate" (*Dissemination* 99). "The medicine," he continues, "is beneficial; it repairs and produces, accumulates and remedies, increases knowledge and reduces forgetfulness. Its translation by 'remedy' nonetheless erases, in going outside the Greek language, the other pole reserved in the word *pharmakon*. It cancels out the resources of ambiguity . . ." (99). The ambiguity was importantly inherent in mustache-twirling Theuth's offer. Like a vaudeville villain, he (at least according to Thamus and Socrates and Plato), had tried to "[pass] a poison off as a remedy" (100), not realizing that others could pick up on the double-voiced irony inherent in his own (*cough*) *spoken* word. Plato is able to conclude that "Writing is no more valuable . . . as a remedy than as a poison" (101). Derrida demurs.

5. Johnson is writing specifically of Paul de Man, here, but the implication is that these charges would apply across the board.

6. Plato's Socrates: "For you apparently it makes a difference who the speaker is, and what country he comes from: you don't merely ask whether what he says is true or false" (*Phaedrus*, pages 157–58; 275C).

Education an article titled "What Was Deconstruction?"[7] (I am surprised this title, if not its mass-produced content in so many other venues, took so long to appear.) Some, like myself, see much less contradiction among healthier deconstructive impulses, Enlightenment thought, and a commitment to social justice. I would argue, cautiously, that a lot of the important social rethinking of the last couple decades regarding gender and race and geopolitics was, in no small part, influenced by the "logic" of deconstructive inquiry. But these last decades have only exaggerated the caricaturist vision of deconstruction as drugging our collective reason and causing the existential horrors of this post-truth era. This, as Johnson argues compellingly—and importantly without hagiography—was precisely what de Man's "deep suspicion of false images of harmony and enlightenment" (360) was cautioning against: the "*aestheticization* of politics" (359)—policy debates being replaced by cults of personality, seen today at levels far above whatever numbers of followers #Derrida or #de Man ever reached.

If whatever is happening now is the "remedy" for, and not the result of, deconstruction—replaced rhetorically by "Theory" and now by "Critical [Race] Theory"—we might ask whether the remedy is worse than the poison. Clever of nature, the epigraph from Joyce tells us. Neither Theory-critique nor anti-Theory-critique is a production of our individual critical genius—a displaced form of political wish fulfillment. Rather, they are functions of a subject position in history, our unconscious now. So are the "post-theorists" (as if there could exist such a space), those who, to purloin a line from Mary J. Blige, would perform "hateration / holleration in this dancery" of deconstruction and other "hermeneutics of suspicion" merely reperforming Derrida's ills of substituting a *they* for the textual *I*, always already quilted by a multitude of voices and stratified by history? How does one account for a philosophical mode that, contrary to the now-fashionable pronouncements of the *they*, feels perpetually aware of its own ilness [sic]?

For my own part, I have spent a number of pages attempting to poke at the nonspace of a critical caesura, the pause between two earlier deconstructive impulses: one, a desire to identify the supposed "presence" of speech as already set in motion by the schema of writing, and the second, understanding lyric in terms of a poetic gesture of speech suddenly turned away from the introspective mind. And why? Because something

---

7. Timothy Brennan, "What Was Deconstruction?" *The Chronicle of Higher Education*, June 3, 2022, https://www.chronicle.com/article/what-was-deconstruction.

still matters when a body cries out for an absence within whatever "texts" have been bookending it. I have tried to maintain throughout that neither poetics nor deconstructive approaches, once one gets past all the melodrama and facile binaries, need work against what Rita Felski and Elizabeth Anker term "postcritique" or what Stephen Best and Sharon Marcus term "surface reading."[8] Whatever their stripes, *Praeceptorus Anglicus* like producing and poking at previous productions of knowledge. Some of my own book's ribs-ripe-for-poking have included supposed distinctions between speech and writing, between lyric and "anti-lyric" modes, between prose (philosophy/ semantic language) and poetry (nonsemantic language)—one seemingly always the thorn in the others' side.[9] Too often, though, critical poking outcries real voices in pain. And poets and poetic rituals live both heroically and unheroically in this space of that mythical nightingale, pressing its breast against the thorn so that our roses can turn red.

Assuming a metaphorical intimacy with an audience, however deferred, can create the discomfort of feeling trespassed upon. You'll recall my "You'll recall"—the opening words of this book—which (notwithstanding its performative wink) assumed such an intimacy, one circle confocal with another, to borrow Bishop's phrasing. This is the excitement and the terror lurking within apostrophic address and the space of lyric poetry: the partial performative

---

8. The rabid, unrelenting, unnuanced rhetoric exhibited at times by "anti-Theory" camps tends to confirm that the ostensible critical diagnoses offered are more likely symptoms of twenty-first-century public engagement. Pointedly but thoughtfully critiquing Felski, Best, and Marcus for their "tropism toward melodrama" in what is now called the "method wars," David Kurnick notes how their work "register[s] the pressure of a broader public by introjecting that public's anticipated indifference or hostility into their style and rhetoric" (351). Neither the neoliberal ripples through academic institutions nor whatever today passes for politics (if one can still call it that) is apparently to blame. Instead, the blame for the humanities and literary criticism's "loss of prestige [is said to lie] not on external factors but on the failure of other scholars—aggressive critique-mongers, depth-obsessed symptom-hunters, paranoid pattern-makers—to appreciate literature properly" (351). Kurnick's patience and understatements are noteworthy. Just like Kurnick, I hope to embody those traits here, in what is an epilogue advocating for mutual presence. See Felski, *The Limits of Critique*, Chicago UP, 2015; Anker and Felski, eds., *Critique and Postcritique*, Duke UP, 2017; Best and Marcus, "Surface Reading: An Introduction," *Representations* 108, no. 1 (2009): 1–21.

9. As I outlined in my earlier introduction and interlude, I tend to approach this aporia through the work of Giorgio Agamben, for whom "poetry [is] the discourse in which it is possible to set a metrical limit against a syntactical one. . . . Prose is the discourse in which this is impossible" (*Idea* 39).

magic of the lyric "I" makes the reader reembody someone else's voice, and the partial magic of the apostrophic "you" allows the reader belatedly to become the addressee of someone else's distant call. Each might be seen as a type of revoicing, its own musical cover, as it were. It is a stepping, for a moment, onto the dizzy edge of someone else's "I," which can at times be a welcome lyric intrusion, every song an invitation to be covered, every "I" a potential "you"—if the "you" wants to take that cautious step.

As I previewed in the introduction, the remainder of this epilogue will be different than the chapters in this book, different than most epilogues. It was cowritten with the Romanticist scholar Manu Samriti Chander, in part while we were alone, in part while we were alone together over Zoom, during this, our COVID era. There were different ways we could have approached this. Rather than have a "back-and-forth" conversation or otherwise meld fragments of sentences into a unified "corrected" version, we wanted to try something new. The resulting form instead had us listening to two songs from our childhood that, in very different ways, relate to questions we wanted to ask about apostrophe and lyric expectations. And then we listened to each other's listening, mapping this all out across two parallel columns, lyrical in sentiment but with a conscious eye toward being overheard. At times, one of us will jump into the text of the other via a footnote when we feel called upon to speak. At other times, we will come together in a joint space to reassess what has been voiced so far or to preview what follows.

*　*　*

One is taught to diagnose the literary in a decisively non-lyric (objective or scientific) manner, but the discipline, oddly though not unpredictably, still embraces many of the romantically lyric notions of scholarly authorship (unified voice, organic and coherent whole, singular argument). In the all-too-brief space of this epilogue, we (the I has now become an ils) hope to embark on a different type of "anti-lyric" turn—two voices and a healthy dose of harmonious and/or disharmonious diagnoses. What matters, now, is mutual presence. Here, for a song or two, we will dance around the lyricization of the critical field while we rethink what might still be to come.

About fifty seconds into the studio recording of "Just Like Heaven," Robert Smith's vocals begin:

> *"Show me, show me, show me how you do that trick*
> *The one that makes me scream."*[10]

DB: In what seems like a direct present-tense address—not a turn away, not an exclamation—the singer appears to be requesting guidance about a magical sexual maneuver, one that on its face might simply be a slight touch of placement, pressure, or speed. But, as we learn after the pause following "scream," the address is a trick, a manner of ventriloquism, brought on by cultural/poetic expectation and the anticipation of linear movement:

> "Show me, show me, show me
>   how you do that trick
> The one that makes me scream,"
>   [pause] she said. . . .

In this inside-out apostrophe, the original words are not the singer's, and the moment is not an address but a narrative recapitulation of a past intimate moment. The words are hers. The words were hers. He is now quoting

MC: About solipsism they were never wrong, the Romantic poets—how well they saw themselves in everything, and everything existed for them. That was the problem with their politics: they could rail against the social ills—poverty, slavery— but they were incapable of allocentrism, incapable of centering the other, of becoming themselves peripheral. And that's the legacy we've inherited, isn't it? A poetic mode that can't really listen, the cowboy who sings a sad, sad song—whose singing drowns out all other voices. That's basically the heart of the lyrical ballad that Wordsworth and Coleridge invented (they didn't actually invent it): the overflow of one man's powerful feeling taken to be universal, the lyrical "I" swallowing up the landscape.*

I think maybe that's the difference between that Cure song and, say, Wordsworth—Wordsworth isn't a

---

10. Twenty-nine seconds into her cover of The Cure's "Just Like Heaven" (different foreplays work for different consumers), Katie Melua reanimates Robert Smith's words almost line for line, but with heteronormative pronoun switches ("the one that makes me scream . . . *he* said").

*DB: After debasing the Tartars and Arabs but before attacking the French, J. S. Mill designates poetry "the natural fruit of solitude and meditation [while] eloquence [that] of intercourse with the world" ("Thoughts" 95). There is nothing inherently wrong with a person walking

a voice invoking himself, while she—the absent body—is essentially conjuring the present singing voice, her words moving its mouth as it once moved her own. The pastness of the moment ("said" "said" "threw") fades into its own past, as the memory comes alive again in the present lyrical utterance: "Show me how you do it / And I promise you I promise that / I'll run away with you / [pause] I'll run away with you." The repetitions accentuate the speech-act nature of the lines, one voice in the moment trying to convince its listener or, more likely, itself of a fleeting dream. But the scene is not even a dream; it's "just like a dream" or, rather, the invoked addressee—always teetering between the second and third person—is just like a dream.**

musician. Robert Smith is used to listening and to responding to what he hears. So he's capable of imagining a voice that isn't a voice, that belongs here and that belongs elsewhere at the same time—a voice that's rooted not in the subject but in the space between subjects. That's where music happens. Especially in jazz—Wynton Marsalis said something about how, in rock music, the rhythm section is enslaved, recruited into repetitive service.

But in jazz every instrument is free to explore, and they all explore together. That's the "trick"; that's how you pull the rug out from under the solitary, lyrical subject (which is of course the liberal subject). It's not indeterminacy—it's not that you don't know what instrument is doing what

---

lyrically alone, thinking. It is the expectation that one deserves to be eavesdropped upon that begins to shade things, and this is before any address, always already mediated by thorny socio-cultural institutions. As a gesture of inclusivity, a call to others, it is wanting—the lyric apostrophe. It is the O of a cowboy lasso, drawing all else in. Both Culler and Johnson warn against this exploitation of address. Culler notes "the crucial though paradoxical fact that this figure which seems to establish relations between the self and the other can in fact be read as an act of radical interiorization and solipsism" (*Pursuit* 146). It is either a projection of the self to fill the world or an internalization of external things—a vanity of power either way. Because the addressee cannot respond, Johnson connects apostrophe to the ideological structure of Louis Althusser's "interpellation," writing that "Apostrophe turns toward anything the poet throws his voice to, and in so doing magnetizes a world around his call" (*Persons* 10). For her, "The speech situation—presence—is about the poet, and his or her feelings about the object; addressing something reveals the nature of the subject, not of the object, but the object is nevertheless affected, drawn into the speech event with the poet" (9). But, to borrow a phrase from a friend, *I wonder* if such is about lyric apostrophe or the stories one has told oneself about it for too many years, creating monuments out of myths. What if the scene of inclusivity is not supposed to be at the moment of address but after . . . and maybe even before? Allen Grossman, the custodian of the poetics of failure—but in oh, such a crucially human way—calls the lyric "the genre of the 'other mind' as it has come to manifestation through the abandonment of autonomy and the displacement toward fiction" (*Summa* 211). It is about the real world, however long deferred, and about ethical responsibility to the other minds occupying it. "The process of creation of human presence through acknowledgement," he writes, "moves through persons across time and is completed neither in the writer nor the reader but in the mutually honorable reciprocity of both" (213–14). The lyric subject, solipsistic though it is, does not exist without recognition. Perhaps the address is returned, only in unexpected ways. And just because you think no one is listening, doesn't mean you aren't overheard.

**MC: "A damsel with a dulcimer, / In a vision once I saw," says the speaker in Coleridge's "Kubla Khan, or A Vision in a Dream. A Fragment": "It was an Abyssinian

To be sure, it is a song about distance: that, amid the raw screams and laughter—each unanticipated nonsemantic vocalizations, meaningful without meaning—that, amid one voice animating another, two lovers could be so far apart. "Why are you so far away," the ventriloquizing speaker asks, before once again offering up the delayed subject and verb ". . . she said." One might naturally assume the following line ("Why won't you ever know that I'm in love with you") remains part of this ". . . she said" but the turn, at least on the written page, is ambiguous—quite possibly the speaker's unvoiced reply to someone who can no longer hear him. Despite its brevity, the song still has enough time to recast the dreamlike-memory-caught-up-in-the-glow-of-the-sexual-act as a metaphorical seafarer/mermaid encounter.

Morning awakens the singer with the same linguistic energy he had once thrust into the mouth of his love. Following the bridge, the return home, he sings,

> Daylight licked me into shape,
> I must've been asleep for days
> And moving lips to breathe her name
> I opened up my eyes

A long-deferred echo of "trick" returns in the dewy reveille of the "lick into shape," but the phrase, in this waking context, feels almost more literal than idiomatic. It is his turn to voice, but all he can muster in his stirring lips (another echo) is a failed conjuring of her name. The end, as if a dream, turns mysterious. The singer is now alone (was (although that can happen, too). It's collectivity—it's every voice doing something different together.

It's a trick insofar as it upsets the lyrical norm that, if it hadn't been for the Romantics, would maybe never have become the norm. I wonder what might have happened if things were the other way around, if the trick had been the norm. But that wasn't the progress of modernity. History didn't happen that way. When the English poet found himself faced—thanks to changes in print technology and a rather dramatic rise in literacy—when he found himself faced with the reality of multiple, conflicting reading audiences, he doubled down on his authority, on his capacity to unite diverse readerships into a coherent whole. He became, in his mind, the man possessed of more feeling than was commonly felt, the legislator of the world. And that sealed the fate of lyric poetry, or at least the strain of lyric poetry I see as dominant.

From then on the lyric could only find freedom in the slip, the accident, the moment of confusion—who exactly is speaking?—that inevitably resolves back into the solitary speaker, alone and palely loitering above a raging sea, aware of his solipsism but unable to escape it.

---

maid / And on her dulcimer she played, / Singing of Mount Abora." The Abyssinian maid, who is a vision inside a vision inside a dream that is a fragment of a poem, is an absent presence. Like the speaker in The Cure song, Coleridge's speaker wants her back, not just as an object of sexual desire (although of course as that) but as a voice that runs through him: "Could I revive within me / Her symphony and song, / To such a deep delight 'twould win me, / That with music loud and long, / I would build that dome in air, / That sunny dome! those caves of ice!" He wants her song to become his "music loud and long."

he ever not?) "above a raging sea /
That," in his own words, "stole the only
girl I loved / And drowned her deep
inside of me."***

*We have tried to clear two very different garden paths through the thorny
reaches of cultural expectation, one that misguidedly imagines that the desires of
an "I" can always overlay themselves harmlessly on an absent, silenced "you."
Here are remedies, if not so much cures. But briars still seem to breach those
prosaic paths. The wound heals, another song tells us, but the scars remain.*

*The other side of this pharmakon we have dosed ourselves with asks that
we now turn to a different cultural toxin. For better or worse, one of the most
unforgettable, hard rock power ballads of the 1980s, comes from a Poison pen:*

> *I listen to our favorite song*
> *Playing on the radio. . . .*
> *And I know that you'd be here right now*
> *If I could have let you know somehow I guess*
> *Every rose has its thorn*
> *Just like every night has its dawn*
> *Just like every cowboy sings his sad, sad song*
> *Every rose has its thorn. . . .*
> Bret Michaels et al. [Poison], "Every Rose Has Its Thorn"

In a reversal of The Cure's song, the singer and his partner "both lie close together / [and yet] We feel miles apart inside." He can't understand the distance ("Was it something I said or something I did?"). Twice, he tells her or us or himself that he tried. Realizing that things are often undercut by their opposites from within, the singer then croons his famous chorus, "Every rose has its thorn." It is no less

Every time I hear the word "every" I look for the exception, and, sure enough, there are thornless roses, and half of Wolf 1069b—an exoplanet, 31.2 lightyears away from Earth—is always dark, no dawn. The real thorn here is the cowboy, whose relationship to his sad song frustrates the chorus's logic of oppositions and parallels ("Just like,"

***MC: Could Coleridge's speaker revive within him the Abyssinian maid's song, the world would shudder: "And all should cry, Beware! Beware! / His flashing eyes, his floating hair! / Weave a circle round him thrice, / And close your eyes with holy dread / For he on honey-dew hath fed, / And drunk the milk of Paradise." The narrative of loss and absence—Smith's narrative—is here a fantasy of successful union between the speaker and his maid. The consequence of this union, the demonic scene of unholy dread, is very much unlike Heaven.

a caricatural bouquet of Deconstruction than a heartfelt sentiment.

By the time of the second verse, they have already separated. Alone, he hears "our favorite song / Playing on the radio." Its reach, as no one ought to deny him, touches deep—not because of lyrical profundity but because it was with him *before*. He probably wouldn't have chosen the song, but that's the risk of letting a box arbitrate your emotional catalogue.

The DJ (they like to talk) offers a banality, seemingly directed toward the grieving soul (or at least that is how other voices are assimilated): like the next song, love is transitory. Universally trite, yes, but it still breeds disbelief. And therein is the agonized lyric condition. Every pain, every loss follows a psychological or cultural formula, and yet, each time, it draws blood. *My pain, we still insist, is different.*

It is unclear whether the figure behind the "I" of the dramatized singer offers his diagnosis in earnest or mockingly (but we probably have a pretty good guess): "And I know that you'd be here right now / If I could have let you know somehow." It is a Hallmark rhyme to go with the card he realizes he should have sent her, along with some chocolate, and those three little words culture tells us every woman wants to hear. But there is no "[pause] she said. . . ." *What about her voice*, one wonders . . . *what about the song she actually wanted to hear on the radio?†*

"Just like").‡ But that was always the point: the wrangler of words is an outsider, "the most unpoetical of any thing in existence," as Keats wrote to distinguish himself from the Wordsworthian solipsist. But, really, what's more solipsistic than self-indulging in one's lack of self? What's more self-assured than "I wonder" or "I guess," when the underlying presumption is that everything you've said is grounded in truth? At which point it doesn't matter if your truth is factual, whether there are strains of roses such as Zéphirine Drouhin that have no thorns, whether what we call the rose's "thorns" are actually prickles.

"Fickle tastes and fickle appetites"— that's what Wordsworth called the preference for "capricious habits of expression" over the common language of common men. Despite what he wrote about how "every"—there's that "every" again!—"great and original writer" creates the taste by which he's enjoyed (a statement about originality Wordsworth copped from Coleridge), it's better, it seems, to be trite than "capricious." So every rose has its thorn because what we accept as common is—Wordsworth again—"more permanent" and "more philosophical." Anyhow, "thorn" rhymes

---

†MC: If we got to hear the absent lover's voice—or the voice of, say Coleridge's Abyssinian maid—if these came to us unmediated by the skinny white guy crooning, there'd be another and another voice left out for us to ask about. That was the point of Gayatri Chakravorty Spivak's "Can the Subaltern Speak?"—or one of the points. And that's true here, too, isn't it? Two voices in an epilogue ask why not three or four or five. To include is to exclude. Which doesn't mean we should turn our backs on inclusivity. Rather, the impossibility of inclusion without exclusion creates the conditions of the ethical imperative (the fulfillment of which would obviate the need for ethics): to keep enfranchising and, in the process, revise the terms of enfranchisement to reflect the new community. The alternative is just to lament with the poets that which cannot be. And honestly, I've had enough of that sad song.

‡DB: The "just like" of The Cure ("You're just like a dream") sounds just like the "just like" of Poison ("Just like every cowboy sings his sad, sad song"). The phrase is analogical,

The singer returns to his chorus of opposites: roses/thorns (bodily); nights/dawns (temporal); and cowboy/sad, sad, song (??). Does the final opposition depend on the idea of the happy cowboy (a cultural norm I am unaware of)? or is the suggestion that cowboys don't sing? or don't emote . . . even if it's not their sad, sad song but simply the one they were asked to sing for a crowd that has heard it countless times before?

with "dawn" and "song," and "prickle" doesn't.‡‡

The couple's favorite song, then, is the cowboy's sad song, which is "Every Rose Has Its Thorn," which is another iteration of the lyrical ballad: the lyrical power ballad. The spontaneous overflow of powerful feeling is scripted and rehearsed, glammed up for a new generation. The question asked isn't so much has anyone ever felt like this but has anyone ever not? The answer is yes, of course: many of us live outside the affective circuits that link Bret Michaels to Wordsworth and (despite his protestations) Keats. We're just imagined out of the narrative, like prickles or dawnless nights.

---

a bringing together of what is so far away. When torn apart, the alienated words fall into connotations of ethics and desire: the latter everywhere across both songs, the former conspicuously absent. It is a crossing at the heart of the poetic gesture of metaphor, its own teetering version of "just like."

‡‡ DB: After reading his naughty text message, Leopold Bloom thinks, "Queer the number of pins they always have. No roses without thorns" (Joyce, *Ulysses* 64; U5.277–78). In Bloom's mouth, it would come out "torns." *Un dessein si funeste, S'il n'est digne d'Bloom, est digne de Michaels.*

One likes the cure more than the poison. And one sides with the occluded voice—the "you," the "she" who isn't given a say. We write together, neither voice drowning out the other. So that—consonantly or dissonantly—the voices do together what neither could do alone.

We write this now in April, over Zoom, virtually close. Earth has begun addressing itself to the era of Covid. We are here together in a moment. How are we here together? The songs remind us why we are doing something, why we are calling out for others. From where does this desire to animate come? It is something desired by both songs. Does one turn to the song? Or further to oneself? Or look to others? Either something is there or not there. . . . Regardless, an audience comes together to dance with the songs. More than the terms, the songs set the stakes for the dance. One can step with it or sashay. Mutual presence is the starting point, already saturated with ethics, commitment. Poems, Anahid Nersessian chances, "model a certain way of being in the world and with others that we might want to call commitment . . . [that is] apostrophe's relational bearing" (135). Songs create community by speaking loss. They create the terms by which we can be together, or, rather, less far apart. They share a desire to hold on to what matters just a little longer, a phantasmic afterlife. If not heaven, then just like it.

Appendix A

W. B. Yeats, "THE STOLEN CHILD"

[*The Irish Monthly* (December 1886)]

WHERE dips the rocky highland
Of Slewth Wood in the lake,
There lies a leafy island
Where flapping herons wake
The drowsy water rats;
There we've hid our fairy vats
Full of berries
And of reddest stolen cherries.
Come away, O human child!
To the woods and waters wild
With a fairy, hand in hand,
For the world's more full of weeping than you can understand.

Where the wave of moonlight glosses
The dim gray sands with light,
Far off by furthest Rosses
We foot it all the night,
Weaving olden dances,
Mingling hands and mingling glances
Till the moon has taken flight;
To and fro we leap

And chase the frothy bubbles
While the world is full of troubles.
And is anxious in its sleep.
Come away, O human child!
To the woods and waters wild
With a fairy, hand in hand,
For the world's more full of weeping than you can understand.

Where the wandering water gushes
From the hills above Glen-Car,
In pools among the rushes
That scarce could bathe a star,
We seek for slumbering trout
And whispering in their ears
We give them evil dreams,
Leaning softly out
From ferns that drop their tears
Of dew on the young streams.
Come, O human child!
To the woods and waters wild
With a fairy, hand in hand,
For the world's more full of weeping than you can understand.

Away with us he's going
The solemn-eyed—
He'll hear no more the lowing
Of the calves on the warm hill side,
Or the kettle on the hob
Sing peace into his breast,
Or see the brown mice bob
Round and round the oatmeal chest.
For he comes, the human child,
To the woods and waters wild
With a fairy, hand in hand,
For the world's more full of weeping than he can understand.

Appendix B

Terrance Hayes, "How to Draw a Perfect Circle"

[*How to be Drawn*, Penguin, 2015.]

I can imitate the spheres of the model's body, her head,
Her mouth, the chin she rests at the bend of her elbow
But nothing tells me how to make the pupils spiral

From her gaze. Everything the eye sees enters a circle,
The world is connected to a circle: breath spools from the
	nostrils
And any love to be open becomes an O. The shape inside the circle

Is a circle, the egg fallen outside the nest the serpent circles
Rests in the serpent's gaze the way my gaze rests on the model.
In a blind contour drawing the eye tracks the subject

Without observing what the hand is doing. Everything is connected
By a line curling and canceling itself like the shape of a snake
Swallowing its own decadent tail or a mind that means to
	destroy itself,

A man circling a railway underpass before attacking a
	policeman.
To draw the model's nipples I have to let myself be carried away.
I love all the parts of the body. There are as many curves

As there are jewels of matrimony, as many whirls as there are
    teeth
In the mouth of the future: the mute pearls a bride wears to
    her wedding,
The sleeping ovaries like the heads of riders bunched in a
    tunnel.

The doors of the subway car imitate an O opening and
    closing,
In the blood the O spirals its helix of defects, genetic
    shadows,
But there are no instructions for identifying loved ones who
    go crazy.

When one morning a black man stabs a black transit cop in
    the face
And the cop, bleeding from his eye, kills the assailant, no one
    traveling
To the subway sees it quickly enough to make a camera
    phone witness.

The scene must be carried on the tongue, it must be carried
On the news into the future where it will distract the eyes
    working
Lines into paper. This is what blind contour drawing conjures
    in me.

At the center of God looms an O, the devil believes justice is
    shaped
Like a zero, a militant helmet or war drum, a fist or gun
    barrel,
A barrel of ruined eggs or skulls. To lift anything from a field

The lifter bends like a broken O. The weight of the body
Lowered into a hole can make anyone say *Oh*: the onlookers,
The mother, the brothers and sisters. Omen begins with an O.

When I looked into my past I saw the boy I had not seen in years
Do a standing backflip so daring the onlookers called him crazy.
I did not see a moon as white as an onion but I saw a paper plate

Upon which the boy held a plastic knife and sopping meat.
An assailant is a man with history. His mother struggles
To cut an onion preparing a meal to be served after the funeral.

The onion is the best symbol of the O. Sliced, a volatile gas stings
The slicer's eyes like a punishment clouding them until they see
What someone trapped beneath a lid of water sees:

A soft-edged world, a blur of blooms holding a coffin afloat.
The onion is pungent, its scent infects the air with sadness,
All the pallbearers smell it. The mourners watch each other,

They watch the pastor's ambivalence, they wait for the doors
    to open,
They wait for the appearance of the wounded one-eyed victim
And his advocates, strangers who do not consider the assail-
    ant's funeral

Appeasement. Before that day the officer had never fired his gun
In the line of duty. He was chatting with a cabdriver
Beneath the tracks when my cousin circled him holding a knife.

The wound caused no brain damage though his eyeball was severed.
I am not sure how a man with no eye weeps. In the *Odyssey*
Pink water descends the Cyclops's cratered face after Odysseus

Drives a burning log into it. Anyone could do it. Anyone could
Begin the day with his eyes and end it blind or deceased,
Anyone could lose his mind or his vision. When I go crazy

I am afraid I will walk the streets naked, I am afraid I will shout
Every fucked up thing that troubles or enchants me, I will try
    to murder
Or make love to everybody before the police handcuff or
    murder me.

Though the bullet exits a perfect hole it does not leave perfect holes
In the body. A wound is a cell and portal. Without it the
    blood runs
With no outlet. It is possible to draw handcuffs using loops

Shaped like the symbol for infinity, from the Latin *infinitas*
Meaning *unboundedness*. The way you get to anything
Is context. In a blind contour it is not possible to give your subject

A disconnected gaze. Separated from the hand the artist's eye
Begins its own journey. It could have been the same for the
    Cyclops,
A giant whose gouged eye socket was so large a whole onion

Could fit into it. Separated from the body the eye begins
Its own journey. The world comes full circle: the hours, the harvests,
When the part of the body that holds the soul is finally decomposed

It becomes a circle, a hole that holds everything: blemish, cell,
Womb, parts of the body no one can see. I watched the model
Pull a button loose on her jeans and step out of them

As one might out of a hole in a blue valley, a sea. I found myself
In the dark, I found myself entering her body like a delicate shell
Or soft pill, like this curved thumb of mine against her lips.

You must look without looking to make the perfect circle.
The line, the mind must be a blind continuous liquid
Until the drawing is complete.

Works Cited

Abraham, Michael. "Elizabeth Bishop and the Schizoaffectivity of Whiteness" *Modernism/ modernity Print Plus*, Volume 6, Cycle 3, February 7, 2022 [https://doi.org/ 10.26597/mod.0220].

Adorno, Theodor. "Cultural Criticism and Society," 1951, *Prisms*, translated by Samuel and Shierry Weber, MIT Press, 1997, pages 17–34.

———. "On the fetish character in music and the regression of listening," 1938, *The Essential Frankfurt School Reader*, edited by A. Arato and E. Gebhardt, Oxford UP, 1982, pages 270–99.

———. "Perennial Fashion," 1967, *Prisms*, translated by Shierry Weber Nicholsen and Samuel Weber, MIT Press, 1983, pages 119–32.

———. "Reconciliation under Duress," 1961, translated by R. Livingstone, in Bloch et al., *Aesthetics and Politics*, Verso, 1983, pages 151–76.

Agamben, Giorgio. *The End of the Poem: Studies in Poetics*, 1996, translated by Daniel Heller Roazen, Stanford UP, 1999.

———. *Idea of Prose*, 1985, translated by Michael Sullivan and Sam Whitsitt, State U of New York P, 1995.

———. "La fine del poema." *Categorie italiane: Studi di poetica*, Marsilio, 1996, pages 113–19.

———. *Language and Death: The Place of Negativity*, 1982, translated by Karen E. Pinkus and Michael Hardt, U of Minnesota P, 1991.

———. *The Man Without Content*, translated by Georgia Albert, Stanford UP, 1999.

———. *Potentialities*, edited and translated by Daniel Heller-Roazen, Stanford UP, 1999.

———. *Remnants of Auschwitz: The Witness and the Archive*, translated by Daniel Heller-Roazen, Zone, 1999.

———. *Stanzas: Word and Phantasm in Western Culture*, translated by Ronald L. Martinez, U of Minnesota P, 1992.

———. *The Time That Remains: A Commentary on the Letter to the Romans*, 2000, translated by Patricia Dailey, Stanford UP, 2005.

Albright, Daniel. *Lyricality in English Literature*, U of Nebraska P, 1985.

Allingham, William. *Sixteen Poems by William Allingham*, selected by W. B. Yeats, The Dun Emer Press, 1905.

———. "Twilight Voices." *A Book of Irish Verse*, introduction and notes by W. B. Yeats, Methuen and Co., 1900, pages 164–66.

Anderson, Linda. "Visual Art" in *Elizabeth Bishop in Context*, edited by Angus Cleghorn and Jonathan Ellis, Cambridge UP, 2021, pages 126–36.

Andō, Midori. "Emily Dickinson's Vision of 'Circumference' and Death from a Japanese Perspective." *The Emily Dickinson Journal*, volume 5, number 2, Fall 1996, pages 221–25.

Appiah, Kwame Anthony. "Strictures on structures: the prospects for a structuralist poetics of African fiction." *Black Literature and Literary Theory*, edited by Henry Louis Gates, Methuen, 1984, pages 127–50.

Aristotle. *Poetics. Aristotle's Theory of Poetry and Fine Art*, translated by S. H. Butcher, Dover, 1951.

Auden, W. H. *Collected Poems*, edited by Edward Mendelson, Vintage, 1991.

Axelrod, Stephen Gould. "Bishop, History, and Politics." *The Cambridge Companion to Elizabeth Bishop*, edited by Angus Cleghorn and Jonathan Ellis, Cambridge UP, 2014, pages 35–48.

Balfour, Ian. "Responding to the call: Hartman between Wordsworth and Hegel." *Wordsworth Circle*, volume 37, issue 1, Winter 2006, pages 15–16.

Barrett, Faith. "Addresses to a Divided Nation: Images of War in Emily Dickinson and Walt Whitman." *Arizona Quarterly*, volume 61, number 4, Winter 2005, pages 67–99.

Barthes, Roland. *Image / Music / Text*, translated by Stephen Heath, Farrar, Straus and Giroux, 1977.

Baudelaire, Charles. *The Flowers of Evil*, translated by James McGowan, Oxford UP, 2008.

Bauer, Mark. *The Composite Voice: The Role of W. B. Yeats in James Merrill's Poetry*, Routledge, 2003.

Bellos, Alex. *Here's Looking at Euclid*, Free Press [Simon & Schuster], 2010.

Benjamin, Walter. *Illuminations*, edited and introduction by Hannah Arendt, translated by Harry Zohn, Schocken, 1968.

———. *Selected Writings Volume I: 1913–1926*, edited by Marcus Bullock and Michael W. Jennings. Harvard UP, 1996, pages 62–74.

Ben-Merre, David. *Figures of Time: Disjunctions in Modernist Poetry*, SUNY Press, 2018.

———. "I'm so vain, I bet I think this song is about myself: The Problematic 'I' of Lyric Poetry." *Metalepsis in Popular Culture*, edited by Karin Kukkonen and Sonja Klimek, De Gruyter, 2011, pages 65–82. [*Narratologia: Contributions to Narrative Theory* Series]

Bennett, Paula Bernat. "'Looking at Death, is Dying: Fascicle 16 in a Civil War Context." *Dickinson's Fascicles: A Spectrum of Possibilities*, edited by Paul Crumbley and Eleanor Elson Heginbotham, Ohio State UP, 2014, pages 106–29.

Benveniste, Émile. *Problems in General Linguistics*, translated by Mary Elizabeth Meek, U of Miami P, 1971.

Berger, Charles. "Bishop's Buried Elegies." *Elizabeth Bishop in the Twenty-First Century: Reading the New Editions*, edited by Angus Cleghorn, Bethany Hicok, and Thomas Travisano, U of Virginia P, 2012, pages 41–53.

Berlant, Lauren. *Cruel Optimism*, Duke UP, 2011.

Bernstein, Charles, ed. *Close Listening: Poetry and the Performed Word*, Oxford UP, 1998.

Berry, Francis. *Poetry and the Physical Voice*, Oxford UP, 1962.

Bersani, Leo. *The Culture of Redemption*, Harvard UP, 1990.

Bevis, Matthew. "Unknowing Lyric." *Poetry*, March 2017. [Accessed: https://www.poetryfoundation.org/poetrymagazine/articles/92372/unknowing-lyric]

Bezanson, Randall P. and Joseph Miller. "Scholarship and fair use." *Columbia Journal of Law and the Arts*, volume 33, 2010, pages 409–70.

Bishop, Elizabeth. *One Art: Letters*, edited by Robert Giroux, Farrar, Straus and Giroux, 1994.

———. *The Complete Poems 1927–1979*, Farrar, Straus and Giroux, 1983.

———. *Edgar Allan Poe & The Juke-Box: Uncollected Poems, Drafts, and Fragments*, edited by Alice Quinn, Farrar, Straus and Giroux, 2007.

Blasing, Mutlu. *American Poetry: The Rhetoric of Its Forms*, Yale UP, 1987.

———. *Lyric Poetry: The Pain and the Pleasure of Words*, Princeton UP, 2007.

Bloom, Harold. *Wallace Stevens: The Poems of Our Climate*, Cornell UP, 1977.

Boland, Eavan. "An Un-Romantic American." *Parnassus*, volume 14, number 2, 1988, pages 73–92.

Booth, Mark W. *Experience of Songs*, Yale UP, 1981.

Bornstein, George, ed. *The Early Poetry Volume II: "The Wanderings of Oisin" and Other Early Poems to 1895 Manuscript Materials*, Cornell UP, 1994.

Brackett, David. *Interpreting Popular Music*, U of California P, 2000.

Brady, Andrea. *Poetry and Bondage: A History and Theory of Lyric Constraint*, Cambridge UP, 2021.

Brogan, Jacqueline Vaught. "'An Almost Illegible Scrawl': Elizabeth Bishop and Textual (Re)Formations." *Elizabeth Bishop in the Twenty-First Century: Reading the New Editions*, edited by Angus Cleghorn, Bethany Hicok, and Thomas Travisano, U of Virginia P, 2012, pages 239–54.

———. "Mapping Elizabeth Bishop's 'Brazil, January 1, 1502.'" *Texas Studies in Language and Literature*, volume 59, number 1, Spring 2017, pages 106–35.

Broumas, Olga. *Beginning with O*, Yale UP, 1977.

Bruhn, Mark J. "A Mirror on the Mind: Stevens, Chiasmus, and Autism Spectrum Disorder." *The Wallace Stevens Journal*, vol. 39, no. 2, Fall 2015, pages 182–206.

Bunker, Matthew D. "Decoding Academic Fair Use: Transformative Use and the Fair Use Doctrine in Scholarship." *Journal of Copyright in Education and Librarianship*, volume 3, issue 1, 2019, pages 1–24.

Burt, Stephanie. "Galaxies Inside His Head." *New York Times Magazine*, March 29, 2015, pages 32–35, 61. [Accessed: https://www.nytimes.com/2015/03/29/magazine/galaxies-inside-his-head-poet-terrance-hayes.html.]

———. "'O Secret Stars Stay Secret': Rock and Roll in Contemporary Poetry." *This is Pop: in search of the elusive at Experience Music Project*, edited by Eric Weisbard, Harvard UP, 2004, pages 200–11.

———. "What Is This Thing Called Lyric?" *Modern Philology*, 2016, pages 422–40.

Butler, Judith. "Personhood and Other Objects: The Figural Dispute with Philosophy." *The Barbara Johnson Reader: The Surprise of Otherness*, edited by Melissa Feuerstein, *et al*, Duke UP, 2014, pages xvii–xxv.

Byrne, David and Brian Eno *et al*. "Once in a Lifetime." *Remain in Light*, Sire Records, 1980.

Cameron, Sharon. *Lyric Time: Dickinson and the Limits of Genre*, The Johns Hopkins UP, 1979.

———. *Choosing Not Choosing: Dickinson's Fascicles*, U of Chicago P, 1992.

Carson, Luke. "James Merrill's Manners and Elizabeth Bishop's Dismay." *Twentieth Century Literature*, volume 50, number 2, Summer 2004, pages 167–91.

Casper, Robert N. "About Terrance Hayes." *Ploughshares*, volume 36, issue 4, Winter 2010, pages 178–83.

Caswell, Robert W. "Yeats' *The Stolen Child*." *Explicator*, volume 25, number 8, April 1967, Item 64.

Cleghorn, Angus. "Bishop's 'Wiring Fused': 'Bone Key' and 'Pleasure Seas.'" *Elizabeth Bishop in the Twenty-First Century: Reading the New Editions*, edited by Angus Cleghorn, Bethany Hicok, and Thomas Travisano, U of Virginia P, 2012, pages 69–87.

Cleghorn, Angus, Bethany Hicok, and Thomas Travisano, eds. *Elizabeth Bishop in the Twenty-First Century: Reading the New Editions*, U of Virginia P, 2012.

Clemens, Justin. "The Role of the Shifter and the Problem of Reference in Giorgio Agamben." *The Work of Giorgio Agamben: Law, Literature, Life*, edited by Alex Murray, Nicholas Heron, and Justin Clemens, Edinburgh UP, 2008, pages 43–65.

Colbert, Soyica Diggs. "Introduction: Do you Want to Be Well?" *The Psychic Hold of Slavery: Legacies in American Expressive Culture*, edited by Colbert, Robert J. Patterson, and Aida Levy-Hussen, Rutgers UP, 2016, pages 1–16.

Coleridge, S. T. *Biographia Literaria*, edited by H. J. Jackson, Oxford UP, 2000.

Collecott, Diana. *H. D. and Sapphic Modernism 1910–1950*, Cambridge UP, 1999.

Colwell, Anne. *Inscrutable Houses: Metaphors of the Body in the Poems of Elizabeth Bishop*, U of Alabama P, 1997.

Conner, Lester I. *A Yeats Dictionary: Persons and Places in the Poetry of William Butler Yeats*, Syracuse UP, 1998.

Cook, Eleanor. *Against Coercion: Games Poets Play*, Stanford UP, 1998.

———. *Poetry, Word-Play, and Word-War in Wallace Stevens*, Princeton UP, 1988.

Costello, Bonnie. *Elizabeth Bishop: Questions of Mastery*, Harvard UP, 1991.

Cotton, Jess. "Unfit for History: Race, Reparation and the Reconstruction of American Lyric." *Journal of American Studies*, volume 55, 2021, pages 523–50.

Crumbley, Paul and Eleanor Elson Heginbotham. *Dickinson's Fascicles: A Spectrum of Possibilities*, Ohio State UP, 2014.

Cucullu, Lois. "Trompe l'Oeil: Elizabeth Bishop's Radical 'I.'" *Texas Studies in Language and Literature*, volume 30, number 2, Summer 1988, pages 246–71.

Culler, Jonathan. "L'Hyperbole et l'apostrophe: Baudelaire and the Theory of the Lyric." [Time for Baudelaire] *Yale French Studies*, number 125/126, 2014, pages 85–101.

———. *The Pursuit of Signs*, augmented ed., Cornell UP, 2002.

———. "Reading Lyric." [The Lesson of Paul de Man] *Yale French Studies*, number 69, 1985, pages 98–106.

———. *Theory of the Lyric*, Harvard UP, 2015.

Cunningham, Valentine. *In the Reading Gaol: Postmodernity, Texts and History*, Blackwell, 1994.

Davis, Skeeter. "The End of the World" [written by Kent, Arthur and Sylvia Dee]. *Skeeter Davis Sings the End of the World*. RCA Records, 1962. LP. A-side.

de Man, Paul. *Allegories of Reading*, Yale UP, 1979.

———. "Lyrical Voice in Contemporary Theory: Riffaterre and Jauss." *Lyric Poetry: Beyond New Criticism*, edited by Chaviva Hošek and Patricia Parker, Cornell UP, 1985, pages 55–72.

———. *Rhetoric of Romanticism*, Columbia UP, 1984.

Derrida, Jacques. *Dissemination*, 1972, translated by Barbara Johnson, Continuum, 2004.

———. *De la Grammatologie*, Les Éditions de Minuit, 1967.

———. *Of Grammatology*, translated by Gayatri Chakravorty Spivak, The Johns Hopkins UP, 1974.

———. "The Purveyor of Truth" ["Le facteur de la vérité"], translated by Alan Bass, *Yale French Studies*, number 52, 1975, pages 31–113.

Dickinson, Emily. *The Complete Poems of Emily Dickinson* [J], edited by Thomas H. Johnson, Little, Brown & Company, 1960.

———. *Emily Dickinson's Poems As She Preserved Them*, edited by Cristanne Miller, Harvard UP, 2016.

———. *The Letters of Emily Dickinson* [L], Volumes I–III, edited by Thomas H. Johnson and Theodora Ward, Harvard UP, 1958.

———. *The Poems of Emily Dickinson* [F], Reading Edition, edited by R.W. Franklin, Harvard UP, 1998.

———. *The Poems of Emily Dickinson: Including variant readings critically compared with all known manuscripts* [J], edited by Thomas H. Johnson, Harvard UP, 1955.

Diehl, Joanne Feit. *Women Poets and the American Sublime*, Indiana UP, 1990.

Donne, John. *The Complete Poetry and Selected Prose*, edited by Charles M. Coffin, Modern Library [Random House], 2001.

Donohue, Pete, Mark Morales and Tracy Connor. "Lunatic slashes MTA cop in the eye, but officer kills deranged suspect in holiday horror outside LIRR station in Queens." *Daily News*, July 4, 2012. [Accessed: https://www.nydailynews.com/new-york/mta-stabbed-face-violent-confrontation-queens-long-island-railroad-station-article-1.1107703.]

Doreski, C. K. *Elizabeth Bishop, The Restraints of Language*, Oxford UP, 1993.

Dowd, Kathy Ehrich. "Carly Simon Says 'You're So Vain' 'Is' About Warren Beatty—Well, Only the Second Verse: 'He Thinks the Whole Thing Is About Him!'" *People.com*, November 18, 2015.

Durantaye, Leland de la. *Giorgio Agamben: A Critical Introduction*, Stanford UP, 2009.

Düttmann, Alexander García. "Integral Actuality: On Giorgio Agamben's *Idea of Prose*." *The Work of Giorgio Agamben: Law, Literature, Life*, edited by Alex Murray, Nicholas Heron, and Justin Clemens, Edinburgh UP, 2008, pages 28–42.

Edelman, Lee. "The Geography of Gender: Elizabeth Bishop's 'In the Waiting Room.'" *Contemporary Literature*, volume 26, number 2, Summer 1985, pages 179–96.

Eeckhout, Bart. *Wallace Stevens and the Limits of Reading and Writing*, U of Missouri P, 2002.

Eliot, T. S. *Four Quartets*, Harcourt Brace, 1971.

———. *The Waste Land and Other Poems*, Harcourt Brace & Company, 1962.

Ellis, Jonathan. *Art and Memory in the Work of Elizabeth Bishop*, Ashgate, 2006.

Emerson, Ralph Waldo. "Circles." 1841. *Essays and Poems*, Library of America, 1996, pages 401–14.

Erkkila, Betsy. "Dickinson and the Art of Politics." *A Historical Guide to Emily Dickinson*, edited by Vivian R. Pollak, Oxford, 2004, pages 133–74.

———. "The Emily Dickinson Wars." *The Cambridge Companion to Emily Dickinson*, edited by Wendy Martin, Cambridge UP, 2002, pages 11–29.

Espy, Willard. *An Almanac of Words at Play*, Clarkson N. Potter, Inc., 1975.

Estes, David C. "'Out Upon Circumference': Emily Dickinson's Search for Location." *Essays in Literature*, 6, 1979, pages 207–18.

Farr, Judith. *The Passion of Emily Dickinson*, Harvard UP, 1992.

Filreis, Alan. "Sound at an Impasse." *The Wallace Stevens Journal*, vol. 33, no. 1, Spring 2009, pages 15–23.

Forbes, Deborah. *Sincerity's Shadow: Self-Consciousness in British Romantic and Mid-Twentieth-Century American Poetry*, Harvard UP, 2004.

Foster, Richard. "The Romanticism of I. A. Richards." *English Literary History*, volume 26, number 1, Mar. 1959, pages 91–101.

Foucault, Michel. "What is an Author?" translated by Josué Harari, in *Michel Foucault: Aesthetics, Method, and Epistemology*, edited by James D. Faubion, translated by Robert Hurley *et al*, The New Press, 1998, pages 205–22.

Freud, Sigmund. *Totem and Taboo*, translated by A. A. Brill, New Republic, 1927.

Frith, Simon, Will Straw, and John Street, eds. *The Cambridge Companion to Pop and Rock*, Cambridge UP, 2001.

Frye, Northrop. *Anatomy of Criticism*, Princeton University Press, 1957.

———. *Spiritus Mundi: Essays on Literature, Myth, and Society*, Indiana UP, 1976.

Furia, Philip, and Martin Roth. "Stevens' Fusky Alphabet." *PMLA*, vol. 93, no. 1, Jan. 1978, pages 66–77.

Galvin, Rachel. "Poetry is Theft." *Comparative Literature Studies*, volume 51, number 1, 2014, pages 18–54.

———. " 'This Song Is for My Foe': Olive Senior and Terrance Hayes Rewrite Stevens," in *Poetry and Poetics after Wallace Stevens*, edited by Bart Eeckhout and Lisa Goldfarb, Bloomsbury, 2017, pages 229–43.

Gasché, Rodolphe. *The Wild Card of Reading: On Paul de Man*, Harvard UP, 1998.

Gates, Henry Louis, Jr. *The Black Box: Writing the Race*, Penguin, 2024.

Gelpi, Albert J. *Emily Dickinson: The Mind of the Poet*, Norton, 1971.

Genette, Gérard. *Narrative Discourse: An Essay in Method*, 1972, translated by J. E. Lewin, Cornell UP, 1980.

Gilbert, Sandra M. and Susan Gubar. *The Madwoman in the Attic: The Woman Writer and the Nineteenth-Century Literary Imagination*, 1979, Yale UP, 2020.

Giles, Paul. " 'The Earth reversed her Hemispheres': Dickinson's Global Antipodality." *The Emily Dickinson Journal*, volume 20, number 1, 2011, pages 1–21.

Gillespie, Robert. "A Circumference of Emily Dickinson." *The New England Quarterly*, volume 46, number 2, June 1973, pages 250–71.

Gilson, Annette. "Disseminating 'Circumference': The Diachronic Presence of Dickinson in John Ashbery's 'Clepsydra.' " *Twentieth-Century Literature*, volume 44, number 4, Winter 1998, pages 484–505.

Goldensohn, Lorrie. *Elizabeth Bishop: The Biography of a Poetry*, Columbia UP, 1993.

Gorski, William T. *Yeats and Alchemy*, State U of New York P, 1996.

Gribbin, Laura. "Emily Dickinson's Circumference: Figuring a Blind Spot in the Romantic Tradition." *The Emily Dickinson Journal*, volume 2, number 1, Spring 1993, pages 1–21.

Griffiths, Dai. "The High Analysis of Low Music," 1999, *Music Analysis* volume 18, number 3, 1999, pages 389–435.

Griffiths, Eric. *The Printed Voice of Victorian Poetry*, 1989, Oxford UP, 2018.

Grossman, Allen. "Allen Grossman—Poetry Lectures #6 [Part 1]—Emily Dickinson's 'I Cannot Live With You' " (Accessed: https://www.youtube.com/watch?v=9CZt-tICoTk).

———. *Summa Lyrica: A Primer of the Commonplaces in Speculative Poetics. The Sighted Singer: Two Works on Poetry for Readers and Writers*, The Johns Hopkins UP, 1992, pages 205–375.

Gurganus, Allan. "James Merrill." *Loss within Loss: Artists in the Age of AIDS*, edited by Edmund White, U of Wisconsin P, 2001, pages 279–85.

Guyer, Sara. "Wordsworthian Wakefulness." *Yale Journal of Criticism*, volume 16, number 1, Spring 2003, pages 93–111.

Gwiazda, Piotr K., *James Merrill and W. H. Auden: Homosexuality and Poetic Influence*, Palgrave, 2007.

Hacker, Marilyn. "Villanelle," *Presentation Piece*, Viking Press, page 89.

Hallen, Cynthia L. "Cognitive Circuits: The Circumference of Dickinson's Lexicon." *The Emily Dickinson Journal*, volume 6, number 2, Fall 1997, pages 74–83.

Hamm, Charles. *Putting Popular Music in its Place*, Cambridge UP, 1995.

Hammer, Langdon. *James Merrill: Life and Art*, Knopf, 2015.

Hariman, Robert. "What Is a Chiasmus? Or, Why the Abyss Stares Back." *Chiasmus and Culture*, edited by Anthony Paul and Boris Wiseman, Berghahn, 2014, pages 45–68.

Harrison, Victoria. *Elizabeth Bishop's Poetics of Intimacy*, Cambridge UP, 1993.

Hart, Ellen Louise. "Alliteration, Emphasis, and Spatial Prosody in Dickinson's Manuscript Letters." *Reading Emily Dickinson's Letters*, edited by Jane Donahue Eberwein and Cindy MacKenzie, U of Massachusetts P, 2009, pages 213–38.

———. "The Elizabeth Putney Manuscripts and New Strategies for Editing Emily Dickinson's Letters." *The Emily Dickinson Journal*, volume 4, number 1, Spring 1995, pages 44–74.

Hartman, Charles O. "The Criticism of Song." *Centennial Review*, volume 19, number 2, Spring 1975, pages 96–107.

Hartman, Geoffrey. *Beyond Formalism*, Yale UP, 1970.

———. *Wordsworth's Poetry 1787–1814*, Yale UP, 2015.

Hayes, Terrance. *American Sonnets for My Past and Future Assassin*, Penguin, 2018.

———. *To Float in the Space Between: A Life and Work in Conversation with the Life and Work of Etheridge Knight*, Wave Books, 2018.

———. *Hip Logic*, Penguin, 2002.

———. *How to be Drawn*, Penguin, 2015.

———. "An Improvisation with Chris Gilbert's 'Chris Gilbert: An Improvisation.'" *The Worcester Review*, volume 33, issue 1–2, 2012, pages 96–99.

———. *Lighthead*, Penguin, 2010.

———. "Line 1: Taped to the Wall of My Cell" *Callaloo*, volume 39, number 4, Fall 2016, pages 805–10.

———. *Wind in a Box*, Penguin, 2006.

Haymes, Greg. "Song Speculation All in Vain." Timesunion.com. [Retrieved on June 10, 2009; originally published in *Times Union* (August 29, 2008).]

Heaney, Seamus. *The Government of the Tongue: Selected Prose 1978–1987*, Farrar, Straus and Giroux, 1988.

———. *The Haw Lantern*, Farrar, Straus and Giroux, 1995.

———. *Poems 1965–1975*, Farrar, Straus and Giroux, 1981.

Hebdige, Dick. *Subculture: The Meaning of Style*, Methuen, 1979.

Hecht, Anthony. *The Transparent Man*, Knopf, 1990.

Herbert, George. "The Country Parson." *The English Works of George Herbert*, vol. 1, edited by George Herbert Palmer, Hodder and Stoughton, 1905, pages 193–323.

———. *The English Poems of George Herbert*, edited by Helen Wilcox, Cambridge UP, 2007.

Heron, Nicholas. "Idea of Poetry, Idea of Prose." *The Work of Giorgio Agamben: Law, Literature, Life*, edited by Alex Murray, Nicholas Heron, and Justin Clemens, Edinburgh UP, 2008, pages 97–113.

Herrnstein Smith, Barbara. *Poetic Closure: A Study of How Poems End*, U of Chicago P, 1968.

Hesmondhalgh, David and Keith Negus. *Popular Music Studies*, Arnold, 2002.

Hicok, Bethany. "Bishop's Brazilian Politics." *Elizabeth Bishop in the 21st Century: Reading the New Editions*, edited by Angus Cleghorn, Bethany Hicok, Thomas Travisano, U of Virginia P, 2012, pages 133–50.

Holander, Stefan. *Wallace Stevens and the Realities of Poetic Language*, Routledge, 2008.

Hollander, John. *Melodious Guile: Fictive Pattern in Poetic Language*, Yale UP, 1988.

———. *Vision and Resonance: Two Senses of Poetic Form*, Oxford UP, 1975.

Holloway-Attaway, Lissa. "The Business of Circumference: Circularity and Dangerous Female Power in the Work of Emily Dickinson." *The Emily Dickinson Journal*, volume 5, number 2, Fall 1996, pages 183–89.

Hopps, Gavin. "Beyond Embarrassment: A Post-Secular Reading of Apostrophe." *Romanticism* volume 11, number 2, Jul 2005, pages 224–41.

"Horse." *Encyclopædia Britannica*, eleventh edition, Volume XIII, Slice VI. [Accessed via: http://www.gutenberg.org/files/39127/39127-h/39127-h.htm.]

Howe, Susan. *The Birth-mark: unsettling the wilderness in American literary history*, Wesleyan UP, 1993.

Hubbard, Melanie. "Dickinson's Advertising Flyers: Theorizing Materiality and the Work of Reading." *The Emily Dickinson Journal*, volume 7, number 1, Spring 1998, pages 27–54.

———. "The Word Made Flesh: Dickinson's Variants and the Life of Language." *Dickinson's Fascicles: A Spectrum of Possibilities*, edited by Paul Crumbley and Eleanor Elson Heginbotham, Ohio State UP, 2014, pages 33–62.

Hughes, Langston. "My Adventures as a Social Poet." *The Langston Hughes Review*, volume 4, number 1, Spring 1985, pages 9–15. [Originally printed in *PHYLON*, Fall 1947, pages 205–12.]

———. *Selected Poems of Langston Hughes*, 1959, Vintage, 1990.

Hunt, Erica. "Notes for an Oppositional Poetics." *The Politics of Poetic Form: Poetry and Public Policy*, edited by Charles Bernstein, Roof Books, 1990, pages 197–212.

Ingram, Claudia. "Lyric Subversions: The Case of James Merrill." *Pacific Coast Philology*, volume 53, number 1, 2018, pages 43–67.

Jackson, Virginia. "Apostrophe, Animation, and Racism." *Critical Inquiry*, volume 48, number 4, Summer 2022, pages 652–75.

———. *Before Modernism*, Princeton UP, 2023.

———. "Dickinson's Figure of Address." *Dickinson and Audience*, edited by Martin Orzeck and Robert Weisbuch, U of Michigan P, 1996, pages 77–103.

———. *Dickinson's Misery: A Theory of Lyric Reading*, Princeton UP, 2005.

———. "Lyric." *The Princeton Encyclopedia of Poetry and Poetics*, 4th ed., Roland Greene *et al.*, Princeton UP, 2012, 826–34.

Jackson, Virginia and Yopie Prins, eds. "Lyrical Studies." *Victorian Literature and Culture* volume 27, number 2, 1999, pages 521–30.

Jacobus, Mary. "Apostrophe and Lyric Voice in *The Prelude*." *Lyric Poetry: Beyond New Criticism*, edited by Chaviva Hošek and Patricia Parker, Cornell UP, 1985, pages 167–81.

———. *Romanticism, Writing, and Sexual Difference: Essays on* The Prelude, Clarendon Press, 1990.

Jakobson, Roman. *Language in Literature*, edited by Krystyna Pomorska and Stephen Rudy, Harvard UP, 1987.

Jameson, Fredric. *The Political Unconscious*, 1982, Cornell UP, 2014.

Javadizadeh, Kamran. "The Atlantic Ocean Breaking on Our Heads: Claudia Rankine, Robert Lowell, and the Whiteness of the Lyric Subject." *PMLA* volume 134, number 3, 2019, pages 475–90.

Jeffares, A. Norman. *A New Commentary on the Poems of W. B. Yeats*, Stanford UP, 1984.

Jespersen, Otto. *Language: Its Nature, Development and Origin*, George Allen & Unwin Ltd., 1922.

Johnson, Barbara. "Apostrophe, Animation, and Abortion." *Diacritics*, volume 16, number 1, Spring 1986, pages 28–47.

———. *The Barbara Johnson Reader: The Surprise of Otherness*, edited by Melissa Feuerstein, *et al*, Duke UP, 2014.

———. "The Frame of Reference: Poe, Lacan, Derrida," *Yale French Studies*, number 55–56, 1977, pages 457–505.

———. *Persons and Things*, Harvard UP, 2008.

———. *A World of Difference*, The Johns Hopkins UP, 1987.

Johnson, David E. "As If the Time Were Now: Deconstructing Agamben," *South Atlantic Quarterly*, volume 106, number 2, Spring 2007, pages 265–90.

Johnson, Thomas H. *Emily Dickinson: An Interpretive Biography*, Atheneum, 1967.

Jones, Douglas. "The Fruit of Abolition: Discontinuity and Difference in Terrance Hayes's 'The Avocado.'" *The Psychic Hold of Slavery*, edited by Colbert, Robert J. Patterson, and Aida Levy-Hussen, Rutgers UP, 2016, pages 39–54.

Joyce, James. *Ulysses*, edited by Hans Walter Gabler, Vintage, 1986.

Kahn, Peter, Ravi Shankar, and Terrence Hayes, eds. *The Golden Shovel Anthology: New Poems Honoring Gwendolyn Brooks*, U of Arkansas P, 2017.

Kalstone, David. *Becoming a Poet: Elizabeth Bishop with Marianne Moore and Robert Lowell*, Farrar, Straus and Giroux, 1989.

———. *Five Temperaments: Elizabeth Bishop, Robert Lowell, James Merrill, Adrienne Rich, John Ashbery*, Oxford UP, 1977.

Kang, Yanbin. "Dickinson's Hummingbirds, Circumference, and Chinese Poetics." *The Emily Dickinson Journal*, volume 20, number 2, 2011, pages 57–82.

Keats, John. *Selected Poems and Selected Letters of John Keats*, edited by Douglas Bush, Random House, 2009.

Keller, Lynn. *Contemporary American Poetry and the Modernist Tradition*, Cambridge UP, 1987.

Keniston, Ann. "The Fluidity of Damaged Form: Apostrophe and Desire in Nineties Lyric." *Contemporary Literature*, volume 42, number 2, 2001, pages 294–324.

Kermode, Frank. *The Sense of an Ending: Studies in the Theory of Fiction*, Oxford UP, 1967.

Keyser, Samuel Jay. "Reversals in Poe and Stevens." *The Wallace Stevens Journal*, vol. 35, no. 2, Fall 2011, pages 224–39.

Kiberd, Declan. "Yeats, Childhood, and Exile." *Irish Writing: Exile and Subversion*, edited by Paul Hyland and Neil Sammels, St. Martin's Press, 1991, pages 126–45.

Kinahan, Frank. *Yeats, Folklore, and Occultism: Contexts of the Early Work and Thought*, Unwin Hyman, 1988.

Klosterman, Chuck. "The Carly Simon Principle: Sincerity and Pop Greatness." *This is Pop: In Search of the Elusive at Experience Music Project*, edited by Eric Weisbard, Harvard UP, 2004, pages 257–65.

Kneale, J. Douglas. "Romantic Aversions: Apostrophe Reconsidered." *ELH*, volume 58, number 1, Spring 1991, pages 141–65.

Koo, Jason. "A Conversation with Terrance Hayes." *The Missouri Review*, volume 29, number 4, Winter 2006, pages 58–78.

Kramnick, Jonathan. *Paper Minds: Literature and the Ecology of Consciousness*, U of Chicago P, 2018.

Kurnick, David. "A Few Lies: Queer Theory and Our Method Melodramas." *ELH*, volume 87, number 2, Summer 2020, pages 349–74.

Lacan, Jacques. *Ecrits*, translated by Alan Sheridan, Norton, 1977.

Laurens, Penelope. "'Old Correspondences': Prosodic Transformations in Elizabeth Bishop." *Elizabeth Bishop and Her Art*, edited by Lloyd Schwartz and Sybil P. Estess, U of Michigan P, 1983, pages 75–95.

Leach, Elizabeth Eva. "Vicars of 'Wannabe': authenticity and the Spice Girls." *Critical Essays in Popular Musicology*, edited by Allan F. Moore, Ashgate, 2007, pages 541–65.

Lentricchia, Frank. *The Gaiety of Language: An Essay on the Radical Poetics of W. B. Yeats and Wallace Stevens*, U of California P, 1968.

Lissner, Patricia Ann. "Chi-Thinking: Chiasmus and Cognition." Diss. U of Maryland, 2007, drum.lib.umd.edu/handle/1903/7687.

Lombardi, Marilyn May. *The Body and the Song: Elizabeth Bishop's Poetics*, Southern Illinois UP, 1995.

Longenbach, James. "Ashbery and the Individual Talent," *American Literary History*, volume 9, number 1, Spring 1997, pages 103–27.

Lurie, Alison. *Familiar Spirits: A Memoir of James Merrill and David Jackson*, Viking, 2001.

MacKenzie, Cindy. "'This is my letter to the World': Emily Dickinson's Epistolary Poetics." *Reading Emily Dickinson's Letters*, edited by Jane Donahue Eberwein and Cindy MacKenzie, U of Massachusetts P, 2009, pages 11–27.

MacKillop, James. *Dictionary of Celtic Mythology*, Oxford UP, 1998.

Manning, Stephen. "Game and Earnest in the Middle English and Provençal Love Lyrics." *Comparative Literature*, volume 18, number 3, Summer 1966, pages 225–41.

Mariani, Andrea. "Orbits of Power: Rings in James Merrill's Poetry." *Exchanging Clothes: Habits of Being 2*, edited by Cristina Giorcelli and Paula Rabinowitz, U of Minnesota P, 2012, pages 58–77.

Marshall, Megan. *Elizabeth Bishop: A Miracle for Breakfast*, Houghton Mifflin Harcourt, 2017.

Marx, Karl. *Capital: A Critique of Political Economy*, vol. 1, 1867, translated by Ben Fowkes, Vintage, 1977.

Materer, Timothy. *James Merrill's Apocalypse*, Cornell UP, 2000.

———. "James Merrill's Late Poetry: AIDS and the 'Stripping Process.'" *Arizona Quarterly*, volume 64, number 2, Summer 2008, pages 123–45.

McCabe, Susan. *Elizabeth Bishop: Her Poetics of Loss*, Pennsylvania State UP, 1994.

McCarthy, Tom. "Tom McCarthy Thinks the Wrong Kurt Vonnegut Book Is Famous," *NY Times Book Review*, 01/23/2022, page 8; [https://www.nytimes.com/2022/01/20/books/review/tom-mccarthy-by-the-book-interview.html].

McClatchy, J. D. "Monsters Wrapped in Silk: James Merrill's *Country of a Thousand Years of Peace*." *Contemporary Poetry*, volume 4, number 4, 1982, pages 1–30.

———. *White Paper: On Contemporary American Poetry*, Columbia UP, 1989.

McGann, Jerome. *Black Riders: The Visible Language of Modernism*, Princeton UP, 1993.

———. "Emily Dickinson's Visible Language." *The Emily Dickinson Journal*, volume 2, number 2, Fall 1993, pages 40–57.

McGarry, James P. *Place Names in the Writings of William Butler Yeats*, edited by Edward Malins, Colin Smythe Ltd., 1976.

McGuirk, Kevin. "Questions, Apostrophes, and the Politics of Seamus Heaney's 'Field Work.'" *Ariel*, volume 25, number 3, July 1994, pages 67–81.

McRae, Calista. *Lyric as Comedy: The Poetics of Abjection in Postwar America*, Cornell UP, 2020.

Merrill, James. "Afterward" in Kalstone, *Becoming a Poet: Elizabeth Bishop with Marianne Moore and Robert Lowell*, Farrar, Straus and Giroux, 1989, pages 251–62.

———. *The Changing Light at Sandover*, Atheneum, 1982.

———. *Collected Novels and Plays*, edited by J. D. McClatchy and Stephen Yenser, Knopf, 2002.

———. *Collected Poems*, edited by J. D. McClatchy and Stephen Yenser, Knopf, 2001.

———. *Collected Prose*, edited by J. D. McClatchy and Stephen Yenser, Knopf, 2004.

Merrin, Jeredith. "Elizabeth Bishop: Gaiety, Gayness, and Change." *Elizabeth Bishop: The Geography of Gender*, edited by Marilyn May Lombardi, UP of Virginia, 1993, pages 153–72.

———. *An Enabling Humility: Marianne Moore, Elizabeth Bishop, and the Uses of Tradition*, Rutgers UP, 1990.

Merwin, W. S. "The End of More Than a Book." *The New York Times*, March 26, 1995.

Michaels, Bret, *et al.*, "Every Rose Has Its Thorn," *Open Up and Say . . . Ahh!*, Capitol Records, 1988.

Middleton, Richard, ed. *Reading Pop: Approaches to Textual Analysis in Popular Music*, Oxford UP, 2000.

———. *Studying Popular Music*, Open University Press, 1990.

———. *Voicing the Popular: On the Subjects of Popular Music*, Routledge, 2006.

Mill, John Stuart. *Essays on Poetry*, U of South Carolina P, 1976.

———. "Thoughts on Poetry and its Varieties." *The Crayon*, volume 7, part 4, April 1860, pages 93–97. [Accessed via JSTOR.]

Millay, Edna St. Vincent. *Selected Poems*, HarperCollins, 1999.

Miller, Cristanne. *A Poet's Grammar*, Harvard UP, 1987.

———. *Reading in Time: Emily Dickinson in the Nineteenth Century*. U of Massachusetts P, 2012.

———. "The Sound of Shifting Paradigms, or Hearing Dickinson in the Twenty-First Century." *A Historical Guide to Emily Dickinson*, edited by Vivian R. Pollak, Oxford, 2004, pages 201–34.

Miller, Paul Allen. *Lyric Texts and Lyric Consciousness: The Birth of a Genre from Archaic Greece to Augustan Rome*, 1994, Routledge, 2016.

Millier, Brett Candlish. *Elizabeth Bishop: Life and the Memory of It*, U of California P, 1993.

———. "Elusive Mastery: The Drafts of Elizabeth Bishop's 'One Art.' " *New England Review*, volume 13, number 2, Winter 1990, pages 121–29.

Mills, Catherine. *The Philosophy of Agamben*, Acumen, 2008.

Mitchell, Domhnall. "Introduction," *Women's Studies*, volume 31, 2002, pages 719–23.

———. *Monarch of Perception*, U of Massachusetts P, 2000.

———. "Revising the Script: Emily Dickinson's Manuscripts." *American Literature*, volume 70, number 4, Dec. 1998, pages 705–37.

Moffett, Judith. *James Merrill: An Introduction to the Poetry*, Columbia UP, 1984.

Moore, Allan F., ed. *Critical Essays in Popular Musicology*, Ashgate, 2007.

Moore, Marianne. *Complete Poems*, Macmillan, 1994.

Morgan, Victoria N. " 'When Bells Stop Ringing': Tracing Dickinson's 'Circumference' through the Traditions of the Praying Circle." *Religion and Literature*, volume 46, number 1, Spring 2014, pages 172–79.

Moten, Fred. *In the Break: The Aesthetics of the Black Radical Tradition*, U of Minnesota P, 2003.

Muller, John P. and William J. Richardson, eds. *The Purloined Poe: Lacan, Derrida, and Psychoanalytic Reading*, The Johns Hopkins UP, 1988.

Murray, Alex, Nicholas Heron, and Justin Clemens, eds. *The Work of Giorgio Agamben: Law, Literature, Life*, Edinburgh UP, 2008.

Nersessian, Anahid. *The Calamity Form: On Poetry and Social Life*, U of Chicago P, 2020.

New, Elisa. "Difficult Writing, Difficult God: Emily Dickinson's Poems beyond Circumference." *Religion & Literature*, volume 18, number 3, Fall 1986, pages 1–27.

O'Donnell, William. "Reading Yeats's Hand." *Yeats: An Annual of Critical and Textual Studies*, volume IX, edited by Richard J. Finneran and Mary FitzGerald, U of Michigan P, 1991, pages 87–94.

Orzeck, Martin. "Dickinson's Letters to Abiah Root: Formulating the Reader as Absentee." *Dickinson and Audience*, edited by Martin Orzeck and Robert Weisbuch, U of Michigan P, 1996, pages 135–60.

Orzeck, Martin and Robert Weisbuch, eds. *Dickinson and Audience*, U of Michigan P, 1996.

Parker, Robert Dale. *The Unbeliever: The Poetry of Elizabeth Bishop*, U of Illinois P, 1988.

Paul, Anthony, and Boris Wiseman, editors. *Chiasmus and Culture*, Berghahn, 2014.

Pearl, Monica B. "The Opera Closet: Ardor, Shame, Queer Confessions." *History, Theory, Criticism*, volume 37, issue 1, 2015, pages 46–65.

Perloff, Marjorie. "Language Poetry and the Lyric Subject: Ron Silliman's Albany, Susan Howe's Buffalo." *Critical Inquiry*, volume 25, number 3, Spring 1999, pages 405–34.

Pinch, Adela. *Strange Fits of Passion: Epistemologies of Emotion, Hume to Austen*, Stanford UP, 1997.

Plath, Sylvia. "Mad Girl's Love Song," 1953, *Villanelles*, edited by Annie Finch and Marie-Elizabeth Mali, Knopf, 2012, page 50.

Plato. *Phaedrus*, translated by R. Hackforth, Cambridge UP, 1972.

———. *Republic*, translated by G. M. A. Grube, revised by C. D. C. Reeve, Hackett, 1992.

Poe, E. A. *Selections from the Critical Writings*, edited by F. C. Prescott, Gordian Press, 1981.

Polito, Robert. *A Reader's Guide to James Merrill's* The Changing Light at Sandover, U of Michigan P, 1994.

Pollak, Vivian R. "Introduction." *A Historical Guide to Emily Dickinson*, edited by Vivian R. Pollak, Oxford UP, 2004, pages 3–11.

Poovey, Mary. "The Model System of Contemporary Literary Criticism." *Critical Inquiry*, volume 27, number 3, Spring 2001, pages 408–38.

Porter, David T. *The Art of Emily Dickinson's Early Poetry*, 1963, Harvard UP, 2000.

———. *Dickinson: The Modern Idiom*, Harvard UP, 1981.

Pratt, Lloyd. *The Strangers Books: The Human of African American Literature*, U of Pennsylvania P, 2016.

Pugh, Christina. "'A Lovely Finish I Have Seen': Voice and Variorum in *Edgar Allan Poe and the Juke-Box*." *Elizabeth Bishop in the Twenty-First Century: Reading the New Editions*, edited by Angus Cleghorn, Bethany Hicok, and Thomas Travisano, U of Virginia P, 2012, pages 274–88.

Quashie, Kevin. *The Sovereignty of Quiet: Beyond Resistance in Black Culture*, Rutgers UP, 2012.

Ragg, Edward. *Wallace Stevens and the Aesthetics of Abstraction*, Cambridge UP, 2010.

Ramazani, Jahan. *Poetry and its Others: News, Prayer, Song, and the Dialogue of Genres*, U of Chicago P, 2014.

Ramsey, William M. "Terrance Hayes and Natasha Trethewey: Contemporary Black Chronicles of the Imagined South." *The Southern Literary Journal*, volume 44, number 2, Spring 2012, pages 122–35.

Rankine, Claudia. "The Art of Poetry No. 102." Interview conducted by David Ulin. *The Paris Review*, volume 219, Winter 2016, pages 139–66.

———. *Citizen: An American Lyric*, Graywolf Press, 2014.

Rasula, Jed. *The American Poetry Wax Museum: Reality Effects, 1940–1990*, NCTE, 1996.

Redfield, Marc. *Theory at Yale: The Strange Case of Deconstruction in America*, Fordham UP, 2016.

Reed, Anthony. *Freedom Time: The Poetics and Politics of Black Experimental Writing*, The Johns Hopkins UP, 2014.

Regan, Mariann Sanders. *Love Words: The Self and the Text in Medieval and Renaissance Poetry*, Cornell UP, 1982.

Rich, Adrienne. "When We Dead Awaken: Writing as Re-Vision," 1971, *On Lies, Secrets, and Silence: Selected Prose, 1966–1978*, Norton, 1979, pages 33–49.

Rodgers, Audrey T. " 'Circumference' in the Poetry of ED." *Emily Dickinson Bulletin*, Issue 31, 1977, pages 15–32.

Rogers, Jude. Review of *Boys in the Trees*, *The Guardian*, December 27, 2015. [Accessed: https://www.theguardian.com/music/2015/dec/27/boys-in-trees-memoir-carly-simon-review.]

Rose, Tricia. *Black Noise: Rap Music and Black Culture in Contemporary America*, UP of New England (Wesleyan UP), 1994.

Rousseau, Jean-Jacques. *Essay on the Origin of Languages*, translated by John H. Moran, *On the Origin of Language*, edited by Moran, U of Chicago P, 1966.

Rowell, Charles H. " 'The Poet in the Enchanted Shoe Factory': An Interview with Terrance Hayes." *Callaloo*, volume 27, number 4, Fall 2004, pages 1068–81.

Rutter, Emily Ruth. "Contested Lineages: Fred Moten, Terrance Hayes, and the Legacy of Amiri Baraka." *African American Review*, volume 49, number 4, Winter 2016, pages 329–42.

Sáma, Metta. "The Burden of Seed, the Seed of Burden: 'Repetitional Schemas' & Pace in Terrance Hayes's 'Sonnet.' " *Mentor and Muse: Essays from Poets to Poets*, edited by Blas Falconer, Beth Martinelli, and Helena Mesa, Southern University Press, 2010, pages 101–106.

"Sanford's Assorted Inks" [advertisement]. *The American Stationer*, vol. 23, 1888, p. 696.

Sastri, Reena. *James Merrill: Knowing Innocence*, Routledge, 2007.

Schwartz, Lloyd. "Dedications: Lowell's 'Skunk Hour' and Bishop's 'The Armadillo.'" *Salmagundi*, number 141/142, Winter–Spring 2004, pages 120–24.

Schwartz, Lloyd and Sybil P. Estes, eds. *Elizabeth Bishop and her Art*, U of Michigan P, 1983.

Sedgwick, Eve Kosofsky. "Paranoid Reading and Reparative Reading; or, You're So Paranoid, You Probably Think This Introduction Is About You." *Queer Readings in Fiction*, edited by Eve Kosofsky Sedgwick, Duke UP, 1997, pages 1–37.

Shank, Barry. *Dissonant Identities*, UP of New England (Wesleyan UP), 1994.

Shaw, Lytle. "Framing the Lyric." *American Literary History*, volume 28, number 2, Summer 2016, pages 403–13.

Shaw, W. David. "Lyric Displacement in the Victorian Monologue: Naturalizing the Vocative." *Nineteenth-Century Literature*, volume 52, number 3, Dec. 1997, pages 302–25.

Shelley, P. B. *The Selected Poetry and Prose of Shelley*, edited by Bruce Woodcock, Wordsworth Editions, 2002.

Sherwood, William R. *Circumference and Circumstance: Stages in the Mind and Art of Emily Dickinson*, Columbia UP, 1968.

Short, Bryan C. "Emily Dickinson's Apostrophe." *Women's Studies*, volume 31, issue 6, 2002, pages 769–83.

Sidney, Philip. *A Defence of Poetry*, edited by J.A. Van Dorsten, Oxford UP, 1966.

Simon, Carly. *Boys in the Trees: A Memoir*, Flatiron Books, 2016.

———. "You're So Vain" [lyrics], 1972, Carlysimon.com [Retrieved on June 14, 2010].[https://www.carlysimon.com/youre-so-vain]

———. "You're So Vain," *No Secrets*, Elektra Records, 1972.

Simpson, Megan. "'I believe all the stories of who I was': An Interview with Terrance Hayes." *Obsidian*, volume 8, issue 1, Spring/Summer 2007, pages 127–36.

Slonimsky, Nicolas. "The Weather at Mozart's Funeral." *The Musical Quarterly*, volume 46, number 1, Jan. 1960, pages 12–21.

Smith, David Nowell. "'I hold it toward you': Alterity in Lyric Address." *Ethics of Alterity, Confrontation and Responsibility in 19th- to 21st-Century British Literature*, edited by Christine Reynier and Jean-Michel Ganteau, Presses universitaires de la Méditerranée, 2013, pages 35–47.

Smith, Evans Lansing. *James Merrill, Postmodern Magus: Myth and Poetics*, U of Iowa P, 2008.

Smith, J. Mark. "Apostrophe, or the Lyric Art of Turning Away." *Texas Studies in Language and Literature*, volume 49, number 4, Winter 2007, pages 411–37.

Smith, Martha Nell. "The Poet as Cartoonist." *Comic Power in Emily Dickinson*, edited by Suzanne Juhasz, Cristanne Miller, and Martha Nell Smith, U of Texas P, 1993, pages 63–102.

———. *Rowing in Eden: Rereading Emily Dickinson*, U of Texas P, 1992.

Smith, Robert. "Just Like Heaven." *Kiss Me, Kiss Me, Kiss Me*, Fiction Records, 1987.

"So Carly, just who is 'You're So Vain' about?" CarlySimon.com. [Retrieved on June 10, 2009.]

Socarides, Alexandra. "Managing Multiple Contexts: Dickinson, Genre, and the Circulation of Fascicle 1." *Dickinson's Fascicles: A Spectrum of Possibilities*, edited by Paul Crumbley and Eleanor Elson Heginbotham, Ohio State UP, 2014, pages 150–68.

Spaide, Christopher. "Multiple Choice: Terrance Hayes's Response-Poems and the African American Lyric 'We.'" *Cambridge Quarterly*, volume 48, number 3, September 2019, pages 231–57.

Spoo, Robert. "Fair Use of Unpublished Works: Scholarly Research and Copyright Case Law Since 1992." *Tulsa Law Review*, volume 34, number 1, Fall 1998, pages 183–200.

Steinman, Lisa M. "Unanticipated Readers." *Poetry and Poetics after Wallace Stevens*, edited by Bart Eeckhout and Lisa Goldfarb, Bloomsbury, 2017, pages 217–28.

Stevens, Wallace. *The Collected Poems of Wallace Stevens*, corrected ed., edited by John N. Serio and Chris Beyers, Vintage, 2015.

———. *Letters of Wallace Stevens*, edited by Holly Stevens, U of California P, 1996.

———. *Wallace Stevens: Collected Poetry and Prose*, edited by Frank Kermode and Joan Richardson, Library of America, 1997.

Stewart, Garrett. *Reading Voices: Literature and the Phonotext*, U of California P, 1990.

Stewart, Susan. *Poetry and the Fate of the Senses.* U of Chicago P, 2002.

Stimpson, Catharine R. *Where the Meanings Are*, Routledge, 1989.

Stonum, Gary Lee. *The Dickinson Sublime*, U of Wisconsin P, 1990.

Thornton, Sarah. *Club Cultures: Music, Media and Subcultural Capital*, UP of New England, 1996.

Thundyil, Zacharias. Circumstance, Circumference, and Center: Immanence and Transcendence in Emily Dickinson's Poems of Extreme Situations" *Hartford Studies in Literature*, volume 3, number 2, 1971, pages 73–92.

Travisano, Thomas J. *Elizabeth Bishop: Her Artistic Development*, UP of Virginia, 1988.

Vendler, Helen. "The Art of Losing." *The New Republic*, April 3, 2006, pages 33–37.

———. *Dickinson: Selected Poems and Commentaries*, Belknap Press [Harvard UP], 2010.

———. *Last Looks, Last Books: Stevens, Plath, Lowell, Bishop, Merrill*, Princeton UP, 2010.

———. *The Ocean, The Bird, and the Scholar: Essays on Poets and Poetry*, Harvard UP, 2015.

———. *Our Secret Discipline: Yeats and Lyric Form*, Belknap Press [Harvard UP], 2007.

———. *Part of Nature, Part of Us: Modern American Poets*, Harvard UP, 1980.

Wardrop, Daneen. "Emily Dickinson and the Gothic in Fascicle 16." *The Cambridge Companion to Emily Dickinson*, edited by Wendy Martin, Cambridge UP, 2002, pages 142–64.

Waters, William. *Poetry's Touch: On Lyric Address*, Cornell UP, 2003.

Watkin, William. *The Literary Agamben: Adventures in Logopoiesis*, Continuum, 2010.

———. "The / Turn and the " " Pause: Agamben, Derrida, and the Stratification of Poetry." *Textual Layering: Contact, Historicity, Critique*, edited by Maria Margaroni, Apostolos Lampropoulos, and Christakis Chatzichristou, Lexigton Books, 2017, pages 49–62.

Webster, Noah. *An American Dictionary of the English Language*. S. Converse, 1828. [Accessed: https://webstersdictionary1828.com/]

———. *An American Dictionary of the English Language*. Revised edition. Harper and Brothers, 1845. [Accessed: https://www.google.com/books/edition/ An_American_Dictionary_of_the_English_La/9BNHAQAAMAAJ?hl=en&gb-pv=1&bsq=degree]

Weisbard, Eric, ed. *This is Pop: In Search of the Elusive at Experience Music Project*, Harvard UP, 2004.

Weisbuch, Robert and Martin Orzeck. "Introduction: Dickinson the Scrivener." *Dickinson and Audience*, edited by Martin Orzeck and Robert Weisbuch, U of Michigan P, 1996, pages 1–8.

Wellek, René, and Austin Warren. *Theory of Literature*, Harcourt, 1949.

Werner, Marta L. "Emily Dickinson's Futures: Enjambment Degree Zero." *jubilat*, volume 11, 2006, pages 102–19.

Wheeler, Lesley. *Voicing American Poetry: Sound and Performance from the 1920s to the Present*, Cornell UP, 2008.

White, Christopher and Quentin Buvelot, eds. *Rembrandt by Himself*, National Gallery, 1999.

White, Gillian. *Lyric Shame: The "Lyric" Subject of Contemporary American Poetry*, Harvard UP, 2014.

Whiteley, Sheila. *The Space Between the Notes: Rock and the Counter-Culture*, Routledge, 1992.

Whitman, Walt. *The Portable Walt Whitman*, edited by Mark van Doren, Penguin, 1977.

Wilde, Lady Jane. *Ancient Legends, Mystic Charms, and Superstitions of Ireland*, Ward and Downey, 1888.

Wimsatt, W.K. *The Verbal Icon: Studies in the Meaning of Poetry*, U of Kentucky P, 1954.

Wolosky, Shira. "Public and Private in Dickinson's War Poetry." *A Historical Guide to Emily Dickinson*, edited by Vivian R. Pollak, Oxford UP, 2004, pages 103–31.

Wordsworth, William. *Selected Poems*, edited by Stephen Gill, Penguin, 2004.

Yaeger, Patricia, ed. "The New Lyric Studies." [Special issue] *PMLA*, volume 123, number 1, January 2008.

Yeats, W. B. *The Collected Poems of W. B. Yeats*, revised 2nd ed., edited by Richard J. Finneran, Scribner, 1996.

———. *Essays and Introductions*, Macmillan, 1961.

———. *Fairy and Folk Tales of the Irish Peasantry*, Walter Scott, 1888.

———. *The Letters of W. B. Yeats*, edited by Alan Wade, R. Hart-Davis, 1954.

———. *Mythologies*, Macmillan, 1959.

———. "The Stolen Child." *The Irish Monthly*, December 1886, pages 646–47.

———. *The Variorum Edition of the Poems of W. B. Yeats*, edited by Peter Allt, MacMillan, 1957, pages 86–89.

———. *Uncollected Prose by W. B. Yeats*, volume I, edited by John P. Frayne, Columbia UP, 1970.

———. *Uncollected Prose of W. B. Yeats*, volume II, edited by John P. Frayne and Colton Johnson, Macmillan, 1975.

———. *Writings on Irish Folklore, Legend and Myth*, Penguin, 1993.

Yenser, Stephen. *The Consuming Myth: The Work of James Merrill*, Harvard UP, 1987.

Zettelmann, Eva. "Apostrophe, Speaker Projection, and Lyric World Building." *Poetics Today*, volume 38, number 1, Feb. 2017, pages 189–201.

Zimmerman, Lee. "Against Apocalypse: Politics and James Merrill's *The Changing Light at Sandover.*" *Contemporary Literature*, volume 30, number 3, Fall 1989, pages 370–86.

Index